BATTLE

We made out a convoy of five freighters plus a *Chidori* escort, a highly effective new antisubmarine ship appearing in numbers throughout the empire. The escort was between us and the convoy and was now on our starboard beam with a small port angle on the bow, closing. This was not the best position for *Scorpion* . . . But there was insufficient time to cross ahead of him.

Three shots at the first target were fired at 1,600 yards and three at the second, range 850 yards, all torpedoes set to run at fifteen feet. Five heavy explosions were heard, and a minute later, a sixth. Meanwhile, the escort and the other two vessels were close on our beam and heading almost directly toward us.

The captain flooded negative tank (to give a quick down angle), rigged for depth charge attack, and went deep. We thought we had 180 feet of water, but before the sound heads could be raised the ship struck bottom at 147 feet with a demoralizing crunch, receiving two close depth charges just as we hit. The sonar went dead . . .

"Paul Schratz has written extensively on national policy and international affairs, but this is the first excursion into the strictly personal field. I like it immensely!"

—Captain Edward L. Beach, USN (Ret.),
author of *Run Silent, Run Deep*

A Military Book Club Selection

SUBMARINE COMMANDER

A Story of
World War II and Korea

Paul R. Schratz

POCKET BOOKS

New York   London   Toronto   Sydney   Tokyo   Singapore

POCKET BOOKS, a division of Simon & Schuster Inc.
1230 Avenue of the Americas, New York, NY 10020

Copyright © 1988 by The University Press of Kentucky
Cover art copyright © 1990 Al Chinchar

Published by arrangement with The University Press of Kentucky
Library of Congress Catalog Card Number: 88-19035

ISBN 0-671-68466-3

First Pocket Books printing March 1990

10 9 8 7 6 5 4 3 2 1

POCKET and colophon are registered trademarks of
Simon & Schuster Inc.

Printed in the U.S.A.

Any commander who fails to exceed his authority is not of much use to his subordinates.

Admiral Arleigh Burke,
Chief of Naval Operations

Contents

Contents

Maps

Preface

Submarine warfare is unique in many ways, different from our preconceptions of strife, different from all previous combat in American history, different even from the visions of war by American military planners at the opening of hostilities on 7 December 1941. And it may be a facet of war never again to be fought by American undersea forces.

Strange as it seems, combat is a rare experience for the man in uniform, even in time of war. Edward Luttwak determined that Americans landing in Normandy in 1944 engaged in actual combat for only a few weeks at most during the Allied sweep across Europe in the eleven months before V-E Day. On the eastern front, where Germans and Russians were in contact for over four years, months passed between the days of intense battle, with rare exceptions such as the Stalingrad fighting which lasted for weeks at a time. Other than bomber and submarine crews, German Panzer troops, and the U.S. Marines, a very small fraction of the tens of millions in uniform accounted for a very large proportion of total days in action.

My distinguished friend and submariner Captain Edward L. Beach, Jr., USN Retired, found that the U.S. Navy before World War II spent a total of twenty years at war with real shooting in only about eleven years and time spent in actual battle only about fifty-six hours. Throughout World War I, no U.S. Navy surface ship fired at or was fired upon by a German surface warship.

In World War II the U.S. Marines were an exception to the limited experience in combat. The average Marine serving from Pearl Harbor to Tokyo Bay spent 120 days in combat. Far surpassing this figure were the submarine forces, both German and Allied.

In the Battle of the Atlantic, the longest and most tragic campaign of the war, the U-boats wreaked enormous damage to Allied shipping at the terrible cost of 28,000 men lost, 85 percent of the entire force. American submarines, fighting a shorter war with a force representing only 1.6 percent of the Navy, accounted for 55 percent of Japan's total maritime losses. Again a heavy price was paid for victory. The loss of fifty-two American submarines carrying 375 officers and 3,131 crewmen either down with their ships or to lingering deaths in prison camps was the highest casualty rate for any element of the U.S. armed forces. Of unique significance, the U.S. undersea warriors sank twenty-seven enemy ships for each submarine lost, the Germans only four.

The average submariner, German or American, operated in enemy-controlled waters, or under direct threat from enemy submarines, aircraft, and minefields during most of his time at sea. The first U.S. submarine departed from Pearl Harbor on a war patrol in Japanese home waters on 11 December 1941. From that day until 14 August 1945, when the last ship was sunk the day before the surrender, our submarines ranged the broad Pacific, penetrating bays, harbors, and seaports of the enemy's innermost defenses, often thousands of miles from the nearest friendly support.

They sank 1,178 merchantmen and 214 warships totaling 5.3 million tons. The warship sinkings included a battleship, 8 aircraft carriers, 11 cruisers, and numerous destroyers and submarines. In addition to the shipping losses inflicted on Japan, U.S. submariners rescued 550 U.S. and Allied aviators from death or imprisonment, landed and recovered spies and coastwatchers, made commando raids, supplied aviation gasoline, ammunition, and stores to isolated U.S. forces, conducted special intelligence operations, launched rocket attacks against enemy shore installations, acted as beacons and weather forecasters for the carrier forces, and photographed beach areas for amphibious landings. The submarine blockade of Japan cut off oil, gasoline, and heavy metals for her industry. The dwindling Japanese air force and navy were forced to rely on fuel made from soybeans; domestic transport was powered by crude charcoal burners.

I wrote *Submarine Commander* partly to express a special debt of gratitude to "the men back aft," the superb chiefs, key petty officers, and the men who were so vital an element in the success of our American submarines. With virtually no choice of the captains or execs under whom they would serve, some great and some less great, they did a masterful job, often under extremes bordering on hopelessness and despair. Their mechanical genius in keeping their intricate warships operating under seemingly impossible conditions may have been equaled but never surpassed. Through utmost misery they never lost their sense of humor, whatever the occasion. After the war, many attained distinguished positions in civilian life yet, whatever their achievements, the war years remain the ultimate experience, a continuing source of pride in a tough job very well done. Like all combat veterans, they recall the comradeship and intensity of life more vividly than the horror and brutality. If their stories of adventure on and under the seas seem to diverge in significant detail, one need only recall that memory is a convenience store often in need of replenishment.

There are a great many people to whom I owe a special debt of gratitude in making this book possible. Former shipmates were invaluable: from the USS *Sterlet*, Robert G. Barker of Watford City, North Dakota; Captain Eugene C. Barnhardt III, USN Retired, of Virginia Beach, Virginia; Judge John J. Callahan of Buffalo, New York; Donald E. Horst of Biglerville, Pennsylvania; George P. Petretti of Dobbs Ferry, New York; and Edward J. Skeehan of Pittsburgh, Pennsylvania; from the USS *Atule*, Hollis F. Church of Avon, Connecticut; Rear Admiral John H. Maurer, USN Retired, of Summerland Key, Florida; Welcome A. Rumbaugh of Gresham, Oregon, and Stefan Zemanek of Binghamton, New York; from His Imperial Japanese Majesty's Ship I-203, *Sasori,* John F. Ahearn, Jr., of Shoal Creek, Alabama, and CDR Allen B. Catlin, USN Retired, of Fullerton, California; and from the USS *Pickerel,* Captain William E. Sims, USN Retired, of Annapolis, Maryland. From the USS *Scorpion,* however, fleshing out official patrol reports depended on memory alone. I am the only surviving officer: the handful of crewmen who were detached before her loss are no longer in contact.

I owe a special obligation to Professor Vincent Davis, Director and Patterson Professor, Patterson School of Diplomacy and International Commerce, University of Kentucky and to Kenneth Cherry, director, the University Press of Kentucky, first in asking me to write the book and then in steering me clear of numerous charted and uncharted reefs and shoals in getting a manuscript into print. No less important was the U.S. Naval Institute, largely flowing from the stimulus to historical research under the new publisher, Captain James A. Barber, USN Retired. Paul Stillwell, directing the oral history program, a well-prepared, sympathetic, and expert interviewer, brought fresh life to many long-forgotten incidents in working out my oral history. The iridescent Fred Rainbow, editor-in-chief, has long been an enthusiastic supporter for my numerous crusades. Nor can I forget Tom Epley, book acquisitions, and Linda Cullen for library support.

For important technical and research assistance I am indebted to Dean C. Allard of the Naval Research Center, Operational Archives, Washington, D.C.; to Dr. Regis J. Ging, of Homosassa, Florida; Terence J. McNamara, of Burlington, North Carolina, and Rear Admiral Daniel K. Weitzenfeld, USN Retired, of McLean, Virginia.

Colonel J. Wesley Hammond, USMC Retired, editor of *Shipmate,* Annapolis, Maryland, kindly gave permission to use "The Voyage of the *Pickerel,*" from the April 1970 issue; the U.S. Naval Institute consented to the use of "Submerged Celestial Navigation," published in the *Proceedings,* April 1945.

One special person remains truly indispensable, my wife, Henri, the guiding light through the adventures herein, the inspiration in getting *Submarine Commander* into print, the word processor expert, grammarian, and primary research source through the hundreds of my letters she preserved over the years.

All the events chronicled here are true, and any errors of fact are my responsibility alone.

1   The USS *Wichita*

Naval War in the North Atlantic

Hvalfjordur, Iceland, December 1941. A few minutes before midnight, as the sixth of December passed into history, I scaled the familiar six ladders from my stateroom to "sky forward," the weatherbeaten compartment housing the antiaircraft director in *Wichita,* where I stood watch as gunnery control officer. Half the five-inch, 38-caliber antiaircraft (AA) gun crews were at full alert with ammunition at hand; the ship was closed up for battle with one-fourth of her crew on watch. Scores of other ships lay at anchor, scattered around the vast fjord, blacked out and invisible. Only the low conversation of the watch, almost inaudible over the pelting rain, broke the stillness. Not for many hours yet would the "Day of Infamy" dawn on the other side of the world in Pearl Harbor.

My 0000 to 0400 watch gave no hint of the dramatic events then rushing to a climax in the Pacific. At our secluded anchorage just below the Arctic Circle, the chance of a surprise attack was remote. Rain, sleet, and fog made flying impossible; the steep fifteen-hundred-foot mountains ringing the fjord on three sides barred surface action; stout submarine nets across the sea entrance prevented U-boat penetration. The ready watch was the normal routine into which the ship had grown since ordered to Iceland with the first contingent of U.S. forces five months before. As I searched the skies from my station seventy-five feet above the sea, wind-driven needles of rain found every crevice in my salt-stained parka, stiff and crinkly from long exposure to sea and wind. Thoughts of war in far-off climes succumbed to immediate personal misery. My somber mood was hardly typical, but then neither were the surroundings. Despite the subdued throb of a complex warship and its seven hundred souls far below me, I felt not only completely alone but terribly lonesome.

Wichita, a new heavy cruiser, had been my home since graduation from the U.S. Naval Academy at Annapolis on 1 June 1939. She was a gorgeous sight at sea: 650 feet long and displacing 16,700 tons, her eight boilers drove her through the water at 33.5 knots, about 40 miles per hour. Mounting nine 8-inch guns in three heavily armored turrets and a dozen five-inch, 38-caliber dual purpose surface and AA guns in twin mounts, plus new 1.1-inch AA mounts, we felt we could outrun anything we couldn't outgun. Experience would soon teach all navies that the antiaircraft and antisubmarine armaments were woefully inadequate, but at least we had the best available.

Flagship of Cruiser Division 7, "the Witch" had been operating out of Iceland on the edge of the European-Atlantic war for five months. The summer months were splendid while the ship was in port. Long hikes or mountain climbs amid spectacular scenery, trout fishing in virgin streams, an occasional ball game or beer bust on the beach all made for a healthy, interesting life.

Missing were liberty and the bright lights of city life. The nearest city, Reykjavik, was about thirty-one miles away and could be reached only by an arduous seven-hour journey over rough, boulder-strewn country lanes, which until a few months before might never have seen a motor vehicle. A duty destroyer made the round trip by sea about twice a week, taking all who cared to go as passengers. At the first chance we were anxious to give it a try. From the wardroom, Donald J. O'Meara, Marvin D. "Doc" Norton, and I, fellow ensigns, classmates at the Naval Academy, and close friends, made the trip in high anticipation.

All we were interested in was sightseeing, a bit of shopping, and a cold beer before the trip back to Hvalfjordur. Shopping was a total waste. Ladies' fur-lined gloves were well made and inexpensive, if one had a special friend who wore size ten. The beer was the biggest disappointment of all. Iceland had been prohibitionist for many years. Beer could be bought only at the two main hotels in town, only with a full meal, only if one had a ration card. In no way deterred, we finally succeeded in buying a round—and only one. The label certified it to be less than 1 percent alcohol; the taste suggested it was brewed from tree bark, and there were few trees in Iceland. In the early months after arrival I made one more trip to town. By then both the desire and the summer had gone by.

Reykjavik was a small town in 1941; the Icelanders were hardheaded, aloof, and intensely nationalistic. Reykjavik was the only place in the world where I was spat on while walking the main street. Some Icelanders were hostile to the British and Americans because we were foreigners, many, especially the youth, because they supported the Nazi cause. Outside the few towns, most lived a stark existence in sod huts in which only the sheep were in on the ground floor, perhaps supplying auxiliary heat for the humans above.

What they resented most of all was the contact of aliens with Icelandic girls. The law allowed trial marriages for a six-month period, dissolvable by mutual consent unless a pregnancy occurred. Illegitimate births caused no stigma unless an alien was involved. If no marriage ensued for any reason, the girl gave the child her family name; there were so few family names the phone book was alphabetized by first names.

Days became shorter and shorter, the sun increasingly rare, and sudden, violent storms more and more the norm even within our protected anchorage. By the end of August, the warships in the area included the U.S. battleships *Idaho* and *Mississippi*, cruisers *Vincennes* and *Wichita*, several auxiliaries and a squadron of destroyers; the British battleships *Ramillies* and *King George V*, cruiser *Hecla*, auxiliaries, and frigates; and a few Polish and Norwegian vessels.

For recreation ashore we finally scrounged enough lumber, equipment, and furnishings to construct three corrugated Nissen huts, one for the younger enlisted men, one for the chiefs, and one for the officers. Two softball diamonds sprang up overnight, but by the time all the cow chips and rocks were cleared away the days were too short or the weather too bad to get ashore. But beer drinking is an all-weather sport, and those metal huts, impervious to wind and weather, were ideal for this climate—as long as we got heat from an old oil stove, electrical power from diesel generators, and muddy water from a nearby well.

On that raw December day the routine of the watch left me largely to my own thoughts, mostly about how I had gotten to Iceland, more about how I was going to get out.

My boyhood in Pittsburgh, Pennsylvania, built around music, sports, and, above all, horseplay, was hardly the ideal preparation for the Naval Academy. I studied the violin from early years and eventually became concertmaster of a fine high school symphony, made the All City Symphony, and won national honors with a chamber group. To keep me out of trouble my guidance counselor encouraged me to write a play on George Washington, which the school eventually staged with me in the lead role. Active with the choral groups, I usually had a lead in the annual operetta, not as the greatest baritone voice but the best available.

My goal was to enter West Point or Annapolis. While struggling for an appointment, I registered at Carnegie Tech in Pittsburgh—now Carnegie Mellon—doubling freshman and sophomore math and physics, then found time to play in the Tech Symphony. When the appointment finally came through in June 1935, I was near burnout. My rugged 185-pound frame had withered to a skeletal 145 pounds.

Most of my classmates at Annapolis also had college experience, but I anticipated no trouble with academic subjects. I joined the Naval Academy Symphony and soon became concertmaster and soloist. I did some writing for the literary club and joined the 150-pound crew. Recovery of weight I had lost at Tech soon made me thirty-five pounds too heavy for that sport. I enjoyed tennis and golf but didn't feel varsity sports were my dish. They demanded near total dedication of time and energy, and with music, sailing, swimming, and a host of competing activities, I was not willing to make the necessary sacrifice. I did well academically, but class standing was more and more influenced by "grease" marks—aptitude for the service—and my undisciplined spirit was far more recognized than appreciated. I graduated in the top third; the yearbook biography, written by a roommate, alleges that I preferred not to be a "star" man (dean's list).

Long before my departure from Pittsburgh, my "one and only" girl friend—OAO—was Henrietta Frank, a petite and attractive brunette. Our families were neighbors and great friends. They assumed we would eventually marry, and that presented a problem. A service life wasn't for everybody, and neither of us was ready. Nevertheless, at the Ring Dance at the end of second class (junior) year, under the influence of a beautiful moon and some Paul Whiteman music, we decided it could be serious.

Orders to sea at graduation went by the luck of the draw. Cruisers were top choice and new construction best of all. I hit the jackpot with *Wichita*. The only flaw was the captain, Thaddeus Austin Thomson. Captain Thad was famed throughout the Navy as a "sundowner," a stern disciplinarian. Affectionately known as "TBT" or "That Bastard Thomson," he had served at the Naval Academy in the Executive Department, involved with discipline, just before my class arrived as plebes. The smoke was still rising. I didn't connect Thad with the Witch until I got my orders. But I hadn't succumbed to discipline at Annapolis, and I thought I could survive Thad as well.

Less than one hundred days after my graduation, the war in Europe was suddenly upon us. On 3 September 1939, the secretary of the navy sent the following message to all ships: "England and France are now at war with Germany. You will govern yourselves accordingly."

War and a future in the Navy dominated our thoughts. The strong "never again" spirit in America about participating in another European war influenced many officers. Captain Thad called all of us into his cabin that day and drilled into us a few inspiring words (which we heard many times and I myself used when my turn came to command): "We took this inanimate mass of steel and breathed life into it. The personality which we stamp on *Wichita* is our personality and will establish her reputation throughout the fleet.

That reputation will last for years, long after our passing. . . . There are good ships and bad ships, some happy and some unhappy, some taut and some sloppy. The character of a ship is the character we impress on her, and I will exert all my energies to shape her character and ours to that end."

Other influences in those days were equally strong in shaping our careers; one, however, was denied us. Americans have romantic visions of Annapolis grads getting married and marching off into the sunset under an arch of swords. But that was not for us. By order of the secretary of the navy, academy graduates were forbidden to marry for two years. I can imagine what the American Civil Liberties Union and similar organizations would say about such a regulation today, applying to regular and not to reserve officers, but there were reasons, however unappreciated. Service life offered a rugged challenge, especially for a young bride trying to make a home, following her husband's ship around the world, and raising a family on $143.25 per month, plus $40.00 housing allowance. The officer starting a new career in an unstable, challenging world couldn't possibly do justice to his shipboard duties even without the normal problems of family life.

To the captain's great credit, he gave us all the responsibility we could handle. After a few "makee-learn" junior officer of the deck (JOOD) watches in port, he qualified us for "top watch" long before our contemporaries in other commands. These were tough duties. A thousand Navy Yard workmen swarmed over the ship, readying her for sea; welders frequently set off fires or fire alarms; and tests of equipment needed to be coordinated. The ship's routines had to be carried out with all the problems of a city. The OOD was the point of contact for everything happening, planned or unplanned.

When we finally got to sea, new responsibilities challenged us, and Captain Thad's tolerance limits rarely included compassion. In seamanship, piloting, navigation, and watch standing, if one fell short, the captain's first thought was to write a letter to the secretary of the navy asking that the culprit's commission be revoked. (Ensigns then served two years on revocable commissions.) We all had our bad moments. I escaped the worst of it thanks to a timely tour out of harm's way in the Engineering Department. Several revocation letters went to the secretary, who wisely transferred the officer to another ship. The letter remained in the officer's record, naturally, to haunt him throughout his career.

On the bright side, the *Wichita* was bachelor heaven. Few in the Navy now have any recollection of the "old Navy" before World War II. Officers were a small elite and enjoyed a prestigious role in society. The enlisted were long-service professionals whose only life was the Navy. That era is gone, never to return. We worked hard and we played hard. Despite her fearsome commanding officer (CO), *Wichita* was a happy ship. Thad's own creed was largely responsible. The officers were highly competent and congenial. Under iron discipline, such a group always thrives. When the iron hand became excessive, it united us in a common misery. Perhaps the captain was an admirer of Machiavelli: "A prince must be indifferent to the charge of cruelty if he is to keep his subjects loyal and united. Having set an example once or twice, he may thereafter act far more mercifully than the princes, who, through excessive kindness, allow disorders to arise. . . . When a prince . . . must command multitudes of soldiers, then more than ever must he be indifferent to a reputation for cruelty, for without such a reputation no army was ever held together, nor was it ever fit for combat."

If the captain taught us much about leadership, his seamanship often taught us what not to do. Here his deficiencies were more than made up by the executive officer (XO), Commander John S. Moyer, a tough old sea dog, fine athlete, first ashore for a party and last to return aboard. Lt. Cmdr. Heber B. Brumbaugh, the "gun boss" and my first department head, was a father figure for many of us. Commander Donald T. Giles, the engineer, knew his job like an old master. Another easygoing, Dutch-uncle type, he too was much admired by the younger officers. Lt. William N. Wylie, assistant engineer, taught me the mysteries of a high-pressure steam engineering plant. I felt close to both Don and Bill; our careers were to intertwine in strange ways.

The Witch was under way almost continuously, and we loved it. We wintered in the Caribbean, basing out of Guantanamo, Cuba, and summered in Norfolk, Newport, or Bar

Harbor—where every mother was trying to marry off her daughter to a sharp-looking ensign. Newport made us experts as small boat officers. The anchorage was several miles from the landing, and there were several sharp turns in the channel. In fog and low visibility—the normal condition much of the year in Newport—a junior officer rode all launches for liberty parties or for public visiting aboard. Picking a safe course through blind fog was a nightmare, particularly when one was responsible for a gaggle of civilians or beered-up sailors.

Captain Thad complicated matters further by using a hotel landing several miles up the bay. When I first checked with the hotel authorities about the landing, they claimed it was unnavigable for the gig at low tide. Their normal landing was in a sheltered cove around a nearby point of land. But they didn't tell Thad. The first time I was boat officer was for a special luncheon the captain was hosting on board. I had the gig alongside one landing waiting to take the captain's lady out to the ship. She was at the other landing with the guests. Lillian Thomson was attractive, a charming hostess—and no less dominating than her husband. Commandeering a small tug, she headed for my landing, laid the tug alongside the gig, and began transferring guests. With a scathing look, she shoved a floral piece in my hands, elbowed the coxswain aside, and personally drove the gig out to the ship. She was a fine shiphandler; she also had a short fuse.

That afternoon Thad sent for me, pointing out with a snarl the proper landing where I was to pick him up in the morning. This gave me three problems. A heavy fog was due to roll in after midnight; the pickup time was at low tide, without enough water to float the gig; and in his present humor I wasn't about to try to change his mind. Next morning, groping my way in to the landing, I cut the engine fifty yards off, and the gig crew poled the boat alongside with boathooks, the keel thumping lightly on the rocks. When the captain appeared out of the fog I ordered smartly, "Man your poles." His added weight in the stern caused a few hard bumps, but we pushed off the submerged rocks and were soon in deep water. He glared but made no comment. We didn't use that landing again.

At sea, the captain frequently held informal dinners in his

cabin with a small guest list, including an ensign or two. Captain Thad, a wealthy Texan, had served several tours of attaché duty in foreign capitals and took great pride in the table he set. He was a superb host and an interesting conversationalist, and his dinner parties were always enjoyable. For a few hours one could forget the other side of his personality, the violent temper and a tongue-lashing of recent memory. All too often we saw a different side of him during the next watch on the bridge at sea, which often became hairy.

Maneuvering with other ships in formation, often at high speeds and in darkness, was nerve-racking. Doctrine called for six hundred yards' distance between ships, but without radar, cruising blacked out at night or in low visibility, maneuvering required a high order of skill. Captain Thad had a poor seaman's eye, unfortunately, which led him to make unreasonable demands on the watch. In that primitive era before radar, distance between ships was checked with a stadimeter, a small coincidence range finder into which one set the guide ship's masthead height and then turned a knurled range knob to determine the range.

If the ships in column were supposed to be at 600 yards, he didn't want 580 or 615, which was extremely difficult when different ships' propulsion plants responded differently. On one especially hectic day, I was the junior watch officer under Ensign George R. Reinhart III, a fine officer and a good friend. I decided to ease George's problem. On the stadimeter, instead of turning the range knob, I moved the knob controlling the masthead height, which left the range unchanged, then reported after each measurement, "Steady on 600."

Everybody on the bridge except Thad could see considerable variation. Finally, even he got suspicious. Leaping from his chair on the port side of the bridge, he stomped over to me, tore the stadimeter from my hand, and put it to his eye. Not a soul breathed. But Thad grabbed the same knob I had been twisting, looked at the range, still steady on 600, naturally, and pushed it back into my hands. There was absolute silence on the bridge for several seconds. Would I, too, be the subject of one of those letters asking the secretary of the navy to revoke my commission? He said nothing, but I never tried that trick again. Even friendship has limits.

The approach of war, particularly the startling success of the German U-boats against British shipping in the Atlantic, was never far from our thoughts. On the day the war started in September 1939, twenty-eight Americans lost their lives when the British liner *Athenia* was torpedoed by the German U-30 south of Scotland. President Roosevelt responded with a limited national emergency and established a "neutrality patrol" by American warships in the Atlantic.

When the "phony war" in Europe abruptly ended with the victorious German blitzkrieg of France and the Low Countries in April 1940 and of Norway and Denmark a few weeks later, the German surface raider and U-boat threat in the Atlantic became grave. The Nazi Wehrmacht controlled the European seacoast from the Franco-Spanish border to the top of Norway, with scores of fine ports for maritime operations against the Allies. Never in her history did Germany enjoy a finer strategic position.

The political situation throughout the Atlantic basin grew increasingly tense. Both Germany and Japan had made significant inroads into Brazilian and Argentine commerce, international trade, and subversion by the "fifth column." Evidence of anti-Americanism became widespread, particularly in Argentina, where bonds with Germany were strong. On 9 May 1940, both officially and unofficially we learned that the fall of the Netherlands to the Nazis created a strong possibility that Germany would take control of the strategically vital Dutch islands of Aruba and Curaçao, off the coast of Venezuela. When three German ships anchored off the islands in early 1940, the Dutch colonials declared a state of martial law. Dutch merchants in Curaçao told *Wichita* officers they expected the United States to take over the islands in case of a German invasion of the Low Countries. The vast petroleum storage tank farms would be vulnerable even to a submarine's guns from a few miles offshore. Control of the islands by the Germans would give them an extremely important submarine refueling facility.

Wichita received abrupt orders to head south on 4 June 1940 to counter a new political crisis in Brazil. Captain J. Phillips Berkeley, senior Marine, leading a heavily augmented Marine Corps detachment, and Don O'Meara and I, leading companies of bluejackets, put on a show of force expressing American support for President Getulio Vargas. Months later we received a special commendation to the effect that the Americans looked so smart one could hardly tell them from Brazilians.

The political tension in no way diverted us from what we did best. The social life was superb. Most of the younger officers were enjoying our enforced bachelorhood at sea or in port. We entertained the Copacabana chorus girls in the wardroom; I was almost seduced in Santos, Brazil, and fell madly in love with a gorgeous lass in Rio, both of us under the spell of the Southern Cross. Despite the language barrier, my late-night description of her deep, dark eyes as "limpid pools" came across eloquently in Portuguese, which my shipmates never allowed me to forget. We junior officers were all social butterflies, but there was little hanky-panky. The Brazilian girls we met followed a strict moral code, the Argentinians even more so. And to a very large extent, at home or abroad, so did we.

Brazil taught us about the gin and tonic and the samba, which we helped popularize in the states. In Buenos Aires, four of us young studs were lavishly wined and dined by the Argentine minister of foreign affairs and his four daughters, thoroughly chaperoned throughout. For an evening at one of the two "acceptable" nightclubs, we first went to their home for cocktails, during which the ladies disappeared, emerging to stage some entertainment for us. They were never present when liquor was served. When we went to the nightclub, the chaperones sat together at distant tables. A pleasant evening of dancing was followed by a late night steak dinner. On saying good night to my charming companion one evening, shaking hands with her in the restaurant lobby, I eased my finger along her wrist in a mild caress. She blushed, gave me a sly wink, and I felt as though I had ravished her.

To reciprocate the hospitality, we often invited guests aboard on Wednesdays, primarily wives and girl friends, for a rice and curry lunch, followed by "rope yarn Sunday"— holiday routine for golf or similar pleasures. Our guests invariably felt warmly welcomed into our gentlemen's club with its obviously high-spirited members.

At the time of our return to the states in September 1940, President Franklin D. Roosevelt and Prime Minister Winston Churchill concluded the dramatic "destroyers for bases" agreement to transfer fifty overage U.S. destroyers to Britain in exchange for long-term leases to eight potential naval and air base sites scattered from Argentia, Newfoundland, to British Guiana. Shortly after, *Wichita* made an inspection tour of Bermuda and other sites for Caribbean bases in Antigua, Jamaica, and Trinidad.

Increasing world tension brought an unprecedented intensity to the 1941 fleet battle problem. The Navy and Marine Corps, after several years of development, tested an entirely new doctrine for amphibious warfare. The British failure at Gallipoli in 1915 convinced most experts that a fortified shore position could not be taken by direct assault from the sea. The Caribbean exercises refuted this hoary belief by developing better techniques for shore bombardment and by establishing the need for specialized landing craft soon to become so vital in the war. The problem involved battleships, cruisers, destroyers, scores of amphibious and replenishment ships, and three U.S. Marine and two U.S. Army combat teams. The intense day and night exercises were exhausting but great sport.

Breaks in the battle allowed us to take advantage of the world's best body surfing on tiny and almost uninhabited Culebra Island, a few miles east of Puerto Rico. The constant trade winds formed an enormous surf rolling across the fine, white sands of Flamingo Beach. Totally isolated, we swam in the nude and were soon more tanned than the natives.

The battle problem also marked an operational test of a new fleet organization. Effective 1 February 1941 the Atlantic Patrol Force, to which *Wichita* and Cruiser Division 7 belonged, became the Atlantic Fleet, coequal with the Pacific and Asiatic fleets, formally creating a "two-ocean Navy." That same month American, British, and Canadian naval officials completed six weeks of consultations in Washington, hammering out much of the basic strategy that was to govern operations throughout the war.

Meanwhile, I was working out a personal strategy. During a short visit to Norfolk in March, I was able to get away to

Pittsburgh for a quick, intense weekend, following which Henri and I announced our engagement. The date on the ring is 3-30 for 30 March; some family members, noting our late night seances working out arrangements, thought it meant 3:30 A.M. I still recall the warm and wonderful feeling, knowing we had pledged the remainder of our lives together. For a marriage date we favored October. But where would I be then? Rumors pointed to operations out of Iceland. Maybe we could have an Arctic wedding and have penguins in full dress as ushers. Or was that the Antarctic?

Little did we know that other actors on the world stage were also shaping our destinies. On 24 March 1941 President Roosevelt authorized Britain to repair her ships in U.S. yards. The day after, Hitler extended his "operational zone" to include Iceland and the North Atlantic westward almost to the southern tip of Greenland; all neutral merchant ships as well as belligerent warships in the area could be sunk on sight. In the same week, all German and Italian shipping in U.S. harbors was ordered seized, and on 30 March the U.S. Coast Guard took twenty-seven Italian, two German, and thirty-five Danish vessels in American harbors into "protective custody." Lend-Lease shipments to Britain began, and British-American naval contingency plans were completed. Then on orders from FDR of 11 April, Admiral Ernest J. King, Atlantic Fleet commander, extended the U.S. security zone farther to the east to include Greenland and Iceland, overlapping Hitler's operational zone, or blockaded area.

On 24 April 1941, the morning press announced in black headlines "U.S. Navy to Patrol Atlantic." The following day, heavy cruisers *Wichita* and *Tuscaloosa*, with two destroyer escorts, sailed from Newport, fully ready for war: "condition watches" (four hours on, eight or twelve off) were set, and the ship closed up for battle with half the AA battery and one triple eight-inch turret manned and ready to shoot at all times. Our orders were to patrol a thousand miles off the coast from the Azores to Iceland, directly through the area where Hitler had promised to sink any belligerent warship on sight. Then on 27 May 1941, following the sortie of the German battleship *Bismarck* into the Atlantic, FDR declared "an unlimited national emergency."

After almost a month at sea, *Wichita* suddenly and unexpectedly was ordered to the Brooklyn Navy Yard for six weeks for installation of a crude air search radar, improved AA gun protection and other war readiness measures such as welding shut the portholes below the main deck. Captain Thad completed his command tour and was relieved by Captain James T. Alexander. The war got better as it got worse. And six weeks in one place looked like a godsend.

In a few weeks the two-year ban on marriage would expire. We might never again have as good an opportunity to tie the knot. Don and Doc set their dates for the first of June but I had a tougher time. The whole wardroom helped me draft a telegram to Henri in Pittsburgh suggesting a June wedding, and we waited anxiously for her reaction. Absolutely nothing happened. I phoned. She laughed, thinking I was kidding or partying too much. Her big sister Dorothy had just set her date for early July, and it was hardly "fittin' " for a younger sister to preempt with a June celebration. I grabbed the train to Pittsburgh to plead my case. Both families realized the special circumstances, and finally we reached agreement. We had a beautiful wedding in Pittsburgh on 21 June at St. Leo's, our old parish church, bought a new Chevy for $400, and went off on a wedding trip through New England and Canada.

The three *Wichita* brides, plus a fourth, the wife of newly reported Ensign John J. "Jack" Healey, set up housekeeping in the same apartment building in Kew Gardens, Forest Hills. The wardroom officers hosted a splendid wedding party for the four couples, Doc and Dal, Don and Jane, Jack and Vi, Henri and me. Following a reception at the officers' club, we enjoyed a superb dinner on the ship with four wedding cakes decorated to match the brides' wedding gowns. Each bride received a beautiful silver gift to grace our new households. As newlyweds, the brides shopped together and prepared the same menus. They shared purchase of items like bread for which they could save a penny by buying two loaves. The men drove to work together and compared notes on married bliss from leftovers to life's dreams. The greatest cloud in my sky was that I had traded off so many duties to work out our marriage that I had the duty and had to remain on board almost every other night.

The day after our marriage, Germany launched a massive

offensive against the Soviet Union. On 21 July, the thirtieth day of our marital bliss, the ship sailed for Iceland and Henri went home to her folks. We had no idea where or when we would be together again. If the time at sea offered hope for us to get out of the hole financially, it was poor consolation. From our now munificent salary of $183.25 a month, $30 went to the wardroom mess for meals, $10 for shipboard sundries, $10 for laundry and dry cleaning, $30 for my government life insurance, and about $15 for clothing and uniforms. Half the paycheck went for shipboard living expenses even if I never spent a cent ashore for travel and entertainment—or for Henri to live on. We were $2,000 in the hole from the wedding and the few weeks in New York. Could I suggest to my lovely bride that she live on what was left and still try to pay off debts? It wasn't easy those days, but I don't recall ever being concerned about it.

Duty as part of an occupation force in Iceland required several sticky political compromises. The cherished neutrality of the 120,000 Icelanders, peaceloving and unarmed, had been violated. In the urgency of war they had requested British and American assistance to preserve their freedom, but cooperation with the belligerent British and technically neutral Americans produced an effective working relationship only because of a happy meld of personalities in the service branches of the two nations. Isolation in a barren and thinly populated fjord offered little contact with the natives.

Separation from my new bride was only the beginning of my troubles. Just before we left New York, Doc Norton was transferred to flight school at Pensacola, and Don left early in October for an eight-week radar school in Maine. Loss of my closest buddies aggravated my own loneliness in this forsaken outpost. A good reason for wanting to get back soon arose—Henri confided that, much to our surprise, we were expecting a young 'un in the spring. Vi had the same news for Jack; he became the target of good natured razzing. I decided to keep our secret for a bit.

The war came closer on 4 September 1941, when the U.S. destroyer *Greer* detected U-652 165 miles southwest of Reykjavik, commenced tracking, and broadcast the sub's position as required by standing orders. A British patrol bomber responded and made several attacks. An hour later the U-boat made two attacks on *Greer* with torpedoes but missed. *Greer* then dropped two patterns of depth charges, which also missed, then at 1500 passed the contact to HMS *Watchman*, arriving on the scene. At 1600 *Greer* cleared the area. President Roosevelt ordered Rear Admiral Robert C. Giffen, commanding Cruiser Division 7 in *Wichita*, to "eliminate" the U-boat. But the U-boat had long cleared the area, and to the great displeasure of the fleet commander, Admiral King, Giffen did nothing. That he was powerless to do anything that had not already been done was less important than the image created in Norfolk and Washington.

Shortly thereafter, *Wichita*, *Tuscaloosa*, and the battleship *Mississippi* sailed for Argentia, Newfoundland, on mysterious orders. Arriving in Placentia Bay, we joined most of the Atlantic Fleet and Royal Navy. Argentia was one of the sites in the "destroyers for bases" agreement with the British. American heavy construction equipment was already hewing out an enormous airfield, and the fleet operating base was becoming a vital key in the Battle of the Atlantic.

Soon to arrive were President Roosevelt, Prime Minister Churchill, and the highest naval and military authorities of both nations for meetings aboard the HMS *Prince of Wales* and USS *Augusta*. From these meetings emerged the "Germany first" strategy and the British and American war aims.

The so-called Atlantic Charter proclaimed that Britain and America sought no "territorial aggrandizement" or "territorial changes that do not accord with the freely expressed wishes of the people concerned." After "the final destruction of Nazi tyranny" had been accomplished, both governments hoped for universal peace, freedom from fear and want, freedom of the seas, abandonment of "the use of force," disarmament of nations threatening "aggression outside of their frontiers," and "a wider and permanent system of general security."

The message carried immense weight to threatened peoples throughout the world. Of greater immediate interest to us, however, was the agreement that the United States would take over convoy escort duties on the "American-Iceland stretch of the Atlantic," making public what had been in our sailing orders from Admiral King for the occupation of Iceland.

On 1 September 1941 the president ordered the Navy to escort merchant ships of any nationality, in effect Allied vessels, across the Atlantic. Germany protested, rightly, that this was a violation of international law, but the policy was already in operation. Admiral King called the American position "a realistic attitude toward events in the Atlantic." For a nation at peace, we were at war in every respect except a formal declaration.

On our return to Iceland, a group of wardroom officers accepted an invitation for a tour and lunch aboard *King George V*. The ship was interesting, but we thought the British were still rather primitive in gunnery—a painful lesson both nations had yet to learn—and especially in damage control involving loss of electrical or hydraulic power. Our stained and oil-soaked blues became expensive reminders of dripping pipes and general lack of cleanliness. But we enjoyed a few beers while relaxing in their comfortably paneled and well-furnished wardroom. We Americans had "stripped ship" of all combustible materials like carpeting, overstuffed furniture, and comfort items presumed to be hazardous in combat even though essential to ease the stark life we were enduring. We returned the Royal Navy's hospitality with cokes—the dry Navy's response to a stronger beverage before dinner—and American steaks as the prime attraction.

To help in our exchange of hospitality with the Royal Navy, Admiral Giffen authorized use of a motor launch hauled out to a boom as a "club." After a few days, however, the foul and unpredictable weather made such a scheme hazardous. For the junior officers, plus anybody senior who dared to volunteer, participation in some of the Limey officers' after-dinner sports often made for hilarious evenings, especially after a few rounds of beverages. The game of steeplechase on the *King George V* involved climbing out a wardroom porthole onto a boat boom, then hoisting oneself (at the cost of a very cold swim in event of a misstep) hand over hand up the stay to the next deck, into a ventilation duct, and crawling through various obstacles to emerge once again in the wardroom. It was great sport but terribly hard on uniforms.

For the enlisted, we had much less to offer. The shore facilities were few enough; boxing matches, smokers, tournaments and contests were limited by the inability to use the topside areas during foul weather and blackouts. As the nights became longer and progressively more dreary, few could enjoy any time ashore. Depression became the common mood. The British Army later reported the bleak and boring environment as the real cause of 128 men losing their lives in Iceland through suicide and "trying to swim back home." The forces afloat didn't keep such statistics, but they shared the problem. Every attempt was made to encourage long hikes or fishing ashore if only to break the monotony. When "daylight" deteriorated to only four or five hours of twilight and the weather became increasingly unpredictable, this diversion too disappeared. Going to sea on patrol or for routine gunnery exercises merely exchanged one misery for another.

Movies were a limited blessing, but showing them on deck caused a heavy strain on the imagination. Starting in early twilight, we had audio but couldn't see the picture; when the picture cleared the order to "darken ship" soon followed. *Citizen Kane*, a great movie with many flashbacks, became doubly impossible when the operator accidentally interchanged some of the reels. At one or two reels per night, half of which couldn't be seen, only a genius could keep track of the plot. Still, it was a touch of home.

We counted the weeks until the ship could get a portable projector for use in the wardroom and crew's quarters. Otherwise, the old Navy standbys of acey-deucey (seagoing backgammon) or cameroon (a version of poker played with ten dice) helped break the boredom. Not many played bridge, and poker was forbidden. Entertainment free of charge via the spectacular northern lights was available on clear evenings. One can't begin to describe the shimmering, weaving, dancing magic of colors that flitted across the sky. The dark waters of the sea reflected the silvery moon. The contrast between the frosted mountaintops and the brilliant northern constellations offered a vision never to be forgotten. All too often the display ended with a vicious storm, the

winds rising from fifteen to fifty knots in fifteen minutes. In
port, boats tied up alongside were carried away recoverable
at peril, swamped or salvaged on the rocky beaches. Any
liberty party ashore risked the nuisance of no boats or a
miserably wet return in driving rain, snow, or sleet.

A sortie to sea by the German pocket battleships *Gnei-
senau* and *Scharnhorst* in October found *Wichita* and *Vincennes* patrolling a line north of Iceland to the Greenland
coast seeking to prevent a breakthrough into the open Atlantic. Shortly after we cleared the fjord, a southerly gale hit
with all its fury. Steaming broadside to the seas, the ship
bucked mountainous waves thundering into her side, breaking up in huge geysers of water, sledgehammering boats and
exposed equipment. A heavy roll and pitch made life miserable everywhere, especially in sky forward, where I hung on
with aching ribs and icy fingers, repeatedly drenched by the
wind-driven spray.

The following day the gale disappeared as fast as it had
arisen. By noon the wind was a gentle breeze and the skies
cleared rapidly. In late afternoon, just before sunset, land
suddenly appeared, a breathtaking vision of the ice-capped
mountain plateaus of Greenland, a gigantic panorama of
pink- and green-tinted peaks rising awesomely from the sea.
So clear was the atmosphere that the peaks were sighted
when they were almost one hundred miles away. The war
was still on, however, and the ship reversed course to
continue patrol. By the next morning the perennial fog and
sleet made an effective search for the elusive pocket battleships impossible. The new air search radar installed in New
York added little confidence. For surface search, we had the
Mark 1 eyeball; for submarine search, nothing. My AA
director crew frequently detected patrolling aircraft visually
at phenomenal ranges in clear weather—twenty-five to forty
miles—but in the fog, search capabilities were minimal, even
for icebergs. The British had better radar; the Germans by
far the better sound gear—so good that even battleships
mounted hydrophones.

When *Bismarck,* then the most powerful battleship afloat,
met HMS *Hood* southeast of Greenland in late May of 1941,
she detected the Britisher by her hydrophones, ranging in
with radar and visually. Opening fire at fifteen miles, she

destroyed *Hood* with one salvo. The lack of either radar or hydrophones on *Wichita* made ordinary navigation hazardous in Arctic waters. She suffered a very near collision when a destroyer whose closest approach should have been not less than twenty miles suddenly loomed out of the fog. Emergency action by both ships caused a miss by less than fifty feet.

Many of us on the firing line in those early days of the war regretted the attitude of isolationism still prevalent in America when war was on our doorstep. I for one greatly admired the skill of the president, his masterful use of "fireside chats," and his use of the power of his office to bring public opinion to support our increasing involvement in the war before the Pearl Harbor attack. Some officers did not share my views. Even in the operating forces isolationism and anti-British sentiments were not uncommon. After all, the military had contingency plans for a war against Britain as late as the 1920s.

Was President Roosevelt deliberately seeking to involve the fleet in a war? Many of us thought so despite the absence of documentary proof. In August 1941 FDR indicated to Winston Churchill that American escort of convoys to Iceland would soon produce an incident leading to U.S. entry into the war. Following the *Greer* episode, FDR countered with his "rattlesnake" fireside chat, in which he misrepresented *Greer* as the victim of an unprovoked attack, when, in fact, *Greer* was clearly the aggressor, not only having vectored the British patrol bomber in to attack but following up with her own attack when the plane missed. The president, as a consequence, ordered the Navy to attack German vessels on sight.

The "shoot on sight" order brought retaliation from Hitler in October, promising that any American ship doing so would be the mark for German torpedoes. Two days before, at 0107, 17 October, 390 miles southwest of Reykjavik, the American destroyer *Kearny* was hit amidships by a German torpedo, killing eleven men and injuring seven others. *Kearny* was one of the American and British destroyers and corvettes escorting a convoy under attack by U-boats that had already sunk eight merchantmen. On 18 October, *Kearny* made a dramatic entry into Hvalfjordur, steaming between the *King George V* and USS *Mississippi* at anchor. The two battleships reversed tradition by rendering honors to *Kearny*. All other ships gave three rousing cheers in half a dozen tongues, echoing across the still waters of the fjord as the brave ship steamed slowly by. Then on Navy Day, 27 October, Roosevelt revealed the existence of a captured map showing German ambitions to set up five vassal states in Central and South America. The map, planted by British intelligence, cannot be found in the public record, but Hitler's *Mein Kampf,* published in the 1920s, carried no less dire threats against the Americas.

Within two weeks of the *Kearny* episode, the war further heated up when the fleet oiler USS *Salinas,* west of Iceland, was hit by two German torpedoes on 30 October, and at daybreak the next day the destroyer *Reuben James,* escorting a merchant convoy, was sunk by U-552 south of Iceland and six hundred miles west of Ireland, with the loss of 115 American lives.

Further evidence of the president's desire to provoke a war occurred in November 1941, when *Wichita* and *Tuscaloosa* were ordered from Iceland without any screening destroyers for our vitally needed antisubmarine protection. We made an aimless cruise to a point about a hundred miles off Londonderry, Ireland. With no escorts, no darkened ship, no zigzagging, and no radio silence, we were cruise ships wandering across the hostile sea, blind and deaf. Many of us thought this a deliberate provocation of Hitler. Whatever the purpose, these actions seemed to show that Hitler lacked the will for battle with American capital ships, a discovery of great value. If true, some capital ships could be released for use elsewhere. Hitler didn't understand seapower and never learned that building a navy required years but creating a naval tradition took centuries.

The *Wichita*'s cruise stimulated the ship's force to build depth charge racks on the fantail adequate to handle the big six-hundred-pounders. Still lacking detection gear, we could now make noise to scare the enemy below, at the risk of blowing off the stern. But we had no way of finding him.

At this time another incident further roiled the international waters. The German blockade runner *Odenwald* was intercepted at sea by the American cruiser *Omaha* and destroyer *Somers* and taken into San Juan, Puerto Rico, on 11 November 1941 under the startling pretense that the ship was engaged in the slave trade. If nothing else, the incident created opportunities for wardroom discussion, but I found I couldn't stimulate much interest in international politics. Few military officers of that era ever voted, seeing the ballot as a violation of the separation of political and military policies in our government. As professionals they accepted their nonpolitical role without question. They placed great stress on being good professionals—good at what one did and unemotional about it.

About this time, the rigorous way of life in Iceland became further aggravated by a shortage of food. Letters to wives commented on the monotony of daily canned corn and beans, which were very liquid, and the sheer rapture one day in getting a fresh leaf of lettuce and an orange. With no wartime logistics plans yet in operation, we were at the mercy of haphazard merchantmen for stores. If we were at sea when a supply ship came in, fruits or vegetables were well picked over before we got back. We lost out entirely once when a U.S. flag vessel, following union regulations, refused to break cargo outside union working hours.

It is hard to imagine today that a major warship could run out of bread. The old stories of the German black rye bread in World War I became a reality when we were forced to use a giant coffee urn to keep a yeast culture fermenting in potato peelings from which we made bread. An ordinary loaf, damp and soggy, weighed about five pounds and tasted rancid even when fresh. It was delicious.

Nor can one imagine today a cruiser on wartime operations in the North Atlantic to be allowed only six suits of foul-weather gear. At my exposed watch station the enlisted men rotated every twenty minutes, the officers every four hours. It was no picnic. Wearing every piece of warm clothing owned or borrowed, we shivered from one watch to the next.

By Thanksgiving 1941, I was halfway to parenthood. I thirsted for details from Henri but mail was often delayed, waylaid, or lost. Nobody else on board knew of our forthcoming blessed event. To celebrate Thanksgiving and five months of married life, I took a long hike in the mountains.

It was clear and cold; a few snowflakes fell on the frozen ground, but the wind had stopped. I walked briskly out the Reykjavik road to the antisubmarine boom, then cut up a steep ravine to the top of a cliff overshadowing the southern shore. Dressed in service blues with topcoat, gloves, and heavy arctics, I was soon huffing, puffing, and perspiring freely. The ravine got steeper and steeper, with large patches of snow and ice. As I topped the crest a blast of wind hit me; the temperature dropped to about fifteen degrees. On the far side of the valley a rutted road could be seen threading its way along a tortuous river. When last I had seen that valley in August, it was green and fertile. Today the brown landscape merged into the scattered shacks and sod huts, a picture of the harsh life these folk must lead in scratching out an existence. It often occurred to me that there were sound strategic reasons for the Americans and British to base in Iceland, but I could never find out what kept the Icelanders there. Years later I readily understood why Iceland was chosen for testing lunar landscape vehicles.

Stepping from rock to rock, shifting the weight of my heavy boots to ease the pain of a few blisters, I surmounted the last peak and suddenly saw the sun. Hanging low over a far range of hills, hidden in a bank of clouds, it was old Sol, sure enough, my first view since returning from sea a month earlier. From the brow of the cliff, the whole fjord lay at my feet. I could count sixty ships at anchor—twenty-two merchantmen, thirty-eight American, British, Polish, and Norwegian warships. Walking out on a rock promontory, I sat down and sketched the vast harbor below. The strong wind blowing me back from the edge kept me safe despite the sheer drop of over a thousand feet. The few farmhouses, grazing cattle and sheep, a bicycle on the road, and the Stars and Stripes waving over the Falcon Club provided a serene facade that disguised the cruel war just over the horizon.

I daydreamed, giving thanks to God for all the blessings bestowed on us. Alone in far-off Iceland, there were reasons why I may have felt sad, but my heart was very light. Somehow Henri and I would be reunited soon and I had everything in the world to make a man happy. If thoughts of the war tried to intrude, I had no concern. Even before graduating from the Naval Academy I had believed war to be inevitable. I wrote a mediocre essay on the path to true peace, mentioning the need for an effective international organization to limit war, and urging that America get her head out of the sand, take her proper place in the world, and prepare for the war already on her doorstep. Dad and Mother thought I was bloodthirsty; certainly their generation had been embittered by the experience of war. But with the Navy already at war and the country soon to follow, I prayed that it would be over as soon as possible. We Americans required a far greater understanding of the peril already at hand.

The krah-krah of some huge blackbirds broke my reverie as they tried to overcome the wind and share the rock shelf. Dipping and plunging, they rushed by time and again to get a toehold, finally giving up with one last raucous complaint. Suddenly alerted that the weather was closing in, I hurried off my pulpit in a brisk half-trot back to the landing.

Safely aboard, I walked into a wardroom bull session on who would go to Bowdoin, Maine, for the radar school that Don and George Reinhart had attended. Much as I wanted to grab the quota, to announce that we were expecting and then to request the school would suggest the wrong motivation and take unfair advantage of the others, who would surely withdraw in my favor.

Another way to get back home, long in the back of my mind, appealed more and more. A new submarine school class would convene in New London, Connecticut, in January. Long ago I had indicated an interest in submarines but had made no specific request. There was a major job to be done on *Wichita* and, having served in every department over two and a half years, I knew every valve and fitting on the ship. Much as my personal side wanted to get back to civilization, my professional side insisted that it was more important to stay.

Such was the situation on 7 December 1941. After starting the day shivering through the midwatch, I returned to my cabin at four, slept uneasily until breakfast, and returned to the wardroom after mass in the crew's mess to scan the shipboard morning press. Shortly, the phone jangled. It was Jack Healey, the communications officer, all agog to report the happy news of telegraphic orders for my immediate detachment to report to submarine school on 2 January. Oh happy day! I went out on deck to find the exec and stir the pot about transportation home. It was just after 1000; a destroyer was fueling alongside; I asked casually if her destination was stateside. It was a nice try but no dice.

At lunchtime, everybody was excited about the orders. I decided it was time to give the officers *the secret*, that we were planning to launch the "class of '39 baby" in March. What a surprise! All were excited except Jack, who grumped all afternoon about my treachery in not putting out our news when he did. Half the joy of fatherhood occurred in that hour.

But the transportation problem still loomed. The exec called me about 1630 to report that a convoy was leaving from Reykjavik the following day, and perhaps I could get aboard. He offered me the captain's gig to chase around the harbor. An old merchantman, SS *North King,* was leaving Hvalfjordur to join the convoy in the morning. Rushing around the rough seas in darkness, with snow and wind biting my face, I strained my eyes to find one rust-bucket among many blacked out ships at anchor. The search seemed hopeless, but somehow we found her. The mate offered passage to Reykjavik and New York if I boarded immediately. I had no luggage and hadn't begun to turn over my duties aboard ship. I watched her sail into the night.

The U.S. Marine barracks on the beach offered a station wagon for the seven-hour trip to the capital, but the roads were impassable. The Witch senior aviator offered to fly me over. With a storm rising and a five-hundred-foot ceiling, that too was impossible. I was fast losing hope for an early departure.

Just as we sat down to dinner, we heard the startling news that the Japanese were attacking Pearl Harbor. All through the evening terse bulletins were picked off the airwaves, but they added very little to the awful news of the tragedy in the Pacific. Deep gloom fell over us as we hazarded guesses about the fate of the fleet and many friends in Hawaii. When I finally turned in I was exhausted—I had had three hours of sleep the night before, and what a day it had been.

Early morning on the eighth, I determined to make one more effort to fly to Reykjavik. Hastily undogging my battle port to check the weather, I could see only rain, snow, and wind; a signal lantern on the bridge reflected off the low hanging clouds, indicating a ceiling of about two hundred feet. My last hope shattered and died. At 1300, just after lunch, general quarters sounded—the British search station in Reykjavik reported an unidentified air contact, obviously false. Just before dinner, however, secret orders came through for the battleship division in Iceland to return to the Pacific. The exec called and asked if I could go immediately.

"I'm on my way."

"What ship?"

"*Idaho*."

With all the officers swarming around to help pack and see me off, I left the ship late that night. I was scheduled to give a lecture to the officers on a revised damage-control bill for *Wichita* on which I had been working for months. As I left the ship for the last time, Lucien "Rags" Ragonnet, the first lieutenant, followed me down the gangway to get all the last-minute details. Aboard USS *Idaho*, the rush of final departure met me. I passed greetings from my recent CO and exec to Captain Conde L. R. Raguet, then found a comfortable bunk in a cabin next to a classmate, John M. "Jack" Reigart, and turned in. When I woke the next morning, the ship was under way, steaming at maximum speed for Norfolk, the familiar snow-capped peaks of Iceland slowly disappearing astern. Visions of sugar plums danced through my head.

2   The USS *Mackerel*

The Gold Dolphins

The reunion with Henri and our families in Pittsburgh was deliriously happy. Then somebody asked where I was headed for duty. When I answered, "Submarines," Mother almost fainted. The morning news carried the story that my hometown buddie Samuel H. "Buzz" Hunter, with whom I had competed for an appointment to Annapolis, had been killed in the USS *Sea Lion* in a bombing raid on Manila, the first submarine casualty of the war. Both Henri's and my family had three sons of draft age, and wonderful as it was to be home, their concern for the future was never far below the surface.

Henri looked great but her pregnancy was becoming obvious. Our very special Christmas gift made for a perfect holiday. All too soon it was time to get on the road again toward New England for my new duties.

We pulled into New London on the first day of the new year and quickly found a large, airy, two-bedroom apartment in a fine old home on Broad Street overlooking a public park. In the center of the park stood a magnificent statue of Nathan Hale. I drew special inspiration from those inscribed words, "I only regret I have but one life to lose for my country." Years later, when U-2 pilot Francis Gary Powers was shot down over the Soviet Union, his considerably less heroic words to his captors did not give the same feeling. No volunteer, he could only whine, "They made me do it."

I checked in at the submarine base as soon as we had made the apartment livable by the addition of a few personal items. Most of my uniforms were still en route from Iceland. But we really needed nothing except each other. The few days together in New York after our marriage made us relish the opportunity to be together in our own home, and this time it would be for three whole months. The two weeks in Pittsburgh had flown by, always punctuated by the dreadful news from the war.

Submarine School was a happy reunion of Naval Academy classmates and old friends, but the dominating personalities were two unsung heroes, Commander Karl G. Hensel and Lieutenant Commander George W. "Silent Pat" Patterson. Deadly serious, they drove us hard. The course had been cut from six to three months starting with our class, and Commander Hensel was determined we would learn just as much in half the time. Submarining for us was a new experience; with much of the surface fleet lying on the bottom in Pearl Harbor, we were anxious to get to work.

The submarine is a strange vehicle, at home neither on the surface nor submerged. Marvelously complex, the "fleet" submarine with which we fought World War II was a tapered cylinder three hundred ten feet long and sixteen feet in diameter, designed to withstand the awesome pressure of the sea at test depth of nineteen tons per square foot. Free-flooding saddle tanks wrapped around the pressure hull, open to the sea at the bottom, provided buoyancy. On the surface the submarine floated on a bubble of air contained in the ballast tanks. To dive, the tanks were vented; to surface, the tanks were blown dry with compressed air. To retain a neutral buoyancy, every pound of stores, equipment, and people moved on or off had to be accounted for by shifting water in the trim tanks to compensate for all changes. Corrections were also necessary to account for the differences in specific gravity of sea water at different temperatures and salinities around the world. The rule of thumb in going through the Panama Canal to compensate for the salty and less dense waters of the Pacific, for example, was to correct the variable ballast by a factor equal to the specific gravity of urine. All changes of weights on or off the ship were recorded in the diving book, and the diving officer, usually the engineer, had to work out his compensation and shift water before each dive. Bow and stern plane operators maintained the depth and kept the ship on an even keel or at a desired up or down angle ordered by the diving officer. The art of diving, like flying by the seat of the pants, involved getting the feel of the boat, heavy or light overall, forward or aft. Some learned it instinctively; a few never got the magic touch.

The rest of the ship served as the fighting and living areas. In the forward torpedo room were a battery of six bow tubes capable of firing either torpedoes or mines, plus storage racks for ten additional torpedoes (or twenty mines), and bunks for the crew snuggled around the torpedoes. A twenty-one-inch by twenty-foot-long torpedo with a warhead of five to six hundred pounds of explosive did not always make an ideal bunkmate, but as the torpedoes were used the racks became available for additional bunks, making the quarters much more livable. In the aft part of the room were the controls for raising and lowering the sound heads and the pitometer log—or ship's speedometer—plus the officers' head and microscopic shower stall.

The next compartment contained the officers' quarters, with a small galley, a tiny wardroom, and three staterooms, each with a wash basin and desk, plus the chiefs' bunkroom, and a tiny office. The lower half of this compartment contained the forward storage battery, 126 cells weighing 1,600 pounds each. The heat from the batteries during sustained operations submerged kept the living spaces warm in the winter, stifling in the tropics.

The control room contained the diving and steering controls and a plumber's nightmare of depth gauges, manifolds, compressors, auxiliary machinery, pumps, ice machines, and air conditioning compressors. Adjacent to the diving officer, the chief of the watch ran the hydraulic manifold controlling the hull openings, his eyes glued to the "Christmas tree," displaying a red (open) or green (shut) indicator light on each hull opening. On the diving alarm, his report of a "green board" meant the hull was watertight and the dive could proceed. Also, in the aft corner of the control room were the radio shack and coding equipment.

Directly above the control room, the conning tower or command center contained the ship control and all the equipment for making an attack: plotting, navigation, radar, sonar, and torpedo firing. In the center of the compartment were two periscopes, forty-foot-long tubes about six inches in diameter. The forward or "attack" scope had a very small window above the surface only 1.4 inches in diameter. The other scope had a window about twice the size and was equipped with an excellent radar. This scope could be adapted for still or movie photography. From the conning tower one ascended to the open bridge, large enough for two officers in the cockpit and, above them, around the periscope housing, three lookouts.

Aft of the control room was the crew's quarters—galley, messroom, bunks for half the crew, two heads, showers, and generally a washing machine. Beneath the crew's compartment lay the aft storage battery, the same size as the forward one, plus frozen food and ammunition lockers. Aft of the crew's space were two engine rooms, each with two diesel engines producing a total of 6,500 shaft horsepower capable of driving the ship twenty-one knots on the surface—about twenty-four miles an hour. Further aft was the maneuvering room for propulsion controls to the main motors below, two motors on each shaft, and finally the after torpedo room, with four torpedo tubes and four reload torpedoes (or eight mines) stored in the racks and bunks for the handling crews.

With rare exceptions, all the officers and men in submarines graduated from submarine school. The course was thorough and demanding. In the officers' course, mornings were spent in the classroom and afternoons devoted to practical work on the attack trainer, the diving trainer, or shiphandling on the old "O" boats. I and most of my classmates were primarily interested in developing our technique in the attack trainer, a dummy conning tower from which we ran problems against zigzagging, escorted targets or warship task forces. The aim was to get into attack position without being detected, firing torpedoes at close range, then getting clear unscathed. Even against a low-speed enemy on the surface, a submerged submarine capable of a maximum of only nine knots, and that for only one hour, was at a severe disadvantage—like a clubfooted man chasing a racehorse. If the enemy zigzagged, the sub commander was often duped into pursuit in the wrong direction to find himself hopelessly out of range before attack position could be gained. To preserve his big advantage of stealth, he used minimal periscope observations, less than seven seconds, and normally exposed only enough scope to see the masts of the ship he was stalking. The trick was to get into torpedo range of about fifteen hundred to two thousand yards without exposing a broad silhouette of the sub to escort vessels, fire a straight shot (with a near zero gyro angle on the torpedo), and escape in the confusion while preserving enough endurance in the battery to break contact and eventually get to the surface to recharge.

All this was a mystery to us young tyros. We had some shiphandling experience and had developed a sense of relative movement in fleet exercises at sea. The submarine attack problem was infinitely more difficult. We slowly honed our skills on the attack trainer, but Silent Pat Patterson and King Kong Karl Hensel were hard taskmasters. They worked closely with the operators controlling the problem topside (above the "conning tower") to set up a wide variety of fully automated problems against a resourceful "enemy." Students took turns as approach officer on the periscope, an assistant to counsel and guide the attack, a torpedo data computer (TDC) operator, and a mechanical plotter in rotation, each intensely interested in the unfolding problem. Commander Hensel in particular was unforgiving of errors, especially mental ones, and was not above a little gamesmanship to capitalize on doctrinal errors and get us into trouble.

Sometimes it worked both ways. I was assistant to John E. Shepherd III on his approach one day. John got himself into trouble by failing to detect a zig by the target group. The target was about to disappear over the horizon beyond torpedo range. Only a big zig toward the submarine would give him a good shot. Suddenly I recalled that the two previous zigs had been away from the sub and that the machine topside was probably not capable of another zig away without going off the edge of the game board. I suggested to Johnny that he wait for the zig toward us and then get a new setup.

Off in the corner of the room, Silent Pat didn't miss a thing. As soon as he heard my suggestion, I happened to see him easing out of the room to head topside. Assuming that he was about to do what I said couldn't be done about another zig away, I immediately suggested to Johnny, as soon as Pat was out of earshot, that we assume another minimum zig away, take the normal approach course at high speed, and get off a quick shot as soon as he got within range. When Pat came back down he realized he'd been outfoxed. But I felt terrible. He was so sincere, so intense, so totally dedicated in his drive to help us excel, I knew I had let him down. In fragile health, he should have been retired for disability; in his zeal to prepare young officers for heavy responsibilities he drove his students to their maximum—and well beyond his own.

The school was competitive, but the competition was self-motivated. There were more openings on operating submarines than graduates, and an officer on any small ship carried great responsibilities, especially on a submarine, where every man was expected to know his job and that of the man next to him. The force never tolerated slackers. A mere word from a CO that a man was unfit for submarine duty marked him for immediate transfer. The captain's judgment was never questioned.

To gain additional experience, we sometimes went back to the trainer at night, accompanied by our wives. The duty personnel set up and ran problems for us, often wild and woolly. It was not unknown for us to have a couple of martinis beforehand, just to keep loose. It was great fun, and one or two of the wives may have become better than one or two of us. Given the limited mobility of a sub, making a successful submerged attack required a high order of skill.

In the early days of the war, submarines were required to remain submerged all day, surfacing at night to recharge. The endurance of the battery was always critical. All the energy to keep the ship operating—propulsion, lighting, cooking, and running equipment—came from the huge storage batteries beneath the living compartments. The total endurance submerged at minimum cruising speed of two to three knots was less than forty-eight hours. The air got foul, carbon dioxide built up, and the oxygen ran short in about twelve hours. A submarine attack was a table stakes poker game. If the attacking officer on the periscope gambled with high speed, eight or nine knots, to close the enemy, the battery—his stack of chips—would be exhausted in less than an hour. Even at low speeds, getting into attack position could deplete the battery so that very little was left for evasion and escape from angry escorts, particularly when the attack was successful. Unless one was miserly in use of the battery and begrudged every wasted ampere and volt, he soon paid the piper. There was no way to buy more chips when his stake was exhausted.

Much sub school time at sea in the "O" boats covered every operation possible in diving and surfacing until each of us could perform the whole operation. Among the most challenging tasks was "bumper drill," making landings and getting under way from alongside the dock. I was fairly fortunate in having considerable shiphandling experience from *Wichita,* but no ship handled quite like a submarine, particularly one of those ancient school boats. Underpowered, slow to respond, and with a round bottom, they handled like a bowling ball. Sometimes they did not respond at all. Standard submarine base practice contributed to the mental stress.

At New London, parking was available for submariners at the head of the finger piers. Should a submarine be brought alongside at too high a speed, or if a backing bell failed to be answered, the heavy, protruding bow on occasion overrode the dock and damaged the car parked at the head of the pier. To emphasize the need for caution in avoiding a possible submarine-auto collision, the first parking space was reserved for the skipper of the submarine, thereby guaranteeing the enthusiastic co-operation of the CO in preventing possible damage to a U.S. naval vessel if only to avoid more serious damage to the family wheels. Insurance claims based on collisions between submarine and automobile in New London were unusual but far from unknown. We all walked away from the sea operations with vivid tales of adventures, crises, and near crises trying to get those awkward and poor-handling ships alongside a dock.

The social life during those fleeting twelve weeks carried a special meaning for all of us. For most it marked our first chance for family life, and at the end of the course, we would scatter far and wide to the call of duty, the wives either going home to their parents or moving to a city nearer the focus of the war to wait and wonder, fighting off rumors and fears of the unknown in the months of festering anxiety for a husband on patrol. Because the future must remain unknown, I couldn't see fretting about it. The days passed with thoughts of tomorrow carefully screened out.

The officers who shared the common bond of the Naval Academy had gone through four grueling years together and two more in a wide variety of experiences around the world since. Our ties were very strong. The wives were great company. Most had been sweethearts through the academy days. They joined every phase of our lives and quickly assimilated their special roles within the Navy family. Promotions to lieutenant (junior grade) came through during sub school with a big $50-a-month increase in pay. In addition, we got submarine pay for every day at sea in the school boats based on 25 percent of base pay extra, adding about $10 a month. It was not much, but we were all hungry in those days. The additional income was not for hazardous duty but as compensation for damage to clothing from acid and grease. Then Congress decided to equate submariners and aviators, who got 50 percent extra for hazardous duty. We suddenly felt affluent.

Henri's term was nearing completion. The baby was due to arrive on graduation day in late March. Frederic B. and Betty Clarke, married like so many of us in June 1941, were in New London, also expecting. We shared many evenings comparing notes. When Henri suddenly began to grow quite large, my first thought was "Golly." That became our private name for our precious little addition to the family. For dad to go off to war just as fatherhood brought its special joys and problems created an unspoken but deeply shared concern. Many young mothers would be paralyzed at the thought of moving out of an apartment and heading home to their parents with little help from the father. Navy wives have been doing it for years. Much as my heart ached at leaving her in the lurch, for every sad departure a deliriously happy return would follow, leaving the pain only a memory. I don't think my zeal to go back to the war lessened with the imminent responsibilities of fatherhood. I felt a strong obligation to do the job I was trained to do, but it was professional and not emotional.

As graduation approached, more and more night hours were spent in deep study for final exams. My concerns were far from the books. Henri suddenly realized that things were not going well with "Golly." A visit to the hospital led to a special series of tests, a second check, and suddenly the dreadful news of the likelihood of losing the baby, and perhaps Henri as well, to toxemia. The next day no sign of life could be detected in the fetus; the sole question was saving the mother. A young doctor called me out of the hospital room that evening to discuss the case and the question of inducing labor to save the mother. My recollection today, in vivid detail, is only of the thoroughly brutal and thoughtless manner in which the doctor presented the alternatives. In anguish I left the hospital with tears streaming down my cheeks. I am not an emotional person. This was the first time since childhood when I could not hold back my emotions, and I never felt so totally alone, even with my dearest wife so close at hand. I felt "they" had her and she was beyond my control. When it was all over, the doctor prescribed no children for at least two years or Henri might not survive another pregnancy.

We called Mother Frank in Pittsburgh; she immediately flew to New London to stay with us for a short time. I revered her just as much as my own mother, and we were delighted. Henri made a slow but full recovery, not without many difficult days for both of us. Sub school classmates, their wives, and friends in the area were wonderful, but they were hurrying off to new duties and could do little except join in our grief. Stern, unbending Karl Hensel sent for me immediately. I deeply appreciated his sincere desire, with his wife, Olive, to be of assistance. He wanted to talk about my orders to sea. An opening for an officer had just come through for the USS *Mackerel*, operating out of the submarine base, which he thought would keep Henri and me together for a while in New London. With a terrible load off my shoulders, I could only mutter my thanks and, with a warm handshake, hurry home to give Henri the good news.

Mackerel was a new submarine built at the Electric Boat Company in Groton, just down the Thames River from the submarine base. She was commissioned 31 March 1941, a year before I reported aboard. *Mackerel,* with *Marlin,* constituted a special class of subs built because some senior submariners thought the 310-foot, 1,850-ton fleet boats then in production were too large to survive in confined sea areas like the Mediterranean. Admiral Thomas C. Hart in particular, commander in chief of the U.S. Asiatic Fleet at the opening of the war and later a U.S. senator from Connecticut, had strong feelings on the need to build smaller submarines. *Mackerel* was 243 feet long, 800 tons, with four torpedo tubes forward, two aft. She was a fine ship operationally, but for the smaller size we paid a heavy price in limited endurance at sea. She was ideal for operations in the Mediterranean, but war across the vast expanses of the Pacific required the great range, endurance, and relative crew comfort of the fleet submarine.

My new CO was Lt. Cmdr. John F. Davidson. Ten years my senior at Annapolis, Captain John was a gentleman and a very good skipper. We soon became firm friends. *Mackerel*'s assigned duties included services to the submarine school to train prospective commanding officers, or PCOs, attending the advanced course in the fine points of submarine attack technique. We were also involved in training antisubmarine units, testing and evaluating new sonar gear developed at the Underwater Sound Lab in New London, and special operations such as training commandos for operations from submarines, all of which added to a fascinating pattern of duties. I was delighted when I was assigned duties as first lieutenant, gunnery and torpedo officer. This meant I would run the torpedo data computer for my battle station in the command center. The long hours of tracking and other fire-control drills in *Wichita* running either the main or AA battery rangekeepers paid handsome dividends. I was determined to become the best TDC operator in the fleet and spent all my early hours practicing on it. And it was none too soon.

The COs and many execs going to new construction, to

first commands, or returning to sea after a tour ashore were all sent through the PCO school. Four weeks long, it was an intensive lecture and under way program designed to give COs the best possible training in periscope technique, attack tactics, and doctrine and to bring them up to speed in all phases of wartime submarining. Again Karl Hensel and Pat Patterson were in charge.

The arduous exercises at sea allowed each PCO to take turns as attacking officer and on the other stations in the fire control party. We were under way before anybody else each morning and often did not get back alongside until the wee hours of the next morning, leaving little time to get in a battery charge and a few hours of sleep before going back out for more of the same. For the young studs it was a rugged routine; Hensel and Patterson, both of whom had passed the ancient age of forty, earned our sincere admiration. I was usually behind the TDC operator trying to preserve the myth of my sudden status as an expert. Nobody aboard had an opportunity to learn more than I.

Meanwhile, other duties took time and effort. We frequently fired exercise torpedoes, and they required constant routining by the torpedo room crews mulehauling them back aboard after each shot. The practice torpedoes were the same as warshots except the warheads had been replaced with bright yellow water-filled heads set to blow themselves dry at the end of the run. Floating to the surface, they were recovered by specially fitted retrievers and toted back to the base torpedo shop for routining and reloading aboard.

The highest motivation driving me, however, was my qualification in submarines and the right to wear the gold dolphins. Regulations required an intimate knowledge of the ship, skill in shiphandling, diving, surfacing, successful torpedo fire, and preparation of a detailed notebook. After a year in submarine duty and when recommended for qualification by the CO, the officer went before a board of three other COs for an oral exam and a practical display of his skills at sea including a torpedo attack on a zigzagging, escorted target. The regulation requiring a minimum of one year at sea was suspended while I was serving on *Mackerel,* but the standards were unchanged.

The war, meanwhile, continued to go badly up and down

the Atlantic seaboard. In January 1942, the first full month
in Germany's war against the United States, 62 ships of
327,000 tons were sunk off the Atlantic coast by only 5 U-
boats. During my few weeks at submarine school, the sinkings off the Atlantic shores totaled 198 ships of 1,150,000
tons and an additional 148 ships in the Caribbean. American
authorities were exceedingly slow to organize defenses
against submarines. Blackouts were unknown. The American shoreline was ablaze with the lights of the cities, and
navigation lights burned brightly. The British experience on
the necessity to convoy ships was ignored. Ships sailed
singly and failed to zigzag. Cooperation between the Navy
and Army Air Corps was poor; the Navy was very short of
escorts and relearned the British experience only when the
slaughter of merchantmen forced changes. Far too few submarines were available for training surface and air antisubmarine forces. One of the first changes to improve the
situation involved *Mackerel*.

On 12 April 1942 *Mackerel* was sent to sea on a war patrol
to hunt U-boats off the coast between New London and
Norfolk. In Norfolk we were to work with the Army on
special mine warfare tests and with the Navy running surface
and submerged exercises for the antisubmarine airmen. As
we left New London at dusk on a gorgeous Sunday evening,
all the officers were on the bridge. Johnny Davidson echoed
the general sentiment, "Just to get to sea to help the war
makes me feel better already."

Entering Long Island Sound, we passed through the familiar tide rips at Race Rock, completed the rig for diving, and
made a quick submergence to check the trim. The shiny,
black contour of the ship returned to the surface shortly and
the regular sea watch was set. I had the midwatch and was
still on duty when we made the morning dive to one hundred
feet at 0450, returning to periscope depth at daylight for
submerged patrol. The officers stood four hours on watch
and eight off, except at night on the surface, when we stood
three hours on the bridge, then three hours below to man
the TDC in an emergency or to decode incoming radio traffic
on the coding machine.

I didn't get to bed the first night until after breakfast and
went back on watch at noon. Just after I got off watch at

1600 and headed for the bunk, the sonar operator reported a screw noise which he thought sounded like a submarine. Nothing was visible on the surface, and *Mackerel* commenced an approach. Shortly a second set of screws could be heard on the opposite beam. We went to two hundred feet and commenced evasive maneuvering for an hour and a half before returning to periscope depth. All was clear. This, my first experience with submarine war, brought the sudden realization that the submarine was the only vessel that could see without being seen, having both powerful offensive weapons and defensive "armor," the layer of seawater as thick as the CO should wish to place between himself and the surface enemy. The periscope, operated skillfully, was invisible to the surface or air enemy; the submerged ears operated in an undisturbed, totally quiet atmosphere wholly free from engine or surface sea noises. Such advantages over the enemy were being proved daily in the unequal contest of the German subs against Allied merchantmen. A duel with another submerged submarine was another matter, however. Each was more or less helpless against the other. Not for many years would the equipment be available for a true submarine war in the depths of inner space.

A few days later, just after sunset, we heard pinging—the active search by an antisubmarine vessel—but could see nothing through the periscope. Coming closer and closer, the screw noises were soon clearly audible through the hull. We were quite sure the source was friendly but that meant little in those early days of the war. Friendly submarines were frequently attacked by our own forces; given the success of the enemy subs, it is understandable that our ships were quick on the trigger. When we were quite close, the captain decided to send the recognition signal on the sonar. There was no response. A repeat still brought no answer. The captain then ordered a recognition flare to be readied in the underwater signal gun while we made preparations to surface. The other ship was now visible through the scope, even in the darkness.

Surfacing suddenly, we scared him to death. Strangely, he had no idea we were in the area, had made no contact on us at any time, and was highly suspicious. The ship was the Coast Guard cutter *Legare*. Convinced we were an enemy, he closed to shouting range for identification. Still unsure, he asked us to repeat words like "valve" and "victor." Still unconvinced, he asked for "something in Brooklynese." The *Mackerel* third officer, Lt. Charles W. "Charlie" Fell, born and raised in Brooklyn, was asked to say a few words. He was totally mute. Prodded, he finally came up with some "youse guys" and similar patois of his favorite borough.

Legare decided to follow us in to Norfolk, but, being slower, she soon fell behind. It seemed unimportant at the time, but it almost resulted in disaster. We were due to arrive off the submarine net at the entrance to Hampton Roads at dawn. The evening was beautifully calm and clear with a slight surface haze. Everything was highly phosphorescent, making our black hull a dark spot in the middle of a halo. The wet hull gleamed when touched or rubbed with gloved hands. Rubbing gloves together lighted many sparkling, glowing points in the cloth.

Just past 2300 a lookout sighted the wakes of two torpedoes approaching from the starboard quarter. Charlie Fell had the deck and put the rudder over hard, just in time to see the wakes whoosh up the starboard side, missing the ship by a few feet. A hazy target was finally made out astern, and two torpedoes were quickly made ready and fired from the stern tubes. I was in the control room and listened to the high-pitched scream of the propellors as the "fish" sped on their way, waiting, waiting for the blast. The target presented a very sharp angle, and in the haze this was a poor shot. Both missed. Disappointment soon turned to horror. *Legare* came on the air in considerable excitement to report that a torpedo had passed close by. We could only imagine the thoughts which must have passed through the captain's mind. Had we almost destroyed one of our own ships? An enemy was certainly present, capable of firing torpedoes, which *Legare* was not. In the hard turn to avoid the torpedoes, the lookouts picked up the only visible target in the area, the *Legare,* which apparently had not been visible shortly before the attack. The wakes we saw placed the enemy submarine almost fifty degrees from the bearing of the Coast Guardsman.

We soon detected Cape Henry light looming out of the darkness at 0330, and we began picking our way around the minefields. Then a lookout reported a strange light to seaward, which after investigation I assured him was the planet Venus rising in the eastern sky. It did look surprisingly bright, fuzzed and magnified in the morning haze. At 0430, a dark object was sighted close abeam to port. It filled the field of my binoculars and hence was about five hundred yards away, with the unmistakable outline of a black hull and conning tower.

The captain ordered "general quarters," and all hands manned their battle stations. Swinging hard right to bring the stern tubes to bear, we challenged the stranger with the recognition signal. There was no response, even after three challenges. The water was too shallow to dive, and we were so close to Norfolk that identification seemed vital. With still no answer, the captain ordered "Fire." Two torpedoes sped out the tubes, shaking the *Mackerel* tail with a slight wag as two tons of destruction sped on their way. They were straight shots at good range and in good position. I knelt on the deck of the open bridge and watched the wakes through my binoculars. The target was clearly in view, and I ticked off the seconds, hardly daring to breathe while waiting for the explosion. Again none came. I didn't see how we could have missed.

We were hearing tales from the Pacific about torpedoes missing on perfect attack setups but didn't figure it could happen to us. I felt doubly sorry for the skipper. He followed up the attack, reversing course to bring the bow tubes to bear, but the other sub, which had been lying to in the surface, suddenly headed for the open sea at a speed we couldn't match, and quickly disappeared. After a short pursuit, the CO decided the chase was hopeless. We were already overdue for our rendezvous at the entrance to Norfolk.

The ship channel had changed since my last visit. New channel markers, apparently denoting minefields, and new navigation lights all looked out of place. Just then an Army plane flew overhead and informed us, "You should be aground."

In a momentary panic, we took a sounding on the fathometer that indicated only one fathom—six feet—beneath the keel. Stopping to verify from the chart that we had plenty of water, we discovered that the fathometer was not working properly. After a minor adjustment, it showed plenty of water. Finally resuming course toward the naval base, we felt the tension slowly easing. The events of the night were hard on the nerves of all, from CO to seaman.

In Norfolk we learned that the USS *Roper,* an old four-piper destroyer, had sunk submarine U-85 by depth charges just off the shore two days before and picked up thirty-two bodies from the water. The remains were laid out in the hangar while coffins were being made. Ship sinkings by the U-boats had been common off Norfolk. Reports flooded in about every twenty minutes of sightings and miscellaneous contacts on submarines, but most of the airmen, who may never have even seen an ocean before, made wild claims that everything and anything was a sub or a periscope. The overwhelming majority of the reports were false; *Mackerel's* mission was partly to show our winged brethren what a real submarine looked like. They freely admitted the exercises did them worlds of good.

That night the captain spoke to an Army colonel about the disconcerting grounding warning received from the Army plane. The colonel replied, "Why, you were right in the middle of our new minefield!" Then the skipper really lost his cool. Apparently some Army official decided to put a minefield in the channel near the big Army base at Fortress Monroe but neglected to tell the Navy, the prime users of the channel. We urged our sister service to try to keep in touch.

The following day we proceeded up the Chesapeake about eighty miles to Cove Point and began exercises with Army and Navy airmen, teaching them to recognize a submarine surfaced or submerged, to spot periscopes, and to track a submarine contact. For eight days we basked in the warm sunlight while on the surface, diving on cue when a plane approached. The under way time gave me a chance to qualify for top watch as OOD at sea and in port, and we were able to train many new men in their jobs. Each evening we anchored off Solomon's, Maryland, on the Patuxent River and went ashore at a tiny village with one hotel and a handwritten phone book—listing "Agatha," "Charlie's," "the garage," "Grandpop," and so on on a single page. We seldom found a newspaper, but the seafood and beer in a tiny tavern were superb. The officers sat around a big table playing "liar's dice" to see who would buy the round, an old Navy ritual. The enlisted men scattered at other tables tried to ply the officers with beverages. Unlike large ships, liberty expired when the skipper yawned and suggested, "Well, men, let's go home and call it a day."

The more relaxed they could make the skipper, the longer the stay ashore. The owner became a co-conspirator, offering rounds on the house for the same reason. The townsmen were equally hospitable, sending bushels of oysters to the ship every day, a big, freshly caught shad with enough roe to last several days, and an occasional bottle of good scotch. With several of us trying to place long-distance telephone calls, the two telephone operators also joined us on their off-duty evenings.

Soon the time came to head back to Norfolk for the next phase of our operations, now with the Army. *Mackerel* was the size of a German U-boat, and the Army wanted us to test the sensitivity and effectiveness of a controlled minefield protecting the harbor entrance against submarine penetration. Thanks to a Naval Academy classmate, Army Lieutenant John F. Splain, our liaison was very effective. John was a chronic seasick case at Annapolis and was offered an Army commission on graduation. The daily trip across Hampton Roads by ferry distressed him to the point that he eventually wound up in the Air Force as a nonflying officer. John was very helpful; we learned much more about the Army mines than expected and were able to offer suggestions for improving the tactical layout of the defenses. The mines were quite insensitive to our passage, including two which we actually pulled from their moorings when they snarled in the propellors.

On our final day in the Norfolk area, Captain Davidson attended a conference with Coast Guard and naval officials on the *Legare* incident. It was decided after study of all the information available that it was *Legare* we had targeted with the first two torpedoes. Her CO said that only violent maneuvers on his part enabled him to avoid disaster, and he suggested that the torpedoes we saw were porpoises. Both the officer of the deck, Charlie Fell, and the lookouts, however, swore that the steady, continuous wake could only have come from torpedoes. The problem of mistaken identity could not be solved, nor was it to be in many similar episodes throughout the war. We were thankful that no higher price had been paid for the experience.

Back in Long Island Sound for some torpedo firing by the PCOs, we were startled on diving one day to hear explosive sounds on the port side. Thinking that a high pressure air line had carried away, we made every check but without success. When we surfaced for an exterior examination of the hull, we heard local radio traffic turning the air blue. A Panamanian freighter reported, "Am attacking enemy submarine, Lat 41-08N, Long 71-31W."

This was *Mackerel*'s position. The "explosions" we heard were the three shots he had fired at us. His report went immediately to the antisubmarine headquarters, including a bomber command at Quonset Point, Rhode Island, whose dauntless airmen were already heading in for the kill. Because *Mackerel* was in the act of diving when the merchantman fired, he thought we were hit and had gone down. Then the Army signal station at Fort Wright off the entrance to New London added to the confusion by reporting, "*Mackerel* damaged; rescue vessel on its way."

He, of course, saw our target vessel in the area heading toward us. The consternation at the submarine headquarters when these reports were received can well be imagined. Captain Davidson sent the target vessel to warn off the merchantman—which he did with great difficulty. By then, every command in the region was trying to get on the air. Only *Mackerel* could ease the tension, but the traffic was so heavy we couldn't break through to make a report. Somehow the bombers were headed off in the nick of time, the merchantman was rerouted to Newport until a board of investigation could be convened, the Army command was brought up to date, and the state of wild excitement at the submarine headquarters finally eased. Not for a long time could we resume normal operations, however. The itchy finger all around occurred largely because six weeks earlier a U-boat off Block Island had used the international call sign of *Mackerel* instead of the recognition signal and was allowed by the Army to proceed south down Long Island

Sound unmolested. When *Mackerel* returned from her late-night operations shortly thereafter, the Harbor Entrance Control Post refused to accept our recognition signal and threatened to open fire. The incident happened just as the signals changed at midnight; he used one, we the other. Only an urgent telephone call to the submarine base convinced him that we were legitimate. Such is the unhappy lot of the undersea warrior, alien to friend or foe.

Looking back on those experiences, particularly the patrol to Norfolk and its near tragic interlude, it is clear that the U.S. forces were a long way from readiness for war. Mistakes bordering on comic opera were made by every command. We were fortunate that the experience was gained without loss of life. I for one determined not to challenge fate so openly when similar situations arose in the future.

The Naval Torpedo Station at Newport had the last word on our two torpedo attacks. Under normal procedures at New London, all torpedoes allotted to the submarines were turned in to the base torpedo shop; the base hotshots accomplished all maintenance and issued torpedoes from the pool as required for training exercises or for war loads on ships outward bound. The four war shots *Mackerel* expended happened to come from the war loading of four different submarines in the area. When I submitted the forms to Newport, requesting that they be stricken from the books and replaced, the torpedo station seemed unable to comprehend how I could have "lost" torpedoes belonging to four other submarines. Torpedoes were not expendable like shot and shell. Each had a service record that followed it throughout its career. Many an officer hazarded his career over inadvertent loss of a torpedo. Nor did my explanation satisfy. It was one of the unsolved mysteries I was happy to pass on to my relief—and he to his.

By late June I felt thoroughly at home in my ship. We had been under way conducting a very high tempo of operations since the day I reported aboard, doing everything a submarine could be expected to do. Then one day I had a big surprise from the skipper. Johnny called me in to his cabin to discuss my progress toward qualification. Thanks to all the midnight oil, my notebook was in the final stages. He said, "Wrap it up as soon as possible. I want to recommend you for qualification in subs." Though the time requirement of a year in subs before qualification had been suspended, the stringency was unchanged. Because of my very short time on board, he warned me that the qualification board would be tough, and I should prepare myself accordingly. I was walking on air.

The big day came late in June. I took our sister ship *Marlin* to sea as OOD, with green crew members in all key positions. Luck was with me. Because they were new, they worked with a special intensity and performed superbly. On the torpedo attack, my luck continued with an "MOT—middle of target" hit. Making the landing on return to port, despite a strong ebb current, was a piece of cake, even with an unfamiliar ship under me. We wetted down my new gold dolphins with a champagne celebration at the club. The quickest qualification known, including time at sub school, was eighteen months. I had done it in less than six.

Qualification influenced my fate in other ways. First, another happy event intervened. My class, which had just made lieutenant (junior grade) a few months before, suddenly learned that we had been promoted to full lieutenant. As a lieutenant qualified in submarines, I was ready to conquer the world. The Navy Department apparently agreed.

One of the PCOs in June was Bill Wylie, my old shipmate from the *Wichita*. Bill had orders to Portsmouth, New Hampshire, where he would place the USS *Scorpion* in commission as CO. When he came aboard *Mackerel*, we had a warm reunion, which soon turned into something else. Within days of my qualification, out of the blue came a set of orders—to "fitting out" the USS *Scorpion* and "on board when commissioned."

I couldn't have timed it better. The extra months in New London carried Henri and me through a difficult period. Now, confident in my mastery of the TDC and the heart of the submarine, I was fully ready for the Pacific war. But leaving New London mixed sorrow and anticipation—sorrow at leaving a happy ship and our many friends in the area and high anticipation over fitting out and commissioning a beautiful new sub and going off to war in the finest ship American technology could produce. And I was particularly proud of those lieutenant's stripes and shiny gold dolphins on my uniform. On a warm summer day in July, we stowed most of what little we owned in the back of the Chevy and headed north through New England to the naval shipyard in Portsmouth, an old and proud yard, which had been building splendid ships throughout most of American history.

3   The USS *Scorpion*

Tragedy in the Pacific

Portsmouth, New Hampshire, is a charming old New England town of tree-shaded streets and stout frame houses topped by widows' walks suggesting long and close ties to the sea. Brief international fame came to the city and the prominent Rockingham Hotel in August 1905 when President Theodore Roosevelt negotiated the Treaty of Portsmouth there, ending the Russo-Japanese War.

The shipyard, reached via a creaky drawbridge over the swift-flowing Piscataqua River, is actually located in Kittery Point, Maine. I assumed that both this and the Portsmouth, Virginia, Naval Shipyard located in Norfolk were built at the port's mouth and named for the adjacent city.

As we drove into the yard for our first look, submarine hulls in all stages of construction filled the building ways and layout areas. Day and night, blinding blue flashes from welding torches lighted the sky; huge mobile cranes maneuvered enormous hull sections into place. From early assembly of components to nearly completed greyhounds of the sea, a dozen submarines were building. For lack of a building way, *Scorpion* and her sister ship, *Scamp*, were laid down in the graving dock and had recently been launched in the first double launching in yard history.

The fitting-out period for a submarine took several

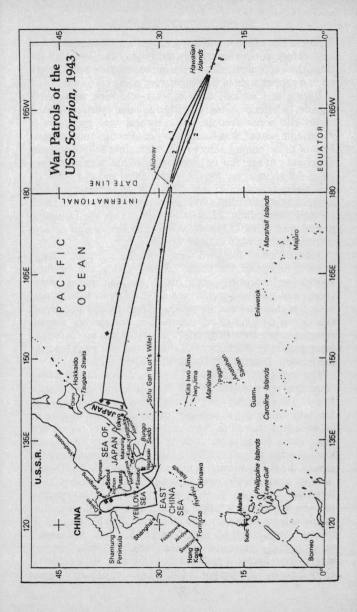

War Patrols of the
USS Scorpion, 1943

months. The officers and key enlisted men began to arrive well before completion to get thoroughly familiar with the ship, the equipment, and operating techniques and to work up to a proper state of training before going off to war.

During this period, both officers and men also had a chance to attend gunnery, torpedo, mine warfare, diesel, radar, and sonar schools. All crewmen were graduates of submarine school; less than half were qualified submariners. Few of those coming direct from submarine school had any experience at sea; few of those qualified had combat experience. All volunteered for submarine duty, and as volunteers in a highly selective service their motivation was extremely high. Their potential, whatever their experience level, seemed outstanding. Most important during the fitting-out period was to mold the crew into a cohesive unit able to respond instinctively in times of stress.

Submarines at the yard were assigned a "living" barge moored alongside the dock, offering galley and berthing spaces for the crew, storage areas, working spaces, wardroom, and galley. Several men soon dropped lobster pots over the side into the Piscataqua River to add occasional crustacean delights to our menu. One enterprising submariner, clearly a New Englander, suggested that an oil-soaked brick placed in the bottom of the lobster pot increased the daily catch. It apparently worked; nobody knew why.

The day I reported aboard happened to coincide with a small reception hosted by the division commander, Cmdr. Leo L. Pace, and his wife, for the officers who had reported for duty on the six submarines of his command. It gave us an excellent chance to meet and greet new colleagues and their wives socially, particularly the officers with whom I was so soon to go off to war. We soon felt completely at ease at the Paces' attractive home in Portsmouth. Old friends Bill and Nancy Wylie and classmate Fred and Betty Clarke were newly arrived from New London. Fred, prospective torpedo and gunnery officer of USS *Sawfish,* introduced us to his skipper, the very congenial and capable Eugene T. "Gene" Sands, and his exec, Joseph W. "Joe" Williams. I was especially interested to meet Frank W. "Mike" Fenno, a submarine hero just returned from the war. Mike achieved early fame by bringing gold bullion and several Army nurses out of the Philippines, foiling their capture by the Japanese. He would become CO of USS *Runner*. His exec, Joseph H. Bourland, another outstanding submariner, would cross paths with me in unusual circumstances.

My attention, however, was riveted on one officer whose piercing gaze met mine across the room—Lt. Cmdr. Reginald M. "Reggie" Raymond, *Scorpion*'s executive officer. From that instant I realized that he was a very special person, the most dynamic and inspiring naval officer I would ever know. Every detail of that first meeting is still clear, even the furniture in the room. There was no doubt in my mind that somehow knowing him would change my life.

Reggie was six years my senior. At the Naval Academy he was frequently in hot water for bending the regulations to his own needs. Because of a major discipline infraction, he was confined and missed his own graduation ceremony. Despite the demerits for disciplinary offenses, Reggie stood near the top of his class, as did his close friend and classmate Joe Bourland. Reggie's resistance to being homogenized in the midshipman mold echoed my own. We both exemplified General George Marshall's credo that if one can't disobey an order, he'll never amount to much as a leader. Part of my admiration for Reggie was instant hero worship; every man in the crew reflected the same feelings. He and I were totally simpatico, and from the earliest Portsmouth days we made a very effective torpedo attack team. Our exuberance frequently got Bill Wylie, a fine skipper, into difficulties. Little did we know the tragic consequences soon to unfold from one of those actions.

Henri and I found excellent housing in Portsmouth. A beautiful old estate had just been converted to apartments, and all the first occupants were submariners assigned to new construction at the yard: Bill and Nancy Wylie, Bert Rodier (engineer and third officer on *Scorpion*) and his wife, Lucille, Gene and Mae Sands, Joe and Madeleine Williams, Fred and Betty Clarke, and, in the newlywed suite, Philip A. and Gigi Beshany. Phil was XO to Walter G. "Wally" Ebert of *Scamp*. The apartments were spacious and very comfortable; the acres of fragrant woods and gardens surrounding the old manor house were delightful for hiking and picnicking. Almost nightly somebody started a barbecue and generally was joined by several other couples. The environment made for close friendships and shared experiences from our earliest days in Portsmouth.

At the office on the barge, drafting a ship's organization and regulations took early priority. The Navy provided a standard organization for each ship type, voluminous and in massive detail, which we hacked down to fit. Even highly standardized diving, surfacing, battle, and emergency procedures had to be adapted to the ship's own style. We stressed simplicity and efficiency.

A major task I wanted to accomplish was a visit to the torpedo station at Newport to find some answers to the dismal reports of torpedo failures coming back from the war in the Pacific. Premature explosions at minimum arming ranges, duds, and repeated failure to get hits on perfect setups drove many skippers to the point of asking to be relieved. The failure of the *Mackerel*'s attack on the German U-boat seemed inexplicable to me, and I didn't want to see it happen again. Both the Bureau of Ordinance and the torpedo station denied responsibility and refused to conduct any tests to determine the real problem.

U.S. Navy torpedoes at the start of World War II were equipped with highly secret magnetic exploders, so secret that nobody on a submarine could work on them. Only the torpedo officer and his senior torpedoman's mate were allowed in the torpedo room when base personnel installed or removed a torpedo exploder. We weren't allowed to touch the mechanism itself. When I got to Newport for classified briefings, I didn't find the exploder all that mysterious. One major weakness, it seemed obvious, was the tiny propellor in the warhead that armed the torpedo exploder after making four hundred revolutions from the time of firing. Instructions called for exactly fifteen ounces of tension on the propellor blades to make sure they were tight enough but wouldn't bind and prevent the torpedo from arming. But the danger of possible leakage of seawater into the exploder, particularly if the torpedo had been taken to two or three hundred feet before firing, seemed a far greater hazard. The slightest leakage of saltwater into the exploder would short out the electromagnetic components and cause a premature detonation. I asked, "What would happen if I tightened those glands to maybe twenty or thirty or forty ounces of blade tension just to make sure they would stay watertight? Will the impeller still be free enough to rotate when the torpedo is fired?"

The station admitted to stacks of evidence using tension up to ninety ounces before failures became excessive. But tension of fifty, even seventy-five ounces, caused no problem. Since so many premature detonations occurred when the warhead exploded as soon as it armed, wouldn't this indicate that the exploders were shorting out? Why not increase the tension and put a change out to the fleet just to be on the safe side? I could get no convincing reply. Such a change would be an admission of guilt, and the torpedo station, under pressure about unsatisfactory torpedoes, chose to deny that any problem existed and to blame the operating forces for poor shooting.

On return to my quarters that night, I sketched from memory the circuitry of the exploder mechanism, then asked my chief, J. T. Fowler, to do the same thing. We compared our drawings, then returned to the exploder lab to recheck a few details—secretly, of course—to make sure we had a good working drawing of the exploder mechanism. It was a serious breach of security but the circumstances clearly left no other alternative. Preparing *Scorpion*'s torpedoes, I prescribed blade tension of fifty, not fifteen ounces. Some probably thought I was mad, but the chief and I were confident the results would bear us out.

Other circumstances influenced my decision. For years the torpedo station had stultified in layers of bureaucratic mold. The United States had not been able to make an effective torpedo from a model in use since World War I, and our torpedoes still, we were soon to learn, suffered from major defects easily discoverable by a moderately bright high school physics student. Servicing torpedoes on ships at sea under regulations dictated by the torpedo station was a time-consuming chore of questionable value. But these regulations applied only to the afterbodies, the propulsion plants, not to the warheads, which forces afloat were forbidden to touch. The propulsion plant had been in use forever, it seemed, and was extremely reliable. There seemed no more need to check the power plant than to check the family car at midnight just to make sure it would start when called on at dawn. The source of the problem was far more likely to be in the new and untested exploder. I ordered my people to make only a cursory check of the propulsion system but to devote great care to the exploders, especially after every unusual submergence. When others in the submarine force learned that the depth-control mechanisms and detonators also suffered from major design defects, Newport, despite convincing evidence of error, added stubbornness to stupidity and held out to the end.

One other problem bothered me at the torpedo station. For years the Navy had been trying to produce a wakeless torpedo. All production models since the 1920s left prominent wakes from combustion gases, often alerting the enemy in time to evade and providing a track of bubbles direct to the submarine for a quick counterattack. Admiral E. J. King, the new chief of naval operations, and many active submariners had long favored a wakeless electric torpedo, but the project had lain dormant at Newport for many years. The great success of the German U-boats with electric torpedoes early in the war stimulated a new interest, particularly when one of the German torpedoes ran up on the beach in early 1942 and was recovered by the Bureau of Ordnance. Under strong pressure from Admiral King, both the torpedo station and private industry were urged to get behind the electric torpedo program, but after early successes, progress came to a standstill. Nor could I penetrate the screen obscuring the torpedo station program. I was only one of many frustrated submariners who thought it a violation of New Mexico scenery to test the A-bomb at Alamagordo when the naval torpedo station was available.

One of the virtues in fitting out a new ship was the opportunity for officers and key enlisted men to work with the yard in getting the ship ready for sea. The yard allowed some flexibility in location of certain equipment to suit the style of the operators. My own fetish was lighting. From experience with the PCOs in *Mackerel* during extensive night operations, I learned the great difficulties in transition from day to night in the conning tower and control room. Navies the world over traditionally used blue lights for night illumination of corridors and operating spaces. Shortly after the war opened, scientists found blue the worst possible choice for night illumination. We learned about the rods and cones in the eyeball and how only the ruby red light of a specific frequency preserved night vision. We learned how to train for maximum visibility at night and discovered great variations in men serving as lookouts. Some with exceptional vision did much less well at night; others could not interpret what they did see.

Instrument lighting was a more difficult challenge. Normal daylight illumination harmed night adaptation, and if one were to go to the bridge at night he would be blinded for many minutes until his eyes adapted. The shipyard furnished tight-fitting red goggles to wear in lighted spaces to preserve night vision. The goggles solved one problem but created another, as the bridge watch and poker players soon discovered. The red suits on the playing cards were not visible through the red goggles. The Electric Boat Company went the next step by manufacturing special cards with the hearts and diamonds outlined in black. Awkward at best, they were only partially successful either by day or by night.

Of somewhat greater operational significance for the planesmen at the diving station, several curved tubes filled with a colored liquid indicated the up or down angle, or "bubble," on the ship, an important aid to depth control. Ordinary lighting worked well by day, but prewar subs had poor instrument illumination at night. To see the bubble when the control room was darkened, the yard devised a heavy, fan-shaped sheet metal framework to focus light throughout the length of the curved tubes, both awkward and ineffective. Recalling a prep school physics experiment in which light rays were bent through a solid, I quickly determined that the same thing would work with a liquid-filled tube and suggested to the yard that a tiny, shielded bulb at the end of each tube would illuminate the bubble at the top of the arc much more effectively than the complicated wraparound light shield. The yard agreed and shortly "invented" the idea. When the proud moment came to show off the Navy's latest and best in submarines on our passage through New London, the only thing that seemed to catch the admiral's eye was the bubble lighting. It quickly became standard throughout the Navy.

I believed that the best lighting was the least. Instrument illumination wherever located must be minimal so as not to destroy night vision. For the same reason, all night lighting should be the proper frequency, not simply variations of color to please interior decorators. Modern automakers still don't realize this. Needless accidents occur on our highways by partial night blindness caused by improper and excessive instrument illumination. In submarine building it took a long time before we got to the point that day and night lighting weren't mutually incompatible.

Experience with the PCOs in *Mackerel* brought another challenge. One of the COs at the yard, Antone R. "Tony" Gallaher of the USS *Bang*, had developed some brilliant tactics for a submarine attack from deep submergence based only on sonar information, without using the periscope. (Doctrine through the early months of the war called for all submarine attacks to be made from below periscope depth.) Tony previously had commanded a submarine operating with the Fleet Sonar School at Key West, Florida, and offered to conduct a seminar for the submarine officers in the Portsmouth area. When Tony took his new command to sea shortly after we arrived in Portsmouth, the skippers present discussed a successor to take over the seminar. To my disbelieving ears, I was nominated. Relieving a senior skipper in a specialty he had developed over several years was one thing; to do so as a tyro of four months' experience in submarines when such seasoned skippers as Mike Fenno and Gene Sands sat in the audience made it easy to be modest.

But I had found Tony's ideas exciting; I had taken careful notes and spent much time analyzing them. The earliest war patrol reports from the Pacific told of many sonar attacks without using the periscope. All were unsuccessful. Had Gallaher's ideas been used, plus a single "ping" range to the target taken just before firing torpedoes as then taught at the submarine school, many would have succeeded. Of greater importance, his concept aimed to cancel out or minimize errors for all attacks and hence was highly useful in attacks at periscope depth or on the surface.

I used the seminar also as a convenient vehicle to test ideas on changes in torpedo routines based on the discoveries at Newport. To add the right degree of saltiness and seniority to my appearance before the first meeting, I aged my new gold stripes and dolphins in oily seawater dredged up from between the piers, and Reggie Raymond contributed a pair of sterling silver lieutenant's bars hand made in the Philippines. Many of the ideas warranted wide promulgation throughout the submarine force. With both CO and XO support, we tried to do just that. I don't know what other success greeted the lectures, but nobody learned more than the teacher.

Some of our ideas were less successful. Probably since the first submarine went to sea, it carried emergency rations and drinking water in pressure-proof containers stored in the overhead of each living space. Tradition since the tin can was invented called for using tinned pork and beans. Under the impetus of war, the Army made great progress in feeding men in the field with varieties of food concentrates such as "C" and "K" rations and of high-energy chocolate concentrates.

Reggie and I discussed the problem with Leo Pace, who suggested that the supply officer order enough for the entire submarine division. That young officer, with more zeal than common sense, soon reported complete success. He estimated the order in Army "units," assuming that a unit was a Hershey bar size. More likely it covered the daily needs of a company or battalion. In due time a freight train wended its way up the New England coast carrying mostly enriched chocolate bars for the submariners. There was plenty for the entire submarine division, perhaps even for all New England. In liquid form, it might have filled an entire submarine. Somewhere in New England today there is probably an abandoned warehouse chock full of surplus chocolate. But high-energy chocolate with pineapple juice in square cans became popular.

The yard also gave us some latitude in decorating. For the officers' and chiefs' living spaces the traditional green felt used for door curtains and the wardroom tablecloth were drab and depressing, particularly at night. We decided to brighten the scene considerably. Henri and the skipper's wife, Nancy, searched New England textile mills for drapery material in tans and browns for use as door curtains and bedspreads, then added a leatherette cover for the wardroom table and durable place settings to reduce the need for linens. The yard added an attractive wood paneling in the corridor where contact with passing arms and shoulders made painted surfaces difficult to maintain. For all berthing areas, we used softer tones in decorating. Yes, it was still a submarine, but it was our home, and our creature comforts were not excessive.

Not long after our arrival in Portsmouth, a black cloud suddenly intruded into our fascinating world. Henri had made a complete recovery from her first pregnancy. We wanted children but couldn't overlook the warning of the doctor in New London that another pregnancy within two years might be fatal. When she mentioned as casually as possible that she was expecting again, a cold knife went through my heart. She had a thorough examination, and the doc assured us that everything looked fine, but try as we could, those dark thoughts kept intruding into our lives. We took several short trips up the beautiful rockbound New England coast, often leaving most of our thoughts unsaid.

One particularly difficult occasion for me was a marriage service for Fred and Betty Clarke. They had been married in a civil ceremony on 1 June, when it first became "legal." With the arrival of Fred, Junior, in Portsmouth, they wanted a church ceremony before Fred left for the Pacific in *Sawfish*. Henri and I served as matron of honor and best man, then as sponsors for the baby's baptism. The private ceremony was held in the chapel of the old Portsmouth Naval Prison. A few spectators in drab prison garb hardly looked like wedding guests. Holding the tiny infant through the ceremony prompted a surge of longing and sudden sharp pangs over our own loss still fresh in our minds.

Commissioning of *Scorpion* finally arrived on 1 October 1942. The officers and men had shaped up beautifully; we had the makings of a superb command. The first dive was always a thrill. Some did it an inch at a time, checking constantly for leaks. Others did it more rashly, only to find the trim way off—the ship went down with a sharp up angle or stayed on the surface with an equally steep down angle. Reggie and I convinced Bill to make the first with the savoir faire of the five hundredth—a quick dive off two engines making standard speed.

Scorpion acted like a lady throughout the training period. All too quickly the day of departure arrived for torpedo trials at Newport and final training at New London. My only mishap at sea was a pair of frozen cheeks while standing a watch on the open bridge. I went below immediately to ask the steward for some ice cubes to rub on my cheeks in the accepted remedy to prevent permanent frost damage. After an impossibly long delay, he brought me a dish of ice cream. He had no idea why I wanted ice cubes, and to this day my cheeks carry small pouches that are quite sensitive to cold.

At this point it is timely to introduce one more *Scorpion* officer, Gilbert L. "Bert" Rodier, Jr. Bert graduated from the Naval Academy in 1935 but resigned his commission shortly after to enter flight training at Kelly Field with the Army Air Corps. As an aviator he led a flight of airmen under a bridge, for which he was dismissed from the Army. He then entered the Merchant Marine and the Naval Reserve and was ordered to submarines when the emergency started. After a tour in an "R" boat, he came to *Scorpion* as the engineer.

Bert's wife, Lucille, was a charming person, far more stable than her husband. Their two children were good-natured hell-raisers. The Rodiers lived in the tower apartment at the Jones Estate, and the children were seen on at least one occasion climbing the parapets outside their fourth-floor apartment. Peril was never far distant; we kept the hospital emergency number close at hand. One day, after completing Christmas preparations, Henri went into town for a few errands, leaving our door unlocked as usual. Shortly after, the Rodier children walked in and went to work. Soon our beautiful tree and smashed ornaments were strewn around the room. Alerted by sounds of uninhibited glee, Nancy Wylie and Marge Raymond decided to investigate. Angered to the point of tears, they packed the youngsters off and began mopping up. When Henri returned, the tree was proudly upright, decorated with newly purchased ornaments. Bert apologized but seemed to find the incident far more amusing than we did. The other three couples adjourned to the Raymond apartment in town for several of

Reggie's superb hot buttered rums, specially heated with a small soldering iron and properly served in a copper mug with a stick of cinnamon.

Final preparations for sea were completed; Captain Wylie accepted delivery of the "Scorp" from the yard, and on a bitterly cold February day we made our departure down the tortuous Piscataqua River and out to sea. Torpedo trials at Newport were routine, but Reggie and I tried to use the opportunity to learn more about the continuing delays in the electric torpedo program. Captain Ralph W. Christie, a veteran submariner, had recently assumed duties as commander of the torpedo station under specific orders to cut through the bureaucratic logjam, first to reduce the critical shortage of "steam" torpedoes in the fleet, then to get moving on the new electric torpedo. Christie was immediately reassigned in a reshuffle made necessary by the tragic death of Rear Admiral Robert H. English, Commander Submarines Pacific, and key staff members in an air crash. Christie had just been selected for rear admiral and left immediately, turning over command to his exec, Captain Frank Fahrion. We could learn only that sharply increased steam torpedo production seemed incompatible with the high priority assigned by Admiral King to the electric torpedo, either the new model by Westinghouse or Newport's own electric model under haphazard development since the 1920s. Newport pushed neither the Westinghouse model on the "NIH" principle (not invented here) nor its own model because of vested interests in the steam torpedo.

At about the time of *Scorpion*'s visit to Newport, Commander Submarines Atlantic decided to bring some operational experience to bear at the torpedo station, ordering the new USS *Lapon* to Newport to assist in the test firing of the Westinghouse model. *Lapon*, with plenty of torpedo experience aboard in the CO, Oliver G. Kirk, and my old roomie Robert C. "Bing" Gillette as torpedo officer, was a fortunate choice.

The Newport trials were completed without incident, and the final training for *Scorpion* at New London was highly successful. Officers and crew performed superbly and earned the blessings and high praise of Commander Submarines Atlantic and his staff. Though it tore at my heartstrings to part from Henri on the dock, we made our fond farewells. I forced any dark thoughts about her health rigorously from my mind. My only consolation was that she was going home to her parents and they would take the best of care of her whatever the need.

On the early morning of 24 February 1943 we sailed from the submarine base down the familiar Thames River channel and headed south. Smooth seas and a following breeze made a seventeen-knot speed possible, and we soon entered the azure blue of the Gulf Stream. Daily training dives and emergency drills were the only breaks in the routine. German submarines were active off the coast, and we kept an alert watch, ready for any eventuality. Arriving in Key West, we received some much desired training with the antisubmarine experts at the Fleet Sonar School. The operations were all hush-hush then, so when people asked questions I suggested that we were searching Florida for the Keys to the Panama Canal locks. This at least changed the subject. We worked hard in the sea exercises, and the unqualified success became a fine morale builder for the last Atlantic leg of the cruise before reaching Panama. The watch settled down well in the standard rotation, and spirits soared.

Monday, 8 March, *Scorpion* transited the Panama Canal to the Pacific. As first lieutenant responsible for deck gear and line handling, I spent most of the day topside in a broiling sun. After the frigid northern winter, most of the deckhands suffered a fairly heavy dose of sunburn, but as somebody suggested, we had a couple of thousand miles to Honolulu to recover. Robert B. Drane, the communications officer, received the worst burn. A handsome gent, prematurely bald, he was sunburned three shades, all of them peeling, with just enough hair to hold the peelings in place.

To get ashore in Panama is always worth a bit of suffering. I searched for table linens in scores of duty-free shops but the word seemed to be out that American sailors had scads of money. I couldn't find a thing. One of our men treated a bar girl to a coke and the bill was $2. If this seems not outrageous today, the reader must remember that his salary then was $21 a month, and it seemed steep to him, even including the small pat on her fanny.

The only day ashore on the Balboa side gave the crew a

chance for a softball game, which we played with zest wholly apart from the natural competition of losers buying the beer. Reggie in particular starred as shortstop in a wild and woolly game. Returning to the ship, he and I strolled up the highest rise we could find—about ten feet—where we stood "silent upon a peak in Darien." Looking across the broad, still waters, we decided that we were ready to join the Pacific Fleet and get down to work.

The war in Europe was slowly turning in favor of the Allies. Despite the great success of General Erwin Rommel, the "Desert Fox," in Africa, the Nazis had been stopped in the great tank battle at El Alamein and the Russians had blunted Hitler's eastern offensive at Stalingrad. The Battle of the Atlantic had reached its decisive point. Both merchant sinkings by U-boats and sinkings of U-boats by hundreds of new radar-equipped antisubmarine vessels reached massive proportions. Shipping losses were not yet being replaced by Allied shipyards, but the American shipbuilding industry was about to shift into high gear.

In January of 1943 President Roosevelt, Prime Minister Churchill, and their strategic planning staffs met at Casablanca to chart the course of the war. The defeat of the Axis in Europe remained the primary goal, but wide differences emerged about Pacific strategy. Admiral King supported a two-pronged effort: one, General Douglas MacArthur's drive from the Solomons and New Guinea to the Philippines; the other, the island-hopping campaign through the Gilberts, Marshalls, and Marianas to China. MacArthur wanted the major campaign from the south and only a diversionary drive through the central Pacific. The British favored a push through Burma, Singapore, and Hong Kong, and a final campaign against Japan by bombing from China. Roosevelt supported the British plan as a supplement to Admiral King's two-pronged plan. The submarine force, in a major change of tactics from the prewar "eyes of the fleet" role, now concentrated on exerting pressure on Japanese lines of communication and a gradual sea blockade of the empire.

The decisions at Casablanca were made largely by default. In the absence of agreement on a single strategic approach, each commander more or less continued his existing campaign. Since new warships rolling off production lines would not be available for combat before mid- or late 1943, however, no mid-Pacific drive was possible before then and there would be no particular stress on the grand strategy until that time. But clearly the time had come to shift attention to the Pacific.

One unusual event marred our voyage west. Nearing midpoint in the passage, we encountered a lone merchantman heading in the opposite direction. As soon as we came within range, he opened fire with a fairly sizable deck gun and came up on the emergency radio frequency to report an enemy submarine. We tried to identify ourselves by searchlight but couldn't raise his attention. Even though his shots weren't very close, it was one more warning that once a submarine leaves the pier, it has no friends and many enemies.

The Hawaiian Islands are beautiful to approach from any direction. The first view of Diamond Head, gradually taking shape on the horizon, the sharp Molokai cliffs to the south, created lasting memories. A stiff trade wind in our faces whipped the deep blue seas into foamy spume breaking over the deck. Sun and sea were pleasantly warm, and the air suggested a tang of forest and sugarcane. Entering the channel and gliding across the still waters past Hickam Field toward the submarine base, we saw everywhere evidence of the 7 December disaster. Great effort had gone into the cleanup, but a thick coating of spilled bunker oil sloshed between the piers and around the scarred, sunken remains of the battleship *Arizona*. It was my first visit to this great bastion of the Pacific; I offered a prayer for those lives lost so tragically here, and I am sure many of my shipmates did the same. The submarine base and the enormous fuel stocks in Aiea Heights above Pearl Harbor had been untouched, however, and it reemphasized the importance of the undersea force doing its very best to carry the war to the enemy until the American arsenal could replace the surface and air forces.

Vice Admiral Charles A. "Uncle Charlie" Lockwood, newly appointed head of Submarines Pacific, met us on the dock and offered a warm welcome to the islands. He appeared delighted to have us on the firing line; we reflected the enthusiasm and good fellowship. In private briefings the admiral indicated to Captain Wylie that torpedo problems were having their effect and he hoped for a solution soon. Equally important, the shortage of torpedoes made it necessary to carry half mines and half torpedoes on our first war patrol.

Some modifications were made to the ship before departure on patrol. The superstructure around the bridge area was cut down to reduce the silhouette, and ammunition handling topside was improved with the addition of two three-inch and one 20-mm pressure-proof ready lockers topside near the guns. Contrary to submarine practice, Leo Pace, the division commander, highly recommended retaining the shields on the 20-mm mounts, not ordinarily carried by submarines, for protection against small-arms fire, ricochets, or flying fragments. This simple precaution later saved the life of at least one gunner's mate.

One seemingly insignificant change turned into a major new weapon at sea. This was the addition of a new device, a bathythermograph, or BT, designed to chart seawater temperature versus depth of the submarine. Designed by scientists in submarine research to help the diving officer determine the amount of water to be flooded in or pumped out to accommodate salinity changes at deeper depths, the BT soon filled a far greater role. The needle on a smoked card made curious tracings of thermal layers in the oceans. Far more important than helping the diving officer, we soon learned that the sharp breaks deflected sonar "pings" when the sub passed from one density to another, sharply reducing the detection capability of antisubmarine vessels. The submariners soon learned to go deep and get below a layer to screen their movements while evading the surface pursuer.

Intensive training off Pearl Harbor included firing six exercise torpedoes against escorted surface units. The loading of twelve Mark 12 and ten Mark 10 mines, plus fourteen steam torpedoes, completed our preparation for war. The patrol area was one of the best, Japanese Empire waters east and south of Tokyo.

One major thought, unspoken but never far out of mind, continued to gnaw at my insides. The doctor's reports about Henri's pregnancy were encouraging. She remained in excellent health, and he could visualize no problem such as had caused the earlier tragedy. But the same thing was true last time, I thought. Then, too, she was doing well until the last few weeks. Her date this time almost coincided with the expected date of our return from patrol. I had two months out of touch at sea to stew about it.

Writing a last letter before departure, I questioned what I could possibly tell a wife whom I loved more than anything on earth when my real concern was more her danger than mine, a subject I hardly dared discuss. I wrote, "If I come back after a dull trip, a soulful message seems melodramatic. If I come back every 2-3 months for a year or two, it seems pointless and repetitive. And if, as is also possible, I don't come back, then it all seems fatalistic and pessimistic. I suppose all I can tell you is that what happens is the will of God. You know as well as I the danger each of us is running in the next two months. If He takes care of us both (or all three), then we can forever be thankful. I mention this next two-month period because it may be the most hazardous we will endure. That much we already know. I know that you won't worry too much. I have always been lucky and may never have a more capable group of officers and men to bring us through. Just remember that everything has always worked out for the best for us and it will again this time. I will pray daily for you and will do my best knowing that you are always behind me."

Departing Pearl Harbor on 5 April, we stopped at Midway Island to stretch our legs and enjoy a cool beer at the Gooneyville Tavern while topping off on fuel. By midafternoon we were at sea again, navigating the narrow channel between Eastern and Sand islands. After dismissing the escorting aircraft at dusk, we soon crossed the International Date Line and were on our own at standard speed on two engines, zigzagging, making a routine dive each day at dawn. A week out of Midway the weather changed sharply for the worse. The wind rose to gale force; heavy head seas slowed us to about seven knots. The seas were breaking over the periscope supports, and the bridge watch was frequently drenched with wind-driven rain, but I thought it still puny compared to a North Atlantic winter gale. It was enough, however, that the Scorp bucked and plunged her pretty nose into green waves, sometimes up to her hips.

Early one particularly dismal morning, a giant comber

rolled the bridge under, cascading tons of water down the hatch to the conning tower and control room. With ankle-deep water sloshing from side to side, the drenched watch-standers, slipping and sliding on the oily steel deck, struggled to regain control of the ship. At that moment, Chief Commissary Steward Tony Manganello, our superb chef, poked his head in from the galley, scanned the cold misery around him, and with a big, toothy grin, shouted cheerfully, "War is hell, gentlemen." Of Italian ancestry, with the happiest disposition the Lord ever gave man, he was the epitome of the morale boost contributed by a top-notch chef. He promised a fine dinner and decorated cake to the first man sighting an enemy ship.

The gale brought one other change. On the way down the coast from New London, Reggie made a ceremony of taking off his heavy underwear when we hit warm weather. His Shreveport, Louisiana, boyhood never left him where cold weather was concerned. Here, just a few days out to sea, the temperature again dropped to forty-five degrees, and back came the long-handles, with the threat that he was going to tape the edges to his skin until we got back to latitude 20. Said I—"Pooey!"

"Enemy contact! All hands to general quarters."

Almost at the stroke of midnight, as we penetrated the Japanese outer defense line north of Marcus Island, a camouflaged, armed escort vessel suddenly emerged in the bright moonlight, three miles off. A quick dive allowed a periscope examination at close range. He wasn't worthy of a torpedo, and it didn't make sense to disclose our position by gun action against a radio-equipped target. But the men were ready and itching for action. I felt a quick pucker, and my palms began to sweat at this first contact with the Japanese enemy. I'm sure the men felt the same way. We hated to pass him by and built up our macho feelings by muttering dire threats against his future. Reggie said it best: "Wait till we come back; I hope you're still there looking for us. We'll be looking for you then." Little did we know how portentous those words were to become.

Reluctantly the Scorp opened the range, surfaced, set the normal watch, and resumed the westward course, closing the Japanese coast. By now the watch had settled into the routine for officers and men of four hours on, eight off. Standing the same hours every day was advantageous in many ways. The officer with the noon-to-four watch went back on at midnight; another had the four-to-eights, the third the eight-to-twelves. While we were in enemy waters cruising on the surface at night and submerged by day, the engineer/diving officer usually stood the four-to-eights so that his watches came during the early morning dive and evening surfacing. The exec, busy with star sights and administration of the training program for nonqualified men, stood no watches. One junior officer was involved full time with coding and decoding duties and frequently needed the assistance of others when the load got heavy. *Scorpion*'s first patrol was in waters shallow enough that she could be salvaged in case of loss, hence we could not carry the highly secret electric coding machine, or ECM. All our communications were by the primitive "strip" cipher, slow and painstaking, usually requiring assistance from other officers available.

To prevent tipping off the enemy by a sharp increase in message traffic before a major operation, the force commanders kept the level constant by adding numerous dummy messages when activities were low. Commander Submarines took advantage of these opportunities to send personal messages such as birth announcements and other news from home. To ease the burden of decoding by submarines not concerned, we were alerted on the personals when it was unnecessary to decode further. The informality in message traffic did much to personalize contact between the big boss in Pearl Harbor and his ships on the firing line and to ease our feelings of being all alone in a hostile world.

The wardroom turned out to be very congenial. The firm bonds of friendship and mutual respect which the captain, Reggie, and I in particular had developed had broadened and matured. Reggie and I thought and acted much alike, and we could visualize our careers following similar patterns. The rumor when we left Pearl Harbor was that he and I would leave *Scorpion* after this patrol and relieve Mike Fenno and Joe Bourland as CO and XO of *Runner*.

Of the younger officers, Bob Drane, a southern gentleman from North Carolina, was "good people" ashore or afloat.

My favorites among the junior officers were probably Ensigns Richmond K. "Dick" Ellis and Robert T. "Bob" Brown. Dick came from York Harbor, Maine, just a few miles north of the Portsmouth yard. I found him a tough opponent on the tennis court. Bob was a prelaw student from Emory University in Atlanta, son of Congressman Paul Brown of Georgia. The skipper, exec and I were the only career, regular Navy, Annapolis types. Bert Rodier's erratic path after graduation set him apart. His unpredictability made it difficult to place full confidence in him when he had the bridge watch.

Life on a sub often rounded off the rough edges in men. Discipline was relaxed but inflexible when matters of safety were involved. One never heard, for instance, the old Hollywood cliché "and that's an order," filmdom's unique way of letting people know they're supposed to do something. Submarine men never needed such arrogant displays of authority. And the men, especially the chiefs and senior petty officers, had their own guileless ways of influencing officers toward preferred behavior.

One officer, who shall remain nameless, had a habit of asking for a cup of hot coffee as soon as he got to the bridge for his normal night watch. Getting coffee from the galley to the bridge in the blackness of night is never an easy task. And after the first sip, our subject invariably complained that it was freezing cold and spat it out. This happened once too often for the watch below, who thought that an officer might better take his cup with him to the bridge like anybody else. To get the point across, one evening a mug was put into the conning tower air conditioning coil for several hours before he came on watch and a pot of molten hot coffee kept ready in the galley. As soon as the OOD ordered coffee, the pot was passed up to the conning tower, poured into the frosted cup, and quickly sent to the bridge. The OOD grabbed the icy cup and swallowed a mouthful, started to complain and immediately lost his voice to the scalding beverage. Neither the incident nor the request ever happened again.

Many submarine stewards had favorite tricks to get a full cup of coffee to the captain on the bridge. Some put the saucer over the cup, then inverted both so they could be handled without leakage. One steward always produced a full cup and a dry saucer. Intrigued, the skipper asked somebody to spy on him to learn the secret. Then he was sorry he asked. Before climbing the ladder to the bridge, the steward took a big gulp of coffee, then at the top of the ladder, spat it back into the cup. This gave me a better idea: I rarely drank coffee on the bridge.

After a few days at sea, the CO decided to shift Bert to the midwatches and me to the four-to-eights. The latter required special vigilance. It was the time when one was most likely to be caught by a sudden twilight air attack or other unpleasant surprise in the tricky visibility. I was blessed with superior vision, especially at night. My only objection to the change was that I had the watch during breakfast and dinner and hence missed the companionship of the wardroom at those times.

Meanwhile, Reggie and I worked out a detailed scheme for the mine plant, including surface and submerged alternatives, depending on brightness of the moon, enemy surface and air activity, sea, and weather. For a number of reasons it was necessary to lay the mines as soon as possible. The location was chosen primarily to interdict the spring ore traffic from the mines in northern Japan serving the Tokyo-Yokohama steel mills. We wanted to get rid of the mines so as to regain full use of the forward torpedo tubes without the clutter and nuisance of the awkward "eggs."

About twenty-five to thirty-five miles off the coast, scores of lighted and unlighted sampans came into view, some radio-equipped and obviously serving as the close-in patrol. One pair of motor sampans gave us a bad two hours, patrolling various courses in formation abreast. The captain went down to 150 feet and ordered "Rig for silent running." Gerald Sweet, one of the best sonar operators in the business, kept us informed on the closing range. Shortly after the first ship passed over the bow, a loud grating, grinding noise shattered the silence and not a few nerves. Men in the forward torpedo room thought someone was pulling the superstructure off. Putting a sharp down angle on the boat, the captain headed for 250 feet, not without considerable difficulty, until the noise ceased with a grinding tear. As we headed back up, the noise recommenced at 230 feet, accompanied by loud rapping on the hull aft. Visions of being snagged by a grapnel, of a fish net fouled in the screws, or of us towing a pair of fishing boats offered few happy thoughts. Worse, could it be a new antisubmarine technique of snagging a submarine in shallow water and sliding a nasty old depth charge down the grapnel line? Caution dictated an early escape by whatever means. We went to 300 feet, pulled clear, and left the area at high speed.

Within the hour smoke was sighted on the same bearing as the trawlers, with the range closing. "Battle stations" brought the crew to the alert as we headed in for an attack. The enemy soon disappeared in the mist, but we continued to close the coast in a gradually increasing rainstorm. Because of the difficulty in preventing detection by the sampan fleet if the mines were laid while we were on the surface, and the possibility of being forced down into our own minefield, the captain decided to complete the task before surfacing. At 1721 (5:21 P.M. to those not of the maritime community) we commenced firing the twenty-two mines in two irregular lines at spacings of six hundred to a thousand yards. Laying mines is backbreaking work for the handling crews, particularly the awkward old Mark 12s, which had a heavy anchor at one end. Each mine had to be fired precisely on signal to produce an orderly yet indiscriminate nest.

The mining operation took two hours. Each mine fired released a heavy shot of compressed air into the sub, and on completion, the air pressure was eight inches above normal. Also, the sub had been submerged for over sixteen hours, and the battery was very low. Men were breathing heavily from the lack of oxygen; any physical exertion caused acute distress. We reached the surface well after dark and cleared the coast at high speed heading for a new area for the remainder of the patrol. It took several hours to rerig the torpedo rooms, now that the mines were gone. Additionally, orders had just come through from Pearl Harbor to bypass the magnetic exploders on the torpedoes and use contact only. The magnetic exploders had not lived up to expectations and were believed by many to be a major cause of torpedo failures. Even with only a partial load of torpedoes aboard, this took a lot of heaving around.

The following morning at 1039, the OOD sighted smoke

on the horizon. The masts of a small freighter soon emerged from the haze, quite close to our track and unescorted. The ship was the *Meiji Maru No. 1,* a converted gunboat of 1,934 tons. The zig plan was rapidly solved, and in a smooth and unhurried approach we gained an excellent firing position. At 1131, three torpedoes whirred from the forward nest and made one solid hit amidships. The target sank immediately, and *Scorpion* had her first kill. This was the first time the great majority of us had heard a torpedo explode. Everything had gone so smoothly it seemed like an exercise on the trainer. It was over so quickly that it was hard to believe that human beings were snuffed out just like that. We surfaced to look for survivors, then resumed patrol down the maru's course in case others used the same route.

Just before midnight, a darkened sampan appeared in the moon streak. Having had many battle surface drills with no target, the CO made a very popular decision to try out the gun crews. The enemy was motorized and fair game. Submerging at three minutes before midnight, we closed the target to 150 yards and "battle surfaced" to greet the surprised enemy with a hail of three-inch, 20-mm and .45-caliber tommy-gun fire at close range. The three-inch flashless ammunition was a great success, blowing gaping holes in the hull, but the 20-mm tracers blinded the gunners and obscured the target.

With the target afire and sinking, we broke off action and cleared the area. After making the usual dawn dive at 0410, we heard two distant underwater explosions; shortly afterward a subchaser was observed echo-ranging and searching the area. Through the morning several pairs of small vessels passed by, towing a minesweeping cable astern. We were over a hundred miles from our plant by then, but if mines were suspected, it was hardly good hunting grounds for shipping. We cleared the area on the surface that night, heading for Shioya Saki lighthouse for a close-in morning search. Again the seas swarmed with sampans, which we avoided only with great difficulty. The flat, calm sea made undetected periscope observation extremely difficult. Our presence could hardly be a secret even without the ship sinking to alert the enemy.

The following morning at 0319, lights of a patrolling aircraft appeared, approaching from landward. We dived when the range closed to three miles, and sound reported high-speed screws almost immediately. Two destroyers making about thirty-five knots were pinging occasionally—and this kind of pinging was not from poor fuel but from antisubmarine sonar on a long-range search. It seemed a good time to go deep and rig for silent running. The destroyers were either suspicious of a possible submarine or searching ahead of a possible ship movement through the area. An hour later they parted, one moving up the coast, the other down. Closing the coast after dawn, we took photographs of the lighthouse and commenced a close inshore patrol. One large tanker was seen moving down the coast with his keel practically plowing a track on the bottom. Nothing else was moving except the ever-present sampan fleet. In water so shallow, we couldn't get close enough even for a long range torpedo shot. It seemed a good time to leave this part of the operating area, after first clearing out some sampans to encourage the others to stay inshore. Another efficient gun action after a battle surface allowed us to set three of them afire as we headed out to sea.

At 0330 the following morning, a radar contact to the south at nine miles soon disclosed two big merchant ships with a destroyer escort, clearly visible in the brilliant moonlight and calm sea. Closing at ten knots, we dived at six miles to make a high-speed submerged approach. The BT indicated that sound conditions were in our favor with a heavy layer close to the surface. We were able to get into excellent attack position undetected. Three torpedoes were fired at the leading ship and one at the second, straight bow shots at twenty-two hundred yards range. Two minutes later, the first of thirteen heavy explosions echoed throughout the ship. An escort with a bone in his teeth roared down the bubble track at high speed. We rigged for depth charge and evaded deep and silent. He apparently made no contact, and we soon returned to periscope depth for a look around.

One maru, stopped and smoking heavily, appeared to be down by the stern; the second was legging it for the beach. The escort soon returned to the cripple to render assistance. We thought *Scorpion* should do the same. As we headed in at six knots speed, making occasional searches for aircraft, things looked bright until the heavily damaged ship began to move slowly toward the beach. The captain decided to wait until pursuit had been abandoned, then surfaced and attempted to regain contact along the enemy track. We surfaced at 1230 at flank speed, twenty knots, in bright sunlight, the wake looming very prominent on the flat sea. Almost immediately the air search radar reported an aircraft at eight miles, closing. Diving when the range closed to five miles, we continued to close submerged for the remainder of daylight. A contact report on the attack cleared quickly to Naval Radio, Dutch Harbor, Alaska, but when relayed by Pearl Harbor on the submarine net, it was badly garbled. It became necessary to retransmit, again giving away our position and southerly course to enemy direction finders homing on submarine transmissions. Course was changed to the west to close the coast toward the center of the assigned area.

Two days later, at 0725 on 25 April, two Japanese *Shigure* class destroyers were sighted at about nine thousand yards, searching at twenty-four knots for five to ten minutes, then making a radical course change and stopping to listen. They were not using echo ranging—a tactic not noted previously in submarine war patrol reports. In a flat sea with excellent sound conditions, an attack was not deemed advisable. We rigged for silent running and watched them proceed southward.

The following morning we submerged at 0343, morning twilight, off Kinkasan light on the island of Honshu. At 0643, the two *Shigure* destroyers were again sighted close aboard. We were making periscope sweeps at ten-minute intervals. Apparently they were using the same tactics and had closed without being detected on our sonar gear while they drifted with engines stopped. We rigged for a depth-charge attack and for silent running but stayed shallow in order not to roil the surface waters with the screw wash. Suddenly the enemy headed directly toward us at twenty-four knots but thundered by directly overhead, the screws echoing throughout the ship. It was a tense moment.

A close reconnaissance near Kinkasan light disclosed twin radio towers but no radar installations. Time also allowed us to give several people in the conning tower a "periscope liberty," a quick examination of the enemy homeland. Perhaps letters to wives and mothers would suggest how "really close" we were to Tokyo. At 1500 a distant column of smoke brought us back to reality. The general alarm and the call to battle stations echoed through the ship. The target was identified as a low-hulled water barge of about five hundred tons, steaming as close to the beach as possible. The attack was broken off.

The following morning, 27 April, a large freighter with a *Shigure* destroyer escort appeared through the haze on a southerly course. We went to battle stations and commenced closing. The target group was shortly identified as a convoy of four freighters steaming in a box formation, with the destroyer ahead. The largest target for attack, *Yuzan Maru*, a passenger-cargo ship of sixty-four hundred tons, happened to be closest. To make sure of this fine target, the captain decided to fire four torpedoes at him from a position on his beam, waiting until the kingposts came into line at a torpedo range of twenty-one hundred yards, then shifting to the second ship in column to fire two more torpedoes. Our last torpedo was held in reserve for the unexpected. On seeing the wakes, the first ship blew his whistle, but all four torpedoes hit, equally spaced from bow to stern. Before we had a chance to observe the second target, the destroyer seemed to rise out of the water, headed our way. We rigged for depth charge and started deep. The first of a series of eight heavy depth charges reverberated throughout the ship—the first the great majority of us had ever heard. Although terribly noisy and quite disconcerting, they were not particularly close. (Depth charges are *always* close.) The BT recorded a beautiful layer just below periscope depth, screening us from the enemy. The pinging indicated that he had no solid contact, and in half an hour we were back at periscope depth for a look around.

Yuzan had reversed heading and lay dead in the water. Down by the stern, she was not long for this world. The destroyer circled, either to regain contact or to pick up survivors; the other freighters had disappeared. Apparently our second attack missed. At 0547, *Yuzan* sank with bow high in the air; we took pictures, then went deep to clear the area. Distant depth charging continued near the attack area, but at 1030, with nothing in sight, we broached to fifty feet to transmit a contact report using the radar mast antenna. With no success, we tried it at twenty feet, and again three hours later, still without success, finally sending it blind. The message was not repeated on the submarine schedule after we surfaced that night, hence the blind transmission had apparently been missed. The report was finally acknowledged at 2136, but because our repeated transmissions surely gave away our position, the captain decided to clear the area to seaward. With only one torpedo remaining—possibly damaged by exposure to deep submergence—our offensive capability was limited. The following evening, Commander Submarines ordered our return to Midway.

The CO's first act, after heading for the barn at flank speed, was to call me into his cabin for a chat. Mentioning the likelihood that Reggie would leave after this patrol for his own command, perhaps with me as his second, he wanted me to take over Reggie's duties as navigator for the trip back. He recognized my great elation at the chance to become an exec so far ahead of my contemporaries but asked for my understanding and discretion because Bert, several years senior to me, might have hurt feelings. I was elated and assumed the new responsibilities with zest. Navigation never lost its fascination for me, and Reggie was a super teacher. With a fine patrol behind us, the future looked bright. Although both of us indicated our strong reluctance to leave our beloved *Scorpion,* Bill felt confident that qualified replacements would be ordered.

The following morning an enemy patrol vessel of about a hundred tons was sighted on the horizon, mounting a single gun atop the pilot house and a heavily insulated cage antenna between the masts. Commencing a gun attack with all weapons, we quickly set him afire, then chased him around in a circle until he was destroyed, burned to the waterline. Once more we headed for home at full speed, ordnance largely expended for a good bag of enemy scalps. All hands were feeling highly optimistic.

Then our luck ran out.

The next morning, 30 April 1943, the superstructure of a small freighter appeared hull down on the horizon. *Scorpion* was then about six hundred miles from the coast of Japan, and three hundred miles northwest of Marcus Island, a

Japanese air and antisubmarine base. We were not far from the point where we had made first contact with the enemy patrol vessel on our outbound passage, the one Reggie in particular had hoped would be in our path on return. Within a few minutes, the enemy was soon identified not as a small freighter but a good-sized patrol vessel. Even without Reggie's and my urging, there was not much question that we had to take this one on with the deck gun. We headed toward him at full speed; he turned and headed toward us. By then we made him out to be a two-masted, steel-hulled vessel of about six hundred tons displacement, 175 feet long, with a wooden superstructure and pilot house. The gun appeared to be an old-fashioned five- or six-pounder mounted on a high platform forward, with two or more machine gun mounts along his ramparts and two depth charge racks aft. Painted gray, number 23 on the bow, he opened fire at about three thousand yards with the forward gun. At two thousand yards the captain swung left to bring the deck gun to bear and opened fire with everything we had. While we were passing broadside to him at eight hundred yards, the deck gun jammed after firing only about fifteen rounds. The enemy was being raked with smaller fire, but the deck gun had been ineffective. Neither point-detonating nor fused ammunition was available to submarines then; I could see later that hull hits with "common" ammunition made a three-inch hole in one side and a three-inch exit out the other.

The captain ordered flank speed to draw out of range while clearing the three-inch gun and replenishing ammunition in the depleted ready boxes. Tommy guns, Browning automatic rifles (BARs), and all ammunition possible were brought to the gun platforms. As we closed for action again, the enemy chased us for a while, then released a heavy white smoke float and turned to withdraw to the south. We assumed it to be a marker for aircraft, an assumption that soon proved correct.

At about 0845, ready for the reattack, we headed in at flank speed. The enemy kept his tail to us for a while, then stopped. Now dressed in white uniforms, the crew had fallen in at quarters. We slowed to ten knots and took course to come up on his stern for several broadsides, then came alongside at close range and stopped. We opened fire at seventeen hundred yards; the three-inch hit the enemy stern on the first salvo and raised a big smoke cloud. By the time we came up his port side at about three to four hundred yards, all guns were firing at best rate with excellent accuracy. The pilot house burst into flames, which later died out or were extinguished. His forward gun was now out of action, but our three-inch gun jammed again when a projectile became separated from the case. The last clearing charge was used and fire was quickly resumed. The same casualty happened twice again, but under the stress of battle, Gunner's Mate Carl Hund coolly muscled the hot projectile out with the extension handle and firing was continued.

Despite our heavy fire, the flash of machine gun and rifle fire could still be seen coming from several points along the bulwarks. Several shots ricocheted off the forward 20-mm gun shield a few feet from me, the fragments injuring two gunners. These were the shields the DivCom had insisted we install at Pearl; they saved at least one life.

Standing alongside the deck gun, I also stopped a ricochet in the center of my chest; the zipper was ripped loose from my jacket as the bullet fused into the metal, but it barely drew blood. A half-inch either way might have told another story.

Then at 0924, Reggie Raymond, while firing a BAR from the bridge railing, was struck in the center of the forehead by an enemy bullet, which passed completely through his brain, killing him instantly. As he slumped down, he was carried to the after end of the gun deck and firing continued. Realizing that we were not sinking the enemy despite the heavy damage, the captain spun the ship bows on and backed down hard to open the range to five hundred yards. The last torpedo was quickly made ready and fired, striking the enemy amidships and destroying him in a terrific explosion. He went down with guns ablaze and his flag flying from the gaff.

At 0945 we secured from battle stations and commenced clearing the area at flank speed. Reggie's body was being prepared for burial at sea when a plane was detected by radar at two miles. He was apparently coming in low out of the sun and was not seen by the lookouts. We dived to 150 feet; two depth charges exploded in our wake. Reggie's body was lost from the gun platform on the dive. Another distant explosion was heard some time later and, influenced by the deeply emotional state of the crew, the captain decided to remain submerged until dark.

Surfacing at dusk, we checked topside for damage. The deck gun, submerged in seawater when the barrel was smoking hot, looked a little odd, but no significant damage could be determined. At 2000 we stopped the engines to lay to on the surface while conducting a religious service for Reggie. Captain Wylie carried out the formal service; he asked me to do the homily. Reggie was the son of a minister, and I found a prayer book in his desk from which I chose some appropriate words, but I had a very difficult time getting them out. For the captain, for me, for the entire crew it was a shattering event. I could not believe that those sparkling eyes, inspiring personality, and superb intellect were forever stilled.

A long moment of silence ended the ceremony. I dropped from the conning tower to the control room. The entire watch, on bended knee at their stations, sobbed quietly to themselves. I thought it appropriate to take a walk through the ship. Here were my rugged, hell-raising shipmates, my beloved heroes, every man in a state of shock, each in his own way trying to pay last respects to the memory of a truly great man. I sought out Bill Wylie to try in some way to ease the very great burden of responsibility I knew he must be carrying. In all truth, I insisted that Reggie and I, the whole crew, wanted that last action, and if anybody should feel responsible, it was I. Bill suggested that I might wish to move into his spare bunk rather than stay in Reggie's cabin. I thanked him for his consideration but suggested that Reggie had been part of my life and would always be part of it; I would be deserting him if I moved. No longer able to hide my emotions, I sought the privacy of my cabin—*our* cabin— and finally gave in to my grief.

The sudden tragedy was hard to believe. I had waked Reggie that morning before breakfast. Little did I know I would read a burial service for him that evening. I tried to resume my duties as navigator, now wholly on my own. Commander Submarines, on learning of our tragedy, diverted us from Midway to Pearl Harbor. Heading for home at full speed, we lost much of one day fighting heavy seas. It was a battle-tested but weary *Scorpion* that moored at the submarine base at 0600 on 8 May. Although it was early Saturday morning, a crowd of visitors, official and unofficial, waited on the dock as we eased alongside. The mood was one of pride in an aggressive and highly successful first patrol, combined with one of deep sorrow at our irreplaceable loss.

As the visitors came aboard the forward gangway, a working party dragged ice cream, fresh fruit, and sacks of mail across the after gangway, enthusiastically aided by eager volunteers. Buses with engines idling were already waiting at the head of the dock to take us to the Royal Hawaiian Hotel for ten days of rest and recreation. Every repair or routine necessary before going back to sea again had been carefully prepared by *Scorpion* experts on the way in from patrol and outlined in the "refit book," a brief of every piece of machinery on the ship. A quick conference with key men from the SubPac staff, the base, the temporary *Scorpion* relief crew, and regular ship's officers allowed a complete turnover of the ship in a matter of minutes. All hands were then free of the war for a few days, returning to the ship once every four or five days for the duty and normal oversight of work in progress. This routine, common throughout the submarine force, proved to be highly efficient.

The Royal Hawaiian, a world-famed luxury hotel on the beach at Waikiki, was taken over by the Navy early in the war for use as a rest facility for aviators and submariners returning from combat. I enjoyed a wonderful corner room with an ocean view on one side and a beautiful tropical paradise on the other, with the famed Diamond Head crater in the distance. (I learned later that several of the men, to confuse the censor in their letters home, referred to Diamond Head as "Club Foot.")

We swam and sunbathed for long hours each day, ate bountiful meals, relished the fragrant walks, and just plain enjoyed life. The dining room was on an open lanai; turtle doves and canaries hovered around the tables begging for crumbs. We tried our hands daily at volleyball, tennis, table

tennis, badminton, miniature golf, bowling, croquet or boxing. We could ride surfboards, sail outriggers and sailboats,
or try snorkeling and spearfishing in the blue waters. Indoor
sports included game rooms, reading rooms, beer and soda
parlors, nightly movies, hula dancers, and just plain goofing
off. The cost was nominal—a dollar a day, meals included;
for the enlisted, twenty-five cents a week.

The first evening was pure heaven. A gorgeous moon rose
through the hanging fronds of coconut palms, a quiet surf
caressing the sandy beach. Then out of nowhere, like news
from home, came Doc Norton, my old *Wichita* buddy, with
Andrew I. Lyman, plebe year roomie and now a sharp-
looking U.S. Marine, and Benjamin C. Jarvis, whose submarine was also in refit. Doc was a hotshot naval aviator,
already decorated for several courageous torpedo bombing
attacks on Japanese carriers in the Battle of Santa Cruz. He
and Dal were celebrating the birth of a son a month ago.
Doc sprouted a mustache for the occasion, more likely just
to prove his ability. It had that sort of stubborn appearance
about it. The lilting sounds of a string orchestra playing
sentimental local songs drifted out to us, adding the perfect
background touch. We had no interest in local wahines,
preferring to reminisce about the past and speculate on the
future.

I had heard nothing from Henri. We had returned from
patrol two weeks early and she still had a while to go on her
pregnancy. Her health was excellent, and she was quite
optimistic. I just wanted to hear her voice. I had planned to
telephone her immediately upon return. Regulations required advance application, and the entire message had to
be approved by the censor, including names and places to
be mentioned and a lot not to be mentioned, plus the time
the call would be made. A "V-mail" letter would have been
about as quick. Only then did I learn that regulations had
recently been changed so that ship-based personnel were no
longer allowed to use the overseas telephone. Instead, I sent
a couple of those sterile, canned telegrams, one on arrival
and another on Mother's Day. Many other Scorps were in
the same boat. Bert hadn't heard from Lucille, three of the
men were awaiting imminent news from their wives, another
was a happy father, and four still had a while to go. Obvi-

ously the men had taken that "new construction" duty seriously.

The endorsements on our patrol report were outstanding. Leo Pace pointed out the gratifying results obtained through intelligent planning and brilliant execution, highlighted by excellent performance of the surface search radar, the remarkable results—quite unanticipated—obtained with the bathythermograph, the excellent material condition of the ship, and the exceptionally smart appearance of the crew on return to port. Of primary interest to me were his kind words on the 50 percent torpedo hits, one of the highest ever by a submarine on patrol. Every torpedo ran hot, straight, and normal, including the one fired in the action in which Reggie was killed. That one had previously been subjected to full sea pressure at three hundred feet, and although routined carefully afterward, we had serious doubts that it would run normally. The exploder was bone dry even after the deep submergence. Would the exploder have resisted sea pressure had we not tightened the impeller glands to four times the required pressure? I thought not and passed the information on to the force torpedo experts.

Admiral Lockwood credited us with four ships sunk and one damaged, totalling over 20,000 tons. Intelligence from Japanese sources reduced it to three sunk and two damaged, but later credited two additional sinkings in the minefield, giving us an impressive total. Both Leo Pace and Admiral Lockwood expressed their deep regrets over the loss of Reggie Raymond. Reggie had served on Lockwood's staff in London before coming to the *Scorpion*. Admiral Lockwood recommended Bill Wylie for the Navy Cross, the Navy's highest decoration for valor, and Reggie and me for the Silver Star, the next highest. Leo Pace, in a special tribute to Reggie, dedicated to his memory one full torpedo nest from each submarine in his division on the next patrol. The reaction to the patrol throughout Pearl Harbor was predictable. Scores of men tried to get aboard for duty, and sea stories about our adventures were on everybody's lips.

Mike Fenno was detached from command of *Runner* as anticipated, but in Reggie's absence, Joe Bourland fleeted up from exec to command. If I couldn't go to *Runner* with Reggie, I was happy to stay aboard *Scorpion*. Bill Wylie would need moral support in the days ahead. And Joe's luck soon ran out. He took *Runner* to sea and was never heard from again. His wife, Peggy, a close friend of Marge Raymond, took an apartment with Marge, and they tried to pick up the pieces together.

Meanwhile, I was looking anxiously for a relief for Reggie. One of the duties of the exec was to transfer about one-fifth of our men to the squadron after each patrol and receive replacements from the relief crews. This was standard procedure. It allowed rotation of the entire crew after five patrols, eased the strain on those at sea, and allowed periodic leave periods back in the states. The transfer of those fine men was always difficult. Experienced petty officers were "traded in" for new men fresh out of sub school, generally with little or no experience at sea. All of them were fine men, too, but an active training program was necessary before they could carry a fair share of the load. These tasks, which I inherited as acting exec, I found to be unfamiliar and time-consuming. Adding the tasks of general oversight of the refit, plus running four departments, soon wore me thin.

Joy of joys, the telegram from Henri finally arrived. We were proud parents of an eight-pound baby girl, born 21 May, and mother and baby were doing fine. No decision had yet been made on a name. Because telegrams could no longer be sent to shipboard personnel, the news came by mail from San Francisco. As quickly as I could, I sent a canned message from a hundred available. I needed only one—Love. I sent Yeoman L'Hereux to the post office to get it on its way. He couldn't see why I wanted to send only one word, but on the back of the blank several other messages had been checked off—someone had used it before I got it—so he added several of those that seemed appropriate, none of which made sense to Henri. Bill offered his very special congratulations. He and I had grown very close in recent weeks, despite the difference in seniority and our rather aloof natures. He sought my advice on a great many things, and though I felt I was sometimes of very little assistance, having someone to talk with seemed to help. An unspoken bond lay between us; I feared we would miss Reggie on the next trip.

A week before we went to sea again, a relief finally reported aboard, Lt. Cmdr. Harry C. Maynard, a classmate of Reggie's and a very bright officer. Harry was a torpedo expert, had spent three years in the Navy postgraduate school from 1939 to 1942, earning a degree in ordnance engineering. He had prewar duty in the old "S" boats but had never served in a fleet boat. From the start we liked him immensely, nobody more than I, if only for some help with the work load. He would have a major job trying to fill Reggie's shoes, and he went to work immediately.

The last day at the Royal Hawaiian featured a native Hawaiian luau. A whole pig was roasted underground, cooking for hours over hot stones covered with ti leaves, then eaten after the usual preparation of songs, hula dances, and games. I found the native dishes strangely fascinating, all eaten with the fingers—enjoyable, delicious, and very fattening. The crew enjoyed the day immensely.

Back on the boat, we commenced working up the new attack team. The three days at sea in advanced training meant continuous drills and torpedo approaches day and night. The rumor held that the training team tried to exhaust the crew as much in three days as during a full patrol, the better to judge their reactions under fatigue. Gunnery drills kept the crew busy. The base had replaced the three-inch gun with a four-inch, and had installed additional ammunition lockers, handlebar controls on the 20-mm guns, and mounts for the .50-caliber machine guns.

Ready for sea at 1300, 29 May, we backed from the submarine base piers into the channel, heading west. The escort was dismissed at nightfall and a course set for Midway, about 1,250 miles to the west. I personally wasn't ready for sea; I still didn't have a name tag on our youngster. But the war had to go on, and following the usual fuel stop at Midway, plus a pleasant lunch aboard the submarine tender, we were soon back out the narrow channel and off into the deep blue looking for new adventures.

The assigned patrol area covered the Yellow Sea between China, Japan, and Korea, and promised good hunting. On passing south of the Tokyo approaches one day just before sunset we gave the crew a treat with a close view of the aptly named Sofu Gan, or Lot's Wife, an island about sixteen feet wide and rising over three hundred feet out of the sea. Passing Tori Shima, south of Kyushu, we entered the East China Sea to be greeted by a beam-ender of a summer gale, slowing the ship to a maximum of six knots. The only relief from our misery came from Tokyo Rose, listened to faithfully by submariners on patrol everywhere. She called us the Black Panthers—the Murderous Black Panthers. She seemed awfully excited about something.

The plan we worked out for area coverage aimed first to patrol the shipping routes between Formosa and Nagasaki-Tsushima, then to take station off Shanghai at Barren Island for a few days before proceeding up the China coast toward the Shantung Peninsula. If good hunting didn't develop, we would then cross the Yellow Sea past Port Arthur and patrol the Korean coast south toward Nagasaki again. The area presented formidable problems. First, the Japanese had laid an enormous minefield to protect the Shanghai-Nagasaki trade routes; much of the patrol would be spent in the middle of it. We lacked any detailed information on the precise areas mined, and had no equipment to detect a mine in our path. Second, much of the China coast was poorly charted, with large blank areas marked "unknown." Shipping generally hugged the coast very close inshore in areas of primary interest. Third, the water throughout the northern part of the area was quite shallow, all of it under 300 feet, much under 150 feet. Good submarining required about 600 feet for unrestricted operations. In evasion after an attack, especially over a rocky bottom, shallow water presented a severe handicap. One other problem was more mental than physical. To reach the Yellow Sea area from Midway, we first passed through the antisubmarine patrols out of Marcus Island, where Reggie was killed, then through the next barrier in the Nanpo Shoto Islands south of Tokyo, then the third in Nansei Shoto, the Okinawa chain, as we turned north around the Japanese home islands into the Yellow Sea. When the patrol area was finally reached, each of those barriers isolated one deeper and deeper within the empire. The nearest friendly force, over four thousand miles from Midway, seemed a long way off.

Navigation offered unusual challenges. Frequent overcasts and haze on the horizon limited opportunities for celestial navigation, and few of the landmarks offered significant help for piloting. Harry was having difficulty. He had never been a navigator, and his nearsightedness made the task doubly difficult. I can't recall anybody wearing glasses while using a sextant. Since he took more time than usual for celestial observations, other problems arose. An open submarine bridge is not an ideal platform for scientific measurements. Rolling and pitching are ever-present; the moist breezes so close to the surface of the sea quickly fog the lenses with salt spray virtually impossible to remove with lens paper alone. Nor does the submarine navigator have the luxury of doing his work at a decent time of twilight, when the horizon is sharp and clear. In the patrol area, submerged all day and on the surface all night, twilight came long before surfacing and ended before the morning dive. The surfacing routine called for the captain to take a quick look around, call up the lookouts, then order trash and garbage dragged up and heaved over the side. Finally the navigator had his chance. If he deserved pity, he rarely got it. I helped Harry when I could and did much of the navigation when he couldn't get a set of star sights. What he lacked most was operational horse sense. He was a scientist more than a seaman.

I was again standing the four-to-eight watches, Bert the mids. But on the morning dives, strange things were happening. Sometimes the ship would dive with an up angle or hang on the surface with a down angle. When we got down, the overall trim was wretched. The weight changes from surfacing the night before couldn't possibly account for the errors. I began studying the diving book in which all the changes were recorded. It finally developed that Bert, all alone on the bridge during the midnight witching hours, would get information from somewhere and order the chief of the watch to flood or pump, causing the trouble on the next dive. After a few scares, I started a new procedure. Every morning when I came on watch, I asked the chief of the watch to restore all the tank readings to where they were at midnight, before Bert came on watch. This took care of the problem. Bert never knew.

Early in the patrol, antisubmarine action was heavy. Distant underwater explosions were heard when nothing could be seen nor any traces of shipping noted. After another heavy storm, and without a navigational fix for three days, we headed north toward Shantung. The first shipping contact was made by radar, a large sailing junk heading for the Korean coast. We went to battle stations, but it was not clear that he was Japanese, and not wishing to disclose our presence by setting him afire, we abandoned the attack. We then headed for Chopekki Point, just north of the present demilitarized zone (DMZ) between North and South Korea. Navigation lights were burning in this area, suggesting that shipping might be moving through.

At 0342 on 3 July, *Scorpion* dived about nine miles off the beach. The wind had died, leaving a light surface fog and a dead flat sea. Two small vessels could be made out indistinctly, either patrol vessels or fishing trawlers, easily avoided at periscope depth. Three hours later, several indistinct objects appeared in the haze, on a converging course, coming up the coast from the south. These soon developed into the tops of several vessels whose hulls were still invisible in the surface fog. Echo ranging could be heard but the source could not be seen. General quarters was sounded, and the men raced to their battle stations.

All the way out from Pearl Harbor, the thought uppermost in our minds was the attack dedicated to Reggie Raymond. Would this be it? The next attack had to be perfect. At a range of about 6,500 yards the enemy was made out to be a convoy of five decrepit freighters plus a *Chidori* escort, a highly effective new antisubmarine ship appearing in numbers throughout the empire. The extreme flat, calm sea made observation difficult, but Bill did a masterful job.

The enemy appeared to be four- to five-thousand-ton coal burners, rusty and ragged in outline. At 4,500 yards the convoy zigged twenty degrees toward *Scorpion* and formed a rough line of bearing about 3,000 yards across. The escort was between us and the convoy and was now on our starboard beam with a small port angle on the bow, closing. This was not the best position for *Scorpion*, presenting a beam silhouette to an escort heading almost directly for us. But there was insufficient time to cross the front ahead of him without further risk of alerting him with a burst of speed. Hence the attack was made on the largest ship, from a position on his beam, using small gyro angles, then shifting targets to the second largest, firing three torpedoes at each and hoping that the spread would catch the third ship, at a greater range but nearly on the same bearing. The three shots at the first target were fired at 1,600 yards and three at the second, range 850 yards, all torpedoes set to run at fifteen feet. Five heavy explosions were heard, and a minute later, a sixth. Meanwhile, the escort and the other two vessels were close on our beam and heading almost directly toward us.

The captain flooded negative tank (to give a quick down angle), rigged for depth charge attack, and went deep. We thought we had 180 feet of water, but before the sound heads could be raised the ship struck bottom at 147 feet with a demoralizing crunch, receiving two close depth charges just as we hit. The sonar went dead, and the shaft, firmly jammed, could not be raised. Fortunately, the shaft had been bent aft; otherwise the attempt to raise it might have brought up a stub, flooding the torpedo room and likely the ship. But if this could be called good luck, we still had a major share of bad.

The *Chidori* dropped five more depth charges, severely jarring the boat, breaking light bulbs, opening valves, and tossing gear into space. The attacks were so close that the captain thought we might be leaving a mud trail on the surface. He stopped the screws, allowing the boat to settle slowly to the bottom in 154 feet of water and sweat out a few attacks from there.

For those without the experience, a good close depth charge attack offers a unique form of punishment. In traditional warfare, battles of tanks and infantry, battles of fleet against fleet, combat connotes noise, confusion, stress, violent activity, chaos. A submarine attack and evasion is quite the opposite. Nothing acts to pump adrenaline into the system. The handful of men who are active work in dead silence. Shoes are removed and, with the normal hum of electric motors stilled, every sound is magnified a thousand times. Few can divert the punishment of his own thoughts and fears. The urge to urinate comes quickly after the call to general quarters, then the only thing active is the imagination. The eerie silence reverses the whole psychological idea of warfare. One is prey to every dark possibility. Every sound takes on an abnormal significance. External noises transmitted through the still water are heard clearly. Dropping a depth charge, the click of the exploder if they're close enough, the sudden rush of propellors passing overhead, each puts a knot in the gizzard. The moment between the click and the boom gives a split second to think about one's past and possible future. It can be emotionally shattering. Sounds are magnified in seawater, and the effect is still worse in shallow water.

Before the war it was commonly believed that a depth charge exploding anywhere within a half mile of a submarine would be fatal. War experience soon proved that submarines were surviving charges as close as thirty, twenty, or fifteen feet. But one can imagine the turmoil created by a major explosion so close. It doesn't seem possible that any ship could survive such abuse, but many survived some godawful punishment. If one were inclined to offer a silent prayer to Andrew I. "Andy" McKee and his superb Portsmouth shipyard craftsmen for building them so tough, even that was deferred until later. If the evasion tactic didn't succeed, the punishment came quickly and one hoped for another chance as the tension built for the next attack. Minutes, hours dragged on, the air became stale, hands and feet felt clammy, the decrease in energy left in the batteries caused concern. Normally, for each burst of speed a price is paid in further reducing the reserve left for escape and evasion until able to surface and get in a battery charge on the diesels. To improve the air quality and ease breathing distress, oxygen can be bled into the boat, but once used it can't be replaced, and the next crisis may be worse. All in all, it takes a certain psychological attitude to be a good submariner.

During lulls in depth charge attacks, I made a point of taking a walk through the boat when I could, ostensibly to check damage but primarily to pass a word of encouragement here or there, to look into the men's eyes and try to search their souls. Submarine war isn't for everybody.

Meanwhile, the bottoming tactic failed. Within two minutes, a chain was dragged over the hull, followed by another close depth charge. Two minutes later, the drag passed over the hull again. We decided that we might be leaking hydraulic oil from the damaged sound heads, making this an unhealthy spot. The skipper went ahead on the screws and made a radical course change. Close depth charges were again heard at 1019, 1028, and 1043; then followed an hour of relative quiet. Returning to periscope depth, we discovered the *Chidori* drifting about the scene of the attack 7,000 yards astern with nothing else in sight. At 1723, a distant and heavy underwater explosion was heard throughout the ship. We continued to clear the vicinity at best submerged speed, and the escort soon passed out of sight. On the captain's "stand easy" normal breathing was resumed by all hands. Was it only a coincidence that cussing suddenly disappeared from the boat and Bibles appeared where I hadn't seen them before? James "The Swoose" Alexander certainly hadn't been wearing a rosary around his neck last time I saw him.

At this time a decision had to be made. Bill thought that since the *Chidori* was still in the area, the remains of the convoy might have fled inshore to shallow water. Because we were without sonar and the visibility was poor it seemed inadvisable to attempt further penetration and a reattack. Bill asked me privately for my recommendations. I suggested that the low convoy speed of eight knots might make it worthwhile to try to overtake the two undamaged ships before they reached Port Arthur, their apparent destination. With full speed on the surface and on a flat sea, we could get into attack position by midnight, make a quick surface attack, and clear the area long before dawn. Then with only a week left in the area, we could return to the Nagasaki-Shanghai trade routes, where the water depth was at least marginally adequate. The hydraulic leakage had been repaired; we could spend much of the remaining time on the surface, where the sonar would not be quite so vital to our survival.

I had to admit that there had been a subtle change in Bill on this trip. It was only natural that Reggie's loss still had him tied in knots. He seemed to have lost some of the zip so characteristic of his earlier style of operating. Perhaps I was only imagining it. Certainly in the attack on the convoy he was cool, totally on top of the problem. I doubt if the other officers noticed a significant change. Part of his problem was a fairly constant pain in his teeth and gums. We all ate plenty of citrus fruits while in port, but the total lack of sunlight caused mild symptoms of scurvy in several people. Bill had been troubled on the first patrol and seemed concerned.

Perhaps I too had changed; certainly Reggie dominated my thoughts these past weeks. After further deliberation, Bill decided the gain from remaining on station for the full duration of the patrol was hardly worth the risk. We headed south, patrolling submerged by day and on the surface at night, finally departing from the assigned area a week early, at midnight, 7 July, passing through the Nansei Shoto Islands on the surface.

Shortly after dawn the next morning, with Akuseki Island five miles to port, we observed two small vessels patrolling or fishing, one on either side of the island. Because the seas were extremely rough, we decided they were patrolling on station. This view may have been confirmed an hour later when a Mitsubishi bomber dropped from the low overcast, heading in for an attack. A lookout picked it up at four miles. We headed for the bottom and pulled off our easterly course at high speed. One distant depth charge was heard as we slowed. Since we were in plain sight of the island, and heavy seas made for a slow dive, it seemed prudent to remain submerged during the remainder of the day.

The next morning at dawn, the quartermaster of the watch sighted a periscope on the port bow at about seven hundred yards. The OOD turned away at flank speed, putting the stern toward the enemy, and prepared for a stern shot. The periscope disappeared quickly, however, and we soon resumed course and speed for Midway. This was the second time in two patrols that our location, determined by a sighting or radio transmission, resulted in our being met by a hostile welcoming party on the daylight circle at dawn.

With only one aircraft contact while penetrating the Nanpo Shoto and Marcus Island antisubmarine patrol areas, we made good speed toward Midway. All hands worked hard to prepare for a smart-looking arrival. We prettied up and flounced the door curtains and laid the Sunday-best table cover, which Henri and Nancy had worked so hard to find in New England dry-goods emporia. Freshly bathed and shaved, clean uniformed and with new insignia, I felt like a nine-year-old going to Sunday school—wearing dolphins and collar marks, shampooed and shined. I tried to wash the salt out of my hair, but combing it was near useless. It was still an unruly mop of cornsilk. But the ship, all admitted, was the cleanest ever in coming off patrol. Easing alongside the tender, USS *Sperry,* at 1800 on 15 July, we were ready for drinks at the Gooneyville Tavern and dinner on board in the commodore's mess. With six hits for six fired, the captain again received warm congratulations on the fine torpedo score.

The first order of business was a determination on replacing the missing sound heads and whether we would have to go to Pearl Harbor for a docking. After a quick survey, *Sperry* decided she could do the job with *Scorpion* moored alongside. It would require pressurizing the forward torpedo room during the whole time the work was in progress, and all traffic in or out of the room would have to go via the air lock on the escape trunk. Never before had such a highly complicated operation been attempted while afloat. But doing the work in Midway would save the ten-day round trip to Pearl and get us back on the firing line that much sooner. On this basis the refit went to *Sperry* as scheduled.

My good news on arrival was a name for our daughter, now almost two months old. Henri had chosen Regina Marie, in Reggie Raymond's honor, and I was ecstatic. I spent hours staring at her pictures—very bright, very cute, with a head of dark hair standing straight up.

But with the good news came also some bad. While we were at sea, *Amberjack* had been lost with all hands. Robert P. "Pete" Blauvelt, a sub school classmate and good friend, served as her torpedo officer. On a previous patrol she had performed a vital mission carrying gasoline into Guadalcanal to help a valiant Marine Corps air support force hang on to a perilous existence on Henderson Field. Pete and Mary Beth had just had a youngster, I learned.

R and R at Midway, we soon learned, was far less luxurious than the Royal Hawaiian but in some ways more enjoyable. The Gooneyville Hotel, relic of the Pan American clipper days when Midway was a stopover on Orient flights, was comfortable and relaxing. The lobby, the lawns, and the grounds were adorned with potted flowers supplied by a group of young botanists trying to plant them throughout the island. On that barren, treeless sand spit only a few feet above sea level, trees and bushes flourished, planted over the years since 1907. We studied one flowering bush, an insect eater, in amazement. The inner cone contained a sweet, sticky covering that attracted flies and ants. A fly crawling under the stamen, as it seemed impelled to do, got wedged or glued in as the flower smothered it. Every flower on the bush was full of wings and legs.

We spent much free time in the tavern, meeting and greeting old shipmates and friends. The fridge was always open and the beer was free. The brands were offbeat export varieties, but one wasn't forced to indulge, and the price was right. Officers could buy a liquor ration of a bottle a week, but with no mix, no ice, and brackish water, most of us gave our rations to the men. Their only other source, through the black market, ran $50 a bottle.

Midway was a wildlife sanctuary almost overrun by birds. Japanese terns, snow white and absolutely beautiful, fluttered through the air constantly; the bosun birds, also white with two long, quill-like red tail feathers—very valuable, used in women's hats—were the most unpopular. Though beautiful, they were raucous and nasty tempered. Walking near a nest invited a bloodcurdling squawk. By far the most unpopular at night were the "moanies," living in the sand and moaning like a baby crying—very disturbing. Everybody's favorite was the wonderful and numerous gooney bird, technically a Leysan albatross. We watched them for hours, the perfection of grace in the air, though sometimes incredibly awkward. If they forgot and made a water landing on sand, they tumbled over in an awkward heap, glaring at the hostile sand. The babies, big as turkeys, were ready to begin flight instructions. A parent, usually the mother, would take five or so chicks and teach them to make the long run to get off the ground, kicking up sand and dust all the way. Some stumbled and fell, bumped into others, or stalled out and landed in a dusty heap. It was funnier every time they tried. All the human emotions passed before our eyes. And many a man, perhaps prone to a bit of overindulgence, returned to his hotel room at night to find a gooney beneath the sheets. What a mess they could make!

In the mating season they made love everywhere, with more mooning in their public courtship than high school sophomores. We found them both affectionate and cruel. Some of us learned the technique of approaching them from behind to scratch their necks to make them purr, at the risk of losing a fingertip or two.

Midway offered fine sports facilities and great beaches. A spirited volleyball game ran outside the tavern almost continuously. The *Scorpion* fielded a hot team and also took on all challengers in softball. On the tennis court, I found a splendid partner in Dick Ellis. Between matches everybody headed for the wide, sandy beaches to swim or cool off. The ever-present trade winds kept the temperature reasonable, but keeping clothing dry was a perennial problem. We gradually wore less and less. I slept nude, pulled on trousers and shirt only for breakfast, shifted to shorts and tennis shoes for sporting events, swam in the nude, and "dressed" for dinner and the movies with sandals, a khaki shirt, and shorts. And swimming nude, we soon discovered, helped to make the coat of suntan look like a much better fit.

At the movies, insects infesting the wood seats feasted on any exposed flesh, leaving rashes that burned and itched for days. The alternative to the nightly movie was the poker game in the Skipper's Hut, running more or less continuously. I enjoyed penny ante poker but these stakes were too rich for my enjoyment, and I was content to kibitz, taking an occasional hand as relief for somebody making a trip to the head. I found the bull sessions with officers passing through and the fascinating adventure stories coming out of the war far more interesting. One of the visitors was Maximilian G. "Max" Schmidt, a *Wichita* shipmate. Max brought news of Don Giles, the former engineer, who left the Witch to become deputy governor of Guam. He was taken prisoner when the Japs landed on the almost defenseless island on 10 December 1941. A letter and photo of Don had come through to his wife. He was in good health but had lost almost one hundred pounds.

During one of my duty days on the boat, a routine battery charge came close to causing tragedy when a relief crew electrician, perspiring heavily from the heat, slipped and fell against two terminals carrying enough electricity to kill half a dozen men, passing in one arm and out the other. A *Scorpion* man, Electrician's Mate First Class E. M. Brack, heedless of his own danger, pulled the man clear and broke contact. Fortunately, help was close at hand. I got there soon enough to see the flesh on the affected man's arm actually boiling. The layer of sweat probably saved him by providing an alternate path for most of the charge. Both men were in shock but recovered quite quickly and were soon back on full duty.

On my next duty, Brack stopped by the wardroom to chat during a trip through the boat, mentioning how good a cold beer would taste. The air conditioning was still off, and the boat was stifling hot. I agreed and said, "Sure, just don't tell me about it. I'll dream about having one too." Thinking no more about it, I went to the movie back aft and, on return, raided the tiny wardroom refrigerator for a bite to eat. There before me were two bottles of beer, cold and inviting. I didn't dare open them while anybody was still awake but relished every drop when the time came.

Jim "Swoose" Alexander was also in my duty section. He had prayed for a Midway refit since Portsmouth days. Very popular and a fine deckhand, he came to my attention from his first day aboard. He had been a champion ice skater in Michigan at age sixteen, and his remarkable agility made him an excellent dancer. He earned his nickname, half swan, half goose, for an outstanding performance as master of ceremonies at the ship's commissioning party in Portsmouth. After several acrobatic acts and a torch dance dressed as a female, he brought down the house with a sidesplitting imitation of Nancy Wylie pulling on a girdle.

For Jim, the visit to Midway was a dream come true. His dad, a SeaBee, was stationed here and spent Jim's duty days aboard. Father and son looked like twins, lean and wiry, both in dungarees, one bronzed by sun and wind, the other pale as a lily from too many months in a submarine. At the Gooneybird Extravaganza, Jim won a $50 war bond for an acrobatic act, upholding the honor of the ship. His wife was expecting their first child in about two months. Their son, to look ahead a bit in time, in later years became a special favorite of his grandfather, but as fate would have it, would never meet his father. Such were the tragic ways of war.

Moving back on the boat to rest up from the rest at the Gooneyville, I received two unexpected surprises. First, the captain informed me he had recommended me as *qualified for command,* and showed me a flowery letter to the bureau for insertion in my record. Again I felt elated and humble. I had less than two years in submarines; some of my sub school classmates had not yet won their dolphins. Harry Maynard was not yet qualified for command.

The second surprise gave me a more mixed feeling. Orders had arrived for me to leave *Scorpion* and return to the squadron staff in Pearl Harbor for assignment to a submarine as executive officer. Bill was quite upset. Harry clearly had not yet found a niche aboard. His navigation required much help, and he had never taken over the Exec's training and administrative duties. Even before giving me the news, Bill sent a telegram to the bureau requesting substitution of either Bert Rodier or Bob Drane for the transfer quota. I felt sure my orders would be changed and made no plans to leave. The next day Fred Clarke got the same orders to leave *Sawfish,* and it looked as though we were needed for something special. Bill sent another telegram to Commander Submarines, but it soon appeared that the orders would stand. The bureau would accept no substitute, and Admiral Lockwood could offer only sympathy. Now it was my turn to feel sad at the thought of leaving *Scorpion.*

Karl Hensel of submarine school fame was then in Midway as a DivCom, hoping to get a submarine command despite his seniority. He had been so thoughtful when we lost our first youngster that I decided to call on him for a bit of advice and also to bring him up to date on the family. Congenial and helpful as always, he thought my chances of getting the orders canceled were slim and that I might as well accept the inevitable. I was strongly tempted to try to help Bill out by expressing my doubts to Hensel about Harry's marginal performance but decided this was not the occasion to go over the skipper's head to introduce such a matter. I soon had good reason to reconsider.

The training period for the third patrol provided an entirely new basis to reopen the subject. I had been formally detached and rode out the training as an observer. Early on the final morning, Harry, at my ardent insistence, finally relieved me fully of all duties as exec and navigator. The final exercise, a torpedo attack against a "heavy" guarded by three escorts, carried us through the morning. When we surfaced immediately after the final attack, I was the first to the bridge. To my horror, coral pinnacles were in clear view beneath us; we were about to go aground. I ordered "all back emergency" but it was already too late. Just as Bill Wylie got to the bridge, we glided slowly onto the reef, with the wind and sea setting us higher and higher. We were in serious trouble. The seas were making; a heavy storm approached. We made every attempt to break free quickly to avert a far more serious tragedy. A tug from the base arrived shortly to assist, and after four or five hours of prodigious pulling and hauling, the ship finally broke clear. The captain's excellent seamanship kept the ship from being set broadside to the beach and made it possible to get free before the heavy weather set in. The screws were undamaged but alas, the same could not be said for the sound heads. Once again they were ripped off, lying on the bottom.

Bill felt his luck had run out. Friday the thirteenth proved to be the final jinx. It was three days before weather permitted a return through the narrow channel into Midway. As we berthed once again alongside *Sperry,* the official warmth so prominent on our earlier arrival had turned definitely chilly. The endorsements on the patrol confirmed more of the same, offering far less enthusiasm than for the first. In the "perfect attack" on the convoy, only five hits were allowed and three ships assessed to be damaged, none sunk. After the war, intelligence from Japanese sources confirmed that the *Anzan Maru* and *Kokuryu Maru,* totalling ten thousand tons, were sunk, confirming Bill's estimate, and for which he received a belated Bronze Star. In private discussions in Midway, the commodore told him he had not given the area adequate coverage, nor did he think the damage sufficient to justify leaving the patrol area early. When I had the chance, I defended Bill as emphatically as I could. The decision to remain in an area where the water depth was inadequate was one of judgment, not of courage, and I think most submarine COs under the circumstances would have acted as he had.

After the Midway grounding, the previous decision took on a new coloring, partly because the grounding seemed so inexcusable. Midway is a tiny atoll rising out of the sea. Just a few feet off the beach, the water drops to unlimited depths. No navigation is necessary if one merely uses a seaman's eye to stay out of trouble. There are no hidden shoals, no other perils of the sea. In the training period, the duties of the officer conducting the exercise, or OCE, required him to choose a safe area in which to operate. When the course he selected required the submarine to cut across the tip of the airstrip to get into attack position, the regulations were clear that, even though the ship commander never loses his responsibility for the safe navigation of his vessel, the OCE has equivalent responsibilities. The skipper of one of the escort vessels in the exercise sent a letter to Bill saying that he recognized that the OCE had chosen an unsafe course, that he tried to divert him, and that he would be happy to testify to this effect in Bill's defense. Bill showed me the letter but said he would not introduce it in the hearing. To the best of my knowledge, he never did.

Scorpion left Midway for Pearl Harbor for repairs and for a board of investigation that convened immediately upon arrival. I was asked to testify; my orders were held up pending the termination of the hearing. In due time, Bill was recommended for a court-martial and Harry for a letter of reprimand. Both were relieved and departed from the submarine force. Bill later distinguished himself in command of a new destroyer, USS *Stormes;* Harry was extremely lucky, I thought, to receive command of the USS *Litchfield* based on Pearl Harbor, an old destroyer used for target and escort services. Bill's relief on *Scorpion,* oddly, was Max Schmidt, who had relieved him in *Wichita* just as Bill and I once before were departing for new duties. Bill himself was totally dispirited. He badly needed a break, some time off with his lovely wife, Nancy, to regain his serene outlook. Shortly before I left, he sang the old sailor's lament: "I'm gonna go back to North Carolina, throw a pair of oars over my shoulder and walk inland until somebody asks 'What's them things fur?' That's where I'm going to settle down."

My departure from *Scorpion* was quite emotional. At morning quarters the crew presented me with a magnificent Swiss Vacheron and Constantin wristwatch, suitably engraved. I badly needed a watch and had seen this one in the post exchange on the base, but the price was exorbitant. I don't know how the men ever paid for it. I realized even then that this gesture was primarily a farewell to Reggie as well and could accept it only with that thought in mind. Mumbling some nothings to that great group of men, I wondered how I could ever repay their trust in me. When the chief of the boat made the official presentation, I couldn't even put the watch on, I was so nervous. Getting married was nothing in comparison, I later told Henri. Leo Pace came aboard, and, far from sharing my embarrassment, he could say only how much it was deserved and how much *Scorpion* would miss my presence on the next patrol.

Fred and I learned that our orders were to new construction as execs, once more in Portsmouth. Fred had already left en route *Pomfret;* I was to get a sister ship, the *Sterlet.* The additional delay awaiting completion of the investigation soon had me climbing the walls as my few days of leave slipped away. I finally grabbed transportation to San Francisco via a returning aircraft carrier, "flying" back at twenty-seven knots. Even with a quick flight out of San Francisco, it was mid-September before the long separation ended in a smother of hugs from mother and bright and happy daughter, Gina. All the sorrows of departure faded in the utter joy of reunion.

4   The USS *Sterlet*

Early Command?

Reunion after seven months' separation fulfilled all our dreams. Henri and our parents met me at the airport, and I couldn't take my eyes off Gina, already quite a little lady at three months. The time at home fled swiftly. So much of my leave had frittered away waiting to be released by the board of investigation in Pearl that all too soon we were again on our way to New England, enjoying the spectacular display of fall colors. The smell of harvest sharpened the air and quickened the pulses. Thanks to an outstanding recommendation on Henri's housekeeping by our previous landlady, Captain H.F.D. Davis, captain of the yard, and his wife, Hazel, happily rented us a charming, modern home they had built for retirement in Portsmouth. We had a signed lease in hand weeks before arrival. We knew the place well. Leo Pace had lived there when we met Bill Wylie, Reggie Raymond, and the other officers of the division on arrival in town for *Scorpion* so many months—or was it years—ago. Happy as we were over the house, there were immediate difficulties with the new division commander, Cdr. Lewis S. Parks, who expected to live there as his predecessors had done.

Hazel Davis, an extremely capable Navy wife, long ago had learned to "wear her husband's stripes." She was

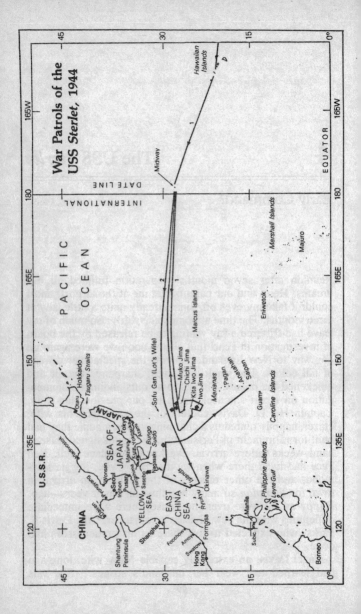

War Patrols of the USS *Sterlet*, 1944

accustomed to sharing his role in positions of responsibility, and the exercise of authority sometimes came too easily. On the departure of Mike and Avis Fenno, our predecessors in the home, she phoned the division office to request that a work detail be sent out to tidy up the place. An ulcerous three striper snarled to his staff, "If the commodore were moving in I'd be delighted, but I'll be double damned if I'll do it for some goddam lieutenant." He sent the work party nevertheless, and we arrived in town innocent of the small tempest already brewing.

The new CO was Orme C. "Butch" Robbins, who had recently completed several Mediterranean patrols as exec of the USS *Shad* based out of England. Aboard *Tautog* in Pearl Harbor on 7 December, he had been hospitalized after one patrol. He had some combat experience and was intelligent and knowledgeable about submarines. First impressions were favorable.

The engineer was Lt. Hugh C. Wright, from one of the "R" boats in Key West; operations officer Lt. Eugene C. "Gene" Barnhardt III of North Carolina; torpedoes and gunnery, Lt. (j.g.) Donald E. Horst, a Pennsylvania Dutchman; assistant engineer Lt. (j.g.) Joe M. Garland, a Mustang—former enlisted man—and two ensigns fresh from sub school, Edward J. Skeehan, a wild Irishman from Pittsburgh, and Robert M. Wright from Florida. I thought the officers looked well above average as a group. They were capable, resourceful, and ready to go to work. I was confident I could add the motivation and experience to build a fine attack team and a congenial wardroom. Their combat experience was limited, but Joe Garland had several patrols under his belt as an enlisted man. Joe, tall and slender, looked like Cesar Romero, complete with pencil mustache. With an irrepressible sense of humor and a keen operational savvy learned in his seventeen years of enlisted service, Joe soon became my right-hand man in every aspect of handling personnel. A few weeks earlier, when Joe first donned that broad gold stripe, he circled in and out of the submarine base gate at Pearl Harbor on his motorcycle, just to relish the salute given him every time by the Marine sentry. For practical horse sense and knowledge of his fellow humans, Joe was a genius.

If the officers were a cut above average, the men seemed every bit as capable. Both the chiefs and "Indians" seemed above average. The younger men, new to the service, were a splendid cross section of America. All were sub school graduates; almost all had specialist training in a host of fields as well. With a little training experience at sea they became fine sailors. Volunteers all, they quickly gained a strong sense of pride in their ship and loyalty to their shipmates. I knew immediately that we were fortunate. An experienced chief attached to the yard with a long and distinguished career in submarines, Chief Torpedoman's Mate Bill Lenning asked for duty aboard to make one war patrol before retirement. We made him the chief of the boat, the senior enlisted man responsible for keeping the entire ship running smoothly.

No sooner had we moved into the Maplewood residence than Lew and Zelda Parks arrived. Surprised to learn of our lease, they began the difficult task of house-hunting. Fortuitously, my orders came through to go to the PCO school in New London—now called the Command Class in Attack Technique—and we suggested that the Parkses live in our place for the month we would be gone.

New London had changed. Without Hensel the course seemed less demanding and less challenging. It offered an excellent forum to discuss new developments in tactics and equipment available to both submarines and Japanese anti-submarine efforts. But at the end of the course, 27 November 1943, we were glad to catch what was left of Thanksgiving weekend in Portsmouth. Lew Parks was bedbound with a very heavy cold, and we hated to move him, but Zelda had him carried out on a stretcher into a large, barren home outside the city, the only place they could find available. We felt heartless, but they insisted.

Fitting out *Sterlet* offered a new experience in many ways. Arriving in town a year earlier for *Scorpion*, a freshly qualified lieutenant, I felt modest about my submarine experience. Returning for *Sterlet* qualified for command, I felt experienced and confident. The captain and I worked well in putting together an effective organization. I initiated the seminar on torpedoes and practical hints in making a submarine attack learned from Tony Gallaher previously. I recommended the tricks he had developed for a sonar attack for all periscope attacks, where, experience proved, they would guarantee more torpedo hits. Always well attended, the discussions produced some spirited give and take from which we all learned.

During my last days with *Scorpion* in Pearl Harbor, the submarine torpedo problems finally neared a solution. Admiral Lockwood took matters into his own hands, firing torpedoes with exercise heads through fish netting. Torpedoes set to run at ten feet depth produced holes in the nets at twenty-one feet. The problem proved to be a design defect of many years' standing, disregarding elementary physics, the venturi effect on seawater supplied to the depth mechanism. Then when the torpedoes started hitting their targets, a new problem arose—duds. Again the bureau passed off the problem; again Admiral Lockwood took matters into his own hands, firing live warheads—despite the cost of $10,000 each—at the Kahoolawe Cliffs in Hawaii. Of the first three fired, two exploded and the third was a dud. Wags suggested that it might have run under the island, but when it was recovered by divers, the neglect of elementary physics once again was apparent. The exploder firing pins, designed to slide up a guide into the detonator on impact, failed because the impact partially crushed the guides and the firing pins couldn't hit the primer hard enough to cause detonation. Why was the fault not discovered earlier? Because prewar penny-pinching forbade expenditure of live ordnance in realistic weapons tests.

The torpedo experts in Honolulu again found a simple remedy. The size of the firing pin was cut down to lighten it and reduce the inertial force, and a new lightweight metal, salvaged from the propellors of Japanese aircraft shot down at Pearl Harbor, was substituted.

The change I initiated in the *Scorpion* of tripling the tension on the exploder impeller blades contributed to a percentage of hits one-third higher than the fleet average and no erratic runs. With the running depth and exploder changes worked out by Admiral Lockwood in Pearl, I thought our torpedo problems were now past history. In addition, the bureaucratic roadblock on mass production of the new electric torpedoes finally succumbed to heavy pressure from the operating forces. With both electric and steam types available, the slower but wakeless electrics were favored for daylight attacks, and the faster, trail-leaving steam torpedoes at night. It had taken two years of war to work out the bugs.

Getting *Sterlet* ready for sea offered few problems. I knew the key officers and leading men in the yard from *Scorpion* days. Our rental of the Davis home also carried unanticipated dividends. Hazel, softhearted where submariners were concerned, soon became a friend despite the generation gap. We were on her party lists, and frequently other shipyard officials included us when few of the submariners from the "waterfront" attended. She also added our name to the list for surplus baked goods at the Portsmouth Naval Prison, generally available free of charge only to those living in quarters on the base.

Another gratuity, though much appreciated, carried the potential for embarrassment. She offered us her houseboy once a week to do the heavy work around the house and occasionally to act as bartender when we entertained. By a strange coincidence, he was a dead ringer for the squadron commander, Captain Charles W. "Weary" Wilkins. The likeness was so great that when either rang the doorbell, I had to allow him the first word of greeting to tip me off on the proper warmth of my welcome.

Meanwhile, progress on the *Sterlet* was gratifying. The yard at that time was unsurpassed in the quality of its craftsmanship. *Sterlet* had a four-hundred-foot test depth, much deeper than *Scorpion,* and had numerous improvements suggested by the experience of war. I was enthusiastic about getting her to sea to try out the marvels of American shipbuilding skills.

Christmas came and went quickly. Over the years, only one memorable event stands out. Henri announced that she was pregnant again. Except that I would be an absentee father, we were delighted. Her health was excellent, and we had no reason to expect anything but a normal delivery. But early in the new year we received news from the Pacific that sent me to the pits of gloom. In February 1944, *Scorpion* failed to return from patrol and was presumed lost with all hands. I thought of all those wonderful people who had made her last dive—Max Schmidt, Bob Drane, Dick Ellis, and Bob Brown, and those superb professionals "back aft," Carl Hund the gunner, Bill Flaherty, my big, good-natured quartermaster, Tony Manganello the master chef, Jimmy Holshouser the hotshot torpedoman, the Swoose. Dick Ellis's family lived nearby in York Beach, Maine. I visited them to express my deep sorrow. The loss of *Scorpion* earned a special note in *Time* magazine. Congressman Paul Brown of Georgia missed his first roll call in ten years. A colleague explained the strangely empty chair. Lt. Robert Thomas Brown, age twenty-four, his submarine officer son, had just been reported "missing in action." His life's ambition was for his lawyer son to succeed him in Congress.

Shortly after the announcement, I received a letter from Bill Wylie in which one statement burned itself into my soul: "I shall always believe that your detachment from the *Scorpion* was a major contributing factor to her loss." Whatever my role, I wish he had never said it. There was no information on her loss until capture of the Gilbert and Marshall islands. Thousands of classified documents fell into the hands of the Navy, including secret notices to mariners showing the exact locations of Japanese minefields. The indefatigable Wilfred J. "Jasper" Holmes, a retired naval officer and submariner, who headed the counterintelligence unit at Pearl Harbor, set up a special group to get the minefield data translated for issue to submariners as rapidly as possible. From these notices Holmes first learned of the new and extensive minefields the Japanese had sewn in the East China Sea. *Scorpion* presumably hit one and sank. If this were really the cause, there is little anybody could have done to prevent the tragedy, but I would have occasion to think often in the not too distant future of the increased hazard of enemy mines.

Another problem at this time demanded more and more of my attention. In our meetings with senior yard officials concerning items of construction and design, the captain seemed to show considerable reluctance in standing up for his officers on differences of opinion with the yard in matters of substance. My relations with the officials were sufficiently harmonious that several asked me why he did not push a bit harder for important changes. With his officers he also seemed prone more to criticize than to praise. The officers were working exceptionally hard, sometimes long into the night. On one such occasion, Don Horst worked with his torpedo gang until about 0400, then fell asleep exhausted and arrived late and unshaven to morning quarters at eight. He earned a royal chewing out, with no chance to explain. I tried to intercede privately with the CO in Don's behalf but felt I made no impression. This was no isolated case; I could see an attitude of discouragement beginning to poison the wardroom spirit, particularly among the reserve officers.

To add to my professional concerns, a wholly unanticipated problem arose during the fitting-out period with the potential for causing considerable embarrassment. Shortly after reporting for duty aboard *Sterlet,* one of the younger officers began a wild romance with the wife of an officer from another submarine fitting out at the yard. "Jim" and "Lily," I'll call them, were soon deep in a passionate affair that provided enough gossip to keep the entire submarine community buzzing. A first-class scandal was brewing and a blowup seemed inevitable. I liked Lily a lot. She was intelligent, an excellent dancer, and fine company. Jim was a superior officer of great potential. I counted the days until we could get away from the yard and be on our way. Following commissioning on 4 March 1944 and builder's trials, we left Portsmouth for the torpedo trials in Newport. The *Sterlet* wives—and Lily—met us on arrival. Her husband's submarine still lay unfinished at Portsmouth.

The famed old Viking Hotel in Newport became our nightly rendezvous. We met every evening in the historic dining room. Jim's parents flew in for a last visit with their son before he went off to war, joining the group around the big open fireplace. Invariably at about nine o'clock, however, Jim made his apologies for an early departure so as to be fresh and alert for his duties the next morning. He then disappeared to a room across Bellevue Avenue at the Muenchinger King Hotel and to Lily. Under way at seven each morning, he barely made the last ferry to the torpedo station, collapsing in his bunk and coming fully alive only when the mooring lines were secured at the end of the day's work.

Finishing the torpedo trials, the ship departed for New London and the last shakedown training under Commander

Submarines Atlantic. When we arrived at midnight in a driving rainstorm, Lily was the only "wife" waiting on the pier. Jim again played fast and loose with working hours, and the skipper finally lowered the boom on him. The officers' club had a big ball slated just before our departure for the Pacific. Among other disciplinary measures, Jim was specifically forbidden to bring "that woman" to the club. He arrived a bit late, Lily on his arm, and headed for the last two vacant chairs, which happened to be at my table. Before I could suggest that under the circumstances it would be best for all if they sat somewhere else, my beloved wife, too well mannered and gracious a hostess ever to turn anybody away for an offense short of treason, welcomed them into the group. I couldn't guess the reaction at the CO's table adjoining, but I thought I would have some explaining to do the next morning. The time had come for us to be off to war again, and nothing would interfere with our having a wonderful time that night.

The dawn brought other problems. The ship was scheduled to move onto the marine railway for some final work on a squeaky propellor shaft, a voyage of about five hundred feet. Jim missed sailing entirely. That's when I finally blew my stack. But another wholly unrelated event intervened.

While in Portsmouth I endeavored to stimulate the imagination and foresight of the officers in stocking spare parts and similar equipment for their future needs in the war zone. If a radar or sonar failed in Formosa Strait or off Honshu, the excuse that the replacement part did not appear on the spare parts allowance list left me unconvinced. Officers and key petty officers were to examine their equipment with extreme care and outfit themselves with spares as necessary whether or not they happened to be on the shipboard allowance. I prepared a memorandum for the officers to this effect, suggesting that the shipyard was really a big post exchange to equip our ship for war, and it wasn't actually stealing. To stress the point, I added, "There is no such thing as a Seventh Commandment in a Navy Yard." The CO liked my memo and gave it the highest praise—he adopted it as his own. Taking it to the division commander, he said, "Here's a memo I just issued to all my officers and thought you'd be interested."

The division commander took it to the squadron commander with the comment, "Here's a memo I just issued," who passed it to Commander Submarines, who passed it to the Atlantic fleet commander, who sent it to the chief of naval operations. The CNO issued it over his signature as part of an information and guidance kit sent to all new construction COs throughout the rest of the war.

On that dramatic morning in New London before our departure for the Pacific, I emphasized how patient I had been with Jim and, I hope, understanding about his affair with Lily. He had let us down terribly, and, given his great potential, I felt especially disappointed at his repeated transgressions against accepted standards of behavior. Looking at me in increasing disbelief, he finally interrupted, "But you gave me permission!"

Astonished, I asked what the devil he was talking about. From his jacket pocket he pulled a ragged copy of the memorandum on thievery in a shipyard. I learned for the first time that, in the King James version of the Bible, stealing is against the Eighth Commandment; the Seventh, which I cited, states, "Thou shalt not commit adultery." All the reissues of my original letter had failed to change the reference from the Douay to the more commonly used King James version. I had approved of adultery, not stealing.

Other problems in the wardroom smoldered throughout the final training exercises off New London. The training officer was Captain Glynn R. "Donc" Donaho, a combat veteran, humorless and a rigid perfectionist, who had fired several execs during his half dozen patrols. Donc was capable but never claimed to be brilliant. While taking *Flying Fish* from New London to Panama a year earlier, he sighted a Nazi U-boat on the surface but made no attempt to attack, merely turning tail and opening the range. Why? His operation order said nothing about attacking the enemy while in transit to Pearl, and he carried it out to the letter. An official fury arose around his head; by the narrowest of margins he retained his command. All operation orders thereafter carried a special paragraph, "Attack and destroy all enemy vessels encountered." Donc compiled an enviable record, but for *Sterlet* he wanted the identical battle organization and attack procedures as he followed, without regard to differences in equipment or personal styles of the skippers. He had difficulties dealing with people so we changed to his system, then changed back as soon as he left.

Sterlet's attack procedures were much like those which Bill, Reggie, and I had worked out for *Scorpion,* the CO generally on the bridge or in the conning tower in overall control, the exec having full responsibility in conducting the attack. Our style was freewheeling, Donc's strongly authoritarian, totally under his control. Having spent many long hours putting an effective team together for *Sterlet,* I was very proud of the progress made. In overall ability, our team was probably unsurpassed by that of any other submarine within my experience. I defended it against radical change by Donc, but to my surprise, I received no support from the skipper. At the end of our training, my disillusionment was complete. I did everything in my power to prevent giving any indication of how I felt to the other officers. Above all, I kept any remote hint of a problem from Henri. In my first letter home after departure from New London, I told her truthfully how sorry I was to leave and that never in my whole career did I feel more like going over the hill than at that time. She accepted it as an expression of love.

En route to Key West for ten days of exercises at the Fleet Sonar School, my navigation skills got a good test. Many submarines, trying to maintain a high speed of advance, came to grief when met by the strong three- to four-knot northward current of the Gulf Stream. I proposed a route much closer inshore so as to catch the favorable countercurrents flowing south. We were informed then that the German U-boats, driven away from the coasts by new antisubmarine activities, had countered by laying minefields at key shipping points from Halifax to Jacksonville, Florida. After a sixteen-hundred-mile passage, including one hundred miles not far seaward of the reefs, we passed through the Florida Straits and arrived at our rendezvous on the minute. I could see that the captain was tense about our position. On arrival he grunted an unenthusiastic approval.

On the way in to Key West, our first welcome came from Frank C. Acker and Fred Clarke in *Pomfret,* just ten days ahead of us at Portsmouth and now operating with the Fleet Sonar School. A former *Scorpion* chief was waiting on the dock. We had left him in Key West for health reasons, much against our wishes. He wanted me to phone Henri immediately to come down to meet us, offering an apartment in town, a car, and whatever else we needed. It was tempting; I compromised by merely telephoning her, always a special treat. He promised to obtain anything the ship needed short of grand larceny. It was a great feeling to realize the depth of emotion for the good old Scorp. I said I had another great crew with me now, but the Little Stirs were not yet as cohesive as the Scorps.

Lt. William R. "Bill" Jameson, who had reported aboard late in the fitting out period, challenged me to a tennis match on our first opportunity ashore. I was able to beat him but he promised all the competition I could handle. Bill was a happy person, capable and in every respect a fine shipmate. Our lack of conditioning seemed far less apparent in the nightly parties at the club. Then, in a friend's station wagon, Bill, Gene Barnhardt, and I drove, or flew, more properly, to Miami, Bob Wright's hometown, to admire the silk-legged scenery. The bus takes five hours; we did it in three. As we drove by the church where Gene and Teeny were married, he was whistling at a girl across the street and almost missed it. It was all good fun, and we thought we earned the break.

The local division commander asked me to give a lecture on antisubmarine warfare for the Key West aviators. Despite a 110-degree, unventilated auditorium, the place was packed and kept me busy with questions for almost two hours. A surprise visitor at that time was Claude L. "Layton" Goodman, my Annapolis roommate for four years, passing through on the USS *Jack* en route to Brisbane. We had several pleasant bull sessions that ended all too soon. Layton was a firm friend, and I needed support.

The route from Key West to Panama offered a series of hot, sunny days, calm seas, and bright, starry nights. The German U-boats had finally been driven out of these waters, and it was almost like peacetime cruising. One day off Tampico, Mexico, I noticed that we would be almost directly underneath the sun at high noon—the subsolar point on the earth's surface would be only about a hundred miles away. I had always wanted to take a subsolar fix using a series of timed sextant observations on each side of the zenith. When the sun passes almost directly overhead, the altitudes approach ninety degrees. An altitude of eighty-nine degrees, fifteen minutes, or forty-five minutes short of the vertical, for example, indicates that the observer is exactly forty-five miles from the subsolar point. A circle of forty-five miles radius plotted from that point on an ordinary Mercator chart will pass through the observer's position; a series of such circles from the subsolar points at each timed observation will all intersect at the observer's position, giving an accurate navigational fix. In addition, the sun reaches its maximum altitude at the instant of "local apparent noon" and gives the navigator a clean latitude line.

Moments before I was to begin observations, however, the captain decided to make a trim dive. I hastened below, and as soon as we were steady at periscope depth, I made my observations, not of sextant altitudes but of bearings of the sun measured by periscope at timed intervals. These were the bearings from each subsolar point and they too intersected at the ship's position. To my knowledge, this had never been tried before from a submerged submarine. The final plot looked quite striking. The Captain was impressed enough to suggest that I write it up for publication in the U.S. Naval Institute *Proceedings*.

Panama, one of the great ports of the world, offered oodles of wine, wild women, and warbling. Here I had a special mission to perform. Because the enlisted men were unable to get a liquor ration in Midway, the likely port for our R and R after the first war patrol, I had done some planning in the yard. Outside my bunk a large sheet-metal locker had been built by the Portsmouth yard between the bunk and the pressure hull as a special storage space, accessible only across my bunk and secured with a lock for which I had the only key. The plan was to use money from the ship's recreation fund to buy alcoholic spirits in Panama for a big ship's party in Midway. The locker would be sealed until that time. Phase two of the plan went off well. We loaded up with much anticipation of the future wingding.

Little Gina celebrated her first birthday a few days before our arrival in Panama, and I tried to find some gifts. Beautiful handmade infant dresses were plentiful. I also ran across Henri's favorite perfume, Guerlain's Shalimar. At $4 for two ounces, however, I decided I couldn't afford it. Silk stockings seemed plentiful but only for big feet and a twenty-inch calf. Many were a royal ripoff. Some advertised as silk offered only silk-reinforced toes. Silk is not supposed to burn, but when tested on board, they went up with a whoosh. They shouldn't lose shape either, but one yank created a six-foot stocking.

Meanwhile, relations of several of the wardroom officers with the CO continued to deteriorate. One night just before we left Coco Solo, Bob Wright invited me to the Club for a few quick ones. I felt frustrated and long overdue to bust out. When we got there, Gene, Joe, Hugh Wright, and Bill Jameson were already hard at work on a round of scotches. We had several more, then after dinner decided to go out in town for a floor show at some shady bistros. With diligence, one can find several of these in Panama. We may have gone to all of them. We all got pretty sloshed before heading back to the ship. Halfway through the evening I let my hair down and finally admitted that I too was having difficulties with the captain's increasing tenseness, hostility, and unreasonableness and that my morale was sagging. That started the real party. Sometime before dawn Gene and I helped carry each other back to the ship. When we got there I suddenly growled in total frustration, "Pee on the *Sterlet*"—and proceeded to do so.

During the time we were ashore, unfortunately, the tide had gone out. The main deck, level with the dock at departure, had now sunk out of sight about nineteen feet below. As I unlimbered, the deck watch took cover, bless his soul, and I felt better immediately. I probably apologized to him; if not, maybe someday he will read these words and finally forgive me. I also try not to make a habit of getting plastered when I go ashore, but that was a doozy. It cleared the air considerably.

The transit of the Panama Canal soon gave us something else to think about. By law, use of a pilot is mandatory. The pilot is fully responsible for the safe passage of the ship under his care. The members of the Pilot Association are highly qualified, but ours had a tough time understanding the unique problems of a submarine. Virtually all ships have heavy metal screw guards to protect the propellors from damage alongside of piers. Submarines have no such protection. Our screw guards were removed during wartime. The propellors, razor sharp and delicate, extended out from the sides of the ship and became vulnerable when maneuvering around docks. The captain warned the pilot as soon as he came aboard of our special design, but the pilot pooh-poohed the very thought that he would have trouble. As the towing engine pulled us clear of the first lock, however, it threw the stern toward the vertical wall of the lock, causing great consternation at the near miss. Remonstrating, the CO drew a sketch of the underwater body to explain the problem in detail. The pilot still seemed unimpressed. Two locks later, the stern was again thrown against the jetty, but this time the noise of the screw scraping the masonry wall could be heard throughout the ship. We radioed ahead to the authorities at Balboa, the Pacific terminus of the canal, and were cleared to dock immediately on arrival.

Our problems were not yet over. After we passed through the Gatun lock, only the antisubmarine net lay between us and the Balboa naval station. But when the harbor authority ordered the heavy metal net lowered, insufficient clearance was allowed for us to pass over it safely, and the heavy cable fouled the port screw, the same blade damaged earlier in the day. We were impaled in the middle of the channel, unable to maneuver, blocking the canal just as two high-priority convoys, one eastbound and one westbound, headed toward us. To determine the extent of the damage, one of the deckhands, Coxswain Bill Jarvis, a strong swimmer, volunteered to go over the side for a look. In a truly heroic performance requiring superhuman strength and endurance underwater, he was able to untangle the cable from the propellor blade and set the ship free before a tug could get under way from the base.

The ship went immediately onto the marine railway; the damaged screw was replaced, and we were fully ready for sea in record time. A board of investigation convened the following morning to assess responsibility for the damage to the screw. The pilot, so cocksure the day before, appeared totally deflated. He was summarily found guilty of dereliction of duty. The captain and I were both given citations for our forehandedness and skill in "limiting the damage to the ship to the irreducible minimum.'' I drafted a citation for special recognition of Jarvis's heroic role, eventually awarded by Commander Submarines.

We were lucky in one more respect. Since commissioning, *Sterlet* had suffered a squeaky propellor shaft, for which the ship had been drydocked at Portsmouth and New London. For no apparent reason, the squeak suddenly disappeared. The strain on the net cable had done what scientific genius could not do. It never again caused concern.

The adventures in Panama still had not run their course. Recent submarine technology had made great progress in silencing the equipment aboard to reduce transmitted noise that might tip off the sub's location to a hostile vessel. Rubber mounts and flexible couplings on pumps and similar equipment sharply reduced noise transmitted through the water. Sometimes tools and other metallic objects, falling into crevices, short-circuited the protection. Submarines, therefore, underwent periodic testing for noise emanation from every piece of machinery on board. *Sterlet*'s final operation in the Canal Zone was an underwater sound test in a tiny, secluded cove in the Perlas Islands south of the Pacific entrance to the canal.

The day of the test, 23 May 1944, dawned sunny and humid with heavy, broken cloud cover conducive to sudden, drenching rainfalls. The tiny, unoccupied island, covered with mangrove and dense tropical timber, offered little help to the navigator. A narrow, circuitous channel led through two sharp turns to the tiny bay where the tests were conducted. Shortly after we entered the channel, the rains started. Navigating from the radar screen in the conning tower, I saw the faint distinction between the radar image of mangrove swamp and the channel fade into nothing. The downpour totally washed out the radar image just at the point for the critical turn in the channel. Nothing could be seen either visually or electronically. Caution dictated dropping the anchor until visibility cleared, but the channel was so narrow that the greater danger was damage to the screws swinging with the current into a coral head. I ordered the course change on pure seaman's eye—guesswork in this case. We made it safely around the turn. The cloudburst let up for a moment, the channel soon reemerged on the screen, and we dropped the hook at the prescribed spot. I went topside for a look around and was stunned at the tiny bay in which we had moored. On all sides the heavy undergrowth rose upward. The channel by which we entered couldn't even be seen. The radar image I navigated by indicated a far wider channel; no radar reflection came from vegetation near the water's edge, only from some distance inland. It seemed impossible that we could have come through the jungle on radar alone. I was very modest in accepting compliments from what seemed to me to be a piece of luck.

Finally, on the last leg to Pearl Harbor, one more incident broke the routine. A leading engineer suffered an appendicitis attack shortly after departure from Balboa. Months before, a submarine pharmacist's mate on the *Seadragon* had performed an appendectomy on the wardroom table, using bent spoons for clamps to hold the incision open. The patient recovered completely, and the incident was widely publicized. The Bureau of Medicine and Surgery, however, became concerned that a wave of similar operations might ensue from others seeking a bit of fame rather than best medical practice. And perhaps the Bureau of Ships was concerned about the willful damage and possible loss of spoons. Instructions were sent out quickly to all submarines that sulfa drugs might reduce the inflammation in the great majority of cases; few would require surgery.

In our case, the doc moved from chiefs' quarters to the bunk alongside the afflicted man, packed the tender area in ice, and cared for him night and day. On our arrival in Pearl, an ambulance with screaming siren roared down the dock to remove the patient. Completely recovered and in the best of spirits, he sat up, waving and smiling to well-wishers on the pier. After cruising across the Pacific at a leisurely fifteen knots, he met his greatest peril when the ambulance screeched off at ninety miles an hour to the hospital. The chief, meanwhile, sleepless and near exhaustion, needed help to find his way ashore for a cold beer.

The base arranged a big ship's party shortly after our arrival. After a few beers, one of the men challenged Gene to a "rassling" match. Gene was up in a minute and had his challenger pinned in two more. A series of other brave but unskilled challengers tried their luck, but he took on all comers until he was so dead tired he was ready to drop. Surprisingly, he won every match. I hadn't known that he was a wrestler at the Naval Academy and a good one. It made him tops in the eyes of the men and set the stage for his announcement that he and Teeny were celebrating a blessed event, a daughter born at her parents' home in New York.

Once again it was time for final training before departure. Surprise of surprises, who should appear as training officer but Donc Donaho. He had been transferred from New London to the submarine staff in Pearl. I was anticipating a very hard time, but good old Weary Wilkins decided to ride *Sterlet* instead. He said some very nice things about the boat and the fine record we were making. I felt confident that ship and crew were at a peak; all I could hope for was that the good luck continued to shine our way.

Our imminent departure brought all sorts of goodies. Movie projectors and a slow-speed record player offered entertainment from Bob Hope and Jack Benny to the Boston Symphony. Crates of paperback books came aboard, all special armed forces editions of the latest and best; an air conditioner was installed in the wardroom to reduce the heat emanating from the storage batteries below, and a big new ice cream machine appeared back aft. Joe Garland was disgusted. "Submarines have gone to the dogs. Even the mess cooks are wearing rubber gloves."

Meanwhile, the war news around the world looked encouraging. The massive assault across the beaches at Normandy commenced in early June and succeeded despite the worst summer storm in forty years. After the appalling wreckage littering the beaches was cleared up, men and equipment moved ashore in a flood for the massive offensive on fortress Europe. Cherbourg would fall in mid-July, the first French port to be recovered by the Allies and the starting point on the road to liberation leading to Paris and the Rhine. Preparations were under way for the invasion of southern France planned for mid-September; in Italy the Germans and Italians had just been driven from the Anzio beachhead in a series of fierce battles.

Although hundreds of new subs were coming off the building ways, the U-boats in the Atlantic had lost the initiative to the Allies as air and surface forces ranged the ocean and hounded the enemy in a cruel and costly war of attrition. Admiral Karl Doenitz, in desperation, stepped up the German air offensive against convoys and expanded the U-boat patrols into the Indian Ocean and off the coasts of Africa. Submarine losses continued to increase notwithstanding, and the toll of ship sinkings finally began to taper off.

In the Pacific, the irreplaceable shipping losses to American submarines gained the emperor's personal attention. A conference with the emperor, the high command and the government convened on 30 September 1943, the first since 1 December 1941. As a result, the Grand Escort Command Headquarters, or GEHq, was created on 15 November 1943 and given operational command over the First and Second Escort Groups, all sea commands except the Combined Fleet and China Seas Fleet, and all naval stations involved in protection of shipping. Commander in chief of the new GEHq was Admiral Koshiro Oikawa, former minister of the navy and senior to all admirals in operational commands. Four escort carriers were added to the GEHq, the first appearing with a convoy escort group just as *Sterlet* was to arrive in her patrol area in July 1944. Also, radar was now commonly in use by oceangoing escorts and quite effective against submarines.

Admiral Oikawa quickly sought to connect the island chains from Kyushu through Okinawa, Formosa, and the Philippines with mine barriers to keep the East China Sea, Formosa Straits, and the South China Sea safe from submarine invasion. Where mining was not feasible, sea gaps were guarded with land-based radars and long-range underwater sonars backed by aircraft and inshore patrol vessels. Unfortunately, no information on the shore-based hydrophones reached the U.S. forces before the end of the war.

In the South Pacific, General MacArthur's team of U.S., Australian, and New Zealand sea, land, and air forces combined effectively to advance 550 miles from Hollandia in north central New Guinea to Cape Sansapor on the western tip, opening the path to the eventual conquest of the Philippines.

Admiral Chester W. Nimitz's initial central Pacific offensive targeted the Gilberts and Marshalls, which fell to the Navy-Marine team after bloody hand-to-hand fighting. Strategically, loss of these islands marked the first crack in the Japanese outer defense ring and opened the way to the future conquest of the Marianas on the inner ring. Of direct interest to the submariners, the Majuro Atoll in the southern Marshalls became a submarine refit base, greatly reducing the turnaround time for boats operating out of Pearl Harbor or Midway. Admiral Raymond A. Spruance, commanding the largest fleet in the world, then leapfrogged to the Marianas, opening the invasion of Saipan, key to the entire Japanese inner defense ring, on 12 June 1944. Success on Saipan would bring Admiral Nimitz's forces a thousand miles closer to Japan than the big support base at Eniwetok. The big Saipan offensive started just two weeks before *Sterlet* departed on her maiden patrol.

The assigned area, the Bonin, or Southern Islands, lay exactly midway between Tokyo and Saipan and hence astride the commercial and warship routing between Honshu and the Marianas. The captain and I were carefully briefed on the forthcoming major campaigns, on Ultra information on Japanese shipping, and on recent but scanty information on the vast new minefields laid in primary submarine operating areas.

Departure from Pearl on 4 July found me in a different mood from the past. The active part of the submarine campaign, now reaching a crescendo, would hardly last more than about six months, I thought. The submarine war in the Pacific was going extremely well. Tonnages of warships and merchantmen sunk or damaged increased steadily; the number of submarine losses in combat—seventeen in 1943, nineteen in 1944—remained fairly steady despite a sharply increased number of boats on the firing line. With the torpedo problems finally behind us, and with superb surface search radar, the submariners had developed the technique of the night surface attack into a deadly weapon wreaking great havoc on Japanese shipping.

I felt optimistic about the skills of the officers. Gene and Don became expert with the TDC; Ed Skeehan, a skilled draftsman, and Bob Wright developed into a superb mechanical plotting team working smoothly with the TDC operator.

To hone their skills, I prepared stacks of canned problems with every possible complexity in enemy zigzagging for daily training at sea. These problems could be administered by the quartermaster of the watch, and I expected each officer to work on them for an hour a day, gradually increasing the degree of difficulty. Our attack team felt confident. Just before departure, however, a steward spilled a pot of boiling coffee on Ed Skeehan, forcing his detachment and hospitalization. Ed was so anxious to get into combat that it was a double tragedy. Fortunately, we were deep enough in talent and experience to replace him on the attack team.

We were very fortunate "back aft," too. The spirit was excellent. Those vital elements of morale, cooks and bakers, overachieved. Meals were a pleasure, well cooked and as varied as possible under the circumstances. We carried about a forty-day supply of fresh fruits and vegetables. With fresh frozen foods now available in quantity, the real problem was pushing away from the table. We had carefully hoarded a frozen food supply from the East Coast, irreplaceable in Pearl, and had stocked up on some fine Argentine beef in Panama. Walter Fedro, a superb baker, worked nights to prepare delicious bread, doughnuts, and birthday cakes—greatly appreciated by the men (and especially the executive officer). The officers' stewards, often a weak point in food preparation, outdid themselves, using imagination in preparing salads and special delights to add variety to our meals. We never had it so good.

After fueling at Midway I set the course for the Bonin Islands, 450 miles south of Tokyo. It was an active area and offered great promise for an interesting patrol. Four days before entering the area, we made radar contact with a U.S. submarine, detected by the search radar interference. *Archerfish*, four days out of the Bonins, identified herself through keying the radar signal, a technique worked out by the operators. The pleasant summer weather allowed daily pointer-trainer-sight setter drills on the four-inch gun and occasional 20-mm firings on flotsam. One particularly useful target was a spare gas tank from an airplane, sighted off Muko Jima just before we entered the area on Sunday, 16 July.

To size up the area, we commenced a surface patrol of the

Tokyo–Bonins shipping lanes. Just after the watch changed at 1600, however, an airplane, coming in fast, drove us down and rattled our teeth with two close depth charges. Welcome to Japan! The detection was made on the SD air search radar with a frequency unfortunately close to the Japanese radars, allowing them to use our transmissions like beacons to home in for attack. We renamed the SD the "Sudden Death" radar.

On surfacing at dusk, we noted a white rocket to the south, and intermittent submarine-type surface radar suggested that somebody might be working over a convoy. We began a high-speed sweep to gain contact, covering best estimates of enemy course and speed. At 0400 the following morning, a contact report from *Plaice* indicated that the convoy had passed within fifteen miles of us two hours earlier. Commencing a new search at flank speed—all the power we could bend on—we made another air search radar contact at 0709 at eight miles, closing fast. A dive off four engines took us down in a hurry, again wearing two heavy depth charges around our necks. Close again.

Over the next half hour, nineteen distant depth charge blasts echoed through the hull. Shortly after the last rumbled through, we surfaced and renewed the search. Three hours later, at 1130, another air search radar contact appeared at eight miles, closing fast, forcing us down to race two more close ones to the bottom. At 1309, after a quick lunch submerged, we again surfaced to resume the search. Three minutes later, the expected air contact, at twelve miles coming in fast, gave us one more opportunity to get down in a hurry. There were four charges this time. Somebody raised the ante. At 1740, trying it on the surface once more, we started a new search from a position nine miles due north of Nishino Shima.

Just before midnight, a report from *Cobia* indicated that for the second time we had missed contact by a matter of eighteen miles. We had one chance left. Our search plan ended at Chichi Jima, a favorite Japanese summer resort before the war. The port, Futami Ko, the most important in the Bonin Islands, was known to be a large convoy assembly point and escort center. If earlier contact could not be made, we could play goalie off Futami and look for trouble. The night was ideal for an attack, moonless and totally dark.

At 0938 the next morning, the periscope watch sighted smoke to the west. The bearing drift indicated that the enemy had probably departed from Futami Ko. We closed at high speed for half an hour, but on the next observation nothing was in sight. Another air contact indicated that something might be developing, however, and one minute after noon, the masts of several ships appeared to the northwest about six miles away. The convoy soon developed into a medium merchantman, small tanker, and five escorts, two ahead, one on each beam and a trailer astern. We had been searching for this convoy for three days over a thousand miles of ocean. Two or three other submarines had hacked at her, and it looked as though the last merchantman was meant for us. She was two-masted, with the foremast shorter than the main. Not realizing this immediately, we assumed we were on her port side and began closing at high speed, only to learn on the next periscope observation that we were looking at her starboard side and she was already well past attack position. On the oily, flat sea, even at slow speed the periscope left large bubbles on the surface visible a hundred yards astern.

Monday morning quarterbacking indicated from the plot that the first observation of smoke had been made at the phenomenal range of twenty-nine miles; the new deck-mounted JT sonar maintained contact for five minutes at ten miles, even though neither the topside sonic nor bottom-mounted supersonic gear had heard anything when range closed to three miles. It was tough to watch him pass out of sight just a thousand yards beyond torpedo range. Another boat soon made contact, however, and two hours later, thirty-six distant explosions were heard. We were in the northern extreme of the assigned area; somebody else either had better luck than we or very much worse.

On surfacing, heading south to the center of the area, we commenced patrol east of Chichi Jima. Shortly after midnight, radar contact sixty-nine hundred yards to the northeast soon proved to be a small seventy-foot launch. We turned tail to evade, and just before midnight a prominent red glow appeared on the horizon in the direction of Chichi

Jima. A Liberator raid on Chichi was announced the following day. Those fires from seventy miles away looked auspicious. Was this the end of the convoy we had chased so vigorously?

At 0414, radar reported contact on another ship at fourteen thousand yards, looking like a large destroyer; we were on his starboard beam. Just as we sighted him he opened fire from guns forward and aft. At the time we were zigzagging by Arma course clock. This was a special clock-operated cam placed over the helmsman's gyro repeater so that the "lubbers line" by which he steered never steadied on a course, continually moving to each side of base course as determined by the cam and almost impossible to track. Further to complicate solving the zigzag plan, we were changing base course every fifteen minutes. Nevertheless, the first enemy salvo landed only 100 yards short, just where we would have been but for a zig. It was half an hour before sunrise, and he had us silhouetted on the eastern horizon, but it is hard to believe he could have opened fire so accurately without tracking us for quite some time. It seemed wise to "pull the plug" and look him over from periscope depth. Strangely, he broke off the attack before he could be identified.

Surfacing at 0515 to clear the area where our presence was known, we moved south to try the hunting closer to Saipan. Only a few fishing sampans disturbed the calm. Late in the evening of Sunday, 23 July, radar contact was made at about five miles. The weather was cloudy and rainy, the first rain since leaving Midway. A small coastal steamer came out of the mist, en route from Haha Jima to Iwo Jima, zigzagging thirty degrees each side of base course on five-minute legs. We worked around to the lee of Kita Iwo Jima at full speed to put the enemy in the brightest section of a very black horizon, then fired three torpedoes set to run at four feet. The phosphorescent wakes of the "fish" could be followed easily from the bridge, one passing under his stack, one under his bow, the third missing ahead. All ran too deep for his estimated four-foot draft; all exploded at the end of the run.

The captain ordered "gun action stations" and opened fire with four-inch and 20-mm guns. Gene and his gunners did their best, but the inky blackness hampered them considerably. One four-inch holed him aft, and a full pan of 20-mm found its mark before we broke off the action because of difficulty in locating the target at a range of 140 feet. Just as the enemy began to abandon ship, he fired one random shot. Listing to port and down by the stern, he soon disappeared from the radar screen. We were credited with a 662-ton coastal steamer *Suruga Maru* sunk, and *Sterlet* was no longer virgin.

On 25 July, submerged off Iwo Jima, we noted a high level of activity; twenty-four aircraft were counted on the airstrip, including eleven fighters, eight bombers, and three transports. We discovered and photographed a mattress-type radar antenna on the north end of the island. A trawler escort vessel mounting two machine guns forward and one aft, depth charge racks aft, and a high crow's nest patrolled idly off the anchorage area, otherwise clear of shipping. Returning to Kita Iwo Jima for submerged patrol, the captain then decided, on surfacing that night, to rig number 4 fuel ballast tank as a main ballast tank. Normal submarine practice calls for using the fuel in the fuel ballast tanks first, then if convenient, converting them to ordinary ballast tanks to gain a bit more speed over the ground. Then we would return to Chichi Jima for five days' submerged patrol off the entrance.

The weather was overcast and rainy, visibility very poor, sea force three with a surface chop. Just as the work commenced on the ballast tank, however, the weather took a sudden turn for the worse, the rain increasing to a torrential downpour in the van of a strong increase in wind and sea.

A submarine deck offers poor footing in the best of times. With strong seas breaking over it, no lifelines for support and no handholds, it becomes treacherous. Gene as OOD became increasingly concerned. Then at 0120, Bill Jameson, working on deck with the team, washed over the side in a very heavy sea. Somebody threw a float light in his general vicinity. Gene backed emergency and twisted to keep the light in sight as it crested the wave tops. When we were two hundred feet from the light, the big signaling searchlight was turned on. From about a hundred feet away, a faint cry from Jameson was heard to starboard. Coxswain Bill Jarvis, the hero in freeing the cable from the screws in the Panama Canal, again volunteered to go to the rescue. In total disregard for his own safety in his determination to save the life of an exhausted shipmate, he had to be almost forcibly restrained from going over the side immediately despite near hopeless odds. With a line secured to his waist, he disappeared into the stormy blackness. After an interminable time, while our fears escalated rapidly, Jarvis was hauled aboard, dragging the exhausted and almost unconscious lieutenant with him. It was a miracle that they found each other. Both were far the worse for wear. Taken below, they were pumped and dried out and given a few shots of medicinal brandy and a warm bunk for the rest of the night. Their recovery was remarkable, and in due time Jarvis received a well-deserved lifesaving award.

Early the next morning a surface contact with an air escort soon developed into three Japanese I-44 class submarines on the surface heading for Futami Ko. The closest point of approach was about sixty-seven hundred yards, well out of attack range. Shortly after, an antisubmarine search group of three trawlers with air cover swept by, close inshore. We went deep, rigged for silent running, and gave them a wide berth. The following morning at 0417, 29 July, another group of three *Chidori* escorts—a type that had given the *Scorpion* such a pasting in the Yellow Sea—was detected initially by sonar, then visually at seventeen thousand yards, making high speed and soon disappearing in a rush toward Chichi Jima. Then at dawn, for the third day in a row, the same trawler sighted off Iwo Jima passed by, also heading into Chichi.

The day was Sunday, 30 July, and *Sterlet* took a short break in the war. Napoleon Finley, the leading wardroom steward and a licensed minister of the gospel, held church services in the forward torpedo room. Finley had asked me if he could conduct Sunday services at sea. I was delighted and attended the first as a matter of courtesy. The homily was inspiring and the service well attended. At my urging, Joe Garland accompanied me. He claimed to be a regular churchgoer, one who attends shortly after birth, when married, and a final visit in the remote future. Yet after the first

Sunday he rarely missed one of Finley's services. By popular request it became a regular part of the patrol routine.

At 2000, 1 August, patrolling north of Muko Jima, *Shark* reported contact on a southbound convoy. We commenced a search at seventeen knots until 2200, when *Shark,* to the north, indicated that the convoy was well to the eastward and would probably hug the island chain all the way to Chichi Jima. We reversed course and increased speed to eighteen knots. At 0149, the SD air search radar made contact at six miles, closing. Making a hard turn with full rudder (at eighteen knots), we headed south. The plane closed to two miles and then began to open, neither of us sighting the other. The entire island chain appeared on the radarscope, but a careful search showed no convoy on either side.

This search was made possible by a new "steerable" unit that had been added to the surface search radar in New London. A submarine patrolling at fifteen or twenty miles off an important enemy port normally used a twenty-five-mile (fifty-thousand-yard) sweep on the radar to examine inner harbors and anchorage areas for shipping. So large a sweep allowed no target discrimination within a harbor at long range. Ideally the operator would like to use his close-in sweep at minimum range, eight thousand yards, to search inside the harbor itself. The steerable unit allowed him to do just that. The outgoing signal was delayed so that the operator could crank his range out as though his four-mile (eight-thousand-yard) sweep originated at any chosen distance from the ship within the maximum range of search. The desired eight-thousand-yard sector could then be examined just as if the submarine were lying in the harbor entrance while searching. The submarine, in effect, was the center of an enormous doughnut; the operator could chew on any eight-thousand-yard sector of the toroid he preferred. We found the new device extremely useful in patrol areas such as ours, dotted with many islands, where shipping, traveling close inshore, could hide from electronic search.

During the early hours of 2 August, we were proceeding down the hundred-fathom curve heading for the familiar position as goalie off Futami Ko and hoping once again to find the convoy indicated by the increased air activity around

Chichi Jima. Navigational lights on Marina Iwa, Muko Jima, and Yome Jima were burning brightly, giving further evidence that something might be in the wind. At 0314 the surface search radar detected a low-flying aircraft at five thousand yards, coming up the starboard side two miles abeam, also heading south. He was flying at about twelve hundred feet altitude, his exhaust visible to the bridge watch as he passed by. At 0910, persistence finally paid off. The masts and four columns of smoke were sighted coming around the north end of Chichi. The target group soon developed into a good-sized passenger freighter and three medium-sized merchants, with one escort ahead, one on the near flank and one astern, and two aircraft circling low over the oily, calm sea. *Sterlet* was four miles off the beach and so close to Futami Ko that if we missed, the torpedoes might go into the harbor. At 1014, while on the firing course and preparing to shoot, all hell broke loose. An aircraft bomb started it, quickly followed by a barrage that rattled our eyeteeth. It felt as though the conning tower was being torn loose. Just ten thousand yards from the dock where the convoy expected to moor, a three-knot current beginning to flood set us directly onto the beach. Rigging for depth charge, we went deep and commenced evasion.

At the height of the first barrage, reports were received from various parts of the ship, corroborated in the conning tower, of a heavy thud on deck. The superstructure began to rattle noisily. The question soon came to mind, did we have a live depth charge on deck that had not yet reached its set depth for detonation? If so, it was hazardous to go deeper. It was no less hazardous to stay shallow. And perhaps most hazardous of all might be the use of enough speed to wash it over the side. A detonation directly underneath the ship would totally spoil our day.

For almost two hours the tension mounted through attacks and reattacks, each pursued with exceptional vigor until they had dropped the last of thirty-nine very well-placed depth charges. Still dreading the possibility that we might be piggybacking a live charge on deck, we returned to periscope depth at 1330. Lunch wasn't much fun that day. Pieces of cork from the inner lining of the pressure hull were everywhere, but the main damage was yet unknown. Throughout the afternoon, patrolling aircraft were noted. The surface appeared clear except for an infantry landing craft leaving Chichi and heading west. Not till 2000 was it deemed clear for surfacing. Caution dictated that we come up slowly and on an even keel until a determination could be made of whether there was an unwanted passenger on deck. That deadly eventuality proved to be false, but other concerns caught our attention as we groped in the dark, not risking too many people on deck.

On deck forward of the conning tower, teak planking two feet long and almost a foot wide had been gouged out an inch deep when hit by a large fragment of the steel case of a depth charge; about twenty square feet of decking over the bow planes was dished in several inches deep, misaligning the bow buoyancy tank vent operating rod and putting the tank out of commission for the rest of the patrol. The forward torpedo salvage line was bent and inoperable; the stern planes were rather noisy and the bow planes very temperamental, rigging themselves in at odd moments; the bridge compass repeater was crushed; the searchlight was grounded out; and the muffler drain on the forward engine room had carried away. That attack really was a lulu. Had it been only a few inches closer, the depth charges would have ruptured the hull. The Japanese evaluated this attack as a positive kill on *Sterlet*. They weren't far wrong.

I entered in the patrol report at that time, "The conduct of a green crew throughout this depth charging was exemplary, despite the fact that the *Sterlet* is still sterile as far as torpedo hits are concerned, having received nothing but punishment for our best efforts to date."

With emergency repairs made, we resumed the search for the enemy. Two days later, shortly after midnight, three trawlers were sighted four miles to the northwest. The moon was almost full and the night extremely bright. An hour of tracking showed the movements of the group to be sufficiently erratic to suggest they were decoys. Since they were too small for a torpedo and too well armed for a shootout, caution suggested a tactical withdrawal. The search radar, always so reliable, made the decision for us by suddenly failing. Gene Romilly, our superb technician, had a surprise for us. On the basis of my Seventh Commandment letter

SUBMARINE COMMANDER

back in the shipyard, he had managed to "liberate" a spare
transmitter and quickly replaced the failed unit just in the
nick of time.

We cleared the area to the north and soon reaped a small
reward. Just as the midwatch came on duty on 4 August,
radar contact was made due north at nine thousand yards.
The target group was soon made out to be a trawler and
patrol vessel escorting a small maru. The ship at first appeared to be too small for a torpedo, but we immediately
began an approach. Working our way to the northeast to put
the target into the moonstreak, we then dived and commenced a submerged approach. Because of the ship's heavy
motion in a seaway, it seemed wise to set the torpedoes to
run at zero feet despite a force four sea. The final look
before firing showed the enemy to be much larger than
originally thought, but it was too late to change the depth
setting. We fired three torpedoes from perfect attack position
on the target's beam, straight stern shots from thirteen
hundred yards and a zero gyro angle on the torpedoes. Three
timed hits blew him to pieces. Two depth charges went off,
detonating as he sank. With one torpedo ready in the stern
tubes, we decided to try a quick shot at the escort but
missed. At 0140 we battle surfaced for a little gun action but
could see nothing but debris. About thirty men were clinging
to wreckage and, surprised to see so many survivors from a
small ship destroyed by three torpex hits carrying 1,350
pounds of explosive, we decided to take aboard a prisoner.
Whatever they knew about the thrills of submarine life had
left them unconvinced. They declined en masse. The entire
group had uniformly close-cropped heads, but little else
about them could be observed in the moonlight. The ship
looked like the *Boyaca Maru* of twenty-five hundred tons.

Clearing the scene, we commenced surface patrol in the
northern end of the area, leaving Chichi well clear for a
carrier air strike set for later that morning. The weather was
rainy and overcast, seas moderately rough. Just before the
1100 air strike, at least fifteen radar contacts were made on
aircraft from two to thirty-two miles. Eavesdropping on the
aviators' frequency, we overheard a contact report on an
eight-ship convoy off Muko Jima. Closing at flank speed for
several hours, we spotted the convoy at 1655 from the high

periscope, about five miles to the east. A new *Asashio* destroyer patrolled ahead of the main body making high speed with radical changes of course, searching along the line of advance. A quick navigational plot showed that we were five miles south of the convoy track so we went to 350 feet and closed for forty-five minutes at eight knots. On our return to periscope depth at 1814, the deck sonar reported high-speed screws, probably the screen on the port flank, but nothing could be seen through the periscope. It was fifteen minutes before sunset and visibility had decreased below five thousand yards. The deck sonar at this time began painting a beautiful sound picture of gunfire, bombs, torpedoes, and at least five sets of screws all around the dial.

We were a submerged spectator to an air show by the zoomies with nothing in sight but tracers, gun flashes, and running lights of an occasional airplane. Since units of the U.S. Fifth Fleet were operating in the area, we were restricted from attacking any ships without positive identification as enemy. Low-angle tracers visible through the periscope suggested that our own surface forces were engaged in the melee. We were lying low, sustained by the faint hope that somebody would come close enough to show his hostile character and allow us to make a quick attack. Three approaches were made on gun flashes, but the harried enemy refused to cooperate.

At 1925 one heavy explosion close aboard rattled the ship from stem to stern. The deck sonar indicated that the cacaphony of sound was moving to the north, hence it must have been an aerial bomb. The new sonar, so badly needed on *Scorpion* when her bottom-mounted heads were wiped off, operated beautifully. At periscope depth in force-four seas, accurate, continuous, and complete information was furnished on everything within at least a five-mile range. We stayed submerged until shortly after the last of heavy and light explosions rumbled through the area about 2200. Only then were we able to secure from battle stations and answer Deacon Finley's plea to enjoy a long-delayed dinner.

Almost from departure from Midway, I adopted the practice of staying up all night and trying to catch what sleep I could by day. It seemed only prudent, even without the increasing concern for the high tension and increasingly odd behavior of the CO. Events happened faster at night on the surface, and I wanted to be close at hand.

My only delay in getting to the bridge occurred when trying to get some star sights after a day submerged. Procedures on *Sterlet* added spice to the navigator's life. The captain delayed longer than any other CO in deciding when it was dark enough to surface. No vestige of horizon was visible when I finally got to the bridge. Waiting in the conning tower with my favorite quartermaster, Doug De-Weese, we tried to preserve our night adaptation against inadvertent use of lighting. As soon as the hatch was opened slightly—"cracked" is the seaman's term—the rush of foul air from below vented through the conning tower from pressure building up in the boat all day. Then the sanitary tanks were blown and vented outboard, usually just as the engines were started up, first drawing a strong suction through the conning tower to air out the boat—and pulling back into the conning tower the same poisonous odors just vented from the sanitary tanks. It was offal. The first breath of outside air assaulted the nostrils as oxygen replaced the human fumes absorbed during the long day submerged. Pure air crinkled the nasal hairs and jangled the senses.

Taking star sights with what was left of the horizon—nothing—soon forced me to become the most adept navigator around in pulling stars out of darkness—and the unhappiest. Most submarine navigators became very good at their art under poor conditions of twilight, largely throwing away prewar doctrine on celestial navigation. On surface ships one may stand around the bridge waiting for the perfect moment with a clear, sharp horizon and bright stars. For sights long after the ideal, submariners were forced to improvise. Some fitted half a pair of binoculars in place of the sextant telescope to magnify the image, an idea poor in theory and worse in practice. The sextant was designed to magnify the horizon and to dim the star so as not to ruin the observer's night vision. The half binocular did the opposite, magnifying the star and dimming the horizon. The star telescope in the sextant could be moved laterally during observations to reduce the reflection from the star and use all the magnification to improve the vision of the horizon.

One other facet of the routine complicated life aboard. As

noted, the odor produced by a submarine on war patrol is unique. Diesel fumes permeated the clothing, a natural by-product of submarine duty compensated for in the extra pay. The odor that really assaulted the sensitive nose, however, was the "Three Fs"—feets, farts and fannies—of eighty-one souls aboard living in close quarters with limited bathing and laundry facilities. (Some thought the USS *Tang* was named after the odor, but there really was a fish by that name.) What we called SO, or submarine odor, the German U-boaters called "fug." I don't know the meaning, but in their far more primitive subs it must have been a good strong aroma.

Air conditioning brought great improvements in habitability. Even though that luxury came to submarines via the Bureau of Ships to improve the reliability of equipment, and not by the Bureau of Naval Personnel to improve habitability, we enjoyed an unexpected dividend in use of the condensate as a new source of fresh water. The ship's evaporators produced adequate potable water for food, drink, and most shipboard needs, requiring only moderate care in conservation; the new source from the air conditioning coils was used almost exclusively for laundry. Our underclothes didn't come out snow white. They were a sweat-colored yellow but this was no problem. Some of the language was off-color too. Clothes looked fine until viewed in the bright sunlight. SO was always with us and little could be done about it, so complaints were pointless.

Surfacing that August night brought no rest for the tracking party. An hour before midnight, radar contact was made to the southeast at thirty-five thousand yards, a ship heading aimlessly away from us at fifteen knots. An hour's chase at flank speed reduced the range only slightly. By then all indications suggested a U.S. warship: the radar interference, the size, and the relatively high speed. We abandoned the chase.

Scarcely an hour later, Commander Submarines ordered *Sterlet* to search for a downed aviator off Muko Jima, whence we proceeded once again at flank speed. At 0300, in the darkest sector of the night sky, an aircraft contact was made at four miles, closing to two, but neither of us sighted the other. At 0605 two ships were sighted ten miles to the east. As we headed toward at flank speed, they turned away at high speed and disappeared over the hill into the morning haze. Again radar interference indicated a friendly. (Where was the surface Navy when we really needed it?)

At 0637 we resumed the search for the missing aviator. An hour later, in the approximate area, a Japanese survivor was found on a raft and pulled aboard. Thinking he might be an aviator able to give some useful information, we soon discovered that his ship, a merchantman, had been sunk by a torpedo plane a few hours earlier. The prisoner, Kim Dang Kee, claimed to be a Korean. He was so frightened and hungry he would have sworn he was the British ambassador or an infielder for the Boston Red Sox if we had asked him. Seeing confession as a guarantee of safety, he anxiously told everything he knew. Joe made a hit with him; when we fished Kim out of the water, he bowed. Joe, seeing him stoop over, bent down also to see if he was reaching for a knife. The prisoner, seeing Joe's bow, thought he had made a friend.

The men taught Kim all sorts of nicknames, making for continuous entertainment. He also earned his keep by doing all the dirtiest jobs on board. He was so anxious to please that some said he would qualify in submarines before some of the seamen. During a later sinking of another maru and a severe depth charging that followed, he kept a death grip on his bunk with fingers and toes, but otherwise he bore up well.

Throughout the day we passed through considerable wreckage and debris, plus many survivors, soldiers and civilians, dead and half dead. So many Japanese rafts were floating around that it seemed likely that the report of a downed aviator could have been mistaken for one of these. At 1900, however, we notified Commander Submarines of "no joy" on the search.

The next morning, Sunday, 6 August, brought a much needed day of rest. We returned to the Tokyo–Bonins route and resumed submerged patrol. Not until a few hours after midnight, at 0243, was contact made on a ship to the south, range thirteen thousand yards. We commenced an "end around" at flank speed, hoping to gain position ahead for an attack at dawn. The moon loomed very bright over a calm sea. An hour before dawn, a second ship appeared five miles ahead of our prey and in his path. It appeared to be an oceangoing tug seeking a rendezvous as an escort. The primary target settled on course 030 at eight knots, not zigzagging. Our best efforts left us still six thousand yards off the track, and detection seemed certain if we stayed on the surface any longer. We were just nine thousand yards away, and only our fine camouflage and four absolutely smokeless Fairbanks-Morse diesels had protected us this far. As dawn broke, our prey reached the site of the earlier wreckage. With a good chance that he might be searching for survivors, it seemed only sporting to add him to the problem. After we dived to periscope depth, the heavy twin screws of the target sounded like a big ship. At 0433, we fired four bow tubes set to run at four feet, straight bow shots, range twenty-six hundred yards. Two good hits were noted by periscope; the screws stopped and never resumed, although sonar had tracked him easily from ten thousand yards. The poor light prevented positive identification, but he was similar to the *Hiyosi Maru* of four thousand tons. Unfortunately, Japanese records could not identify this sinking.

Almost immediately the escort loomed into the periscope field, becoming larger by the second as he ran down the torpedo wakes. Coming hard right and making ready the stern tubes, we watched him drop the first depth charge, well short, and open fire at the periscope with machine guns. When the range closed to eight hundred yards, we fired three "down the throat" shots at him. In the stress of the moment, time did not allow a change of depth on the torpedoes and all missed underneath. Over the next three and a half hours, fourteen more depth charges were dropped singly. We gave him an "A" for effort and persistence, but he was definitely on the scrub team. Sound conditions were excellent, and we helped him still further. An after ballast tank had pressure in it and the stop was leaking so noisily it blotted out the sound all around the dial. Negative tank was still full; I ordered Hugh not to blow it dry but to pump it down. The superstructure, damaged in the 2 August depth charging, added a few more decibels of rattles. Then the starter on the trim pump failed, and we had to bleed high-pressure air—

very noisy—screeching into the auxiliary tank to level off at 560 feet, considerably deeper than Andy McKee and the Portsmouth shipbuilders ever dreamed we should go. Nevertheless, our pursuer never came close, making all his runs in the same water and dropping all charges well aft.

If the impression is gained of the ship calmly going from one task to the next during these stressful happenings, that impression is entirely incorrect. We were as calm as could be expected; that does not mean we were calm. By 0815, after a sleepless night, we were back at periscope depth, all clear. Two search planes flew by later at close range, and distant depth charging echoed through the still waters. Something was brewing; I wanted a part of the action.

At 2026 on 8 August, radar contact was made on another maru five miles to the north. The pip indicated a large ship heading west at nine knots, zigzagging on ten-minute legs. Steaming without an escort on a course taking him nowhere, he looked suspicious. We were still near the position of yesterday's attack, and a trap did not seem unlikely. More likely, the carrier attacks in the area may have run the enemy so short of escorts that he hoped to run this ship through our area unescorted, which his direct route seemed to substantiate. Wisdom seemed to lie in the assumption that Lady Luck was with us. Events soon proved she had a real smile for us. Moonrise occurred just as the zig plan was solved, and the night soon became bright enough to check zigs visually at thirteen thousand yards. To eliminate small errors in the setup, the target assisted us by keeping himself in the moonstreak with little outside help.

At 2217, we dived twelve thousand yards ahead of the maru and continued to close. Both deck and bottom sonars made immediate contact and verified the propellor count at 120 rpm. The sea was again flat calm, and a shallow depth setting of only one foot could do little harm—and we still couldn't believe our good fortune. Just an hour before midnight, we fired four bow tubes, straight bow shots with an eighteen-hundred-yard run. Four perfectly timed hits equally spread along her 417-foot length destroyed the target in ninety seconds. Boilers and everything else blew up, leaving only floating boxes and bales where the ship had been. Two depth charges went off, falling off the stern as she sank. All hands in the conning tower got a look as she went down. As we surfaced at 2315 in a sea covered with debris, a strong odor of bunker fuel and carbide permeated the air, but no survivors could be seen. The target was similar to *Mansei Maru* of 7,770 tons.

Patrolling along the Tokyo route continued for several days, but other than the daily sighting of the morning Mavis patrol plane, no other ship contacts could be developed. At noon on 15 August, we headed for the eastern part of the area and resumed patrol. The following morning, a round, silvery object appeared to the southeast, visible for more than thirty minutes. As navigator I assured all that it was not a planet but likely a meteorological balloon, 175 miles northeast of Chichi Jima. At 0125, 19 August, we made radar contact five miles due north. Friendly radar interference indicated a U.S. submarine. After identifying and exchanging area information with *Shark,* we commenced a coordinated search across possible convoy routes on this, our last day in the assigned area.

At 1700, 19 August, *Sterlet* headed for the barn at fifteen knots, making daily dives during twilight and maintaining a speed of advance of twelve knots. The trip home gave me plenty of time to think about the increasing loss of control of the CO under the high state of tension during the patrol. His unaggressiveness and the gradual disaffection of the officers placed me squarely in the middle of an acute and worsening situation. Bill Jameson insisted that he would not go to sea with the captain again. Joe was not far behind.

In a way I had contributed to the problem. I had offered to write the patrol report for the captain and wrote it largely as I would have conducted it. It surely sounded more aggressive than the facts warranted. For many of these "aggressive" acts, the CO was not on the bridge or in the conning tower, either going below for a bite to eat or for other reasons then unknown to me. Leo Pace and Commander Submarines both were to note in their endorsements to the patrol report the "aggressiveness, excellent planning, determined effort and gratifying results" of *Sterlet*'s first patrol, "worthy of a veteran." How could the *Sterlet* officers object to a lack of aggressiveness in the face of those comments by the reviewing seniors? It is true that the attack team performed superbly, but the CO's role was supervisory. I do not intend to disparage the character of an individual no longer able to defend himself; the supporting evidence, to my great distress, would continue to emerge.

I was torn by loyalty to the command and my responsibilities, possibly in conflict, for the safety of the other eighty men aboard. I had reached no decision toward resolving the internal conflict when we arrived at the submarine base, Midway, on 26 August. The enthusiastic welcome over a highly successful patrol soon produced a Silver Star for the captain and Bronze Star medals for me and Gene Barnhardt. Gene and Don Horst were recommended for qualification in submarines; I thought Joe thoroughly deserved it too, but the skipper decided that he and Bob Wright should wait until the next patrol.

During the R and R period in Midway, one of the highlights was to be the big ship's party at which we were to break open the special beverage supply purchased in Panama and carried halfway around the world. We played some football and volleyball, then the bar was opened just before a delicious steak lunch, offering not just beer but name-brand beverages. With some formality, I carefully located the special key and opened the locker outside my bunk. Lo and behold, it was empty—absolutely, totally, inexplicably empty. I couldn't believe my eyes. At all times the key had been kept in the captain's safe, to which only he and I had access. Looking into this intriguing mystery a bit further, we soon found the answer. There were not one but two access doors to the locker. One opened into my stateroom, the other into the chiefs' quarters directly aft of my stateroom. Somebody learned about my plan while we were in the shipyard and talked the yard into adding an extra access door from the chiefs' quarters.

Had the chiefs been having gilley parties at sea, drinking up the ship's stock? Since the men themselves were the only losers, I was content to let kangaroo justice catch up with the culprits in its own time. Nothing else could be done. And so the ship's party toasted our success with beer rather than booze and I came in for a lot of good natured ribbing.

After the steaks disappeared, I joined in a few games of horseshoes and a game of softball, then went down for a swim. Dragging my weary frame back to the Gooneyville Lodge, I met the skipper, Gene, and Hugh, just starting a tennis game, and leaped in as a fourth. The sun was blazing hot, and the cement court burned through the soles of our tennis shoes. After three fast sets, the skipper called a truce. We returned to the beach for an hour's relaxation.

While horsing around in the surf, I almost killed Hugh, inflicting what he thought was a chest full of cracked ribs. A quick x-ray on the sub tender showed only a strain. He had a tendency to pamper himself with medicines and tonics; I thought the roughhousing would do him good. Hugh developed into a fine officer, a zealous engineer, and an extremely capable diving officer. Having apparently been somewhat of a mama's boy, his experience on the *Sterlet*, I thought, made a man of him. He later asked me to be sure to report to Henri how I crushed him in the sand, severely wounding his emaciated body and almost doing him in with my 400 pounds of brute flabbiness. My weight on return from patrol was actually near a normal 188. Many of us gained or lost up to twenty-five pounds with no apparent relation to stress or quality of food; I had lost a few.

Henri once again dominated my thoughts as I sweated out the days until early September. On the possibility that I would be at sea when the news came in, I had advised her to wire Commander Submarines directly. When the happy news arrived, he put it on the "Fox" circuit so that it went not only to Midway but to all submarines. The commodore on the tender sent a messenger direct to the hotel to break me out of the sack, arriving with the good news just as Leo Pace telephoned. Little Henrietta arrived on 3 September, and both mother and daughter were fine. I didn't realize that the entire submarine force was in on the news until the communications officer on a boat arriving from patrol congratulated me. He knew because he had the chore of decoding the message. One of my cares drifted away quickly with the good news.

The difficult task of transferring fifteen men to the relief crews and receiving generally unqualified replacements was easier this time. I capitalized on Joe Garland's superb understanding of his fellow man and made him my assistant personnel officer. Only qualified men were transferred, usually in critical ratings; the men suggested as replacements were top quality high school graduates, well schooled but with little or no experience at sea. Joe scarcely looked at the records of the men suggested by the squadron for our review. Running his finger down the squadron files, he pulled out all the thick service records. The usual sequence ran, "Is this man available?"

"Yes."

"He's had a court-martial and been busted for direct disobedience of orders. That shows he's got the courage of his convictions. We'll take him."

The next man may have been busted for drunkenness; Joe added, "But look at his quarterly marks. He can do a superb job, and there's no liquor where we're going. We'll take him." On one busted for insubordination Joe said, "That was a fouled-up ship; we can handle him; I need him in the engine room."

We were buying experience on the cheap, confident that these men knew their jobs and would perform well in a good organization. Joe was invariably right. By the time we left the ship, *Sterlet* had become a haven for the rejuvenated.

One of the men transferred was the chief of the boat, Bill Lenning, the ancient mariner who had asked to come aboard in Portsmouth for a last tour before retirement. He had done a fine job for us but was forty-seven years old and was clearly slowing down. I did what I could for him—wrote him up for a commendation and gave him a sendoff letter which I hoped would get him back to Portsmouth rather than to serve out the war in Midway. But the choice of who was to leave the ship was always tough. One of the men almost cried, asking me to cancel his orders. Censoring the mail of those scheduled to leave was still worse, even if it was flattering to learn how badly they wanted to stay aboard.

The real problem arose with the officers. Bill Jameson had specified that he would not go to sea with the captain again and would leave submarines if orders to another boat couldn't be arranged. The CO went to great lengths to butter him up with no success. Eventually he was the only one to leave. But the evenings at the Gooneyville did nothing to ease my concern. The officers, except the CO, usually sat out on the veranda of the tavern in nightly bull sessions. The mood was downcast. Several, their inhibitions eased by a few beers, later told the CO that if I ever left the ship, they would never stay aboard under him. Although I tried zealously to prevent such discussions, they more and more became the focal point of any action to be taken. Privately I agonized over what action to take. Should I go to Leo Pace? He had always been friendly, but loyalty to the command tore me both ways. As long as I was aboard I thought the safety of the boat was not in question. Again, how could I justify an accusation of timidity in the face of the commodore's belief in the aggressiveness of the patrol? I saw no other conclusion but to "tough it out."

Another action by the CO generated considerable comment. When we captured the prisoner, Kim Dang Kee, much of his personal gear and clothing was given out as souvenirs. On arrival in Midway, however, the captain asked for a return of all the souvenirs, which he then sold to the post exchange to be marketed over the counter.

Meanwhile, the refit by *Proteus* had gone well. Battle damage was repaired and all equipment checked out by sound tests and routine drydocking. Ready for sea, we departed Midway on Monday, 18 September 1944. After an all-night run, the port stern tube, which had been repacked by the tender, began to leak. A dive to deep submergence proved the leak serious enough to warrant return to Midway.

Back on the marine railway at 0600, a sliver of wood was discovered in the stern tube packing. Fully repaired, we returned to sea for a test check at 1145 and were on our way once again. The patrol area this time was the Nanpo Shoto Islands—the Okinawa chain. The battle for the recapture of the Philippines was set to open in all its fury on 10 October. Our assigned area, lying between Japan and the Philippines, again promised to be a busy one.

Four days out of Midway a heavy typhoon and beam-end seas caused heavy rolling and pitching, making the bridge extremely wet and uncomfortable. One gigantic comber overwhelmed us and sent a twenty-five-inch pillar of solid green water down the hatch to the control room. No electrical equipment shorted out, proving the seaworthiness of our submarines. The large well at the foot of the hatch and a strong drain pump suction eliminated the menace in short order. The main induction, supplying air to the engines, remained almost entirely clear of water when the bridge was an overflowing bathtub.

While making a routine dive during the typhoon, we almost lost a man. Herbert Meitzler, a lookout, barely heard the "Dive, dive" or the klaxon over the shrieking wind. When he leaped for the guard rail to swing himself down to the bridge, he jammed his foot in a limber hole around the periscope shears. By the time he was able to pull free, the conning tower hatch had slammed shut and the quartermaster was dogging it down. Nobody else in the conning tower heard his cry for help but, unsure, I ordered the hatch opened and a very scared petty officer tumbled down with the whole ocean helping to push him through.

On 28 September, we received an Ultra contact report on a convoy crossing our track from the north, which we could reach in a day and a half. Heading to intercept at sixteen knots through the night, we gained a few miles ahead in case we were forced down by air patrols during passage northeast of the Bonins. The level of enemy air in these waters raised a strong possibility of further harassment. Luckily, the only aircraft sighted was avoided by a quick dive.

At 0330 on 30 September, Lot's Wife, that odd pillar of stone, appeared on the radar at fifteen miles. Shortly after, a ship appeared near the base of the pillared rock, soon made out to be a large steel-hulled trawler with a well-deck and a raised superstructure fore and aft. As we approached at high speed, he disappeared behind the rock, emerged on the other side, then reversed course again. When the range closed to seven miles, he showed his stern and chugged away to the south. He didn't appear to have seen us, but less than an hour later an air patrol at six miles forced us down, as did another at fourteen miles an hour later.

Back on the surface at 1000, we sighted a ship to the southeast at fourteen miles, soon identified as the same trawler, now heading northeast. Another air contact at twenty-five miles at 1300 forced us down when the range closed to nine miles. The air and surface activity suggested that our long-sought convoy might be moving through the area. It seemed prudent to stay down for a few hours to allow the airmen to go home and us to complete our rendezvous with the convoy. No contact was made throughout the night, however. The trawler probably called in the dogs, using the prominent landmark to establish our position and known course.

Sunday noon, 1 October, a contact report from *Trepang* indicated that we had missed last night's convoy by a very narrow margin. Intermittent submarine radar interference had been noted several times, but neither a radar target nor a contact report was received despite the new UHF radio installed at Midway.

Following a delayed lunch, I joined the full house attending Deacon Finley's church services in the forward torpedo room. No matter what one's religious preference, the hour of meditation was well spent. Erudition is where one finds it, and Finley had a fine mind. His homilies displayed wisdom, warmth, and wondrous understanding of the human condition. And I certainly needed wisdom to confront the worsening conditions with the captain and to prevent affairs in the wardroom from going further downhill.

On entering the area, we noted the seven-hundred-foot peaks of Kikai Shima and the towering twenty-three-hundred-foot Amami O Shima rearing prominently into the sky, but no surface activity could be detected. Distant explosions were heard several times in the evening, however, and we headed in that direction for a submerged patrol off Tokuma Shima. A midnight radar contact at eight miles was held for several minutes and suddenly disappeared. No explanation seemed satisfactory. It was not a plane and definitely not a cloud pip, and the range seemed a bit long for a surfaced submarine which had suddenly dived.

The CO decided to conduct a photo reconnaissance of nearby Tokuma Shima the following morning, the last day to be spent in this part of the area. The inshore area dawned somewhat misty, but taking what the gods offered, we closed to three miles off the beach and began a standard photo survey of the east coast. Then the area east of Okima A Shima beckoned for four days of submerged patrol. The fringe of a typhoon struck with moderate fury about the same time and hung around for three days. We patrolled at one hundred feet with a periscope sweep every hour. On the surface at night little could be done except to buck forty-foot seas and hang on.

For the big assault on the Philippines on 10 October, Commander Submarines assigned *Sterlet* a lifeguard station off Chen Wan, the main harbor of Okinawa, during strikes by the fast carrier forces. Proceeding to the area for a close-in reconnaissance of the harbor beforehand, we sought primarily to locate swept channels through the mined entrance. A round of photographs of the entire inner harbor disclosed no shipping, but a large sailing vessel stood out of the harbor at dusk, looking for all the world like a fine gun target. Remaining submerged until 1920, we surfaced close to a small fishing fleet. I tried to dissuade the CO from using these wretched people as gun targets. They were poor fishermen making a meager livelihood; they were Okinawans, not Japanese. Fishing vessels with engines and radios often filled additional roles in carrying food and war supplies to the various combat forces. Those were generally manned by Japanese and were legitimate gun targets. Fishermen under sail rarely performed such acts of war, and submarine force policy favored avoiding them. I failed to make the point, and the CO picked out a target and headed in, opening fire with 20-mm cannon and machine guns at a range of about fifty yards. The target, a small banca with an estimated displacement equal, in the words of the patrol report, "to half that of the executive officer," broke in two and sank. Plans to take the remainder of the fleet under fire had to be abandoned; on the first shot all the fishermen doused their lights as quickly as if a master switch had been thrown. In the inky blackness it was impossible to locate a new target, and the possibility of fouling a fishing net discouraged groping around. The decision came easily to clear the area and head for the morrow's lifeguard station.

I stayed clear of the bridge during this action. The "enemy" sunk was about the size of a rowboat, with only one occupant. Its destruction could not further the war effort in any way. The comparison of the target's size with that of the executive officer I had written into the patrol report to express my disapproval. The episode brought my relations with the skipper to a crisis. I was angry with myself that I was unable to dissuade him. My concern mounted over his timidity in the face of a legitimate enemy and false bravado in the face of helplessness. Although I kept my opinion to myself, I objected to the day wasted conducting the photo reconnaissance in the fog off Tokuma Shima, a small island with an airstrip of no significance, and I objected to the subsequent waste of four days patrolling off Okima A Shima at one hundred feet, far away from the action building up around Okinawa, where important warships might be fleeing to safer waters.

As long as the CO allowed the fire-control party to run the attacks, almost without interference, I could keep things fairly well under control. But the heavy depth charging off Chichi Jima on the previous patrol had its effect. That he was under great stress became evident even before leaving Midway. Late on the night before departure he had called me into his cabin to read letters written to his wife. I didn't care to read highly personal correspondence, but in these letters he lavished praise on the officers—these same officers who had just gotten a royal chewing out for their various shortcomings, these officers who were demoralized, including the exec, for lack of an occasional kind word.

Before we reached the patrol area he called me into his cabin repeatedly for late-night sessions until they became a ritual. He would ask me to sit down—usually on the small electric heater with my back cramped against the sink. A submarine cabin is a very small place, and I had to sit there interminably while he, lying in his bunk, mumbled unintelligibly. I'd ask for a repeat five or six times and still couldn't understand; he just wasn't making sense. Then I simply let him ramble. There was no conversation; he just mumbled—and mumbled. I prayed for an interruption, for any excuse to allow me to escape.

His actions during enemy depth charging were occasionally bizarre. As things went from bad to terrible, more and more I had to think of the very difficult choice of relieving him and taking command myself. To aggravate the problem, we were very early in the patrol. A long time remained at sea. From the briefings before departure, I knew that the big offensive against the Philippines and the showdown with the Japanese fleet were just over the horizon. If I did relieve him, for what reason could I justify it? If I sent a report to

Commander Submarines, what would Admiral Lockwood do? I couldn't imagine him leaving the captain on board to complete the patrol. It seemed likely that we would be ordered to rendezvous somewhere to get him off the ship lest something worse happen. I knew only vaguely of his earlier relief from a submarine and hospitalization in the first months of the war. I suspected it too may have been stress related. But no surface units were nearby, and he couldn't be sent to another submarine. *Sterlet* was badly needed on the firing line at the time. We were in a vital strategic area between the Philippines and the Japanese mainland as the greatest naval battle of all time took shape in Leyte Gulf.

I had no concern as to our ability to carry on in his absence; we were already doing so. The system for surface and submerged attacks had the exec conducting the approach, the CO in overall control concerned largely with the general safety of the ship. If I relieved him, no change would be required. I believed then that we were successful in keeping information on wardroom problems from the men back aft. But every small incident made the problem more difficult.

Many nights I spent hours on the bridge seeking the best solution when no choice seemed feasible. I couldn't discuss it with the officers until I had made my decision. I knew I had their total support, but the question of loyalty to command loomed large to all of us. Was I being rash even to think of relieving him? He had three times the experience in submarines I had. Few of us could be classed as old seadogs. A week before, I passed my twenty-ninth birthday. The average age of the eighty-one officers and men aboard was only twenty-two. I finally came to a decision. No alternative seemed to offer fewer problems than it created. I resolved once again to tough it out, but to be prepared for anything. Was I thinking mutinous thoughts? Not under the circumstances. Once I had made my decision, the Lord seemed to intervene quickly in our behalf.

Tuesday, 10 October, marked the opening of one of the major campaigns of the war against the crumbling Japanese Empire. The assault on the Philippines, so long promised by General MacArthur, finally became a reality. With the Marianas in Allied hands, the major air support for the Japanese defenders on Luzon must come from Japanese bastions on Okinawa and Formosa. These airfields would be under heavy attack by the carriers, commencing at dawn. At 0520, *Sterlet* dived on her assigned lifeguard station, ready for any eventuality. Surfacing at 0610 to man the fly-fly frequency on the VHF, we were driven down within minutes by a big Japanese "Betty" bomber. Back on the surface at 0655, we saw the first wave of Allied planes heading for their targets. The two fighter planes covering us checked in at the same time; we passed them the dope on the Betty and soon learned that it had been splashed.

At 0830 our services were requested for an aviator downed fifty-four miles to the south. Heading toward the position at flank speed, we learned at 1005 that he had been recovered by a float plane. Moments later, however, the float plane capsized taking off into heavy head seas. Again we reversed course to head for the site at maximum speed. Exactly an hour later we recovered Lieut. (j.g.) R. L. Dana, pilot of the cruiser scouting plane from USS *Biloxi,* and Lieut. (j.g.) A. J. Ferrenda from VF-13 in USS *Franklin,* both in excellent condition. We used Dana's overturned float plane for target practice with the 20-mm, aided by a few devastating bursts from the fighter cover.

As soon as we found some dry clothes for Dana and took away the chill with a mug of hot coffee, he volunteered to man the VHF on the bridge. His assistance in translating the mysterious lingo of the birdmen was vital. In addition, he knew the air group calls so that we were able to use returning groups to search for reported life rafts near their routes. Part of the problem was linguistic. To capitalize on the Japanese difficulty with the letter *l,* pronounced *r,* voice calls usually included several *l*'s, invariably making tongue twisters out of every routine transmission. Reaping rizards, it was rough.

Moments after the rescue, report of another downed aviator south of Okinawa gave us the chance to use our air fleet, sending a cruiser scout plane and one of our fighters to investigate as we chugged along at flank speed trying to keep up. Their report that nothing was in sight was quickly followed by another, this time of a pilot who failed to come out of his dive and was beyond any assistance we could offer.

Just before arriving at the first lifeguard station, we took a few moments to note and photograph the devastation ashore. Heavy smoke rising from several points on the island united to form one fiery black and orange mushroom cloud clearly visible forty miles away. These fires continued throughout the night, dying down only to burst out again and again. The Japanese commentator who later admitted slight damage to shore installations made one of October's most conservative estimates.

Eavesdropping via the VHF, we suffered through the vivid firsthand descriptions and agonized pleas for help in the heavy Japanese attack on our escort carriers. Two were sunk as well as three destroyers that tried to turn the Japanese battleships back with a torpedo attack. Then three destroyer escorts charged the battle line—one of them, the USS *Raymond,* named for Reggie—closing to fifty-five hundred yards with only a five-inch popgun to drive off a mighty enemy task force. She damaged two heavy cruisers, and the force turned back, saving the escort carriers from destruction. I later sent the CO of the *Raymond* a note of congratulations on the brave attack, so typical of the man his ship memorialized.

At 1550, a damaged torpedo bomber vectored to our position made a skillful water landing ahead. Although the plane sank almost immediately, the occupants popped out in a rubber boat. Lt. R. G. Freeman and second-class petty officers R. P. Perry and A. J. Valisen from VT-14 in USS *Wasp,* all uninjured, joined the submarine force. Then we immediately reversed course toward Okinawa at flank speed to a position one mile south of the island looking for another survivor.

At 1800, a pilot in a rubber boat close to the beach could be seen making no headway against the sea setting him further onto the shore. We were already well within the hundred-fathom curve but decided to go in anyway. The captain remained on the bridge; I conned the ship by radar and fathometer from the conning tower. The captain's order to stay outside fifty fathoms—three hundred feet of water— gave me immediate heartburn. I could see the officer through the periscope, plying a tiny oar against a mighty ocean. Ten fathoms of water is little different from fifty. How could we get so close, then turn away and abandon him? I crossed my Rubicon, which I suspect was also about five fathoms deep. One major element was in my favor—that part of the coast had recently been mined by the Japanese. It was probably safer inshore of the minefields in shallow water where no submarine would dare go. The mines were more likely to be in water from fifty to one hundred fathoms deep, but this was pure speculation. If we got in safely, the greater problem was to get out again. Retracing the exact track would be impossible.

Having made my decision, I started fudging reports to the bridge on fathometer readings of the depth of water below the keel, keeping the reported depths close to fifty as the water shoaled to forty, thirty, twenty—and then less than ten fathoms. I reported merely that the depth was steady. The thought passed through my mind that this was the same trick as fudging the stadimeter readings on *Wichita* back in the Thad Thomson days to protect the officer of the deck. But a man's life was at stake here, and by now we were so close to the beach that natives in shacks could be seen eyeing us curiously. In the uneasy stillness, shouts and sounds of life could be heard clearly. The bluffy contour of the coast gave the impression that we were in the shade of the trees. I was afraid we actually were. But no sign of hostile activity could be seen ashore; the Japanese and Okinawans were too busy elsewhere.

At 1816 we picked up Lt. (j.g.) J. R. Amussen, "the Moose," from VB-14 in USS *Wasp*. He had been shot down once before in Manila Bay and rescued by a destroyer. To say he was grateful to get aboard puts it mildly. As he came into the conning tower, I asked him where he wanted to go. "Anywhere you say," he replied fervently.

"What do you want for dinner?"

"Anything you say."

"Where's your hometown?"

"Anywhere you say."

Wasting no time, we retraced our path out to sea at high speed, thus ending a very special day at the beach.

The four new officers in the wardroom were a godsend. A bridge, poker, acey-deucey, or cribbage game ran almost continuously. When the CO walked in one doorway, most of the occupants soon found reason to leave by the other. Only a few days earlier the CO had ordered some of the junior officers to eat breakfast with him. But the tension between the captain and the officers was broken. Our guests were gregarious, well-informed, and intensely interested in learning all about submarines. We put them all on watch mainly to keep them occupied and out from under foot. On their first Sunday aboard, every one of the birdmen, for whatever reason, appeared at church services. I too attended, for good and sufficient reason.

A week of patrol in the island chain north of Okinawa, marked by frequent aircraft contacts visually, by radar or radar receiver, made all hands feel ready for action. About that time, 15 October, Commander Submarines ordered us to patrol the center of the area scouting for Japanese fleet units en route to or from the Philippines. Three days later, in midmorning, sonar contact was made on screws at long range. The tops of three warships were soon made out at twenty-nine thousand yards range—almost fifteen miles away. Soon the enemy force could be made out to be two *Atago*-class heavy cruisers and one *Tenryu*-class light cruiser screened by six escorting destroyers, with one cruiser-type aircraft circling overhead. The enemy was using a 60-degree constant helm zig plan on base course 320 degrees at eighteen knots. He had apparently come through the pass between Okinoyerabu and Yorou Shima. We were far off the track, and only a large zig toward would give any hope for getting off a shot. The navigation plot indicated that he was heading toward the relative safety of the Inland Sea, and his likely course change would be a zig away, which he did. After a half hour chase we reached a minimum range of eight thousand yards at 20 degrees abaft his beam. We took photographs and sadly watched these prime enemy targets go rapidly over the hill. One escort started pinging at the end of our speed run; a distant depth charge was heard, but he indicated no further awareness of our presence.

Shortly past noon, just before we were to surface to send a contact report, the air search radar reported a pip at eight miles. When all clear at 1300, we surfaced to report the enemy disposition, course, speed, and position to Commander Submarines. An hour later two long-range aircraft contacts were held for several minutes. At 1430, with the transmission finally acknowledged in Guam, we dived and resumed periscope patrol. The carrier forces greatly appreciated this very timely report.

Within the hour sonar had a good contact on screws, verified visually as an "unescorted" destroyer eleven miles to the southeast. The BT trace indicated no layer to four hundred feet; the recent typhoon had stirred the seas to break up all subsurface temperature gradients. In other words, the waters were superb for tracking by both the submarine and the antisubmarine forces, and evasion after an attack would be very difficult. We went to battle stations and tried to gain attack position. The enemy, alerted either by our radar or by the contact report, patrolled somewhat aimlessly in our general area, five miles away. Though we continued in his general direction, he failed to close. In the isothermal water the surface-mounted sonar again performed superbly.

That evening after we surfaced, atmospheric conditions seemed to affect the surface search radar as well. At three separate intervals, close-in contacts were made, one at thirteen hundred yards, two at fifteen hundred yards. The pips were clear and distinct, generally tracking at about twenty-four knots and, more often than not, heading directly for the submarine. Too close for a plane, too fast for anything but a PT boat—or a hostile seagull—these "phantoms," terribly nerve-racking, soon became part of the routine, especially on surfacing. After a few scares, the captain asked me to man the radarscope every night on surfacing. I soon found that if the first quick sweep showed a phantom, then I reduced the strength of the outgoing signal to see if the image faded. A legitimate contact at such close range would not fade and would be quite distinct. Many years later, in the Vietnam war, I suspected immediately that the alleged PT boat attacks on the USS *Maddox* (on which the Senate "blank check" resolution was based) were also phantoms. They occurred in the same general region under much the same atmospherics. Many other submarines noted the phenomenon.

On 19 October, on orders to cancel the scouting line, we returned to the Amami O Shima area for submerged patrol.

The following day, off Tokumo Shima, a large transport plane landed on the Tokumo airfield. Three other planes were visible, all fighters, but no unusual activity seemed in progress. Late the following day radar contact was made on a small ship at eight thousand yards, heading south at seven knots, not zigzagging and unescorted. The radar was at peak condition, and the low range of initial contact made it doubtful the target was worth a torpedo. Detected visually at four thousand yards, a small spitkid of about a thousand tons, it seemed almost worthwhile. We fired three bow tubes set at two feet; one was seen missing ahead, one astern. So he wasn't worth a torpedo after all. An end around at flank speed got us near attack position once more at 2300, just as he made a sharp course change to head for the shallow passage north of Tokuma Shima, cutting us off at the pass. The passage was so shallow it proved beyond doubt that he wasn't worth a torpedo, and we broke off the attack. Then for the next hour or so the phantoms were at us again, offering tracking practice much less vital at the moment than sleep. Each disappeared, annoyingly, after only a few ranges and bearings. And when the phantoms retreated, the fishing fleet took over to preserve the high nuisance value.

The phantoms continued through the next two evenings, one in bright moonlight invisible at three thousand yards. At 0319 on 25 October, however, a solid radar contact at fifteen thousand yards soon proved much more substantive. A very large gasoline tanker and another large tanker or freighter close on his starboard beam had an escorting destroyer trailing about five thousand yards astern and two patrol chaser escorts keeping rather haphazard station on the flanks. The enemy course was southwest at nine knots, zigzagging on ten-minute legs. Deciding to attack the big ships on the first pass, we planned to get a shot at the destroyer on a second attack. Light conditions were ideal for our camouflage. The black horizontal surfaces and black and gray mottled vertical surfaces produced near invisibility so that we hoped to get both attacks off before diving at dawn.

As we headed in for the first attack at 0405, the escorts kindly went to the other side of the formation. Dead on the beam of the tanker at fifteen hundred yards, we were about to commence shooting when the target group zigged. I should have anticipated this when the escorts changed station in advance of the convoy course change. Going to flank speed, we cut across the bow of the tanker, showing him a full silhouette at twelve hundred yards. Perhaps we could wake up his lookouts in just a few moments. Stopping to hold the range steady, we fired four stern shots from a position on his starboard beam but scored no hits. With ideal firing position, enemy course, and speed accurate on a cold setup, this was hard to believe. Six minutes later, we heard four end-of-run explosions of our torpedoes. To our amazement, all the escorts immediately proceeded to the scene of the explosions, leaving a completely clear field for the target group. We could now class the stern shots as "tactical," a ruse to confuse. At 0430 we fired six bow tubes at the two overlapping targets, very close together in range, straight shots from just abaft his beam, range three thousand yards. Three timed hits were observed in the large tanker, one in the other ship, followed by the most devastating explosion imaginable. A tremendous ball of fire lighted up the sky. The ship's bow leaped fifty feet into the air. In the conning tower, bright as day from the explosion and ball of fire, I was about to give a cheer, but the shock wave from the blast drove the words back down my throat. A fully loaded, ten-thousand-ton gasoline tanker disappeared in a matter of seconds.

Shifting to the second target, we pulled clear to reload. She had lost steering control and slowed to four knots, but the pip was still very large on the radar screen. Fifteen minutes later, at a range of six thousand yards, the pip disappeared from the screen as quickly as if somebody had wiped it from a slate. Only the destroyer and two small escorts remained, milling around the scene of the explosion and depth charging in a very vicious manner. Seventeen charges were counted, the last a blockbuster that rattled the ship at eight thousand yards.

No time remained for an end around to attack the destroyer before dawn, so we cleared the scene, hoping to make a submerged attack after sunrise. At 0518, the destroyer came around to the east. To prevent being left out in the cold, we came to course 070 at flank speed to stay on his new track. At 0535, with dawn breaking all around, we could no longer escape detection on the surface but continued to close submerged. The three escort vessels might be picking up survivors; we decided to wait and hope for a crack at the destroyer if he came near. At 0543 he headed our way. Identifying him as a *Mutsuki*-class, we made the bow tubes ready. Just before reaching the firing bearing, however, he reversed course and rejoined his friends. At 0715, an airman joined the hunt. The air and surface search continued through the morning while we watched the cat from the mousehole.

At 0830, the *Mutsuki* seemed to abandon the search and headed for us. Again we began an approach, but the closest point, forty-five hundred yards looking up his kilts, left us far out of it. In this attack, we were credited with destroying a 600–675 foot, 10,000-ton tanker and a 7,500-ton freighter.

Before things settled down to normal, Don Horst, the watch officer on the periscope, suddenly found himself out-staring a Japanese zoomie. By his stuttering description, he could see only fuselage, part of a wing, and the red nose of the plane, even with the periscope in low power. We went deep to let matters cool off, came back to periscope depth half an hour later, and Rufe was still circling. Going deep again while he burned more holes in the sky, we were suddenly surprised at 1420 by a very close depth charge. Again we went deep posthaste. Since the strong current in the Yokuma Kaikyo almost countered our forward move-ment, course was reversed to let the current work for us, surfacing finally off Taku Shima, well clear of rocks, shoals, and air surveillance. Because of the difficulties of navigating at the mercy of the elements, this was hardly recommended for normal practice.

The continuing pattern of surprise attacks from the air during both *Sterlet* patrols caused increasing concern. We knew the Japanese could home in on our air search radar and were cautious in its use. Many times the airman flew down the periscope, where detection visually or by radar receiver was nearly impossible. Had the Japanese developed a magnetic anomaly detector like our MAD gear for use against a submerged sub? There was no information avail-able from intelligence material on board or from classified briefings before our departure. Yet no other explanation seemed to satisfy. We later learned that the Japanese *had* developed MAD, but it was so heavy initially it seriously overloaded the plane. Removal of its steel armor for flyability also improved magnetic sensitivity but made the plane vulnerable to gunfire.

Two weeks later, on 14 November 1944, *Halibut*, with *Pintado* observing, was bombed with several blockbuster explosions, damaging her so severely she had to be withdrawn from service. Comparison of the accounts of the two skippers, I. J. "Pete" Galantin and B. A. "Chick" Clarey, left little doubt that the detection and attack had been made by MAD-equipped planes. But future knowledge helps very little in present crises.

At 2218, we made radar contact on a large ship fifteen miles to the west, heading toward Japan, probably via Bungo Suido into the Inland Sea. A dim red light on the ship could soon be made out, raising momentary hopes that it could be an aircraft carrier. That hope died when the special markings of a hospital ship became clear. Since other traffic could be expected to be returning to Japan from the major fleet action under way in the Leyte Gulf, this section of the area looked attractive as a focus of the patrol for the next few days. After surfacing on 26 October, we identified *Croaker* by keying the surface radar and closed to exchange information. The two COs decided to split the patrol area, *Croaker* to the east, *Sterlet* to the west.

On 29 October at midnight, *Sea Dog* put us on the track of a task force of two battleships escorted by four destroyers heading for the Tokyo area on course 050 at twenty-two knots. The battleships were at the center of the formation with screens on the four-thousand- and six-thousand-yard circles. Heading in at full power, we could expect contact as early as 0230. Arriving at the reported position, we commenced a search along the enemy's track. At 0415 we hit the jackpot—radar contact to the west at twenty-five thousand yards. I sent contact reports to *Ronquil* and *Besugo* and commenced tracking. On initial contact we were on the starboard beam of the formation, twelve miles off the track. At emergency full power, with the ballast tanks blown dry to coax out another quarter of a knot, we were gaining position very slowly, so slowly it seemed unlikely we could get into attack position before the enemy force reached Bungo Suido. The enemy was clearly in view in the three-quarter moonlight; we figured we were not likely to be detected outside twelve thousand yards. At 0500 we reached a minimum range of thirteen thousand yards, at which time the enemy changed course to the north, showing us nothing but churning wakes. Both *Besugo* and *Ronquil* were even farther off the track.

None of the boats in the pack detected radar in the enemy force. Later, studying the plot, it seemed likely that the Japanese used a radar detector capable of receiving our surface radar emissions and merely ran circles around us. This chase was a particularly bitter pill for me to swallow. On receiving the initial contact from *Sea Dog,* I left orders with the OOD that on making contact, he should immediately come to course 050, paralleling the known enemy track, and go to full power. In this way we would lose no distance off the enemy track and would keep pace with the enemy while we solved the torpedo problem. When contact was made, however, the CO happened to be in the control room and immediately ordered the officer of the deck to put his tail to the enemy at flank speed. By the time I got to the conning tower, commenced tracking, and changed course to parallel the enemy, we had drawn so far off the track that we never recovered the distance lost by turning tail, and hence never got into attack position.

The following evening, radar contact was made on a ship at 12,700 yards, heading east at seven knots, not zigzagging, and unescorted. In the moonlight the target seemed to be a small freighter, possibly even a destroyer. To avoid the possibility of the enemy using a radar detector, we shut down both radars and tracked him visually, checking the setup with a quick radar range at ten-minute intervals. Tracking a nonzigzagging enemy in this manner was simple. At 2153, we dived eight thousand yards directly ahead of our prey. His speed increased, then decreased just before we fired, unfortunately. Three torpedoes from the after nest set at four feet, and a fourth with enemy speed increased to ten knots, all missed.

Feeling that he was too small for a torpedo, we surfaced

and opened fire with all weapons at a range of twelve hundred yards. The guns performed superbly, the four-inch getting about 60 percent hits, the machine guns putting up a murderous barrage that soon set a bright fire amidships. The ship appeared new and smart looking, steel hulled, and about two hundred feet long. Three machine guns were mounted above the bridge and possibly a large gun aft. At 2344 the target sank, riddled by countless holes, an oil fire burning fiercely on the water. Clearing the area until the fire burned out, we returned to recover a prisoner. No volunteers could be found, but a new Kapok life ring was pulled from the oily waters; the small, thousand-ton maru had disappeared. The postwar assessment failed to record this kill, hence it must have been less than five hundred tons, the minimum recorded. We hereby claim the kill of a four-hundred-ton maru.

At 0330 on October 30, we received a contact report on a ship near our track, 110 miles distant. Commencing a high-speed search, we arrived at the site at 1400, but no enemy appeared, only *Silversides* or *Salmon,* both nearby. So many submarines were congregating on the line of retreat of the Japanese warships that we needed a traffic light. At 1530 *Salmon* reported the position of a large tanker and two escorts, then *Silversides* reported that *Trigger* had put a torpedo in the tanker's stern, stopping her dead in the water. *Burrfish* reported that she was closing to attack. *Ronquil,* without a star fix in several days, came within hailing distance to get a navigation check from me. *Trigger* then brought us all to attention with a report of a battleship in the vicinity. Salivating commenced over such juicy targets. Just before midnight, gun flashes to the northeast attracted our attention, soon disclosing the long-sought tanker, dead in the water and down by the stern. The escorts had gone, making this close to the simplest attack of the war. Almost without changing course we charged in and fired six bow tubes for at least four solid hits. The target went down like a rock. Evasion required only picking a path through the debris-strewn seas and continuing course and speed for Midway.

Meanwhile, *Ronquil,* also closing for attack, arrived from the west as we departed to the east—and just as the escorts returned from their wild goose chase after *Trigger*. The damaged tanker had sunk, but they found *Ronquil* and pinned her down for the next three hours under a prolonged attack of fifty-four charges. *Ronquil*'s navigator was my very good friend Lincoln Marcy to whom I had just given our dead reckoning position. With my position as his own, he ran down our track but we took the prize and he took the punishment. Yet with submarines all around us, nobody had yet found any evidence of the battleship reported earlier by *Trigger*.

That mystery took a long time to resolve. Wolfpack submarines used a radio code with simple two-letter substitutions for common tactical terms. *Trigger* hadn't seen a battleship. The message she intended to send was, "Enemy bearing north 12 miles from position" such and such. When the radioman took the word *bearing* from his wolfpack code book, he accidentally grabbed the word above it, *battleship*. In a tiny, semidark radio shack in the confusion of battle, such mistakes can happen. (Clausewitz called this the fog of war.) The report he actually transmitted decoded as "Enemy battleship north 12 miles from position" such and so. It made equally good sense and got a lot more attention.

In the meantime, all was not well with the remainder of our pack. At 0230, 31 October, *Besugo* reported *Salmon* severely damaged, lying to on the surface with a fifteen-degree list and unable to dive. We raced toward the reported rendezvous, soon joined by *Silversides*. John S. "Jack" Coye, as senior skipper, set up a search plan. At 0948, an aircraft appeared on our radar receiver, but we stayed on the surface to draw a possible attack away from *Salmon*. *Salmon*, meanwhile, had jury-rigged a radio transmitter and was able to send weak signals at timed intervals on the 500-kc distress frequency. At 2225, after twenty hours of agonizing search, a red rocket appeared in the east. We headed toward at flank speed and quickly made radar contact on *Salmon*, and shortly after on *Trigger*, closing from the east a short distance behind us. The first message from *Salmon* was, "You sure look sweet to us."

Salmon's exec, Richard B. Laning, came aboard via a rubber boat. His first words stuck in my memory: "Hi, Paul, old buddy. What can we do for you?"

Salmon's crew was extremely lucky to be alive. A very

heavy depth charging had dished in the pressure hull,
knocked one engine off the base plate, severely damaged all
radio and radar equipment, and caused major structural
damage throughout the ship. Exhausted and forced to the
surface by three escort vessels, she took them on with the
deck gun, picking her way in and out of rain squalls. At the
peak of the gunfight, a box of galley stores was inadvertently
passed topside as ammunition. Dick claimed that on a close
pass by one of the escorts, the gun crew threw potatoes at
the enemy, using oranges for tracers. I doubt this. We never
had oranges that late in the patrol.

Commander Submarines' orders were to take off the crew
and sink the hulk or escort her to Saipan. In event of attack
en route, we would dive, then surface later to pick up
survivors. Hence I asked Dick if we could take off some
nonessential men to ease the burden on facilities. He emphatically refused. "We've fought her this far and we're
going to fight her back to Saipan."

Then, a few minutes after midnight, a new danger arose.
Suddenly a lookout shouted, "Torpedoes on the starboard
bow." *Sterlet* went ahead flank and paralleled the wakes as
they whooshed by, close aboard. It was high time to get
moving. *Trigger* and *Sterlet* took station on the bows of
Salmon, and our small force headed for Saipan. At daybreak, *Trigger* moved ahead to the horizon as an advance
scout, and *Silversides* took the other distant flank. *Salmon,*
under Harley K. "Kenny" Nauman, struggled to get additional machinery in operation. When she got a third engine
on the line, the force was able to speed up to sixteen knots.

At 1415, 1 November, air cover from Saipan checked in to
control the friendly skies, reporting that on the way out they
had shot down a snooper just south of us. Two days later,
without further incident, the tall mountains of Saipan came
into view, and at 1440 a surface escort joined the formation.
At 2010 *Sterlet* moored alongside the USS *Holland,* an
elderly submarine tender sharing refit duties with *Fulton* in
Tanapag Harbor, Saipan.

The day before we arrived, the captain called me into his
cabin. He informed me that on arrival he planned to ask for
my detachment. He had apparently given considerable
thought to the reaction of the senior submariners at the

potential refit base. He knew my comments would carry considerable weight but that he could keep the other officers under control in my absence. The *Salmon* episode and the unplanned stopover in Saipan presented him with a golden opportunity to leave me in the boonies.

Immediately on arrival he went to the squadron commander in *Fulton* and reported that I was hot for combat, didn't want a rest period, and preferred to go back out immediately on another boat. To me he promised a satisfactory fitness report in my record on condition that I say nothing about *Sterlet* problems. My last words to him were, "You know you'll never take the ship on a war patrol again without me on board."

I finally unburdened myself to Gene. I had never criticized the CO, and since I had been allowed full freedom in all our attacks, he and the other officers were greatly surprised at the seriousness of the breach. With deep sorrow in my heart I walked through the boat to make my farewells to a superb crew. Next morning, long before anybody was up, I took a motor launch from the *Holland* to take me across Tanapag Harbor to the other tender, the *Fulton*. Almost nobody saw me leave; only the deck watch knew it was my detachment. Walking into my new quarters aboard *Fulton,* 3 November 1944, I felt mentally and physically exhausted. The continuing tension of the past year left me dispirited, discouraged, and somewhat bitter about the sudden turn of events. I wondered how deeply the squadron commander in Saipan would look into *Sterlet*'s command problems and how forthright I could be in response to his inquiries.

I had barely gotten settled in my cabin aboard *Fulton* when a delegation of *Sterlet* officers and men visited me to express their profound sorrow on my detachment and to wish me a fond farewell. Knowing how hard it was for them to arrange a boat and get away during all the turmoil, I was deeply moved.

Shortly after lunchtime, Joe Garland returned with several key people to present a farewell remembrance from all the officers and men, a beautiful Swiss travel clock. I was astonished as much as pleased. Where could even Joe have found such a beautiful gift, complete with engraving, in this barren outpost? He apologized that it wasn't more elaborate.

I felt like crying tears as big as snowballs. The clock, chromium and red leatherette, gave day, date and month on one face, time on the other. The first thing that popped into my mind, wholly irrelevant, was how nice it would be for Henri and me to use on our second honeymoon, when the war was finally behind us, to replace the ancient, battered relic of a travel clock we had been using.

When I saw the respect and honest affection on the faces of those fine men, my morale got the boost it sorely needed. For the first time I realized how good it felt to be free at last of the continuing unpleasantness during all these months. I regretted that those left behind must continue for a while in the same dispiriting routine, but I felt sure the CO would be very circumspect during the trip back to Pearl, where *Sterlet* was now scheduled for refit. He would have to answer the inevitable questions about my sudden departure. Joe again told him this was his last trip to sea with him. Others followed, and there would be no easy explanation to seniors in the remote chance that he would decide not to give up his command.

Above all, I wanted a loving letter from Henri, and that was impossible. Mail for *Sterlet* was heading for Midway; the ship was heading for Pearl, and I was in Saipan, soon to be heading out to sea. It would take forever to catch up. The change of address I sent out immediately would take two weeks to get stateside and another two for return mail to find its new destination. By that time I would be long gone to another assignment, wherever that might be.

Sterlet departed from Saipan for Pearl Harbor with a covey of other submarines, arriving there on 30 November. En route they made a sweep through the Bonins, then a detour to Midway for emergency medical assistance for a man wounded by accidental discharge of a firearm. For this patrol, *Sterlet* was credited with the large gasoline tanker, a large merchantman, a small maru, and a patrol escort sunk, and given one-third credit for the second large tanker which *Salmon* and *Trigger* had attacked before *Sterlet* administered the coup de grace. Postwar credits claimed the large maru made port, and the small maru, from which we recovered debris, was credited to the aviators. The captain was recommended for the Navy Cross; I had the memories. At the end of R and R in Pearl, the thought of going to sea again was too much for him. He asked to be relieved from command. He soon disappeared from the submarine force; I never saw him or spoke to him again.

5

The USS *Atule*

Minesweeper?

I watched the sun rise over Tanapag Harbor on that early November day aboard *Fulton*. The morning air carried a tangy fragrance across the calm waters. Somewhere near the top of 1,554-foot Mount Tapotchau a Japanese flag flew unseen to any but the few surviving occupants still holding out in the network of caves and bunkers.

Saipan was critically important to both sides, the key to U.S. conquest of the central Pacific, the keystone of the Japanese inner defense perimeter. U.S. troops had stormed ashore on 15 June after a spirited bombardment by fifteen battleships and heavy attacks by carrier aircraft. Vice Admiral Jisaburo Ozawa sent the greatest Japanese fleet ever assembled to aid the defenders. Four days after the initial landings, some five hundred aircraft were launched from the Japanese carriers and airfields in an all-out assault. In the "Great Marianas Turkey Shoot," four hundred Japanese planes were lost; one hundred U.S. planes were lost, most of them ditching or crash landing on the carriers when they ran out of gasoline on their return flights. The destruction of three Japanese carriers—two to U.S. subs, one to torpedo planes—and most of their pilots inflicted a blow from which the Imperial Navy never recovered. The loss of Saipan's Aslito airfield and four satellite fields on adjacent Tinian

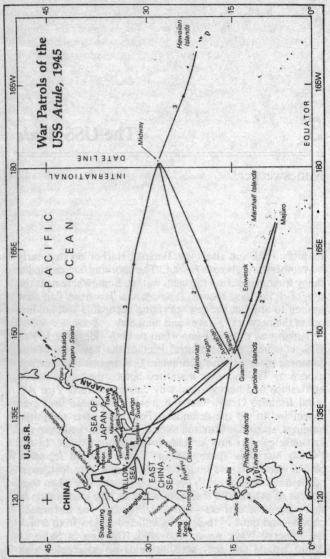

War Patrols of the
USS Atule, 1945

Island took away a major military staging base, the most important air complex between Tokyo and Truk. Much of Japan's dwindling supplies of sugar, corn, vegetables, and whiskey from the Suntori distilleries came from Saipan.

During June and July Vice Admiral Takeo Takagi was ordered to send every Japanese submarine available to defend the Marianas. A dozen were lost to little or no purpose, including Admiral Takagi himself. The submarine force never recovered from the disaster. Priorities on new construction shipbuilding went elsewhere. The submarine program was changed from fleet boats to scores of small *kaiten* midget submarines to be used against the anticipated Allied invasion of the home islands. The remaining fleet submarines were adapted to carry either the *kaiten* or suicide torpedoes for use against the U.S. fleet. Despite the best efforts of the defenders, the island was declared secured by the American forces on 9 July. Prime Minister Hideki Tojo had personally guaranteed the successful defense of the island to the emperor. When Saipan fell, Tojo and his entire cabinet resigned. The disaster could not be hidden from the people and convinced many, including the emperor, that the war could not be won.

Holland arrived in Tanapag harbor in August, *Fulton* shortly after, and the new afloat submarine base was immediately open for business. The capability for full submarine repair and logistic support in the forward area allowed a new patrol routine. Refits would occur alternately at an advance base—Midway, Majuro, or Guam—or at Pearl Harbor, using Saipan for topping off or emergency repairs.

Japanese combat remnants holding out in the mountains made occasional foraging raids, causing a few casualties to men from ships in the harbor—including submariners—rubbernecking or souvenir hunting. I was as anxious as any to get ashore and have a look around. At first chance, several of us commandeered a jeep or hiked around, fascinated by the charred relics of tanks and equipment destroyed in the bitter struggle. The limestone hills were pockmarked with caves scarred by flamethrowers, their inhabitants still frozen in final death throes. The first day ashore we visited the internment camp at Charan Kanoa, where Japanese civilian workers from the destroyed sugar mill, their families, and others tried to resume life behind barbed wire. My lasting impression is of thick, grubby flies everywhere, on faces and feces, on food or swarming over rotting animal carcasses. The flies had been introduced into Saipan as a natural enemy of a local pest, but they immediately declared a truce, then went forward and multiplied, soon becoming far worse than the pest they were supposed to eliminate. I watched a native put a bowl of thin soup to his lips, several fat flies bathing in it, then suck it through his teeth, putting down the bowl, empty except for the ugly insects.

The huge air complex developing on the southern end of the island offered a major point of interest. Army engineers put top priority on expanding Aslito airfield into a huge B-29 bomber and fighter base. Everybody on the island wanted to rubberneck; an ironhanded West Pointer decreed that every vehicle of any description passing through his area would carry coral. Whether a jeep or a general's car, they paid the price of admission, and the skyline changed day by day. Soon fighters zoomed off freshly rolled, dusty strips; by mid-November B-29 bombers launched their first Saipan-based raid on Japan.

Days of scavenging along the beaches and interior always ended at 1630 at the "Officers' Club," hastily erected for the fleet on a low promontory overlooking the harbor. The club opened daily at 1630 and closed at 1900, so that all users could get back to their commands before nightfall and its hazard of Japanese raiding parties. Only beer was served; refrigeration was limited to a single large reefer that kept the contents far below freezing. Each day sufficient beer was set out early enough to be somewhat thawed by 1630 but not too warm by 1900. Regulations for tropical export beer required the use of formaldehyde as a preservative. When the beer froze, the formaldehyde distilled to the top. We fell into the "club" each day, hot and sticky from our brisk walks around the island, and couldn't wait to get a long sip of beer. It was mostly formaldehyde, and the overusers soon found they were embalming themselves. They quickly went berserk, causing wild, free-swinging battles before they could be brought under control. That stuff sure hit the spot.

With many boats passing through, the friendship and sympathy of old friends greatly helped raise my morale.

Fellow execs Johnny Shepherd of *Trigger,* Linc Marcy of *Ronquil,* Charles F. "Chuck" Leigh of *Silversides,* John D. Harper of *Shark* (lost two weeks later), Howard A. "Howie" Thompson of *Scabbardfish,* and Dick Laning of *Salmon*— and their skippers, I soon found—were solidly behind me. The COs who knew my boss were surprised not over the break but that he lasted as long as he did before it came. Frederick A. "Pop" Gunn, Howie Thompson's skipper, tried to get me aboard *Scabbardfish* for a patrol as a PCO but couldn't swing it before heading out again.

As my sagging morale struggled to return to normal, a nagging physical problem added to my concern. Despite my iron constitution, the emotional strain of the past year caused my weight to drop to 173, lower than it had been since plebe year. More bothersome was a severe case of "periscope eye" from long hours on the periscope or squinting through a sextant. During the last days at sea my left eye had weakened to the point that I could distinguish little more than light from dark—I, who frequently earned the nickname Hawkeye, now was half blind. After a thorough examination on the tender, all the doc could do was produce an ugly pair of glasses, which I detested.

Meanwhile, the Japanese made one last hostile effort against the island. One day at high noon a dozen Japanese Zeros made a sudden low-level attack on ships and the airfield. They had secretly restored an airstrip on Pagan Island about a hundred miles away and moved in planes. For several days, usually at noon and midnight, a group of fighters flew over Tanapag, shooting up everything in sight. Since there was neither a carrier nor a known land base within range, the first attack achieved complete surprise. The twice-daily attacks kept us busy until the last plane was splashed. The display of pyrotechnics, searchlights, criss-crossing tracer fire, flares, and rockets over the harbor at night was unbelievable, but the accuracy of the fire by the defenders was not impressive.

Few of the ships at anchor were frontline combatants. Many, like *Fulton,* were support ships whose specialists could spare little time for gunnery drills. Since the *Fulton* AA battery was the same five-inch 38s with which I had spent so many hours in *Wichita,* I offered my services to run the AA battery, an offer quickly accepted by the CO. I thoroughly enjoyed the tracking exercises and control of the guns, my first experience banging away at live targets. We didn't shoot any down but our accuracy improved mightily in a day or so. Meanwhile, U.S. fighters and bombers soon smoked out the airstrip on Pagan and put it permanently out of commission.

I had few duties formally assigned while waiting for orders. Wishing to stay occupied, I initiated a routine check of TDCs and other fire control equipment on every sub coming alongside for repairs. After all those hours of loving that toy, I wanted to use my experience for the general good. I used my file of training problems and checked each submarine over carefully, finding many mechanical errors, some significant. Any officer who wanted a wardroom bull session on attack tactics always found me ready. The skippers were genuinely appreciative.

Part of my interest in spending time on the submarines rather than on the tender came from the differences I saw day by day in the officers and men aboard *Fulton* from what I was accustomed to in the boats. The tenders had serious problems in maintaining high-quality personnel. Rejects from the submarines went to the tenders and could rarely be sent anywhere else. The rest of the Navy didn't want submarine castoffs; they had their own to worry about. The spread of experienced regular Navy officers was also very thin. As a result, time-honored customs, so necessary in building the "band of brothers" spirit in a close-knit unit, fell by the wayside. To me, the shipboard life was different, disappointingly so. Nobody denied the remarkable job the tenders did. The display of American genius was unsurpassed. The Japanese knew; they called our submarine tenders "America's secret weapon." What I saw lacking were little things that create big impressions.

The wardrooms on navy ships of every maritime nation are gentlemen's clubs, a place for stimulating discussion by mature, well-traveled, and well-read individuals. Mealtime in the wardroom highlights the shipboard life. But here I found meals to be fifteen- or twenty-minute affairs at which everybody bolted his food and bolted from the table. Outside their jobs, they found little to talk about, few shared escapades and adventures on the beach to live and relive. By the nature of their service, they knew precious little about each other's wives, families, or outside interests. The ideal cannot be endless bull sessions, but mealtimes should offer food for the mind as well as for the body.

Specialists in the trades, most knew little of naval tradition and lore of the sea. Because they lacked a background of mutual ties and experiences, their conversation was largely shop talk or local news, the same as one might find in a cafeteria with a casual passerby. The department heads associated little with the endless waves of ensigns; the ensigns were too often fat, flabby, and little informed of service life. Conversation lagged, even with a great war going on around their ears. Meals became pit stops in a busy day. Few division officers knew their men or understood their problems; they showed little interest in making the ship their home. The vast expansion required by the war created many specialists and few professional seamen. Remarkably, standards of performance suffered little.

Fulton in Saipan earned a special nickname. Submarine tenders at advance bases had access to steaks and no booze; the hospitals on the beach had nurses with access to booze and few steaks. It was not uncommon for late afternoon motor launch trips to the beach to include a few sailors in clean uniforms carrying $50 and a blanket. A rendezvous could easily be arranged with a female companion carrying a bottle of booze and a need for companionship. On the beach under a canopy of stars they could commune for the night while sharing their various offerings.

Nor did such activities exclude the officers. The "O" Club ashore closed at 1900 each evening—but not completely. A few suites were available for after-hours parties. The beer had been returned to the freezer for another day, but the hard stuff came forth for a round or two by a select few senior submarine officers and their peers in nurses' uniforms. Then they would go back to the ship for some delicious steaks and a movie on deck. Who knows? Maybe they too had offerings over which to commune. The *Fulton* came to be known, in envy perhaps, as the pigboat "Pussy Palace."

As often happens, relaxation of some shipboard standards

encourages relaxation of others. The men deprived of the above-mentioned fringe benefits soon sought alternatives within easier reach. The *Fulton* engine room crew decided that if booze was not available, they would produce their own and have a private gillie party on board. Using a secret formula developed for such occasions, a cabal of sailors began a batch of brandy deep below decks. In a new fifty-five-gallon GI can—trash can to the layman—they concocted a mixture of forty pounds of sugar, raisins, maraschino cherries, yeast, distilled water, and a few other ingredients. After a few days, the lid was soldered on to make it airtight. To get the tropical sun to work its wonders on the mystic brew, when the word was passed through the ship to bring all GI cans topside for airing, the batch was carefully carried up on deck and just as carefully struck below each evening. After a minimum period of aging, the conspirators gathered to reap the reward of their industry. Unfortunately, the chief master-at-arms, the executive officer, and squadron medical officer also descended on the scene, took the culprits into custody, and confiscated the evidence. Somebody had blown the whistle, proving that there is no honor among thieves. The evidence was carefully examined to prove the allegation of manufacture and possession of alcoholic spirits on board. Privately I learned that it tasted delicious and was certainly less harmful than the embalming fluid being passed off as beer at the "O" Club every afternoon.

The rebellious spirit permeating *Fulton* emerged in still another way. One evening shortly before Thanksgiving, when the officers and their covey of invited female guests walked aft for the movie on deck, only three or four enlisted men showed up. No other entertainment was scheduled that evening nor any other activity that could possibly interfere. The chief master-at-arms reported that the men had been ordered not to attend the movie in protest of something by somebody not yet determined. The following morning, only a handful showed up for breakfast. The pattern of planned absence at one meal and the movie was repeated for the next two days. If a reason emerged, it was both unknown and unimportant. By chance, an officer from the Third Marines on Saipan, veteran of several hard-fought island campaigns, happened to come aboard for a social visit. On learning of the sit-down strike in progress, he made an immediate suggestion: "I have any number of men who envy you the soft life on a submarine tender. Find me the leaders and let me administer a bit of discipline for a few days."

Three malcontents were soon produced. At dawn the following morning they began carrying coral from the seashore up to the division camp, then late that afternoon began carrying it all back down again. They lived off Marine rations and in two days prayed for return to their ship. The protest was over; I never learned the cause. Yet I developed a fondness for the *Fulton* and the great job she was doing to keep the submarines on the line. Perhaps my feeling was only anticipatory—sixteen years later I was to command her, the first tender to be equipped to make nuclear repairs in the new atomic Navy.

The duty in Saipan offered a fascinating interlude, but I was anxious to get back to a submarine. My departure from *Fulton* came as hastily as my arrival. The USS *Atule* arrived alongside on 2 December, just a month after I had left *Sterlet*. Her exec, Richard H. "Dick" Bowers, a year senior to me, had orders for immediate detachment to command the USS *Sea Cat*. I was nominated to relieve him. I had heard the rumor late the night before but received my orders only forty minutes before *Atule* was due to go to sea. In a wild rush to clear up all the accounts on the tender, recover my laundry, dry cleaning, and pay records, and complete the myriad details necessary to get detached, I threw my gear on board *Atule* with only a few moments for a turnover with Dick. Fortunately, he had every possible detail ready for my scrutiny. We had spent an hour or so the night before "just in case." He, of course, was just as hot to get detached and off the ship. One can imagine the turmoil. As he walked up the accommodation ladder to the tender, the mooring lines already taken in, the engines idling, I shouted one last question: "Wait, Dick; what's the destination?"

"Majuro," he replied from the top of the ladder.

This may be one of the few times when the navigator of a warship doesn't know the destination two seconds before departure. There are words to describe my reaction to duty on *Atule*, but I don't know them. I was elated to be back aboard a submarine, and I had lucked out on a great one.

Her skipper, Commander John H. "Jason" Maurer, Naval Academy '35, had a fine reputation. A Washingtonian, his dad was a professor of international law at Georgetown University. *Atule* was Jason's first command; previously he had served with the distinguished Samuel D. Dealey in the *Harder* and helped compile an enviable record. Dealey had been lost when *Harder* was sunk by a minesweeper on 24 August 1944 after sinking sixteen ships totaling fifty-four thousand tons, including four destroyers and two frigates. Maurer had departed not long before that date for command of *Atule,* a new construction boat from Portsmouth, named for a Hawaiian fish.

I soon met the department heads in "the Fighting O'Toole," the engineer, Lt. Cmdr. Sidney W. Thaxter, a prominent New England attorney; gunnery, torpedoes and TDC operator Lt. Hollis F. "Tony" Church, another New Englander and an engineer in civil life; Lt. Jack W. Hudson, a Texan; and Lts. (j.g.) Charles N. Pettit, an Iowan, Fred A. Oyhus from Montana, and Glenn O. Olson, an Oklahoma oilman. *Atule* was in the latter stages of her first war patrol during which she sank the pride of the Japanese merchant service, the huge *Asama Maru* of 16,975 tons, on her maiden attack, plus a freighter and two destroyers, totaling 26,000 tons. After topping off on fuel in Saipan, her destination was the new refit base at Majuro, a coral atoll and lagoon in the Marshalls just four hundred miles north of the equator.

Celestial navigation in that exotic part of the world was a delight. I found adventure picking my way through the southern constellations. The southern latitudes have fewer clouds and more brilliant stars hanging low in the heavens than the northern skies. Guiding us through the tropical waters, they added calm and serenity to my Kantian "contemplation of the starred heavens." Relaxing on the bridge, the gleam of the astral diamonds mirrored on the calm sea, created the feeling of being suspended at the center of a spatial universe, our phosphorescent wake astern a celestial contrail across the cosmic vastness. Entranced, I was inspired one clear night to try to shoot every navigational star and planet in the heavens. Of the 110 listed in the almanac, I believe I shot fifty-five stars, the moon, and three planets. The navigational plot made a striking picture.

Admiral Charlie Lockwood chose Majuro as an advance refit base shortly after the capture of the Marshall Islands and personally picked Myrna Island in the atoll for the submariners. The vast lagoon inside the ring of coral islands could accommodate several fleets. Its narrow entrance passage to the open sea was easily defensible against penetration by a hostile submarine, and a Japanese air or surface attack in this remote area was no longer possible. The highest point in the islands reared only about fifteen feet above sea level. This caused one minor variation in personal habits. To minimize any possible source of water pollution from human waste, some medical authority decreed that solid and liquid waste could not be excreted together; urine was to go down some pipes at one spot, feces at another. Only a bit of thought was required and we were happy to pay this small price for a passport to paradise.

The lush growth of coconut palms, breadfruit, papaya, and dozens of other tropical delights made it impossible for anyone to starve even without tapping the abundance of the surrounding ocean. At night the trade winds provided a constant breeze, and the starry skies were so bright they looked artificial. Sleep, with the rolling surf just outside the cabin, was heavenly.

Before I could even take a look around, however, I almost had to pack up and leave. Just after our departure from Saipan, orders came through for me to go to USS *Batfish* as exec, and on arrival in Majuro a message was waiting for the skipper to nominate either me or Sid Thaxter for the job. Jason didn't want me to go, and he felt that Sid was not fully qualified. After much haggling, he finally won out with the big boss; neither of us went. But that still left the problem of seniority. I mentioned to the CO that Bert Rodier in *Scorpion* had been senior to me and it caused no problem, nor should it with Sid. Sid agreed, and when his promotion came through, he delayed accepting it so as to avoid the problem of being senior not just in date of rank but in wearing an additional stripe on his sleeve. And I was glad to have him aboard. A Harvard lad, gregarious and well traveled, he might not have been the greatest engineer, but there was plenty of talent around. Off the ship I found him congenial and a fine tennis player. His sister, Phyllis Thaxter, was a rising movie star, but Hollywood to us then meant a scratchy, often spliced, second-rate movie each night, usually starring a horse.

The first day in Majuro, Tony Church and I chose an uninhabited island in the atoll for some target practice. Tony was an ardent shooter, carrying his own piece. We had fun knocking down coconuts—green and just the right season for drinking the milk. Beautiful tropical birds fluttered all around; we aimed only at seagulls and never came close. Then I went fishing for several hours, noting much too late that my half-inch of hair gave far too little protection to my scalp. The blazing sun soon made my head feel like a safety valve trying to lift. Then, back at the club, the drinks were flowing, leaving me tired and sleepy. I walked down to the beach for a midnight swim in the warm, phosphorescent water under a sky full of stars. When I finally turned in, for the first time in my life I slept through breakfast. Bunks were made up and decks scrubbed, and I still snoozed my life away. Never had I slept better or longer.

Christmas 1944 was approaching, and several sacks of gifts arrived. In this area one didn't wait until Christmas Day to open them. Where mold, mildew, rust, and baggage smashers were constant enemies, one salvaged what he could immediately, sharing the wealth with the less fortunate. Since no mail could catch up with me for quite a while—already I hadn't heard from Henri in three months—the other officers made up Christmas presents for me. A three-month-old *Time* magazine without wrapper was deeded to me, plus two totally useless official letters from the Bureau of Ordnance, some new charts of the Atlantic from the Hydrographic Office, a coconut, and a stack of outgoing mail to be censored. It was great fun; all I could say was that when Easter came I would have all sorts of Christmas gifts and they would have forgotten theirs.

My real Christmas came a few days later, when Jason and I were invited to visit the island on the far side of the atoll, where the natives lived. Several times each year, the Red Cross made inspection tours of the islands. They invited two sub skippers and their execs to join. With us were Gordon W. Underwood, CO of *Spadefish,* and his XO, Theodore M. "Ted" Ustick, a Naval Academy classmate of mine. The visit was a step back into a past era. The way of life had changed little over the years, influenced only slightly by visits from missionaries encouraging somewhat more extensive use of clothing.

From about the age of puberty all the males moved into a bachelor pad outside the village, the girls to another on the other side. Ties with the families continued, but the main stress seemed to be a preliminary to choosing a mate. Every male had sexual relations with every female of his age group within wide limits. As a result, yaws, a tropical variation of syphilis, was widespread.

As we walked from the boat landing toward the village, Ted and I passed the local laundry—four or five women under a tree beating clothes with sticks. They were just across the path, Main Street, and I watched with a curious eye. One young belle looked in my direction, quite coyly I thought. She began using her charms, including lowering her dress to bare a small, shapely breast, which she waggled at me shyly. Could it have looked other than shapely to us warriors so long removed from society? I nudged Ted, but as soon as he looked she called off the show and became a prim maiden again. He claimed that she recognized he meant business. I thought the incident, in the town square at high noon, was quite seductive.

At noon the villagers assembled in the town center to sell the trinkets they had made since the last market day. The king of Majuro presided, paying each inhabitant in turn what he judged the curios were worth. To his left sat the king of Wotje, a neighboring atoll, who had been driven from his kingdom by the conquering Japanese early in the war. Both looked very dignified in silk top hats, shorts, and spats over shiny hightop shoes. Some of the articles were crude, but many showed high skills and would bring good money when marketed by the Civil Affairs Committee in Honolulu.

Meanwhile, the *Atule* refit was going very well. Walter L. Small, a year my senior and a longtime friend, was the temporary CO. The day we got back from the native island, Walt had a surprise set of orders to command *Sterlet*. We had a long chat about the boat; I assured him he was very lucky, but I hoped Joe and Gene were still aboard. Bill Jameson, who had left *Sterlet* after the near drowning incident, was in Majuro on his new boat and heartily seconded my enthusiasm. For some reason, however, Walt never got the boat; it was given to Hugh H. Lewis, a reserve officer, the first to get a frontline command.

The stay in Majuro gave me the chance to indulge in my love of flying. The naval aviators on another island in the atoll arranged for me to fly a combat mission to dump some explosives on several of the Japanese held islands bypassed in the campaign across the central Pacific and now slowly dying for lack of logistic support. In an old gull-winged PBY flying boat, the birdmen showed me a very scenic trip. The last island we flew over was Wotje. I decided to drop a special calling card from the king on the invaders and, like Gulliver, used the only weapon at hand. I urinated on it.

Christmas really arrived when the long-delayed mail reached me, my first letters from home in many moons. Pictures of the family and lots of news about Henri and our parents made a wonderful gift. I had barely finished devouring them when it was time for the eggnog party at the club. It took quite a number of storage eggs to find enough good ones, but the result justified the effort. Then many of us went to midnight mass on the tender, an inspiring sight under the stars with a thousand men singing the familiar Christmas carols. The padre, a stirring speaker, had been in the forward areas with the Marines. His vestments were stained with rust, mildew, and vestiges of five shades of mud, which no amount of laundering would ever remove. Perhaps it only added to the drama of the message he delivered. Jason and I went together, and for the first time in many months I finally felt I had recovered my normally rosy outlook on life. The war was far off; I felt totally at peace with the world.

The time had come to go to sea again. The workup went very well. The new attack team stood out in intensive training exercises of a new type—with a wolfpack in coordinated action against a convoy. I felt I should have done a much better job during those hard, hard days and nights, but overall I felt satisfied. More important, I gained great respect for the skipper's ability, and my personal liking for him increased as well. We worked together like a charm, a detail noted most enthusiastically by the division commander, who rode with us as chief observer.

For her second patrol, *Atule*, with *Pompon, Jallao,* and *Spadefish*, became part of "Underwood's Urchins," Group Commander Gordon Underwood in *Spadefish*. We departed Majuro on 6 January 1945, and events started off with a bang. Less than six hours out of port, while traveling in a total bombing restricted lane, *Spadefish* was bracketed by two aerial bombs from low-flying TBMs (Navy torpedo dive bombers) and made a quick dive. *Pompon,* next in line, also dived, but to prevent a tragedy, *Atule* tried to exchange recognition signals, finally succeeding by the time the range closed to half a mile. *Spadefish* soon surfaced and announced that only his spirit had been damaged.

The period at sea gave me some much needed time to adapt the *Atule* training program to my style. I was fortunate in having a very capable predecessor to set up the organization. But Dick Bowers used far more personal control than I. I favored making training the direct responsibility of the department heads and division officers, who after all were involved with the new men on a day-to-day basis. I talked to the men about their submarine qualification if they fell behind; but I prodded the department officers and petty officers to monitor progress. The ideal was to train the junior officers to do my job as well as their own and to do both so well that the ship ran smoothly in my absence. Then I had extra time to write letters to my beloved Henri and our children. On only this last point did I find any divergence with Jason.

The captain admitted to a very convenient superstition. He didn't write to his wife, Billie, while at sea. She agreed as long as he came back. Since we were both convinced that we'd survive the war, everybody seemed to be happy. Long ago Reggie Raymond tried to convert me to his system. Reggie wrote no long letters, stressing numbers rather than tonnage. Marge preferred opening letters at various times to enjoy each individually. If he wrote long letters, she was apt to read them hastily and without the intensity given a short missive. I was impressed with both schools but continued to write at sea as the urge or opportunity arose. My only regret was the requirement for censorship, which eliminated from discussion much of the life on board a submarine and its highly colorful devotees.

The other task I customarily worked at en route to a new area was a strategic estimate of what to expect and how to get the best area coverage. For the current destination in the Yellow Sea–East China Sea, I had an additional advantage of having made a previous patrol there in *Scorpion*. The major shipping centers were Shanghai, Tsingtao, Dairen (Port Arthur), Seoul, Nagasaki, and Shimonoseki. Shipping lanes ran from Formosa and the South China Sea, along the China coast to Shanghai, from Indonesia and the Philippines through the Nansei Shoto Islands to Nagasaki, and from the Japan Sea through the Straits of Tsushima to Nagasaki. Analysis of tonnages, seasonal variations, strategic cargoes, and enemy naval and air activity were made from intelligence material on hand (before destroying it on entering salvageable waters), from the operation order, and from intelligence briefings before departure. With this background, the captain and I were able to derive a plan for area coverage; it is interesting that for every patrol I made, the area coverage and development of the resources received favorable comment by Commander Submarines. The only exception was the *Scorpion* Yellow Sea patrol when Bill Wylie left the area prematurely after the grounding.

On 14 January, radar landfall was made on Anatahan Island at 45 miles, and shortly before noon the "Urchins" moored alongside *Fulton* in Tanapag Harbor for an overnight fuel stop. On departure the following morning, USS *Bang* and USS *Devilfish* joined the formation in place of *Pompon* and *Jallao*, who were delayed. On the second day out, Commander Submarines reported a life raft with a single occupant near our track ahead. Closing the position at high speed, we soon located a yellow oxygen bottle with heavy marine growth, indicating a long time in the water. A second amplifying report placed the raft 60 miles closer, with three survivors, one wounded. At the new location at 1744, we fired a green rocket and commenced a search. At 1819 a third report placed the raft 120 miles to the northeast. Temporarily abandoning the search, we headed north to rejoin the Urchins, but a half hour later received new instructions to search for twenty-four hours at the scene of the first reported contact. We turned back at high speed, and an all-night run put the ship again in position, only to be instructed to abandon the search. The position of the survivors was never accurately established, unfortunately, and lives may have been lost for lack of navigational data.

Something happened that surprised me after I joined *Atule*. Always a light sleeper, I suddenly began sleeping like a log. On one occasion the diving alarm six feet from my head failed to rouse me; I even had to be called a couple of times for morning stars. And for no apparent reason, I felt my performance as navigator and personnel administrator was not up to my standards. Small mistakes I had never made before bothered me considerably because I could find no reason for them. I knew I was trying to do my best to reflect the confidence Jason had in me. It was a long time before I recovered my customary zip.

At noon on 19 January, fifteen B-29s passed by on their way north. The wolfpack commander established VHF contact with them, and we each manned the lifeguard frequency for the next six hours in case our airborne brothers needed assistance. The skies were full of aircraft, and the voice radio became more and more important. Increasing numbers of aircraft of all descriptions were being detected by radar, radar receiver, or visually, and we had great difficulty in identifying friend from foe. Jason and I asked Fred Oyhus, the radar officer and an electronic genius, what could be done. Few submarines used the air search radar anymore because it acted like a beacon to enemy fliers. The Japanese homed in on the signal with seeming ease. I wanted to know why we had to put out a continuous radar signal. Why couldn't the radar be keyed, somehow, to send out a short pulse, for example, just enough to see if a plane was within range but not long enough to give him a homing signal?

Fred, a true scientist, answered any technical question with a "Yes" or a "Yes, but" and then outlined the price to be paid for the desired result. After some thought, he said it could be done, but the major problem would be to make the blip visible on such a short signal. It might be necessary to soup up the voltage on the radar screen to increase its image retentivity. The incidental problem of illegally modifying shipboard equipment Jason and I dismissed as tomorrow's concern. True to his word, Fred disappeared into the pump room to emerge a few days later with the new gadget. The souped-up screen worked well. To protect the operator's eyesight Fred added a tinted screen over the radarscope. Now, instead of a steady outgoing signal, the radar transmitted a single pulse of eight microseconds. The results were encouraging and seemed immune to enemy receivers. A more sophisticated version soon became standard throughout the force.

Late in the afternoon on 20 January the Urchins transited Nansei Shoto, the island chain dominated by Okinawa, then headed north past Nagasaki to enter the assigned patrol area. Sampans and junks cluttered the seas, plus an occasional patrol craft lying to or searching at low speed. An effective periscope search became difficult. At sunset on 23 January, *Atule* headed north along the coast of Korea for a daylight submerged patrol off Chopekki Point—where *Scorpion* had grounded so many months before. Just before the group commander ordered the Urchins to continue patrolling this area until 27 January. The weather, meanwhile, caused increasing difficulties for the topside watchstanders. Snow flurries fell throughout the day, and our Majuro suntans faded quickly as the hunt went on for warm clothing. The temperature had fallen sixty degrees in two days and I felt great. The air had a snap to it, and I could feel it singing through my system. I spent hours on the bridge, but as Jack noted, "You can go below when the snow and sleet falls; we get to enjoy it up here for four hours out of every twelve."

Celebrating the frosty weather in the wardroom, the chef and our fine stewards put on a special meal. I added the background with one of our new recordings on the large discs prepared for the armed services—slow speed, half an hour per side. It was a special Christmas performance with good music and comedians Fred Allen, Jack Benny, W. C. Fields, Bob Hope, Jimmy Durante, and others. We laughed hard and often. *This* was my idea of a gentleman's club.

The following day at 1500, however, our blood began to flow a bit more warmly when a maru was sighted to the east at 21,000 yards, unescorted, heading west at eight knots. When the range closed to 16,000 yards, we dived and commenced a periscope approach. The enemy soon disappeared in a snow squall, but, broaching shallow enough to expose the radar, we headed in for a bow shot. The enemy was seen to be very light in the water, so Jason decided to try a stern tube shot using the electric torpedoes for better depth control at a shallow, three-foot depth setting. At 1658, we fired four torpedoes at a range of 720 yards, small gyro angles, from a position just abaft his beam. Jason watched two torpedoes hit, the first abreast his stack, the second near his mainmast. The enemy was an engines-aft medium freighter, described at the time as "new as a 1945 dime." It was in fact the mint-new 6,688-ton *Taiman Maru No. 1*, heavily compartmented for maximum defense against torpedo attack. She settled rapidly by the stern; the survivors manned two motor lifeboats launched from the fantail with great speed. Both boats cleared the heavily damaged tail section just as it broke off and disappeared from view with a rending and tearing heard throughout the ship. The forward half popped up like a cork, appearing little the worse for wear despite loss of the working end of the ship.

Atule opened to three thousand yards and surfaced to give the men a look and to finish off the wreck with gunfire. With the bridge force up and ballast tanks partially blown, the target suddenly came to life with well-directed 40-mm gunfire from mounts near his bridge structure. Sightseers dived for the hatch as Jason cleared the bridge, then fired one steam torpedo from the bow tube nest. The "tin fish" broached repeatedly as it steamed toward the enemy, passing just under his bow. With 40-mm shells bursting like giant firecrackers to the right, left, and ahead, it seemed prudent to retire hastily and plan the next phase of the action. We cleared the area and circled to the northwest to put the hulk up moon, then headed in after dark to try the deck gun.

On a dark and bitterly cold night, stations were manned at 2055 for gun action. The deck was covered with ice, and the gunservers had difficulty toting shells from the ready locker to the gun. The target was beautifully silhouetted in the moonstreak, and at six thousand yards, the captain's command rang out across the still waters: "COMMENCE FIRING."

Nothing happened. The ice-covered firing mechanism was frozen and the safety pin inoperative. One shot was finally kicked out by hand. The target began blinking a signal light to westward, perhaps to an arriving escort or salvage vessel. The gun crews were ordered below. When the range closed to five thousand yards, the ship went to battle stations torpedo. Closing to one thousand yards we fired one more steam torpedo, set to run at three feet, a straight shot on his starboard beam. The torpedo again porpoised along the surface but ran straight and true for a hit amidships, or better, a hit in the middle of what was left of the ship. This hit, just forward of his bridge structure, vented a few more bulkheads and started the hulk down by the bow on its final plunge, the bridge rearing into the night sky before settling into the depths. The ship was empty, with good damage control, and tough to sink. Sailing on her maiden voyage, she got less than fifty miles from her home port of Inchon, Korea, when her short but interesting career came to an end. *Atule* cleared the area on the surface, retiring to the north, then set course to return to Chopekki Point.

By midnight the radio antennae were heavily coated with ice several inches thick. Diving at dawn to clear the ice off the topside, we surfaced after breakfast on a brilliantly clear, cold day to patrol the traffic lanes across the northern Yellow Sea. From the high periscope watch while we were on the surface, one could see almost the entire upper Yellow Sea. Many fishing floats and much debris cluttered the water, but a heavy blizzard soon struck with remarkable suddenness and nothing could be seen.

The following day, 26 January, we surfaced in midmorning in bitter cold, with heavy snow near blizzard strength whistling through the bridge. Just before noon, the horizon suddenly cleared, revealing the Shantung Peninsula on the Chinese mainland. We closed to the twenty-fathom curve, noted the water change from light green to yellowish brown, and turned south before it shoaled further. The wind at twenty-five to thirty knots drove flurries of snow and sleet through every crevice in one's clothing. The topside began icing heavily from freezing salt spray.

The charts of the China coast were inadequate, with many unexplored areas left totally blank. The muddy water looked suspicious. I wanted to take a sun sight to check the latitude and notified my quartermaster to meet me on the bridge. Chief Charles Birck arrived topside wearing a heavy parka, fur helmet, galoshes, and heavy mittens; I arrived in my usual below-deck wear—open-toed sandals and skivvy shorts. One thing I had mastered from the *Sterlet* was the necessity for speed in celestial navigation in a submarine. At that precise moment, however, Jason wanted to take pictures of our snow-covered exterior. The photos looked good, except for one individual seemingly at ease in a totally inappropriate costume. I didn't learn for many years that the bridge watch was mightily impressed by the new exec and his "fastest sextant in the west."

Throughout the afternoon several fishing trawlers were sighted, all heading for the lee of Shantung. That night we wished we had too. Diving again to clear the ice from the topside, we surfaced into a pooping sea, almost rolling the bridge under from aft. In the heavy column of water pouring down the hatch came a fish, three feet long, trying to fight his way into the galley fry-pan unaided. The hatch was pulled shut before much water was taken in, but the temperature was dropping and the gale winds, straight out of Siberia, drove icicles of snow into every crevice. Officially, it was a nasty night.

The following evening, a report of a convoy, received from *Pompon* three hours late, set us on the chase at four-engine speed. With characteristic suddenness the seas abated, and a full moon cast cold shadows on the dying whitecaps. Just before midnight, *Pompon* corrected his position report, adding that both he and *Spadefish* were attacking from the starboard flank. We should have made contact, but not until 0230 was smoke sighted to the south. We headed to intercept at flank speed before he reached the sanctuary of shoal water. Explosions echoed in the distance. At 0250 a terrific explosion blew a column of water high enough in the air to create a saturation-strength radar pip at sixteen miles.

At 0302 we made radar contact on a ship to the east at 19,200 yards, a medium transport attempting to clear the scene of the attack toward the western shoals. A few minutes later, we dived in his track at 16,000 yards. The enemy was clearly visible to the naked eye. At 0340, sonar reported distant echo ranging. An escort was apparently rushing in to rejoin the formation. To get in an attack before the escort arrived, we went in at full speed, but, five minutes later, the target changed course to the north and the escort was sighted coming up on his port quarter. When the range to the target had decreased to 5,000 yards, the escort closed to 1,500 yards, slowed, stopped pinging, and took a sounding. This made me uneasy. If his concern was about the depth of water, how did he think I felt about ours? Or worse, perhaps he was merely determining how shallow to set his depth charges. We couldn't even risk a sounding. When he resumed pinging, our sonar operator reported that he was developing contact. At this time we were directly ahead of him, trying to cross his bow to get between him and the target. Crossing the bow of an alerted escort at 1,000 yards is neither wise nor healthy, particularly in less than ninety feet of water. We eased toward him to reduce the silhouette slightly and to attack from abaft the transport's beam, but the escort continued on a near collision course as the transport passed within the safety of the ten-fathom bank. Stymied, we couldn't overtake him before dawn, nor could we hazard an attack on the surface.

As soon as he drew clear, we surfaced, just after dawn. The approach had taken us five miles inside the twenty-fathom curve, in uncharted water much too shallow for minimum maneuverability submerged. Immediately, a new column of heavy smoke could be seen on the horizon to the southeast. We headed toward it at flank speed, hoping to find a cripple from the attacks by our wolfpack partners. An hour later, calls were exchanged by radar with both *Pompon* and *Spadefish*. The smoking ship was burning fiercely throughout most of her length, *Spadefish* standing by her victim. Wishing her luck, we cleared the scene and returned to our assigned area, picking the way carefully through patrol craft and trawlers returning from the melee. Wreckage of a small wooden vessel and a floating raft were noted, indicating earlier submarine successes in these waters.

On 29 January, we crossed the Great Yangtze Bank thirty miles southwest of Socotra Rock, and a new phenomenon entered our catalog of concerns. Shortly after breakfast a floating mine was spotted, apparently torn loose from its mooring cable. Two ammo pans from the 20-mm failed to detonate or sink it. The patrol report for the rest of the day read:

1043 Detonated mine with 30 cal. machine gun fire.
1110 Sank mine with 30 cal. machine gun.
1145 Sank mine with 30 cal. machine gun.
1315 Sank mine with 20mm.
1435 Sank mine with 20mm . . .
2352 Floating mine was avoided by Officer of the Deck. Passed thirty feet off the starboard beam. . . .
0030 Floating mine bounced disconcertingly down the port side of the ship, plainly heard by bridge watch and officers in the wardroom.

These were moored, contact mines which, according to the Geneva Convention, were supposed to disarm if they broke free of their moorings. When the mines were encountered at sea, many questions came to mind. Did the Japanese observe the Geneva Convention? Even so, if a mine had a great length of cable when it carried away, would a defusing mechanism still work? If a mine had three inches of barnacles or moss on it, could one still have faith enough to bet his life on the disarming mechanism working properly? We were soon to learn that about half detonated when hit by gunfire. What about those we didn't see, as when cruising on the surface at night?

The mines were not toys. The Japanese had planted one of the largest fields in history trying to protect their shipping against marauding U.S. submarines. One of the most heavily mined areas was the trade route from Nagasaki to Shanghai, the area we were then patrolling. Here *Scorpion* and *Escolar* were lost, most probably to mines. *Swordfish* was lost to a mine off Okinawa where *Sterlet* made her close-in rescue of the Moose. Could we expect to operate for a month in a heavily mined area and totally disregard that they were in place solely to counter the submarine threat?

The mines were spherical, about thirty inches in diameter, with four to six horns visibly protruding from the upper surfaces. A rolling, pitching submarine with only an open sight against an almost wholly submerged target had to move in close, to seventy-five or a hundred yards, and allow a team of sharpshooters to cut loose. If the mine detonated and the big orange ball appeared, all hands ducked behind the bridge fairing and got drenched with icy water and hot mine fragments. What would happen in the dark of night when they couldn't be seen? The answer to that question was not long in doubt.

The red outlines of known mined areas on the chart coincided closely with our patrol area. Probably the mines were set deep enough to catch a submerged sub and not shallow enough to be struck by surface shipping. Therefore it seemed wise to stay on the surface when possible. It was hardly necessary to remind the bridge watch to become doubly alert. Apparently the contractor who supplied the Japanese with mooring cable for their mines unloaded some lousy goods on the Imperial Navy. Every storm passing through the area tore many loose to float to the surface as new hazards.

A few days of fruitless patrol off Nagasaki created a new challenge for Fred Oyhus. *Atule* had no steerable unit on the surface radar such as I had used so effectively in *Sterlet* to search inside of harbors and anchorages while we steamed several miles offshore. When I asked Fred if he could make one at sea, this remarkable officer had it in full operation in only a few hours. Thus equipped, we headed west hoping for better pickings off the China coast and the unknown mud flats close inshore off Shanghai, hoping to intercept north-bound traffic en route to Japan.

The weather again worsened, with heavy winds, sleet, and snow driving in from the north. When the seas abated, the mines reappeared in our track, torn loose by the storm. Thirteen more were sighted, five of which were exploded and seven sunk by gunfire. The last one of the day passed close aboard, but minesweeping operations had to be canceled because of darkness. We were within the known mined area south and west of Daikokuzan Gunto, and Japanese shipping apparently avoided the area.

On the morning of 6 February, while we were on the surface, an Emily bomber broke through a low overcast at three miles, five hundred feet astern. We dived, receiving a light bomb while passing ninety feet. Surfacing shortly after in a heavy snow squall, we headed for a new patrol area off the south coast of Korea, looking for traffic transiting the Straits of Tsushima. The steerable unit on the radar showed the anchorage off Amba Gunta to be all clear. Local navigational lights were burning normally, suggesting that inter-island shipping might be moving through the area. Then at 0751, nine depth charges exploded not far off, all dropped in quick succession by an unseen, unknown enemy. Nothing further developed.

Occasional patrol vessels and big antisubmarine patrol bombers were encountered over the next few days. One of the bombers appeared to be tracking us using magnetic MAD search equipment. With another storm swirling about, *Atule* dived to enjoy lunch on plates instead of in our laps. As we prepared to surface, the OOD noted a bomber circling at a thousand feet altitude. Two hours later, another bomber was noted circling inside of two miles. Even in very poor visibility these planes apparently could track us successfully with the MAD gear. Heavy air and surface patrols and no shipping told their story; we decided to try the China coast for better hunting.

On the surface at 1337 on 12 February, Charlie Pettit on the high periscope watch detected a destroyer heading westerly at about twenty thousand yards, zigzagging on five-minute legs at a speed of ten knots. When the range closed to sixteen thousand yards, the enemy headed directly toward us and increased speed. Then the quartermaster suddenly saw a dive bomber coming out of the clouds on the starboard bow, heading in for an attack. Because the cloud cover was low and broken, double aircraft lookouts had been posted. Making a steep dive off four engines put some heavy traffic down the hatch for a few moments. Two well-placed bombs shook us up, one as we passed 75 feet, the other at 125 feet on his second pass.

This appeared to be a coordinated "man and boy" attack team, except that the airman jumped the gun just a bit. When the destroyer closed our diving position, he began echo ranging. We tried to clear the area at eight knots to prevent his making contact. Three hours later he was still searching. In the shallow water, he thought he had something. He made three attacks at twenty-minute intervals, dropping five depth charges on each attack. He appeared to be attacking and reattacking the spot where we had dived, or possibly a wreck on the bottom. It is easy to believe that there is no such thing as a distant depth charge, but none of these fell close.

By dark we were well clear. On surfacing, we immediately noted a strong enemy aircraft signal on the radar detector, driving us back down as two explosions rattled the deck plating aft.

Returning to the China coast on 14 February, we heard distant explosions that continued throughout the day. Surfacing at 1917, we received a report from a China-based plane of a battleship force to the south. This seemed unlikely, but we headed toward it on three engines, detouring to detonate three mines and sink a fourth. At 1550, we dived for a Nell bomber on the starboard beam at five miles, heading in with bomb bay doors open. No bombs were dropped, but an hour later he was still circling overhead. After dark we tried to make up for lost time but the following day, Naval Group China had no further information. This group, the Sino-American Cooperative Organization or SACO, under Commodore Milton E. "Mary" Miles, USN, was based in Chungking, China. The colorful Miles served under Chinese Communist General Tai Li and frequently traveled through China disguised as a Buddhist monk. A senior submariner on the staff coordinated intelligence for the subs and assisted in providing rescue services by the subs for downed aviators.

Bang and *Sunfish* were in the area also groping for information. Surfacing at 1845, we avoided a mine dead ahead and turned north at flank speed toward a new position on the enemy task force, arriving off Saishu To Island at dawn for submerged patrol. On surfacing that evening, we continued north at flank speed toward the enemy.

At 0127 a mine was struck flush on the bow with a jar heard and felt throughout the ship, turning out a good percentage of the crew. The sound of a thousand-pound (explosive) sledgehammer hitting a steel hull is not soon forgotten. After the first impact, it bounced several times down the side, busily exploring limber holes with its horns. When heartbeats returned to normal, a quick survey showed no obvious damage. Then *Sunfish* returned us to the other war with a contact report on three ships, which we soon located 11 miles to the north. The three ships were apparently two destroyers and a patrol craft heading east at nineteen knots. At this time *Sunfish* was ten to twelve miles west of *Atule*, and *Bang* to the southwest. None of us was in position to make an attack, hence we patrolled across the track in hope that the destroyers were sweeping ahead of the battleships and cruiser. No other contact could be developed, and the futile 850-mile pursuit was abandoned. Time in the area having expired, *Atule* also headed for the exit. We were not to leave, however, without a few parting shots by unfriendly air.

Before transiting the Okinawa chain, we were forced to dive several times, once by a Betty bomber coming out of a low overcast at five hundred feet, three thousand yards away. Thirty seconds later, while still at forty feet, a very close bomb rattled the ship from stem to stern. This was the third time during this patrol that we were bombed by airmen coming in low and close during low visibility. In no case did we have contact on the radar receiver, suggesting a MAD search or enemy use of a higher-frequency radar not covered by our equipment. Even Fred Oyhus couldn't offer much help. When I requested an omnifrequency detector, his "Yes, but" indicated that the equipment would fill the whole control room and part of the conning tower.

At 0500 on 26 February, *Atule* again moored alongside *Fulton* in Saipan. After a quick fuel stop, course was set for Midway, where we arrived for refit at 0940, 7 March. Standing with the dignitaries awaiting our arrival was a tall lieutenant, his Irish visage rising above the crowd, a wide grin almost disappearing into an unruly shock of gray-black hair. It was none other than Ed Skeehan, whom *Sterlet* had left behind after his accident with a pot of boiling coffee. Ed had recovered completely and even managed to steal some home leave in Pittsburgh while recuperating, bringing firsthand news of Henri and our families. We also learned, to our great delight, that Ed was to be in charge of the *Atule* refit. In record time we were clear of the ship and off to the Gooneyville Tavern for a beverage and a bull session—the proper way to start any refit.

Ed was a superb example of a wartime reserve officer, highly successful in business, a volunteer for submarines and hot to get into combat at an age when his civilian accomplishments could have guaranteed him a position of responsibility in a more sedentary role in the war effort. He was immediately accepted by the "Fighting O'Toole," and we began scheming to get him aboard for duty.

A stack of back mail caught up with me, and I soon begged off to get to my room at the Gooneyville Lodge for a bit of privacy. And a splendid room it was—freshly decorated corner room with large windows and french doors opening onto a balcony. Overhanging fir trees made it cool and shady by day and wonderful for sleeping at night. Midway is blessed with gorgeous weather most of the year, and we were soon back at the daily sports ritual.

Commander Submarines congratulated the ship for an aggressive, tenacious attack which sent the new maru to the bottom on 23 January and credited the killing to *Atule*'s scorecard. The tonnage of floating mines—twenty-three sunk and two struck by the ship out of twenty-nine encountered—wasn't included but added additional color to the battle flag. Our experience in hitting the mine stimulated an excellent cartoon, framed and mounted in the submarine force operations center in Pearl, our hair standing on end. More seriously, the increasing hazard of mines in submarine operating areas caused considerable head-scratching.

I hoped, while in Midway, to get some news of my chances for command. Several members of my Naval Academy class had been given command of fleet submarines, but they were old boats used for training in the Pacific area or returning to the Atlantic Fleet for the same thing. Many of us '39ers had borne the brunt of the war, and the high command feared that too many would be burned out by the time we were ready for command. All those with two patrols since a new construction tour were eligible for a system of rotating "school boats," spending half the time in the forward area, half on the West Coast for training the thousands of aviators and surface sailors in new ships and squadrons heading for the war zone. Despite the great attraction of having my own command, my enthusiasm was tempered. I didn't want an old boat running training routines. Execs of new, front-line combatants were an exclusive fraternity, and I didn't want to leave the front until the war was over. In at the start, I planned to be there at the finish.

Just before I joined *Atule*, the personnel bureau asked for volunteers from my class for the Naval Postgraduate School in Annapolis. Fred Clarke, who had been forced to relieve his CO, Frank Acker, on *Pomfret*'s second patrol because of Acker's acute illness, got the best of both worlds. He was given command of *Seal* and very shortly thereafter received orders to postgraduate school. It was a good policy, but again I didn't want shore duty in time of war. The request for volunteers indicated that they wanted to take us off the firing line, but I felt it more important and valuable for me to remain where I was.

There was another factor. As explained by Clay Blair in *Silent Victory* (Philadelphia: Lippincott, 1975, pp. 588–89):

> At Admiral Lockwood's insistence, all fleet boats remained in the hands of Naval Academy graduates for the first three years of the war. He reasoned that reservists, now composing about 50% of all wardrooms, were not nearly so experienced as Academy graduates. Few reservists had held responsible jobs in the boats, such as exec, and Lockwood believed it was unfair to give command to a reservist when able men then serving as execs—from the class of 1939, for example—with five, six, or seven war patrols under their belts (plus two years in peacetime surface forces) were still being denied.

I would miss out on a command to give a reserve officer a chance, so my strong desire for a combat command seemed temporarily thwarted in every direction. When Jason and I talked about it a few days before arrival in Midway, he offered to fly to Pearl to plead my case. I deeply appreciated the offer, and, happy as I was with him in *Atule*, I began to count the days.

On the tennis court I lost a favorite opponent when Sid Thaxter left for surface ships. He realized he had reached his peak in submarines and would be far better employed as a judge advocate somewhere. Jack Hudson fleeted up to his job as engineer and diving officer, where his great talents quickly made him nearly indispensable. Jack also wielded a wicked tennis racket, having held a national ranking while in college. Tennis became our favorite sport, next to beer drinking.

With Sid's departure and the routine transfer of another officer to the relief crew, the path seemed clear, we thought, to get Ed aboard. Jason went to work on it immediately. He was also using his influence toward getting me a command. No plane was available for a flight to Pearl Harbor but a better alternative soon emerged. *Atule*'s next patrol called for outward routing via Guam, where Admiral Lockwood had moved his headquarters. We could talk to the big boss personally on the way through. This would mean staying on the *Atule* for another patrol, and then detachment in Guam or Saipan to wait for a command in the forward area, far preferable to waiting in Pearl Harbor as part of the million or two servicemen now sinking the Hawaiian Islands under their weight.

During the final preparations for sea, we learned that Ed Skeehan would not go with us. Ed had made himself too valuable in his zealous work with the relief crews; others had been waiting longer than he. Despite the best efforts Jason and I could exert, we failed. Ed was broken up, thought he had gotten a bum break, and promised "to be a bad boy." That night the Wild Irishman really hung one on. The highlight occurred when, fueled by some eighty-proof spinach, he tried to emulate Popeye and smash through a wall, leaving his silhouette in the broken plaster. Unfortunately, the Gooneyville Tavern, built to withstand heavy gales roaring across the tiny island, was much more resistant than a Hollywood movie set, and Ed carried the abrasions and bruises for a long time. Shortly thereafter he joined the *Tirante,* another fine boat, and got his wish for a combat patrol. In his stead we got Lt. Earl G. "Woodie" Woodward, an upstate New Yorker who soon proved to be a boon member of the wardroom fraternity. In "real life," Woodie was a restaurateur; wardroom meals soon reached unscaled heights of culinary delight.

Christmas arrived while we were in Midway. A pile of packages chasing me all over the Pacific finally caught up. Their sad condition gave us a lot of laughs but not much else. I was being razzed about a butchering the local barber had given me, leaving only a half-inch of fuzz on top. The first gift I opened was a bottle of hair oil. Since I had no hair to oil, one of the less rude suggestions was to rub it into my navel as they do to babies. All the packages were crushed or broken; several had been rewrapped but were without cards or other identification. A cardboard cylinder of broken glass left us mystified. Two fruitcakes, badly mauled, were OK if a bit rancid. The saltwater taffy from Henri had melted into one large, sticky, gooey wad of tasty paper. Since it reminded me of the many happy times we had enjoyed in Atlantic City back in the *Wichita* era, I enjoyed every chew. A can of cookie crumbs smelled good; we served them under ice cream. The box of dried fruit survived, but ants or little bugs with wings infested them and I had to pitch the mess over the side. The promised box of cookies from my mother hadn't arrived, and—as I write more than forty years later— probably will not.

By the time we were ready to return to the lists again, the progress of the war looked encouraging. The European campaign was nearing its close. In a letter to my wife back in the Iceland days, I had predicted that the "inevitable" war in Europe would last four long years. Now, three and a half years into it, a hot rumor swept Midway that Germany had thrown in the sponge. We all had a big celebration; the radio station on Midway, its puny signal spanning the entire one-mile length and breadth of the island, promised to stay on the air all night waiting for confirmation.

In the Pacific a lot remained to be done. The Japanese were taking a terrible shellacking but still represented a mighty force in the field. Jason and I learned that the campaign against Okinawa would open the day of our departure; plans for the invasion of the Japanese home islands were well in hand, but the Japanese were largely unchecked in China and to the south in Burma and Indochina. The submarines had nearly driven enemy shipping from the seas. What was left was being fought over with the carrier airmen.

The mission for the forthcoming patrol reflected the change in the tide of war. More and more submarines were being allocated to lifeguard services, a role that grew almost by accident and now represented a major morale factor for Army and Navy airmen making flights deep into enemy territory, secure in knowing a friendly submarine would reach them even if it needed keel wheels to drive up on the beach.

Yet sad news from the front always lurked nearby. *Trigger*, which had operated with *Sterlet* in the *Salmon* rescue, was lost with her fine skipper, Dave Connole, a superb officer, and her exec, Johnny Shepherd, my classmate at Annapolis and sub school. Edward Ackerman, one of the first in the class to get a command, went down with his submarine, the USS *Kete*, stopping a torpedo from a Japanese submarine while he was en route to Okinawa. Finally, Layton Goodman had gone down with his ship, the *Barbel*, operating out of Brisbane. Layton had been my Naval Academy roommate, fellow fiddler, and closest friend in the class, and I felt his loss deeply. His mother was a widow, he the only son. I knew his family in Newport News, Virginia, and just couldn't accept the terrible news. For weeks I consoled myself that he might have gotten ashore on one of the many islands in the South Seas. I spent much time after the war investigating some strange happenings at the time of his loss, all to no avail.

Just before our departure, another item long in preparation finally reached completion. The subsolar fix shot during the *Sterlet*'s transit down the coast of Mexico interested the Naval Institute *Proceedings*, but first, security required that I use neither my name, the precise location, nor the name of the ship. For a nom de plume I opted for my first and Reggie's last name, but even that gave problems, so I compromised on Henri's maiden name. As the months rolled by, I finally cleared the galley proofs and sent the final draft off for publication as the last act before we left for sea again.

After the usual farewells on 1 April, Easter Sunday, we were off into the deep blue. Our destination was Bungo Suido, the major entrance to the Inland Sea and the heart of central Japan. The area was just east of my last patrol area in *Sterlet*. I knew it better than the streets of downtown Annapolis. I should have; I spent more time there in two patrols than I ever did in Annapolis in four full years at Canoe U.

The carefree life which Jason and I maintained on the O'Toole brought on a heavy problem. I had gained twenty pounds since leaving the *Sterlet;* other officers were also gaining. The presence of a baker who spent all night turning out a continual stream of pies, cakes, doughnuts, and twenty loaves of fresh bread a day helped the morale of others but destroyed mine.

I do not mean to imply that the war was now a piece of cake. The bitter campaign for Iwo Jima had been fought and won in February. We knew only too well the determination of the Japanese to fight to the death and the need for eternal vigilance. As long as the Allies demanded unconditional surrender, we could see no possibility that the Japanese leaders would give in before total defeat. The war was in its decisive stages, and the savagery with which it was fought on both sides increased rather than decreased.

In the three days before the assault on Iwo Jima on 19 February 1945, Admiral Marc Mitscher's Task Force 58 destroyed 150 Japanese aircraft in strikes against military targets in the Tokyo area. In coordination with the Navy attack, 200 of General Curtis LeMay's B-29 bombers destroyed two square miles of highly inflammable residential areas of Tokyo, killing eighty-four thousand people and wounding forty thousand others. This new phase in the brutality of war, now involving indiscriminate bombing of population centers, was described in a Pacific Fleet intelligence survey that came aboard in Midway. The experience in Europe showed that a factory could be rebuilt in eighteen months but a worker still took eighteen years. The airmen's primary target in the incendiary raids, hence, was the Japanese labor force, the civilian population living in their flimsy wood and paper homes.

I found it difficult to believe that this could be put in print as a deliberate aim of U.S. national policy. I had been educated in parochial schools and saw myself as a man of moral principle. I felt a repugnance in carrying hostilities indiscriminately to women and children. The submarines were conducting a ruthless unlimited war, also involving death of noncombatants in violation of Judeo-Christian standards of morality. But at sea, little else could be done. I thought of these things many times when nuclear arms became weapons of war.

Guam carried a particular fascination. Here Don Giles, my old engineer on the *Wichita,* had started and ended his war on 10 December 1941 and now languished in a Japanese prison camp on Formosa. The new submarine rest camp on

Guam, named Camp Dealey in honor of Jason's former skipper on *Harder,* offered a superb beach and recreational facilities, but occasional Japanese stragglers were still being flushed out of the jungle. The road to Dealey was a massive, slimy mudhole. On a steep hill just before one reached the camp, supplies moved forward only by a continuous tow-chain of large trucks moving down one side and hauling trucks up the other. The transformation of the island into a major fleet base was a logistical miracle. Supply ships arrived by the score, piling up mountains of war supplies of every description. But at the moment, Jason and I were more interested in an evening near the beach with old friends, exchanging war experiences, and perhaps talking of home and family more than anything else.

Atule departed Apra Harbor, Guam, on 12 April en route Bungo Suido. *Gato* shared the patrol area, and by mutual agreement she covered the east entrance to Bungo and the southern coast of Shikoku the first half, *Atule* the western approaches and the coast of Kyushu, then we would switch. Lifeguard missions, nineteen each for *Atule* and *Gato,* necessitated some departure from the plan. In addition, good coverage of the entrances was maintained by both boats throughout the patrol. The Japanese added several hazards—new minefields, submarines in transit and patrolling out of the big base at Kure, and the new MAD-equipped antisubmarine patrols.

Two days out of Guam we were back at our adopted trade. At 0550, 15 April, a mine directly in our track was exploded by gunfire. Then we interrupted the routine at 1300 as all hands observed, with the rest of the fleet, five minutes of silence as a memorial tribute to the late President Franklin D. Roosevelt. He was the only U.S. president to serve during our entire adult lives, a period when the United States had developed from the depths of depression to the most powerful nation in the world, and the Navy in particular had a warm feeling for him.

Late that evening orders arrived for lifeguard station for the following morning, thirty miles to the southeast. We were on station early, and the B-29 air cover, a so-called Superdumbo, appeared at 1120 and exchanged calls. Cruising on the surface at this point in the war produced an electronic nightmare. U.S. fleets of all descriptions, carrier strike forces, battleship groups, amphibious assault groups, antisubmarine forces, underway replenishment groups, countless aircraft, and a continuous bridge of ships of every description from the states to the forward areas drove us electron-happy. With no doctrine for emission control, radar signals saturated our scopes, frequently blanking out whole quadrants in the direction of Okinawa, where the majority of the surface Navy was hard at work. Any hope for an effective electronic search routine became quite wishful. Our new radar receivers detected frequent and strong Japanese emissions from shore stations ringing us from the southwest to the northeast. In a wardroom bull session we put the problem to Fred Oyhus. Fred's earlier modification to the air search radar, to prevent the Japanese homing in on it like a radio beacon, worked fine. Now we needed help against radar saturation from so many ship transmissions that they severely limited our tracking ability. The most likely torpedo target in the Bungo Suido area was a Japanese submarine on patrol or moving in or out of the big Kure naval base.

Could he build a directional receiver that would make it possible to locate and track a Japanese warship passively by "listening" to his radar signals to get us into attack position? Second, could such a directional antenna intercept signals from Japanese shore radar stations for navigational use as an electronic lighthouse?

The first problem concerned us more than a little. The ship spent all day on the surface, easily visible from ashore. Why wouldn't the enemy send a submarine out from the Kure Naval Base to take a potshot at us as we steamed around in circles all day, retreating only a few miles to sea at night until the next call from the birdmen to be back in the same place the following morning? The Japanese at that time were building hundreds of two- or six-man midget submarines in Kure less than a hundred miles away. To make it harder for them to track us, all U.S. subs used extreme zigzag plans that kept the helmsman steering like a madman. But too many of the advantages still favored the enemy.

Fred's resourcefulness met the challenge easily. Out of the pump room soon came a portable reflector and adjustable dipole constructed by some capable machinists under his direction. Looking like a cross between a snow shovel and a TV antenna, "The Thing" was mounted over the Target Bearing Transmitter (TBT) on the bridge with a portable coaxial cable leading down the hatch to the control room. The TBT was then used to transmit bearings to the fire-control system for an attack or to me for navigational purposes. The major objection was the cable running down the hatch, a hazard not every CO would tolerate when enemy aircraft forced us down many times daily, or where a periscope sighting might require an equally quick dive. Yet it worked satisfactorily for navigation; two friendly aircraft were detected, and on the return home, the island of Midway radar station was detected at long range with an accuracy of about fifteen degrees. It was hardly good enough for navigation. A permanent, positive directional antenna system was badly needed. The German U-boats and Japanese I-boats already had directional radar receivers, which they used with excellent success.

For two solid weeks we wore ourselves into a frazzle diving from aircraft or trying to solve the riddle of continuous saturation signals from nearby radar sources. On several occasions dives were made to escape bombers zooming overhead at extremely low altitudes. Why they didn't drop bombs or use machine guns was another riddle. Then, while we were patrolling the coast of Kyushu, the answer to the heavy air activity came to us. We were directly in the path of aircraft raiding Okinawa from airfields in Kyushu and Shikoku; each wave of planes forced us down as they flew overhead going south and on returning northward. So often were we forced down that sometimes we dived at noon just to enjoy a peaceful meal without interruption.

Even with the intensive air activity, mine warfare never ceased. Every day brought a sighting, a sinking, or a scare, and our tally continued to mount. And, thrashing around at night, when the buggers couldn't be seen, where were all those mines we saw by day? If we hit another like that sledgehammer experience in the previous patrol, could we again count on it not to explode? Many of those we saw now were new models, with no growth on them, indicating a very short time in the water. These thoughts were not sleep inducing. Could we have realized it, wise counsel would have suggested, "Patience, you will soon know." Alas, we soon did.

To date our services as lifeguard were unneeded. One possible rescue was chased down in *Gato*'s area without success; *Pogy* beat us to another ditching and rescued ten aviators. A couple of rescued aviators meant a successful patrol. If two subs ever closed the same contact there might be an awful tug-of-war as each tried to be the first to pull a survivor aboard. At 0613 on 4 May, twenty miles south of Ashizuri Light, the port lookout sighted a large enemy submarine on the surface to the south at about eight miles. The seas were rough but the visibility was perfect, allowing the captain, exec, and OOD to verify the enemy character before we dived to attack. We took the normal approach course at full speed, and the first two looks through the periscope showed a radical turn away and an increase in speed to twenty knots. That was all we got from what was to be the one and only ship contact during the patrol.

In the post-mortem, we decided that he either had just surfaced or was trying to gain position ahead of us for an attack. Since we had detected his radar signal on our receiver just at the moment of visual sighting, it seemed more likely that he had just surfaced and, on detecting us, cleared the area to the west at maximum speed. As soon as he was clear, we surfaced and crossed the Suido to cut him off from another approach into the east channel. We were fortunate in being between him and port, but after diving on the new station at 1115, no further contact was made.

The following morning our luck changed. Heading in for the assigned lifeguard station, we were forced down by an aircraft contact at 0419, surfacing on station at 0730. At 0759 we were again forced down by a Japanese Jake and Rufe who apparently hadn't gotten the word on the B-29 air strike soon due on target. Sighting our B-29 Superdumbo air cover at 0855, we surfaced and established radio communications. An hour later Jake and Rufe reappeared, coming in on the starboard beam. The Dumbo had just checked out and headed home, disappearing southward as the enemy came in from the north. We recalled the Dumbo immediately, then discreetly dived to periscope depth to watch the show. Jake passed directly overhead, close enough for us to distinguish the tail fins on the bomb between his floats. In the meantime, Dumbo had gone to battle stations gun action; the big ship spun around like a fighter and charged into the fray. Awed by the sight, Rufe turned tail and fled, leaving his teammate to tackle the monster alone.

The fight was short and unequal. The panorama through the periscope was an unforgettable scene as the action unfolded, low over the water and less than two miles away. The CO at the periscope acted as commentator, giving a play-by-play account throughout the ship by all communications systems—mostly by direct voice. At 1006 Jake dropped his bomb, then began a twisting, weaving retreat until stopped by one short and devastating barrage from the B-29, the tracers plainly visible from *Atule*. He burst into flames aft and crashed into the sea in a sheet of exploding gasoline and bomb. At 1009 we surfaced. The Dumbo thanked us for the assist and again headed for home.

As we reached the scene of the crash at 1020, one survivor was calling for help, but of the remaining two, one had been decapitated and the other was dead and floating face down in the gasoline covered water. The survivor, Lt. Masayosi Kojima, a naval observer, was pulled past the grisly corpse and floating head of his teammate and hauled aboard, crying in English, "I surrender."

He was suffering from shock, second-degree burns of the face and hands, flesh wounds on the neck and arm, and gunshot or crash wounds in his right ankle. How he escaped alive from the exploding plane was amazing. Our "doctor," Chief Pharmacist's Mate Archie Sierks, was examining him on deck when a stentorian voice from the bridge asked, "What shape is he in?"

"Burns face and hands, deep lacerations on his legs, semi-shock, and can't tell if anything internal, captain."

"Throw the bastard over the side. We can't save him."

"No, no, I fine," cried the lieutenant, waving his arms in proof.

The doc, true to the best ethics of his profession, asked for a chance to dress his wounds, and "Bungo," as he was immediately nicknamed by the crew, was helped below to the after torpedo room. We then received the surprise of our lives.

In addition to English and Japanese, Bungo spoke German and French, and he certainly was no ordinary POW. He was wearing about three layers of clothing and from a dozen pockets poured identification, seven packs of Japanese and one of British cigarettes, ration books, club tickets, diary, notebook, flight record, and, of prime importance, two magnetic detector traces from his antisubmarine search gear and notes concerning them. Proving he was a man of the world and ready for anything, he also carried a thick wad of currency, a vial of perfume, and several condoms.

The speed of this operation was unusual. The elapsed time from initial sighting, reporting the contact, diving, the attack, surfacing, and rescue of the POW covered only twenty minutes. And an hour later—ho hum—we detonated another mine. About that time, Captain Maurer went aft to interview the prisoner; as soon as Bungo saw him coming, he turned his head toward the bulkhead and feigned sleep.

Bungo was terrified. Trussed in a straitjacket for safekeeping and given a bunk on an empty torpedo cradle, he was sure we were preparing to fire him out the torpedo tube. A burly guard, Keith Hayter, towered over him with a huge .45 pistol on his hip. Hayter claims today he had no idea how to shoot it, but the effect was the same.

Bungo recovered quickly from his injuries. At his first meal he stared in disbelief at the quantity and quality of the food. That night the menu called for steak, mushrooms, fresh frozen peas, ice cream, and the works. He couldn't understand how we had such food so far from home. Never having tasted ice cream before, he soon became a nut for it. To keep his attitude correct, however, crewmen would occasionally work the grinding wheel near his bunk to hone a large knife, occasionally glaring fiercely at the prisoner manacled to the top bunk.

The familiar Jake plane again appeared overhead as preparations were made for surfacing, then was sighted three more times at fifteen-minute intervals, on north-south and east-west courses. Preliminary interrogation of Bungo revealed that he was on antisubmarine patrol when we detected him and was making a bombing run when shot down.

He admitted that his plane would not have left base that day if they had known B-29s were in the area. We learned from the traces of his magnetic recorder that the Japanese equipment was very similar to our own MAD gear, so similar that the spools of recording paper seemed interchangeable. Of major significance, the traces he provided from tracking *Atule* indicated a sharp loss of sensitivity on certain magnetic headings, which gave the submarines a major advantage in evading an air search. We passed the information immediately to Commander Submarines.

On 7 May, just before dark, we detonated a floating mine with only four rounds of .30-caliber ammunition. This was a new peak in efficiency for the mine-disposal squad. The patrol report adds, "The state of training and morale of this group, composed entirely of volunteers from among old Naval Officers, is very high."

Two days later we celebrated the announcement of V-E Day in Europe by conducting a photo reconnaissance of the Kyushu coast from Muroto Saki to Hane Saki at five miles off the beach. This section of the coast might be important for an amphibious landing in the forthcoming Operation Olympic, the invasion of Kyushu set for late fall. Two days later, another giant mine was seen close off the coast, looking at least three times the listed forty-one-inch diameter. It had six horns and a cover plate bolted on top. Tony was doing the honors. After a few rounds, he could see three or four holes in it and said, "I think it's going to sink, captain."

Jason said, "Give it one more."

Tony swore we had drifted to within fifty yards of it, and he sure didn't want to see it detonate with his pate the only one exposed. He obeyed the captain but, truth be told, aimed wide so as not to have this one go off in his face. Lots of sighs of relief went up when it failed to explode.

Then it was the Navy's turn again for new carrier strikes. At 0742, survivors in a lifeboat were reported close offshore in the Inland Sea. At 0915, two enemy destroyers were reported eight miles away and heading toward us. The fighter cover over the survivors strafed the destroyers until they were out of ammunition, requesting assistance from the carrier in the meantime. We then requested permission from the carrier to send our own cover to the rescue. With permission granted, they disappeared like twelve-year-olds after the fire engines, negotiating the hundred miles in record time. By noon the situation was under control. Our cover, with additional help from the carrier, strafed the destroyers and set them afire as they retreated northward. The Kingfisher float planes arrived on the scene, recovered the survivors, and were on their way back to the carrier.

This remarkable rescue, equivalent to an enemy landing inside New York or San Francisco harbors to save a countryman, indicated the degree to which control of the air had been gained over Japan. The *Atule* fighter cover then lucked out in finding a small freighter near the scene which made the fatal mistake of coming into their gunsights. While they were absent on their errand we kept busy by sinking a mine and, when they returned, detonated another as a special pyrotechnic display, then did some giant porpoising on quick dives and surfacing to complete our "show and tell." At 1730 they headed for the birdfarm; we prepared for the local enemy and their plans to entertain us.

Occasional fun and games notwithstanding, the submarines didn't enjoy the best of all possible worlds while lifeguarding. The air cover was great while the raids were in progress, but to make the submarine easy to find for a damaged aircraft trying to ditch in the sea, the lifeguard stations were always close to a prominent landmark. Of necessity we operated on the surface, where we were just as visible to an enemy sub as to our friends, and in clear view from the hostile shore.

The lifeguard subs were a great boost for the airmen's morale. Fifty percent of all downed birdmen were rescued; the score would have been higher if others could have survived and been able to reach the sea. One naval aviator was shot down three times and rescued three times by submarines. Ensign George Bush was among the Navy pilots pulled from the sea by a submarine and saved for a distinguished career in public life.

So complete was the destruction of enemy air in the days of coordinated B-29 and carrier attacks that we had our first peaceful night free of aircraft alerts since entering the area. We returned to the Kyushu coast for close-in examination of

Toi Misaki, then surfaced at noon to detonate a mine, very clean and new looking with no growth. Tony, who had detonated the previous monster with only four rounds, took only two rounds of .30-caliber ammunition on this one for an all-time low.

On the return home, three more mines were detonated, the last the scariest of them all. When it was sighted, dead ahead, the OOD backed emergency and threw the rudder over. When the captain and I got to the bridge, it was very close, *very close* under the forefoot. The CO ordered, "Give it everything you got, maneuvering room."

The rudder had absolutely no effect. The fleet submarine, like most ships, backs into the wind. Both wind and sea here were from dead aft. The ship was in irons, in the grip of Neptune. As the bow rose on a sea, the mine disappeared from view. As it came down, the mine reappeared, very close aboard to port. It disappeared a second time under the bow, then reappeared very close to starboard. The third time the bow rose on a swell, the mine didn't reappear. Pulses raced; tension built up, but the backing bell had finally taken hold. The mine was dead ahead, missing us by one foot. I said, "Captain, that was close." But no words came out.

When this one finally sank under a hail of lead, tension was still high. The last of forty-four destroyed from fifty-two sighted in two patrols, this at least should have given us membership in the United Mine Workers Union.

On the return trip I spent much time polishing up the patrol report. It was a good heads-up patrol, but to qualify for the combat insignia, the standard required "significant enemy shipping . . . sunk or a comparable mission accomplished." It was important to us, especially to the enlisted men, because it added a battle star to the submarine combat insigne each man earned with his first successful patrol. Not many people in a submarine have chances to earn individual awards; the combat insignia did the equivalent.

Long ago I learned from reading patrol reports that many skippers are more powerful with the sword than the pen. Jason was very modest in describing his exploits, letting the deeds carry the message. On this patrol the only enemy contact was a few peeks at a submarine several miles away;

we rescued no aviators while lifeguarding. The rescue of Bungo, while of considerable intelligence value, was hardly a Rosetta Stone. I wrote the report with only minor changes by the skipper, and these would have been bigger if the other officers hadn't asked him to leave it as written.

The report of the last mine was a point of difference. I had half a page of narrative as above, which was certainly no exaggeration, but he finally overruled all of us with the bland statement, "1748—Sank floating mine." He had a point. "We weren't out there roaming the oceans looking for those little baubles that couldn't shoot back."

On 21 May Gina celebrated her second birthday. I was not far from the spot where Reggie was lost, and I sent her a special letter commemorating the day, along with a poem I found in a ragged old magazine.

> Dolphins guard thy infant slumbers,
> Davy Jones thy sandman be,
> For thy father's gone ahunting,
> In the jungles of the sea.
>
> Moonless nights and sunless days
> Doth he stalk the watery ways
> Where the pale anemone
> Decks the gardens of the sea,
> Where the coral's lacy fan
> Waves in courts unmarred by man;
> Where the shark and dolphin play
> There thy father hunts his prey.
> Where the great whales rise and blow,
> There thy father tracks his foe,
> With periscope for magic eye
> To watch the ships go swiftly by,
> With darker magic tuned to hear
> The pulse of foeman drawing near.
> He'll come home to thee at last,
> Broom triumphant at the mast.
>
> Dolphins guard thy infant slumber,
> Davy Jones thy sandman be,
> Child of war thy father's hunting
> In the jungles of the sea.

Atule arrived in Midway on 25 May to take on enough fuel to get us to Pearl Harbor for rest and refit. By now I had learned that boats arriving late afternoon in Midway are allowed to stay overnight, so my navigation skills brought us alongside at 1400. Had we been ten minutes earlier we would have been back at sea before sunset; ten minutes later we would have missed ten minutes of good fellowship at the tavern. Proper planning gained a pleasant evening at the Gooneyville Tavern visiting with old friends almost until departure the following morning at 0900. Bungo was turned over to the Marines on arrival, blindfolded and thoroughly scared at leaving us. Eventually repatriated, he was scorned by his peers for surrendering. Nevertheless he entered the postwar Japanese Defense Force and eventually retired as a rear admiral.

At 1030 on 30 May we moored at the Submarine Base Pearl for a well-deserved rest after fifty-nine days at sea. On the dock were Commodore Weary Wilkins, always warm and friendly, and old friends Mike Fenno and Vernon L. "Rebel" Lowrance. Anxious to hear of our exploits, they immediately dragged us off to the *Sperry* for lunch. Several people recalled the fine job *Sperry* had done replacing the *Scorpion* sonar domes in Midway two years before. The impossible job of those days was the routine of today.

The incoming mail included a check for $28.40 from the Naval Institute for the article on the subsolar fix, my first as an author. At the evening bull session at the club with Bing Gillette, Charles R. "Honey" Clark, Jr., Howie Thompson, and a few others, somebody mentioned the article in conversation, wondering who the author, "Paul R. Frank," was. When I confessed, they were surprised, more so that I had to use a pen name.

The incoming mail also brought a note from the Red Cross that my brother-in-law, Dr. Regis J. Ging from Pittsburgh, had donated a pint of blood in my name. When Jason, Tony, Jack, and the others learned that their poor, anemic, two-hundred-pound shipmate was storing up blood transfusions, it became table talk for days. I shared in the levity but I deeply appreciated Rege's thought.

The orders to command, my main interest, also came through. I would be detached from *Atule* and proceed to

Guam with Submarine Squadron 36 in *Sperry* for a command as soon as one was available. I was number three on the list. When Jason and the O'Tooles heard, they beseeched me to stay aboard for one more patrol. Jason promised that if I did, he'd give me a strong boost for a new construction boat. Since it would then be a year and a half since I left the states, his may have been the best advice. Strongly tempted, I accepted this alternative if no relief could be found.

Shortly after we moved into the Royal Hawaiian some very pleasant news came our way. Three or four families on the beautiful island of Maui frequently invited recuperating submarine officers to spend a few days with them. Jason, Woodie, Jack, and I were nominated for a four-day visit. All transportation was perfectly arranged by the manager of the Royal Hawaiian, with cars, boats, and planes warmed up and ready for each leg of the trip.

In Wailuku we were met by Mrs. Frances Allen, whose husband Ray managed the Wailuku sugar plantation. Jason and I stayed with Ray and Frances, Jack and Woodie at a forty-thousand-acre ranch in the mountains. The Allen home was a gorgeous stone mansion with wide lawns, spreading eucalyptus trees, lily ponds with Japanese bridges over them, and a riot of flowers in bloom everywhere—gardenia, fuchsia, orchids, hibiscus, birds of paradise, and hundreds of others I couldn't begin to name. The wide lanais around the home opened onto a panorama sweeping down to the beach and the brilliant blue ocean beyond. To the south a fertile valley led to the vast ten-thousand-foot Haleakala crater in the distance, and to the north two precipitous, cloud-shrouded peaks guarded the entrance to the rain forest in the Iea Valley. Add a tennis court and swimming pool, mango, breadfruit, avocado, orange, grapefruit, and lime trees, plus the friendly chatter of mynahs, cardinals, bluejays, and many exotic birds flitting about, and we were in heaven.

Dinner the first evening included thick, luscious T-bone steaks and mushrooms, fresh corn, fresh tropical fruit, fresh blackberry pie, and fresh milk—deeelicious! Friends dropped in later, and we played games but mostly just got acquainted. Frances roundly trimmed me for $1.50 at cribbage—which doesn't happen often. The following morning

Jason and I played tennis, then swam a bit, shot some skeet, drove up the beautiful Iea Valley with Frances, enjoyed cocktails with the commandant of the Naval Air Station, then enjoyed another of those perfect dinners—broiled pheasant this time. In the evening, I won a couple of bucks at bridge with Frances's sister as partner, and Jason won ten at poker with host Ray and the men.

We finally got a chance to shop, finding some beautifully made clothing for Henri and the two daughters, and then were ready for a swim at the Allens' private beach—an eight-room bathhouse with three beautifully furnished suites and the usual sweeping lawns and flowering shrubs.

The third day, we drove up to the rim of the Haleakala crater to see the sunset, then enjoyed dinner in the clouds. In addition to the breathtaking scenery from this two-mile-high aerie, we enjoyed the *bracken*, a phenomenon seen only here and in Switzerland. A complete circular rainbow can be seen in the crater, with the observer's shadow in the very center. Each viewer sees only one shadow, even though five or six may be standing side by side looking at it.

On a beautiful spring evening, a panorama of mountains 125 miles away towered skyward; pheasant and mountain goats rustled in the underbrush, yet the miracle of the evening was the organization of the whole trip. Frances made all the arrangements for the party of seventeen people, including Jack and Woodie and their "family," some Marine colonels, Red Cross girls and friends, and supplied all the food, drink, and transportation. Dinner, served five hours after we left home, included a twenty-pound rib roast piping hot, fresh baked beans, an iced salad, fresh pumpkin pie, and numerous other delights. The food was kept hot in an electric roaster in the trunk of their big Packard limousine.

I particularly enjoyed the mixed company. Could it be possible that this was my first chance to converse with a young lady in over a year? The group was extremely congenial, and a sudden wave of homesickness almost did me in. When the stars came out, I slipped away for a few moments of fond meditation, high above the clouds, dreaming of Henri and the faraway family I hardly knew. Fortunately, nobody noticed my short absence, but I will always carry a special bond of warmth and appreciation for Ray and Frances for making these treasured moments possible. I really needed the break in routine they offered. Now well into my second year since departure from the folks in Pittsburgh, in a few days I would head west again for still another duty tour on the far side of the globe. But I was determined to see the war through. I was a professional: this was the job I was trained to do.

Jason and I returned to Pearl in time to read Commander Submarines' endorsement on the patrol report. Praising the well-planned, heads-up, and smart patrol, regretting the lack of shipping or other attack opportunities, he nevertheless authorized the award of the combat insignia. A lot of people wondered how we did it.

The track chart of the patrol earned special praise. As in all my patrols, I had done it with drawing instruments, lettering guides, and five or six colors of ink. The wardroom officers shared the credit for the report, feeling they had influenced the skipper to accept my dramatized version rather than his straight factual prose. Jason and I were riding high. Neither of us had yet had an unsuccessful Pacific patrol. To show his appreciation he presented me with a truly beautiful and complete set of drawing instruments, which I cherish to this day.

The O'Tooles did their usual fine job in the athletic competition. I tried to help out with tennis, softball, and volleyball, so after winning in all sports the men asked if I would accept the trophy for the ship. The photograph of the winning volleyball team showed more horseplay than ability, but the beer was flowing by then. Many commented—facetiously—on our gaunt and haggard appearance after so many weeks in close confinement under the sea.

Near the end of the refit, my relief appeared, John B. Dudley, a classmate and an outstanding officer. Johnny had just relinquished command of an "R" boat in Key West; he would be exec and PCO, which means that he would leave *Atule* after one patrol and then wait for his own command. His arrival made it certain I could not stay aboard, and I made my preparations for departure quickly. At a special ceremony, the ship presented me with a purse with which to buy war bonds for the children, plus "a permanent seat in the wardroom bull sessions." Again I was embarrassed. The men couldn't afford these gifts, but there was little I could do about it. They were generous by nature, and their hearts were always in the right place. Early that morning, 29 June, I made my farewells, my sad parting from Jason and all the O'Tooles. Jason and I walked down the deck and across the gangway, arms on each other's shoulders. This truly was a most congenial group of shipmates. With a big lump in my throat, I watched silently as the sleek ship backed away from the dock and headed out to sea.

Walking aboard the *Sperry,* I was hoping for a real surprise. For several weeks there were rumors that I once more had a good chance to get command of the *Sterlet.* At the last moment, however, it didn't work out. She was in a Pearl Harbor squadron that had quite a number on the list waiting for a command; my chance would come from Squadron 36 in Guam. Two days after the Fighting O'Toole headed west, I followed in *Sperry,* en route to Apra Harbor, Guam, arriving there 12 July 1945. The trip was pleasant and relaxing. My only surprise, on the last few days before arrival, was that we weren't zigzagging. Surely the experienced submariners running *Sperry* knew its value. A few weeks later a Japanese submarine would send the USS *Indianapolis,* not zigzagging, to the bottom with an enormous loss of life.

In Guam as a PCO, my main duties were temporary command of boats in refit, supervising the work, getting subs under way to shift berths, moving them in or out of the huge floating drydock, offering technical assistance on new equipment being installed, and in general representing the regular CO in his absence—and praying for my chance.

One of the first subs passing through Guam on her way out was *Sterlet.* We had a great reunion. Gene Barnhardt and Bob Wright were the only veterans left and reported everybody happy in the wardroom now, although sorry I didn't get command. Gene was now the exec, Bob the TDC expert. Bob reported having recently heard from our old CO, enclosing a five-dollar bill he presumably owed for a bet he had overlooked. With a wry smile, Bob handed the fiver to me for a (fictitious) bet he had lost to me. The next day at mass the priest took up a special collection for the local Chamorran bishop in rebuilding churches and schools. I pitched in the five, feeling it would do the most good in Bishop Omura's hands.

The most surprising news concerned Joe Garland. Joe had gone back to a school boat in New London but was hospitalized for tuberculosis immediately after and discharged from the service. After griping about the Navy for twenty years, he fought like a tiger to stay in. That confirmed bachelor also decided to get married, having found an absolutely delightful lady fully worthy of him.

One day the tender had to shift berths to accommodate the major construction of new docks and other facilities. Six submarines had to be moved simultaneously. Shiphandling with a crew who had never worked together sometimes offered unusual thrills and always a surprise. I moved one sub and tied up to a mooring buoy in the outer harbor, then got another and moored it alongside. With two hours to kill before we could go back alongside the tender again, I sounded swimming call and most of us stripped and dived over the side. A few moments later, the USS *Tirante*, returning from patrol, passed quite near us. There on the bridge was Ed Skeehan, just returning from his first patrol. We gave a hearty, bare-assed welcome. I foresaw a big reunion that night. Ed was happy. He had earned his combat pin and had been selected to be the new diving officer for the next patrol.

Suddenly I was the only PCO in the squadron. It was great to head the list, but with no other qualified shiphandler around, my duties began to escalate. I fully earned my pay. Another day when multiple subs had to be moved, I was in one or another for ten straight hours, with no brekky, no lunch. The need, with a catch-as-catch-can team, to be continually alert made it very tiring, especially while parboiling and stewing under a blazing sun and alternate driving rain.

On Guam I found time to visit the U.S. Marine cemetery, where rows and rows of white crosses, and the occasional Star of David, offered their silent testimony to the losers in the brave battle for a piece of turf. Many Marines were present, taking the day off to pay their last tribute to buddies no longer around the mess tent. Officers, burly sergeants, privates, and plain Marines walked down the lanes carrying flowers to decorate a particular plot, aided in many cases by humble native men or women.

I've seen these cemeteries on Saipan and Tinian and Majuro and Oahu; every island out here has one, but I never saw one without wondering if the folks back home—all of us—will remember ten years from now these men who never made the trip home. I wasn't discouraged, but, as I wrote Henri, "Sometimes I take a very pessimistic view of the ability of the people back home to win the peace as well as the war. These poor fellows are sure going to be awful let down if we don't."

My time on Guam gave me the chance to learn more about the air war on Japan. Three other submariners arranged to ride a Superdumbo covering the lifeguard sub; this wasn't what I had in mind. I wanted to make a combat mission over Japan on one of the massive night fire raids. I requested orders to ride the Dumbo, but when I met General LeMay at Northeast Field on Guam, I showed him only the top half of the authorization "to make a B-29 mission." He looked no further before putting me in a Pathfinder plane, one of the three lead planes over the target, the top navigators who find the spot and drop the first bomb load to light up the drop area for the rest of the flight.

The target that night was near Nagasaki, a maximum-range effort for the B-29s from Guam. A total of 350 B-29s made firebomb raids that night, dropping twenty-two hundred tons of incendiaries on three cities with a total population of 377,000. I went through the briefings with the regular crews and happened to catch the first use of a new psychological weapon—announcing the target in advance. Radio Guam began telling the Japanese that five of ten named cities would be hit, thereby encouraging mass absenteeism and work stoppage in ten cities rather than the five actually targeted. Also, having made two war patrols off Nagasaki, I was far more familiar with the terrain, the economy, and the defenses than the briefers—although they were very good. One item surprised me. Shipbuilding, naval bases, and warships got no mention from the briefers even as targets of opportunity if the main target was weathered in. I soon learned that destruction of naval targets had no effect on destroying the "will to fight" or on the economic collapse of the country and therefore held no priority in the airmen's strategic plan.

After the briefing I drew my gear—flak suit, parachute, Mae West, night ration, rubber boat—which pushed my displacement to about 250 pounds dead weight on the plane. Then we learned that the prevailing fifteen-knot trade winds had reversed. The runway plan couldn't be changed and we would take off down wind. The planes took off at one-minute intervals. Large markers every couple of hundred yards along the runway gave the minimum speed. If a plane fell below minimum, he dropped out and another took his place at the end of the line. We never had quite enough speed at any of the markers, and, reaching the end of the paved runway, we were still bearing down hard when we hit the coral strip. Another few hundred feet and a small shack loomed into view dead ahead. The pilot "humped" the big plane over the shack, clearing it by inches, then zoomed downward to regain air speed before hitting the ocean at the foot of the small cliff. With ten thousand pounds of incendiaries aboard, it would have been quite a splash. Interminably, we finally started to climb. The tail gunner muttered, "John, do I have to fly clear to Japan and back with this load of s—t in my pants?"

It broke the tension, but it took hundreds of miles before we gained any real flying altitude. Passing over Iwo Jima, we headed directly for the target. The navigation, I thought, was superb. What a long way we'd come since those primitive raids on Wake two years before!

Over the target I thought it would take two or three runs to complete the drop. No way; one pass and it was all over. The Japanese AA fire as we approached the target was impressive. I heard claims of losses but never learned for sure. In a few moments it was all behind us. But the tremendous holocaust of fire and smoke rising two miles into the night sky was simply beyond imagination. Ideally the planes dropped on the perimeter so that the burn was toward the center, shutting off the oxygen and uprooting giant trees as everything was drawn into the vortex. I could see why the loss of life was so high.

One of the other targeted cities that night was on the Inland Sea near Kure. On our return trip we flew within about 150 miles of Kure and could see the giant volcano of flame rising into the night sky, reflected brightly on the aluminum surfaces of the planes in the formation.

After the long sixteen-hour, thirty-two-hundred-mile flight, there were no bands, no oranges, no ice cream, no mail waiting—and no depth charges to duck after the attack. But a double shot of whiskey, hot coffee, and doughnuts served by two Red Cross ladies made a reasonable substitute. It was a fantastic experience. I thought the B-29 raids were probably the finest example of tactical planning in the war. But the moral implications of indiscriminate bombing of cities I found difficult to put out of mind.

Having made a night raid, I wanted to make a day raid on Tokyo, and again used my "authorization" with General LeMay. It was now 8 August 1945; I got to the field, went through the briefing, and drew my gear. Just as the call came to man planes, the raid was suddenly canceled. The weather was perfect; the real reason soon emerged. I returned to my quarters on the tender about midnight. Two hours later I was awakened by a big Marine showing me a message from Commander Submarines to General LeMay revoking my permission, and requesting my presence at Admiral Lockwood's headquarters "at my earliest convenience." It became "convenient" at about 0600, and the day, already unforgettable, soon became much more so.

When I arrived at the submarine force headquarters shortly after dawn, the place was a beehive. The Russians had declared war on Japan, and Russian troops immediately marched into Manchuria and northern Korea. The first atomic bomb had been dropped on Hiroshima two days before; the second was to be dropped on Nagasaki the following morning. Japan had put out a peace feeler through Swiss and Swedish channels—which caused the cancellation of the B-29 raid—and in Guam, four submarines were arriving from or departing on patrol. Yet with all these earthshaking events happening, the submarine force was most concerned with my flying bombing missions, and called off the war for a few moments to investigate and take proper action.

My first contact that dramatic morning was with Rear Admiral William D. "Happy Jack" Irvin, the humorless communications instructor at sub school so many years before. My offense was that as a recipient of highly classified Ultra intelligence information I was forbidden to overfly enemy territory. Given the gravity of even using the word at the time, this was a serious offense. I had not deliberately violated the regulation; I had simply forgotten about it. My offense apparently came out in the open when General LeMay recommended me for an Air Medal. Based on the same evidence, the submarine force suggested a general court-martial. After much discussion, not much of it on a "boys will be boys" level, it was decided to pit one recommendation against the other and forget both. I received no Air Medal and no general court-martial. The award of a medal would be prominent recognition of an obvious violation of security regulations, and the submarine force wanted no part of it.

When Henri learned that I was making combat air missions, she blew her stack. I suggested to her that since the submarine force wouldn't send me home, I might make thirty-four more missions and get home on aircrew rotation. I wasn't rejecting her concern. I recognized that the problem of wives waiting at home was far tougher than ours. In a considerably lighter mood, another wife had expressed the sentiment quite aptly.

I'm getting awfully tired of the sexless life of a saint,
I'm thinking mighty seriously of writing a complaint.
To the OPA in Washington or whoever writes the laws,
To tell them the system has one too many flaws.
They provide a substitute for everything we lack;
They take the dough for war bonds and we can't get it
    back.
They ration all the canned goods; sugar stamps they
    redeem,
But where in hell can a Navy wife let off a little steam?
She knits for the Red Cross and does V-mail till she's
    dead,
But that's a poor substitute for being alone in bed.
Of course we write our love letters until we fairly burst,
But does he get his mail direct? The censor gets it first.
I buy my bonds dutifully and write poems for a laugh

But don't you lose the point of this—I want my better
    half.
So with all this New Deal red tape and OPA complex,
There's still no stamp in my ration book redeemable for
    sex.
You can take my stamps for sugar and another one for
    shoes,
But give me back my husband, *please,* before I blow
    my fuse.

The peace feeler from the Japanese soon had its effect in
the squadron. On 12 August, Commodore Lew Parks, the
senior submarine squadron commander in the forward area,
sent for me to tell me I was selected to be part of a force to
leave for Japan as soon as possible after the cease-fire, and
to take over a Japanese submarine to take back to the states.
His news sounded fantastic. The chances of getting a normal
command seemed to be fading. The new construction program had been cut back to nothing, and as the war neared
its close many senior submariners, who had done their share
earlier and gave up commands for a little home life, now
suddenly wanted a peacetime command. Those still in command were hanging on, seeing no comparison between sea
command and a shore job somewhere. The loss of submarine
pay by going ashore made it still less attractive. To reduce
the list of those waiting for command, the admiral first
decided to limit command to the top half of '39 or senior. I
would be included but this would be a severe blow to a lot of
fine people.

The news of the surrender came on 14 August. We received the word about 1600, just as several of us left the ship
for a quiet afternoon at the club. Despite what one might
expect at the end of a long and hard war, things were quieter
than usual with no apparent difference from the day before—
no whistles, sirens, fireworks, or celebrations. I met two
destroyer COs, friends from academy days; we talked about
many things, little about the peace. It was simply taken for
granted. We had fought a tough, cruel enemy and won; we
were glad it was over. When I got back to the ship for dinner,
I felt only acute loneliness for my family and a strong desire
to get on with the world in a peaceful era.

The following morning I was on the move again. At 1230 I had just finished a pleasant Sunday lunch when the commodore sent for me and told me to pack my bags and be ready to leave by 1300. I flew through packing, getting clear of mess bill, laundry, tailor, paymaster, doctor, and the rest, and was on my way to Squadron 20 and the USS *Proteus* for transportation to Japan for the surrender, there to take command of a Japanese submarine.

I had just scrambled aboard the *Proteus* when I learned of a message to all submarine COs in the area asking if they wanted to make the trip to Japan and let us PCOs take command of their submarines while they were gone. Classmate Lloyd R. "Joe" Vasey almost lost out. I was next in line. Only the lack of time saved us. We sweated through preparations for getting under way, counting the minutes. The long blast on the whistle as *Proteus* slowly backed clear meant we were safe.

Already I was figuring ahead—get a submarine command and head back to a West Coast shipyard to rebuild it as necessary to meet U.S. fleet standards. I guessed that H-Day on the West Coast—for Heaven and Henri—would be in early fall. My eyes turned toward Tokyo. Not for months had I felt more lighthearted. The final chapter, the culmination of the war, was at hand. But I was heading west with the setting sun toward the land of the Rising Sun, not east toward home.

6

The Demilitarization and Occupation of Japan

Admiral Chester W. Nimitz, commander of the Pacific Ocean Areas, had invited Admiral Lockwood to attend the surrender ceremonies on the deck of Admiral William F. Halsey's flagship, the USS *Missouri*, and to designate a dozen submarines and the submarine tender USS *Proteus* to be present for the ceremony. Departing Guam immediately, 15 August 1945, and steaming steadily toward Tokyo at eighteen knots, *Proteus* from commodore to cabin steward was a hotbed of rumors. Nobody knew what Japanese forces still survived or what reception they, a proud people, were preparing for the American conqueror. An early intelligence bulletin told of diehards, particularly in the army, refusing to accept the surrender. There was not much we could plan on.

Nobody could recall when a previous victor in war had occupied Japan. Commodore Matthew C. Perry and a small naval squadron had opened Japan to the West in 1853. His experience seemed totally remote. We were excited about setting foot on Japanese soil, but the cultural differences of East and West were extreme. We could only speculate on the response of this fanatical, even self-destructive people. That very morning we heard that rumors of Allied landings in western Japan caused terror-stricken women to flee to the hills, some carrying cyanide for use in emergency. Fifteen

American airmen in prison in Fukuoka were taken out of their cells and beheaded. The submarine blockade of the Japanese home islands had reduced food supplies to starvation levels. At least one local plan to resist the American invasion called for the elderly to turn in all food stocks and commit suicide. We had few expectations of a serene welcome.

On 21 August *Proteus* joined the Third Fleet south of Tokyo Bay. Even for the old hands the display of naval power was awesome. From one horizon to the other, fleets of flattops, battleships, cruisers, amphibious ships, destroyer squadrons, support forces, and ships of every description, so many as to stun comprehension, all headed for the most important rendezvous in U.S. naval history. On 27 August two I-400 class submarines surrendered at sea and were brought into port. These were massive six-thousand-ton monsters, big as cruisers, three times the size of our subs. Each ship carried three seaplanes that could be launched from catapults. The Japanese had experimented with aircraft-carrying submarines since 1922; the idea still came as a surprise to naval intelligence. Designed to raid the U.S. coasts to drop bacteriological bombs on the populous cities, or to make hit-run raids on the Panama Canal, they came too late for use in these roles. An interesting sidelight occurred in bringing one of the submarines into port. The Japanese skipper, with charts of the minefields and a U.S. prize crew on board, refused to enter the Inland Sea unless a Japanese pilot conned his ship and another ship led the way.

The next day, 31 August, *Proteus* moored in Yokohama Bay and Commodore Parks ordered a select crew ashore to take over the Yokosuka Naval Base. Leading the group were the two division commanders, Rob Roy MacGregor (who had tried to get me to sea with him after I left *Sterlet*) and Bernard F. "Bernie" MacMahon, former CO of *Drum,* and I, backed by a dozen enlisted volunteers. We left *Proteus* in the late afternoon, in the rain. On the ten-mile trip to the naval base, we were soon drenched to the bone by heavy seas breaking over the bows of the launches. The only food the tender could scrounge up on short notice was a slice of

Spam and an apple. The pot of coffee was soon a cold blend of polluted sea water. Nobody cared.

Arriving alongside the ancient docks, everybody wanted to be the first ashore, but nobody wanted to scramble up the oily steps and trigger a booby trap. Once somebody stepped fully on a plank, the others immediately joined, then waited for the next brave man to try another step. We had no idea what to expect from the Japanese. The first people ashore, we tried to be ready for anything. The yard, pitch dark and gloomy, appeared to be abandoned. Somebody decided to build a fire while we contemplated the next step. Several oil-soaked rattan fenders, used to prevent damage to ships coming alongside a dock, were soon burning briskly.

As we crowded around for warmth, suddenly a series of explosions blew hot coals all over the place. It sounded like machine-gun fire. With a whoosh everybody fled in panic around the corner of the nearest building. But no enemy appeared; the hollow reeds of rattan burned briskly, and when the inner cores reached combustion, they exploded violently. When calm was restored, we soon found the administration building and, still concerned about finding no occupants, began looking for intelligence materials—that is, souvenirs. The occupants had fled in a hurry, leaving everything behind. Finally reaching the submarine headquarters, we found half a dozen skippers, far more tense than we, waiting to turn over their commands—and get a proper receipt. (Bureaucracies are the same everywhere.) The submarines were old, but a number of midgets and *kaiten* suicide torpedoes had been assembled for use against the U.S. invasion forces. As soon as the skippers left, we looked for a place to spend the night, sleeping on benches, tables, or desks. Some slept in a geisha house where the only inhabitants—bedbugs, lice, rats, fleas, mosquitoes, and a few other specimens—kept us scratching for weeks.

We came alive at five, glad to be up and about, even though the Spam and two apples this time, with a glass of tomato juice, didn't arrive until 1100. (Logistic support for this microcosm of invasion hardly reached expectations.) The day's work consisted of demilitarizing midget subs, piggy-back subs, PT boats, human torpedoes, suicide subs, ordinary torpedoes, mosquitoes, and fleas, anything that had a capability against the U.S. fleet. Under terms of the surrender agreement, all offensive weapons had to be out of the water. They had been dumped indiscriminately on docks and piers, most lying on their sides. We worked in teams, a submariner and a demolition expert, each knowing his own trade and nothing of the other's. Japanese submarine construction was foreign to both, and the *kaiten* were too cramped for both to work side by side. By turns we crawled into the blackness of the stinking, filthy interiors and quickly decided the problem of defusing the craft was in the other's area of expertise. Not knowing one pipe or fitting from another, how could we determine which was the detonator and whether or not it was booby-trapped? The entire bow section of some of these craft were warheads, designed to go off on contact.

After alternate spells of fear and panic, we discovered that the detonators had been removed, but every one had to be individually checked, always with the thought that a wrong action might demilitarize us as well. The whole job had to be done before the surrender terms were signed on the *Missouri* quarterdeck the following day. That great moment in history for so many people was less important to us than a hot shower and scrubdown to ease the bites and stings, then a big dinner and a good night's sleep between clean sheets.

For the historic signing to end the most horrible war in history, I was among those who didn't quite make the party. The submariners were celebrating nearby, listening to the ceremony on the radio while christening the new U.S. Submarine Officers' Club, Yokosuka. Rob Roy MacGregor and Bernie MacMahon had already slipped off to Tokyo, visiting the emperor's palace even before General MacArthur arrived. Frank C. "Tiny" Lynch, Jr. and I took the train to Yokohama and Tokyo, asking the conductor to stop once or twice to give us a better view of burned-out cities in the most awful desolation and destruction ever wreaked by man. (Bodies were still stacked in the Tokyo rail station.) Frank, tall and athletic, was CO of the *Haddo* and a former shipmate of Jason Maurer in *Harder*. Together we were about the size of four of the late enemy, and they seemed most anxious to assist. The people we saw were curious but completely docile, fearful, and aloof.

Much remained to be done in Yokosuka. A primary concern, the recovery of submarine prisoners of war and information on submarine losses, drove us to extraordinary efforts. What we found discouraged us greatly. The *Grenadier* and *Perch* crews had survived almost intact; twenty-three survived *Sculpin;* only nine escaped from *Tang*. In the *Sculpin* sinking, forty-one had gotten off, but eighteen of those were lost when a Japanese carrier returning them to Japan was sunk by Robert E. M. "Bob" Ward and the *Sailfish* in the middle of a wild typhoon. Of forty-three U.S. submarines lost at sea in combat in the Pacific, survivors were recovered from only nine. Several known losses resulted when erratic torpedoes made circular runs and destroyed the submarine itself. About the *Scorpion,* none of the prisoners had heard anything. We obtained the locations of the 468 sinkings of U.S. submarines the Japanese had "confirmed" and took grim pleasure in correlating these attacks with many of our own close calls. I had been "sunk" four times, once in *Scorpion,* twice in *Sterlet,* and once in *Atule*. This exaggeration I could put up with.

Two classmates were included in the early survivors, Jacob J. "Jake" Vandergrift, Jr. who had gone down in *Perch,* and Alfred J. "Sonny" Toulon, Jr. from the *Grenadier.* As plebes at the academy, Sonny and I had walked countless hours of extra duty for conduct offenses. Both Sonny and Jake were in terrible shape; like all the prisoners they suffered from beri-beri, malaria, malnutrition, and skin diseases. Al in particular was emaciated and confused, had lost 50 pounds from his original 170, and suffered a terrible case of "rice brain"—memory loss—from the wretched prison diet. He also had an ugly gash on his forehead. One of the greatest shortages in prison camp was soap. One had the feeling of never being able to get clean. Ironically, when the B-29s started dropping food packages to the prisoners a few days before the surrender, Al was hit on the head with a case of soap. He and several others were flown to Guam for a few days' recuperation at the submarine rest camp before heading back to America. On the plane from Tokyo, Al carried a large tin of dry mix, a dehydrated whole milk product, and every hour he spooned down a mouthful straight out of the can. Much to our amazement, he made a complete recovery and soon earned his own submarine command.

Before leaving Tokyo, I talked with Commodore Parks about my prospects for command. He advised me to get back on a boat as an exec and try to get command when the wave of COs headed for shore duty, or when half the force was decommissioned or placed in reserve commission. When I reached Guam, however, Commodore Stanley P. Moseley immediately asked for my services on his team preparing to leave for the demilitarization of western Japan. My experience in Tokyo would be of great value to him. Both Admiral Lockwood and my own squadron commander turned it down, however, because I was needed in Guam as the only qualified CO then available for command. With so many senior submariners working to get me a command, I felt somewhat better. Perhaps Jason Maurer's earlier advice was best of all, to stay aboard *Atule* and hope for a command after one more patrol. John Dudley, who relieved me, was pulled off after one patrol and given command of *Skate*.

Yet the situation was so fluid nobody could predict anything. Proving the point, the following morning another prospective CO in Commodore Moseley's group was suddenly ordered to relieve me and I to take over his duties in the Demilitarization and Occupation Force for western Japan, leaving shortly for Okinawa and then Sasebo, Japan. This having been my fourth change of duty in ten days, I gave up on ever receiving mail again. That morning I had walked clear out to the cable station to wire Henri my new address; when I got back to the ship it had changed. But I was pleased to go west, grasping at one more straw, yet participating in a major historic event. Every reserve officer in Guam was counting "points" to see if he had enough to quit and go home; I was credited with twenty-five months in combat areas, had a ton of points, totally useless for a regular officer.

I hadn't had a letter from home in a month; perhaps I can be forgiven for suddenly feeling miserable and forlorn, tired, homesick, and sharply disappointed by the turn of events. The fifteen inches of rain falling on Guam in four days didn't help a bit. Our youngest daughter Henrie, whom I hadn't met, had just passed her first birthday; our parents were celebrating important anniversaries, and I was mired in the boonies on the opposite side of the planet. Then I learned that my pay accounts had been missent back to the *Proteus* in Tokyo. My chances of getting paid again seemed remote.

In a highly restless state of mind, I carried out my orders and moved to the *Euryale,* a converted merchantman serving as a submarine tender. The following day, 16 September, we headed west for Okinawa. I hoped my flea and rat bites from Tokyo would heal before I got the next set. I was so full of typhus and cholera serum no blood came out anymore.

My new boss was Captain Delbert F. Williamson, known at sub school as "Diesel Dan." He was one of my instructors, also famed as one of the hardest graders on work assignments. I had done an exercise using his own "gouge," or answer sheet, my drawing instruments, and multicolored ink for the sketch and turned in a beautiful piece of work. I hoped for a 4.0; I got a 3.2. He was a very pleasant individual, and we had a fine association, but I couldn't imagine what standard of performance would earn me a 4.0 on my fitness report. It turned out to be one of the most glowing I ever received.

The voyage to Okinawa was very relaxing. Almost forgotten were the delights of a waxing full moon, movies on deck, no zigzagging, and a pleasant cabin with a fine view of the sea. Reading through some delayed intelligence information on the defenses of Okinawa, I received a start to discover a chart of the minefields, two of which we had penetrated in *Sterlet* for the rescue of Moose Amussen. Our instructions were to "presume the area to be mined." My early plan for Okinawa was to stand on Cham Zaki and look out over those minefields.

Ashore in Okinawa was a great expectation for many, me not the least. We arrived on the rainy end of a typhoon and rode a jeep through swamps and rutted paths called roads. Sand, coral, mud, and rainwater stung my face. I could barely open my eyes. Despite the wretched roads, Okinawa had much to offer the visitor. The country was dotted with massive stone and concrete burial vaults, many destroyed and desecrated in hand-to-hand fighting for the island.

I felt sorry for the Okinawans. They are related to Polynesians, definitely not Japanese or Chinese. Their culture was still distinct despite their having been under the heel of one or the other for centuries. The houses in the villages were strongly built of concrete and stone, roofed with tile over the thatch, and secluded from the narrow lanes by four-foot stone walls. Their tiny farms each had a concrete pigsty and a huge stone mortar and pestle for grinding rice and nuts. Everything gave the impression of timelessness, at least until the tornado of death swept through after the American landings. Here 24,000 civilians had died along with 99,000 of the 110,000 defending Japanese troops. American casualties totaled 23,420 killed and 75,631 wounded. In one U.S. Marine division, about 3,500 Marines landed and 2,900 fell in eighty-two days.

In the countryside, I watched some youngsters washing the two-wheeled family cart and horse in a rice paddy. Then several women washed themselves, hair included, in the blue-black ooze. This was the day I got to Cham Zaki, hitchhiking my way through clouds of dust, finally to reach the spot overlooking the *Sterlet* rescue. Looking down from the cliff made it seem much closer. The native shacks from which the people had watched the rescue were now heaps of charred rubble, the radio towers twisted into rusty scrap metal. The heaviest fighting occurred around Naha and Shuri Castle, now also destroyed. Scores of Japanese dead lay everywhere, bloated and stinking in the sun. Some were desecrated by young firebloods, who removed gold teeth and ears, which they carried around in a rag or bottle. Too young to fight the war, they had macho ideas on how to win the peace.

I made a short flight to Ie Island, where the esteemed columnist Ernie Pyle was killed, then tried to arrange a flight to Formosa or Shanghai with some aviator friends. The first day, torrential rains killed pleasure flying and mired in everything else—jeeps, trucks, and staff cars. Riding an open truck, I was soon a moving icicle of mud. The next morning, however, a flight to Canton and Shanghai was laid on. But at the last moment I was recalled for the imminent departure of *Euryale* for Japan.

The military government urged the people to stop the

traditional use of human waste for fertilizer—night soil, as it is known throughout Asia. In their communal life, Okinawan men and women seemed totally uninhibited. They had no private lives. Those I met seemed friendly, especially the children, who would do anything for a jeep ride. Occupation policy, contrary to the "no fraternization" in Europe, encouraged social contacts. Insisted on by General MacArthur over strong objections, it demonstrated a freer and kindlier way of life and became the secret weapon in the successful demilitarization of Asia. It eased much potential bitterness among the defeated populations. MacArthur also refused to accept two hundred specially trained U.S. Army officers for the occupation, using his own staff instead, causing serious problems with Washington.

With the minefields now cleared adequately for *Euryale* to enter western Japan, we were on our way. After watching Buckner Bay and the scenic northern mountains of Okinawa fade in the distance as we took departure, I turned in to finish my night's slumber. Lo and behold, I awoke shortly and found a letter from my wife on my bare tummy, just as if she herself had waked me. A long and affectionate one, it was sorely needed. I almost needed a cold shower before going back to work.

On 28 September the *Euryale,* or "O'Reilly" as we called her, with all watertight doors dogged and steaming close behind a minesweeper, anchored in Gotto Retto, just off the entrance to the Japan Sea. Sasebo is not far from the Straits of Tsushima, where Japanese Admiral Heihachiro Togo annihilated the Russian fleet back in 1905. Both sides remember it vividly. One of the world's great natural harbors, Sasebo Bay lies in northwestern Kyushu, the mile-wide entrance flanked on both sides by imposing five-hundred-foot cliffs. The bay extends twenty miles north and south, six miles east and west. A line of hills protects the entire bay from the bitter winds that come screeching out of China, Mongolia, and across the Sea of Japan. Sasebo then was a city of 250,000 and had been mauled heavily by American bombers late in the war. Here the Japanese submarine force made its home. A major fleet repair facility, the huge drydock was undamaged and could handle any possible need.

Toward sunset the O'Reilly moved into the inner harbor,

passing many relics of Japan's recent naval might. Burned and aground in shallow water were three big Japanese carriers, two submarines, two destroyers, and many other ships; shore facilities were severely damaged. In Sweeper's Cove a couple of dozen submarines, almost the entire force surviving the war, lay moored to the large buoys, manned by roughly half the normal crew strength. Totally unexpected, lying serenely at anchor, was the USS *Wichita*, almost alongside our mooring. The last time I had seen her she was at anchor in Iceland, the farthest eastern U.S. advanced base when the war started; now she was at the farthest western base as it ended. Then I was on my way home; now I hardly knew what fate held for me.

Looking over the remnants of the Japanese submarine fleet, the common thought was, "Here are all their subs, men; let's blow 'em up and be on our way home tomorrow."

The problem was not so simple. First we had to demilitarize or dispose of the scores or hundreds of suicide craft littering the shores. Second, an Allied commission of Americans, British, and Russians had to reach agreement on the fate of the remaining fleet units. When the Americans discovered that the ultramodern I-200 class reportedly could make twenty-five knots submerged, the antisubmarine people drooled over the possibility of using two of them for advanced training. The British expressed no particular interest, but the Russians wanted an unspecified share of everything. Third, the intelligence experts wanted to analyze some of the six-man subs, which, with the I-200s, represented the best shipbuilding capability of the Japanese at the end of the war.

Our primary interest was disposal of the submarines. The surviving units, including the useless cargo types, were grouped into three divisions, one for each of the three of us waiting for commands: John P. "Speed" Currie, John R. "Red" Mason, and me. The three I-200s, the only fully modern attack submarines built by the Japanese, earned our primary attention. The most noted Japanese submarine was I-58 under Captain Mochitsura "Iki" Hashimoto, who had sunk the USS *Indianapolis* after she delivered the A-bomb to the Army Air Corps on Tinian Island. Hashimoto was the senior skipper in my division.

At first opportunity I gathered the senior COs to talk about Japanese fire-control doctrine and their equivalent of the TDC. Based on this and other information, I drafted a study that eventually became part of the official record. Shortly after, Hashimoto was ordered to Washington, D.C., to testify at the trial of Captain Charles B. McVay, CO of *Indianapolis*, over the loss of his command. That morning, Iki came to me in great distress: "What they do to me? Shoot me in public square?" I reassured him that no such thing would happen. He gave me his beautiful Swiss A-chronometer as a special gift. Figuring somebody would get it anyway, he felt he might as well get some leverage out of it.

On 29 September, Diesel Dan and I made an inspection tour of the base and the town of Sasebo. Most conspicuous was the total destruction of the business district by a B-29 raid. The hardship on the people was terrible, but they looked better and were friendlier than those in Tokyo. All saluted or bowed when we passed, and all cooperated willingly. The first day any of us went ashore, the city was totally deserted. The Japanese had been advised by their government to expect waves of rape and pillaging, just as their troops had done in Nanking and other Chinese cities.

For the sexual onslaught of U.S. occupation troops, the deputy prime minister had ordered the recall of every former prostitute, taxi dancer, masseuse, and waitress to volunteer for "sex amusement centers" wherever sizable groups of GIs were to be stationed. About five thousand were considered necessary for the expected three-hundred-thousand-man American occupation force—"to act as a shock absorber in order to prevent the rape of our wives, sisters and daughters."

Although such happenings were not totally unknown in every army, the Japanese couldn't believe that most American military wanted some sightseeing, some picture taking, a couple of glasses of beer—almost unobtainable in the towns—and a chance to pass out a few candy bars to the children. Strict orders went out from Admiral Halsey personally, "No incidents," threatening dire punishment, and there were very few. Liberty was limited, curfews were strictly observed, and problems were minimal.

After the first day, old men appeared in the streets, the children a day later. Only after several days was a woman to be seen. All were dressed in shapeless, ragged *mòmpe* or working kimono, showing everywhere the effects on the civilian economy of total war since the 1930s. No woman wore a bra; nobody needed one. But we'll get to that later. With little danger of pillage and ravishing, every train soon brought people swarming back to the cities. We, meanwhile, began the work of demilitarization, traveling by jeep over rough, rutted, and very muddy country roads to reach some of the beached *kaiten*.

Kyushu had been targeted for Operation Olympic, the U.S. invasion of Japan planned for 1 November 1945. It then would have become the springboard for Operation Coronet, the invasion of the main island of Honshu in March of 1946. I couldn't see how the Japanese could possibly defend their land with such a miserable network of rail and roads. In Okinawa, for example, huge American bulldozers leveled hills and paddies to make airstrips. When the dozers sank from sight in the paddies, they used them as piers to anchor the steel mats used for runways essentially floating atop the paddies. In these basics of war, Japan still moldered in the primitive technology of the nineteenth century.

The underground caves, shops, and torpedo warehouses— miles of them—were dark, low ceilinged, dank, damp, and eerie. Torpedoes and electrical equipment were pushed into caves with water dripping on them; yet the few concrete-lined, air-conditioned caves contained glass fishing floats impervious to moisture. The organization of stores and supplies was so intricate that nobody understood the system. Elementary safety precautions were unknown. Torpedoes and ammunition, detonators and boosters, depth charges and powder cans, already deteriorating, were all stored in the same building. We heard that an ammo dump had blown up in the Tokyo area killing four and wounding forty, with no evidence of sabotage. Sasebo had a similar incident, killing fifty. One of my early tasks in Sasebo was a lecture to all officers on precautions to prevent accidents.

The estimate that half a million American casualties would have been sustained in the invasion of the home islands, I soon realized, was very high. Even given the fanatical character of the resistance, a nation whose air and naval power were destroyed couldn't defend itself with pitchforks against flamethrowers. Fuel stores, war logistics, food stores, and the people were exhausted. Army tanks couldn't struggle along on charcoal converters, as the city buses did. The ersatz fuel made of soybeans worked fine, even on U.S. diesel submarines, but the vast underground storage tanks were empty; shortages late in the war had already forced pilots to go into combat with less than an hour and a half of solo flying.

I visited a friend on a seaplane tender to arrange a sightseeing flight over the Inland Sea and the island of Kyushu, and then accepted his invitation to join him at the "club." These aviators were smart. They loaded beverages and mix into a motor launch, along with a steward, then picked a scenic spot offshore, and the club was open. We found a site near an isolated village where it seemed possible no white man had ever visited. Near our parking space was an outdoor bathtub, a concrete trough with a grate below for heating the water. As we watched, grandpap took his bath, assisted by two youngsters, a boy and a girl, followed by the father, eldest son, and the rest of the family, all in the same water and oblivious to our presence. Finally the two youngsters had their turn. Meanwhile, other family members were doing Sunday chores, fishing, washing, harvesting the garden—and occasionally urinating in the front yard—the latter not just a Sunday custom. The terraced rice fields in the hills beyond, the utter stillness of evening under a bright crimson sunset, created an unusually picturesque rural landscape.

October first was remarkable, not for being my thirtieth birthday with lots of wonderful mail from home, but because I was flat on my back with fever and a very sore arm. My health record arrived after having been missent to Tokyo, and the doctor immediately noticed that I hadn't had typhus and tetanus shots, very important in this area. He administered repeats of those I had taken in Tokyo. The first ones didn't count because my health record hadn't caught up, and an officer's word was no good in the world of a civilian doctor on contract to the Navy. The only consolation was the mental picture of a rat biting me and spitting it out with a distasteful "Ugh" on chewing nothing but serum.

The days dragged by slowly with much time wasted driving over wretched roads, transacting all business through interpreters. I began to form insights into the character of the people, concluding that an Occidental could never understand the Asian mentality. Driving through the total destruction of the heart of a city, smelling the odors of putrefaction from still trapped bodies, I wondered how the people could treat us with no evidence of hate or ill-feeling. We walked darkened city streets alone at night without fear. Their cooperation was remarkable. That day a young lad about seven years old stopped us to offer a saki cup as a souvenir, a very good grade of china (called porcelain in Japan), and refused any payment, asking only for a cigarette. Everybody begged for cigarettes, but they offered to pay for them, even for a butt.

One of the most interesting sights was the Japanese army demobilization camp on the beach near our anchorage. American tank landing ships, or LSTs, brought in thousands of veterans and their families from China for separation processing. Hundreds of men, women, and children swarmed over the ships. On the main deck, long metal troughs had been built with saltwater from fire hoses providing continuous flushing. Some were urinating or defecating in them; old crones washed clothes, and the children played in them with makeshift boats.

Disembarking at the delousing station, they stripped off all their clothes for fumigation, then walked through a deep footbath while the delousing team with long-nozzled hoses gave them a thorough scrubdown. Coming out the other end, each man, woman, and child was given a GI skivvy shirt draping down to the knees, the Japanese equivalent of the GI Bill benefits. Free to proceed home, or more likely to join the homeless, they walked or swarmed over teeming railroad trains and soon disappeared, hanging onto every protuberance or riding the cowcatcher. Pathetic? Yes. Hopeless? Only temporarily.

On 9–10 October, the great typhoon hit. *Euryale* had to shift moorings into the outer harbor, then put two anchors down in a double moor. Despite the protection of the surrounding hills, the ship creaked and groaned as never before. An LST dragged both anchors and, with full speed rung up, drifted by us less than a foot away. Winds reached 200 knots, but we couldn't verify the figure; the wind indicator flew apart at 160. On Okinawa, where the center passed, the beautiful officers' club built late in the war by the SeaBees atop a steep cliff was blown over the edge. To build the club they had scrounged every piece of material, including slot machines and a stock of alcoholic beverages. When the surrender came, they sold shares to every incoming Army officer for a hefty price and went home rich. After the big wind, the Army had to start over, assessing a new levy to rebuild, with much pain and hard feelings. The club survived for many years, however, as the RyCom (Ryukyu Command) Club, very popular throughout Asia. The typhoon was extremely costly: 250 lives lost, many ships aground, and millions of dollars in damage.

By early November the preliminary demilitarization of western Japan was completed. Our teams had driven hundreds of terribly rough miles chasing down enemy suicide units, destroying stranded and damaged submarines, and looking for submarine intelligence material of interest to the service. Phil Berkeley, my old Marine buddy from *Wichita* days, was now a colonel with the Fifth Marine Amphibious Corps in Sasebo. Phil provided me with the various passes and keys to warehouses to aid my search. Naturally we did a bit of souvenir hunting along the way. At that time, orders arrived for *Euryale* and the squadron to shift operations from Sasebo to Kure, a major Japanese submarine building yard on the Inland Sea. The day before departure, I walked into the wardroom for lunch and found a copy of an anonymous "poem" at every plate.

Schratz's Raiders

Listen my children and you shall hear
Of Schratz's Raiders and their brilliant career.
Early each morning before break of day
These brave men are up and on their way.
Each man a veteran of combat and danger;
Each man at least a Lieutenant Commander.
They strap on their pistols and guns and knives,
And leave farewell messages behind for the wives.

In Case They Don't Get Back.
While skeetshooters and clam-bakers are still in the
    sack
The Raiders are off for the morning attack.
Sometimes in boats, more often in jeeps,
They reach the objective while the enemy sleeps.
Their flag is their symbol of daring and fight—
Three brass balls on a background of white.
White for their purity, honesty, and innocence,
Balls for their rank, position, and ignorance.
This colorful group, not afraid to die
Shall be immortalized in the public eye.
   In Case They Don't Get Back.
Paul Schratz is their leader, brave and strong.
He'll make full Commander before very long.
Many battles he's fought and all of them won,
For among Schratz's Raiders, one loss and you're done.
Bobby Gibbs is second in command
His supply of southern charm exceeds the demand.
For among these commandos there's no room for
    gentlemen;
They'd rather find enemies—and strenglethem.
Live for today, get it while you can,
They must not be cheated, they know to a man.
   In Case They Don't Get Back.
Their strategy is simple, their objective plain:
They must probe the heart of the enemy's domain
To find hidden stores of goods piled in caves.
Destroy or capture or end up in your graves.
Guns and swords, and gyros and brassieres,
They pile in the jeep—loaded to the ears.
And start the long back, dangerous to be sure;
But with never a worry—so brave, so bold, so pure.
They stop off at the "O" Club to reinforce on the way,
With beer for a nickel they drink up their pay
   In Case They Don't Get Back.
They return to *Euryale* and sneak up the stair,
To deposit their treasure in Looter's Lair.
They post a watch, and admission to the den
Is the rank of Commander, or 50,000 yen.
They dress for dinner and eat with the guys,

But the thrill of adventure twinkles in their eyes.
With all hands at the movie, they return to the lair,
And divvy up the treasure until each has his share.
Then off to their cabins, loot piled to their ears,
They count up the take—their goddamned SOUVENIRS.
    In Case They Don't Get Back—FOR MORE!!!!

The author to this day is unknown to me. Copies reached every corner of the ship, and once again it seemed wise for me to take a low profile. The team enjoyed the notoriety, but in fact there was little souveniring. It was a chore to carry anything back, and because of strictures against looting, shipments of war booty rarely got through the mail. Nor did I even want reminders of the war. What I found, I gave to others, and it wasn't much.

Because of both American and Japanese minefields, much of the route to Kure was closed to all navigation. The Shimonoseki Straits were closed so we had to steam around Kyushu Island and into the Inland Sea through Bungo Suido, past the spot where the Fighting O'Toole had gently penetrated, the last submarine to transit before the establishment of a *kaiten* suicide submarine unit in Kure. A narrow channel had been swept; as we passed, minesweepers were at work on both sides of the channel. The whoooom, whoooom of detonating mines reverberated throughout the ship; more than forty must have been set off that day. Two doubtful areas where B-29s had mined the area were navigable only at minimum speed. *Euryale* was the first to penetrate; we exercised great care. The scenery through this area may be the best Japan has to offer, its Riviera. Steaming past Beppu and Oita at slow speed, we were far enough offshore to escape the odor of man, close enough to enjoy the fragrance of pine forests.

On my first chance ashore I took a boat to Mizaki Shima, mainly to go through the battleship *Hyuga*, burned and lying on the bottom, a victim of carrier raids. The main deck was above water, but the devastation by fire and bombs was fierce. We climbed the foremast structure through the admiral's quarters, conning tower, flag bridge, navigating bridge, signal bridge, main battery control station, AA control, radar station, and finally arrived atop the main battery range-keeper and radar mast in the foretop. Japanese ships were built like building blocks piled on a barge; the foretop rose 130 feet above the water.

I had a special reason for wanting to see her. She was the flagship of the force heading back to Japan when *Sterlet* had the last chance to get in a shot and lost it when the CO turned away. Perching like seagulls, we could still see oil seeping from crushed tanks far below, leaving a wide slick moving to sea across the glassy, rain-drenched waters.

Then the commodore and division commanders made an inspection trip (the official term for sightseeing when a junior officer makes all the arrangements and doesn't get to go). We first visited Kure, a completely destroyed city with a pall of heavy smoke from underground fires still smoldering in the huge coal stocks. Across the bay, two new *Katsuragi* class carriers, the battleship *Ise,* and cruisers *Izumo* and *Aoba,* lay on the bottom, burned to the water's edge. The *Izumo* was well known to old China hands. Flagship of the Japanese fleet in Shanghai before the war, she always anchored for safety as close as possible to the U.S. consulate. The Chinese tried to sink her in 1938, killing many natives in the attempt, but she survived until her luck ran out in the last days of the war.

The battleship *Haruna,* carriers *Hosho* and *Unryu,* two more cruisers, destroyers, gunboats, escorts—an entire Japanese fleet was there, entombed in shallow graves. In the naval base, twenty-six submarines lay at anchor waiting for us, and eighty-four midget submarines in drydock awaited the destruction order. Most surprising was an old World War I four-piper destroyer, the former USS *Stewart*. In drydock in Surabaja when the war came, she overturned on the keel blocks in a bombing raid, then was repaired and put into service by the Japanese. From Kure her former American owners took her to sea and sent her to an honorable death.

At the Japanese Army Immigration Station, several army supply submarines lay at anchor. Here we learned one more story of the severe rivalry between the Japanese army and navy. When the army asked the navy to use submarines to carry food and urgent medical supplies to army units cut off by the U.S. offensives across the Pacific, the Imperial Navy, claiming lack of ships and manpower, became first reluctant then hostile. The army, left with no alternative but to build its own supply submarines, refused assistance or even blueprints from the navy. Lacking shipbuilding facilities, the army used a boiler factory in Korea for the task. The ships looked like boilers and sailed like boilers. Only one got into the war; it was sunk off Lingayen, raised by the U.S., and sent to the states. Technically they were the "YU" class; we named them the "YU Fathead," "YU Dope," and so forth.

Then our speedboat headed for Hiroshima at full throttle. Only when the Japanese escort began screaming for a change of course did we realize that he was trying to steer us clear of a minefield. With a heavy fog rolling in, we decided to defer Hiroshima for another day. But much of interest was visible on the waterfront. Moored at the army base was an army aircraft carrier, nearing completion when destroyed in the A-blast. Because of poor tactical air support by the Japanese navy to aid the sorely pressed army, the army decided to build its own carrier, a monstrosity that never got to sea.

It was high time for the raiders to get back to work. My exec, Robert I. "Bob" Gibbs, and I examined some midget submarine construction in caves on an island off Kure, then visited the Torpedo Experimental Station, where we sought a few specimens of two new torpedoes the Japanese were developing. Unfortunately, the entire station was a mass of rubble, twisted wreckage, and still smoking fires in a small mountain of coal. One section of a torpedo lay alongside a fifty-foot crater, where a building had stood, and just twenty-five feet from two B-29-launched mines, fully armed, that missed the water on the drop. Since the expiration date for Purple Hearts had probably gone by, we passed the problem of the new torpedo to the mine disposal and intelligence teams.

The destruction of the island full of midget submarines presented problems. The method suggested to me was to burn through the hulls with a cutting torch. This seemed naive. Anybody could weld them up as fast as we could cut them. Commander John L. Detar, the exec of the tender, urged privately that we use controlled explosives. With his assistance, our four young demolition experts in the squadron soon commandeered from the army all the necessary gear and loaded it into launches. Off we went, complete with explosives, incendiaries, sledges, motor generator sets, and a wild gleam in the eyes of more than one of the wrecking team. Doc William R. "Bill" Hunt, a boon friend and fine surgeon, went along. He had the greatest thrill of his career when somebody pointed to a new diesel generator awaiting installation on a sub and handed him a big sledge. There must be a destructive instinct in all of us.

To destroy the submarines, I decided to experiment with the use of controlled explosives, setting one up with a charge in the control room. The explosives caused little more than a "poof," but the destruction was total. The pressure hull puffed up like a balloon; inside was a spaghetti of piping and pumps. Perfect! Much encouraged, we set up a series of about a dozen more timed to go off at one-minute intervals. What I didn't know soon brought me to grief. These young demolition experts, trained and sent far from home to do their job, were very disappointed at the lack of fire and brimstone in the controlled explosion. Without consulting me, they decided that instead of one charge they would double it and in addition put doubled charges forward and aft as well.

The first went off with a sharp flash of fire and a horrendous explosion. The hull split; burning fuel and rubber rose in a new mushroom cloud over the city of Kure. Flames shooting up the conning tower hatch focused a massive torch on the roof of the huge warehouse, setting heavy timbers on fire. Then the second one went off—and so on through a dozen more, each spreading the previous destruction. Choking clouds of smoke forced the afternoon PBY mail plane to use landing lights to set down on the water five miles away. The warehouse, burning merrily, set the barracks on fire, another building, then the firehouse. Japanese officers suddenly appeared from nowhere, asking in great indignation, "Who's going to pay for this disaster?"

The thought had occurred to me, too. Then somebody reported the commodore's barge approaching at high speed. I had to get the Japanese clear before he arrived or I would be double-dipped in kimchi. On a stray piece of cardboard, I wrote out a receipt for the Japanese commander for fifteen submarines, a warehouse, barracks building, and fire station and signed it Charles A. Lockwood, Vice Admiral USN, Commander Submarine Force, Pacific. The Japanese officers exited right as the commodore entered left. Seeing his career also going up in smoke in a direct violation of Admiral Halsey's order, he shook a bony finger under my nose and shouted, "Who's going to pay for this disaster?"

I had already faced the question but couldn't use the same answer. He added, "You stay here until every ember is out."

By then the hulls had turned cherry red. The hard rubber battery jars burned fiercely; fuel and luboil tanks created dense clouds of oily black smoke mixed with poisonous yellow fumes from the sulfuric acid, burning furiously throughout the night until only a pile of slag remained. It was quite colorful, I thought. I shot some excellent color movies of it.

Under cover of darkness I got back to the ship at 2300 that night, having had no food since breakfast. Johnny Detar came to the rescue. He became my undying friend over the holocaust and immediately aided my conspiracy to get back to the really big job at Hiroshima for a good look around. (I had to go secretly lest they accuse me of that one too.) No leave or liberty was granted in Kure, and Hiroshima was out of bounds for all military personnel. Bill Hunt as a physician was particularly anxious to go, so Detar gave us a set of orders to make an official survey. We hitchhiked to the roadblock outside Hiroshima, flagged down a military police patrol, and asked him to drive us around on the grand tour— easy if you have enough gall and a few oak leaves.

The devastation at Hiroshima was awesome. Where other cities turned to rubble, here we saw dust. By the jeep speedometer an area eight and a half miles north-south, and six miles east-west offered the most god-awful mess imaginable. Only a handful of buildings still stood, one a seven-story newspaper office with a small tower on top. We went to the tower to take photos, but no camera can record the total desolation. Even the debris had vaporized in the blast, and the effect on people was profound. A marble bridge showed shadows of people etched into the paving just as they stood when vaporized.

For the first time in Japan I saw sullen people who avoided contact or who were anything but servile in assisting us. I have no imagination to conceive of the eighty thousand dead; the living dead carried their own vivid message. The death of a family is a tragedy; the death of a city is a statistic. No woman in the vicinity had menstruated since the bomb, we were informed. I saw a boy with ugly red keloids disfiguring his face and bald head. I tried to photograph him but didn't have the gall to ask him to pose and I doubted the film would work anyway. We were told the radiation level was still too high; movie film would be ruined.

I carried the film magazines in a special lead wrapper, popping them into the camera for each shot and back into the wrap. We soon learned that these fears were groundless; the radiation lasted only a few hours. We talked frankly with our guide-interpreter, a former Japanese army officer. Though he had lost his wife and two children in the blast, as a military man he justified use of the bomb. Perhaps no other reply was possible for him under the circumstances, but others who knew they could speak freely gave the same message.

My team had the unpleasant task of inspecting the I-402, one of the huge six-thousand-ton plane-carrying monsters. The ship had a figure-of-eight hull, carried 238 men and 38 officers, and was so filthy we could hardly walk through it. The CO was hospitable. Of his twenty-four years of service, fifteen were in submarines with five commands. (The most senior U.S. submarine commander at the end of the war had about ten years' service and was on his first or second command.) I-402 had made one patrol, off Brazil. For food, sacks of rice were everywhere, even layered over the deck plates in the engine rooms. The rats loved it, but the engines, lacking gaskets, sprayed fuel oil over everything with each stroke of a piston. The ersatz soybean fuel spillage turned rancid with a vile odor. The engine rooms were like the insides of a septic tank. The sub had only one head—a hole in the deck—and no showers below decks. Many preferred to improvise. During long dives, the improvisations added to the overall aroma. Noting no first aid facilities, I asked the skipper what they did to treat cuts, bruises, or minor injuries. He said simply, "We piss on them."

That killed the conversation. I asked Bill Hunt later if I could have misunderstood this uncivilized custom. He replied, "About 90 percent of antiseptics have crystals of urea in them somewhere. You might remember this. In a future emergency, it might prove useful." I was about to mutter that if the emergency involved a lady it might require delicate handling, but I decided to change the subject.

The I-402 had undergone captain's inspection just before our arrival. The report on the condition of the ship was so typical that I made some notes. Equipment such as the gyro, engines, fathometer all rated "Perfection." The last paragraph stated:

	Item	No.	Remarks
General Arm	Fire Apparatus	6	Perfection
	Washtub	3	Perfection
	Canvas hose	96 mtr.	Perfection
	The tip [nozzle]	1	Perfection
Surgeoncy Arm		0	
Paymaster	Tableware	310	Perfection
	Cooking Tools	2	Perfection

The CO courteously offered every assistance. On my departure he presented me with a small gift, a beautifully carved ivory cougar on a teak base. Then he asked a favor—would I send a message to the senior officer present for him, requesting permission to return to Kure? After some double talk and chuckling on both sides, the reason emerged—he wanted a sex cruise.

In Kure harbor, as generally in Japan, women were rowed out to the ships by loving fathers capitalizing on their daughters' physical assets. Or the government took care of the men by sending the "SeaBees," as we called them, the Consolation Battalion to service the troops. I first saw this custom in Sasebo when an old man rowed two females out to each of the submarines in turn. The girls disappeared down into the forward torpedo room and reappeared out the after torpedo room hours later.

While examining the eighty-four midget subs in a drydock in Kure, we learned that other visiting Americans were interested in undersea warfare. Major Alexander P. de Seversky, the airpower pioneer, came by with a team of photographers. All those submarines filling the huge dock made quite a sight. He was then writing a book on how airpower won the war, and this picture gained wide publicity. I always liked to hear that kind of talk. After three years in combat, I learned that anybody who wanted to win any war single-handed had my blessing, as long as I'm not one of the "hands." It took the best of all the service arms to win this time, and it will again. The zealots have their role, just as long as we don't take them too seriously.

With one task we had little success. Shopping was almost nonexistent in Japan. Even with our advantages of travel into the boonies and through cities well off the beaten path, we could find little. Kure, we thought, was the last chance. Bill Hunt and I tried it together, in the hills beyond the city. We made out well enough in pidgin Japanese to go door to door, talking to everyone we passed. We met a group of women and caused quite a stir when we stopped to talk. They had no "kimono wo" for sale but they darted off to their homes, returning with small gifts for us. These were poor people and we felt genuinely touched by their sacrifice. Seeing a cute little girl in the group, I showed the mother a new family picture I had just received from Henri. What a hit it made! As they passed it around, jabbering and laughing, we could see their amazement to learn that the American ogres could be family people like themselves.

A short distance beyond, we came to a very fine manor. Seeing a young lady in the yard, Bill started off with his "Doko, con ichi kimono wo—" She replied, "I beg your pardon." Bill, so engrossed in his Japanese that he didn't recognize English, tried again. Then we all burst out laughing. Born and raised in Los Angeles, she had returned home after high school. Her family was one of Japan's wealthiest, related to a former premier. We were invited in, asked to lunch, and entertained for several hours. The lunch came from their slender stock of sweet potatoes, garnished with crystals of sugar like rock candy—the first they had served in two years. I put out of mind any thoughts of how the yams had flourished on night soil and concentrated on happier thoughts.

The old prince, a distinguished man with a long life in a

Japan of a happier era, delighted in talking about his country and ours and spoke freely on all subjects. He told us of the order, before the surrender, for all people to vacate the streets and bar the doors and windows before the arrival of the brutish Americans. Knowing the arrogance and savagery of their own forces, they expected the same and were amazed at what they saw. In truth, the Americans were superb. With no liquor available and very limited liberty, even the unruly 2 percent had little chance to blow off steam except within their own compounds. Any rowdiness would have reflected against MacArthur; their exemplary conduct aided him considerably.

While we were talking, two of the maids came in all aflutter, chattering to the prince. He apologized for the interruption, then said to me, "I offer you my sincere apologies. My maids have been doing laundry for U.S. Army enlisted men. Two of the men came by to pick up their laundry, and the maids didn't realize there were Navy men in the house. I apologize for allowing Army people under my roof while you are here." That's what I call interservice rivalry—the kind that had seriously undermined the Japanese war effort.

We discussed the decision to drop the A-bomb on Hiroshima. He echoed the same feeling I had received in discussions with submarine officers. The Japanese army and navy could probably not have faced surrendering under the threat of conventional weapons alone. They realized fully by then their technological shortcomings. The A-bomb allowed them to save some of their dignity in defeat by claiming they didn't lose the war; only this scientific stuff beat them.

Before we left, we mentioned that we were trying to purchase something to take back home. The prince asked his daughter to bring out some priceless heirloom china—three large platters—offering us two of them. The third, he said, had to stay in the family to be passed down to his son; all had been with the estate for five generations. He wanted no money, only a symbolic gift we could offer "on which to start building the new relationship of Japan and America." We had nothing with us; the only thing in the ship's store was a camera, possibly, and we promised to return the following day. We finally purchased two of their kimonos, accepted some other gifts, and took our departure, racking our brains to think what to bring back.

We had scarcely left the courtyard when a little girl ran up and took my arm, asking us to follow. She had waited for us nearly five hours to take us to her home. They wanted to see my family picture again. Showing the picture around, they pointed to Regina and offered a very beautiful kimono for her, plus a fine red silk one for her mother. They apologized that they had none small enough for our youngest but they found one for Bill's wife, Helen. They wanted no money but would accept some sugar; we finally forced them to accept three dollars in scrip.

Returning to the manor the following day, we expressed our regrets that we could find no appropriate gift. I could have offered a camera but the prewar image of Japanese photographing American installations from behind every lamppost somehow deterred me. Would this be the germ to start a new world war? I couldn't go through with it and regretfully returned the superb ceramic piece.

During my absence, all Japanese submarines in Kure, plus the three with American crews in Tokyo, had been ordered to Sasebo. There they would stay until the Allied commission decided their fate. And the commission hadn't yet convened. Days went by; it was already the end of October. I could no longer count the months since I left the states. I hadn't visited our parents in Pittsburgh in over two years. Sisters and brothers were marrying and enjoying family gatherings of which I never would be a part. It wouldn't be bad if the very important task we were doing could be finished so we could get on with a new world. But the pace was so slow and uncertain it seemed the job would never end. We still counted on the *Euryale* being in San Francisco for mothballing by Christmas. Red Mason tried to get some dope from the submarine detail officer in Pearl Harbor about our future; he was assured that we were "untouchable." We were Admiral Lockwood's private property.

Two key men on my team got good news. Bob Gibbs and Bill Hunt, both reserve officers, received orders to inactive duty. Bill had a medical practice in Duquesne, Pennsylvania, and Bob planned to enter Emory University in Atlanta to study medicine. As a parting favor, the Raiders liberated a fine Japanese microscope and a set of chemical weights to start Bob on his medical career. The three of us had become close friends; I was sincerely sorry to see them go.

A new squadron medical officer arrived just before Bill departed, a college buddy of his and a noted eye specialist. He was just what I needed. My severe case of "periscope eye" showed little improvement; treatment by a specialist was necessary. At the time of the surrender, any close work very quickly left me able to identify only light from dark; I had essentially no vision in one eye. While in Japan my sight improved slightly because I was doing no close work. Doc Robert Hogsett made a careful examination and could see no disability except astigmatism in one eye, easily correctable. He suggested that one wears glasses for only three reasons: if he can't see without them, if his eyes hurt without them, or if he happens to like his appearance with glasses. My case fitted none of these. I dropped my glasses over the side, promising not to mention eyesight again for fifteen years. If I never regained the visual acuity of my youth, within six months I learned to cope and crossed it from my mind.

On completion of the job in Kure, *Euryale* made tracks to get back to Sasebo before the arrival of the rest of the submarines. Unfortunately, one struck a mine near Shimonoseki and was wrecked beyond repair; another struck a mine in Bungo Suido and was lost with only one survivor; a third went aground just south of Sasebo. The Americans were also having trouble. The USS *Bridge*, a refrigerator ship, left Sasebo just as we entered and struck a mine in our wake, receiving serious damage.

It was quickly decided that one of us PCOs and a prize crew should meet each incoming sub at sea, inspect it, and help pilot it into the anchorage. Going over in my mind how many close calls I'd had with mines in the last two years, I thought this duty would be pushing my luck. I put such thoughts out of mind. U.S. ships passing by in the channel were probably curious about these weatherbeaten excuses for submarines, Japanese colors flying and a Japanese crew on the bridge, plus one American.

Two of the incoming subs missed the rendezvous, proceeded independently to a secluded cove, anchored, and went ashore. When I arrived on board, the exec thought he could get under way in "five days, about." I ordered the skippers to return aboard, get their crews off the beach, and get under way immediately. In about thirty minutes they were en route to join the rest of the underseas fleet. The Japanese were doing things about the way I would if we had lost the war, and we, unfortunately, too often followed the whims of the bureaucracy. With twenty-nine subs now in Sasebo, men were standing watches all over the place, interfering with each other, primarily to create the semblance, if not the substance, of efficiency.

I hadn't yet seen Nagasaki, where the second A-bomb was dropped, and finally wangled another official duty trip. The bomb damage was awesome but by Hiroshima standards less spectacular than expected. Primarily to see the countryside in the full glory of fall colors, I traveled by rail. The train winds along the shores of Sasebo Bay almost the entire way. We passed through the world-famed Nagasaki orange groves, where little boys handed us fresh fruit through the train windows in exchange for cigarettes. As a nonbeliever in nicotine for either pre- or post-teens, I disappointed them, but they gave me the oranges anyway. They were probably full of radiation, I thought, but delicious.

The next morning we had scheduled a trip to Shimonoseki, the northwestern entrance to the Inland Sea, for a demolition job. I noted wryly that the prescribed method now was with explosives, but I was not one to gloat. Participating was my new exec, Allen B. "Buck" Catlin, replacing Bob Gibbs. The pre-dawn train from Sasebo was frigid. Japanese trains were heated by body warmth. In November it's not enough, in July, too much. Arriving in Moji at 1400, we were driven to a small luxury liner, which the Chinese ran from Shanghai to Hankow before the Japanese took her over, now used by the U.S. Army for officers' quarters. A Japanese staff, retained on board and paid by their government, did miracles with "C" and "K" rations plus a little fish and rice. Beer, saki, and gin were also supplied by the Japanese, convincing us that the Navy had missed something. We completed the destruction in record time so as to get back quickly to that beautiful ship. I tried to photograph the blast, but it was near sunset and I was too close, actually *inside* the column of water and fuel oil. At the ship, we went to a dance attended by fourteen, count 'em fourteen, Army nurses. Most seemed spoiled by overadulation, but we gave silent thanks to the Japanese government for definitely unspoiled beer and saki.

Shortly before midnight somebody suggested going to a geisha house. I had heard the somewhat cynical explanation that women's rights in Japan at that time had progressed only to the late thirteenth century. Women were chattels. They couldn't pull as big a load as the horse, but they pulled more than the dog and had the marginal advantage that one could sleep with them. Companionship they were not. For this purpose it was necessary to create the geisha, an entertainer in a profession for which they are rigidly trained. They laugh at all jokes, not because the jokes are funny but because they're trained to laugh. They keep the men's saki cups full, light their cigars, dance, put on skits, and serve in other ways. The American word symbolizing the good life then was "in like Flynn." The geishas caught on quickly and after each sip of saki, they toasted "in rike Frynn," to the accompaniment of much laughter.

Even with half a buzz on from the night's drinking, I found this too much to stomach. Their floor show was a stilted ritual with a significance or artistry wholly unknown to us clods from the West. Most of us tried a few dances with them, which were just as ritualized, lacking spontaneity or any honest emotion beyond that of a robot. Only when Buck Catlin, tall and lanky, tried to teach them to jitterbug was it funny, mainly because they fell out of character and almost laughed at each other. Of the many great gifts brought to Japan by the American culture, the improved status of women must stand near the top.

On our return to Sasebo, another example of the dreadful status of women greeted us. A ship had just arrived and anchored astern of *Euryale,* a Japanese escort vessel returning about seventy-five prostitutes from a "SeaBee" consolation battalion in Okinawa to their native Korea. These pitiful creatures, diseased, many pregnant, were tough as tungsten. I had some work to do in the harbor alongside and took an interpreter, Robert White, to assist. We could have spent the day talking with them. The women were actually little worse off than most in Japan, which means that slavery lived and flourished. We couldn't imagine how they would ever pull their lives together again.

A note awaited my return. The former *Wichita* Marine, Colonel Phil Berkeley, invited me to join him for dinner the following evening. I had met his boss, General Holland M. Smith, with the Allens in Maui back during *Atule* days. Unfortunately, I had to beg off for a big meeting on the fate of the submarines. Hiram Cassedy, who had taken command of the big I-400, was flying to Tokyo the following day to shake down some information on disposition of the submarines. I should have gone with Phil; Hiram failed completely. Phil also arranged a flight for me to Beppu, the Japanese Riviera on the Inland Sea, the site of the famed giant Buddha. The trip sounded so good that the senior aviator decided to take two planes—tiny Piper Cubs—and join us.

The route across Kyushu runs through a six-thousand-foot mountain range, very high when flying a plane with a ceiling of seven thousand feet. I also wanted to get some photos of Mount Aso, an active volcano. Two jeeps met us on arrival and took us around the town and through the ancient moated castle at Oita, hardly a common sight in Japan. A tiny but elegant stone building next to the castle, built to house the emperor's picture, was untouched; the castle was heavily damaged and burned by the B-29s.

The Army graciously wined and dined us at a luxury hotel they were enjoying. We were barely able to resist the temptation to use the hot springs for a "hotsy-botsy" bath. After a leisurely tour of the Buddha, we headed toward home. On the return my pilot and I peeled off to photograph the volcano. The weather was perfect, crystal clear and with no wind. We flew low over the lip of the crater, and I got some superb movies looking into the core. Then we passed over the town of Omuta on which I had made the B-29 raid, finding it totally wiped out. If I had feelings of doubt then about my participation, they were lessened by my living in Japan these several months.

The return to Sasebo came just in time for me to participate in a few volleyball games at the Submarine Club we had set up outside the base. A simple farmhouse assigned us by the local government had a large center room we used for socializing, gaming, and the inevitable songfest each night. Part of the refreshments came from the stock of Emu bitters—fine Australian beer—which the *Euryale* brought from Down Under. Some refreshments also came from a warehouse with about forty thousand cases of Japanese beer and saki which the Raiders had liberated to help slake our tongues after exercise.

We had given the farmer a shovel, "Gift of the U.S. Navy," making him so happy he wept. He probably gave it to his wife with all the fervor we would attach to a dozen American Beauty roses. Armed with tools ancient and modern, he (she) and his (her) neighbors spaded up the vegetable garden to make us a very attractive volleyball court. Soon more and more Japanese locals came to see the games, cheering on the players and taking still greater pains to beautify the court. We dubbed it "Currie's Coliseum." The farmer offered to help tend bar, but our fear of dysentery limited his aid to trash removal and cleaning the head. The club became the village center. A big communal washhouse and dining hall adjoined the club. People returning from the fields at night bowed as they passed, the ladies smiling slyly and bowing deepest of all.

When life got dull, Edward D. Spruance, commanding one of the big I-400 boats, could always be counted on to raise our spirits. On one liberty he and I had made together, we planned a bit of shopping, then a visit to a geisha house for an evening of music and entertainment. Ed, son of Admiral Spruance, was a wild man who shared little with his staid and proper parent except great natural ability. Going ashore in the Japanese admiral's barge he had commandeered, we took his jeep to a geisha house in Arita, about ten miles outside Sasebo, well beyond the out-of-bounds limit for all military personnel. After sitting around sipping saki and watching the entertainment, Ed became curious about why Japanese girls were so small-breasted, claiming that he and I were better endowed than any of them. Verification was simple and quite scientific. Language in these instances was no barrier; it merely spiced up the exhibits with conversation. Ed's theory was that Japanese girls didn't use cotton for what nature had forgotten, but used the tight obis around the waist to force a few ounces of flesh from their middle up or down to give them a figure.

With this question resolved satisfactorily, Ed responded to an urgent call of nature. He stepped out the rear door and into a big honey pot full of night soil, sinking up to his bosom—er, chest. When he returned, even the women couldn't stand him. It spoiled the party. Nobody would dance with him. He dropped off his clothes, except Lil Abner boots and skivvy shorts, and we headed for the jeep. Arriving at the landing about 0700, we found his barge stranded high and dry by the outgoing tide. I commandeered a rowboat to get us to the tender. We struggled up the gangway to arrive on deck at the stroke of morning quarters, with the entire crew on parade during the national anthem. The stench still reached halfway to Chefoo; as quickly as possible Ed was pushed into a shower.

On Thanksgiving my morale hit a new low. The commodore called a conference at 0900. Orders had come through to take over two more submarines for return to the states to evaluate them as high-speed targets for the antisubmarine forces. Speed Currie was senior and got the first; Red Mason, next senior, got the other. This meant that we would be delayed further until the two new boats, the ultramodern I-201 and I-203, could be made ready for the long voyage home. I lost all around. Not only was it the last chance for a command but the return home for all of us would be delayed. I tried to remember a holiday when I felt more depressed. I went to a special mass on the hospital ship USS *Samaritan* and talked with the padre afterward. He tried to cheer me up, but to be the senior PCO in the entire Pacific was no consolation when no command was available.

Misery loves company. The mail brought an official notice that all reserves were exempted from paying tax on income earned from the government during the war, but regulars were required to pay. The regulars also lost the $1,500 tax exemption granted during the war, and, the ultimate blow, we lost submarine pay for our present duty because we were not "serving on board a U.S. submarine," as required to qualify for hazardous duty pay. The old saw about the regular being indispensable in war and forgotten as soon as the fighting was over held true once again. We thought

Congress might at least have waited until completion of our hazardous duty in Japan before lowering the ax. The commodore appealed the decision, but we lost the pay in the meantime.

I took my usual cure for the blahs, arranging a sightseeing flight in a big Navy PBM over the Tsushima Straits and southern Korea, then around both shores of the Inland Sea, Hiroshima, Kobe, and Osaka. Returning after a 750-mile flight, I found a really sweet letter from Henri waiting. My blues disappeared. If they were replaced by a wave of homesickness, it was at least a much more wholesome alternative.

That night the commodore hosted a special party at the club and came back singing a new song titled "When Do We Leave Here?" Two lines caught my attention: "We destroyed all the midgets, / And gave the Commodore fidgets." He contributed the lines himself. Obviously I was forgiven. I also heard from Wakayama that every sightseer passing through the Kure area was toured by the midget holocaust. Now that the Japanese weren't going to make an incident about it, the time had come to claim it as a great day's work. I could visualize the commodore back in New London telling what a big time we had blowing up the Jap fleet. I was out of the doghouse, but at odd moments I wondered whatever happened to that receipt signed by "Admiral Lockwood." To this day it has never surfaced.

On 30 November, a week and a day after Thanksgiving, Red Mason got orders to shore duty in Washington. My moment had finally arrived. I became the new captain—technically, officer in charge—of the I-203. My exec was Buck Catlin; the engineer, Lt. John Drumm; the communications officer, Lt. John A. "Jack" Ahearn; electrical, Lt. Robert Prine; and the "gofers," Lts. (j.g.) Doug Gillam and Robert P. "Nick" Nicholson. I knew them well and was delighted. Getting a new ship of revolutionary design steady for sea so quickly was a stupendous job. But at long last I had a command for which I held total responsibility. I was ready for anything.

The I-203 officers had been working and playing volleyball together daily. By chance, the big match with the *Euryale* team happened the day after the decision to send the two boats back to the states. We were all set. In the hottest games played yet, we won two out of three, the commodore cheering us on and the CO of the tender backing his team as an excited Japanese audience cheered both teams from the sidelines. It gave us the league championship, and we thought it a fine omen.

Then I learned that Bill Wylie was due to arrive in Sasebo. He had done well since leaving *Scorpion*. A fine command tour in destroyer USS *Stormes*—including a hit by a kamikaze off Okinawa—earned him command of Mine Division 7, the new minesweepers in Sasebo. Bill arrived by plane only to find the division had left six hours earlier. He got back in the plane and chased them home. Some thought his six-hour tour was one of the better ways to see Japan in those days. I had planned a proper reunion with Bill and Phil Berkeley, including a tour of the subs, cocktails at the club, and, at the commodore's invitation, dinner with the cabin mess. Except for Bill's absence it was delightful.

7

The Sorry *Sasori*

I-203, a Sen-Taka or high-speed submarine, was similar to
the German Type XXI, both designed as ultramodern attack
submarines capable of very high bursts of speed to break
contact with the enemy. Completed in May 1945, I-203 was
259 feet long and displaced thirteen hundred tons. The
designed underwater speed was about twenty-five knots—
almost three times that of the American fleet boat. She was
about 50 feet shorter than a U.S. fleet submarine, and her
draft three feet deeper. A very high length-to-beam ratio
contributed to her high speed. After sea trials, bow planes,
and huge stabilizer fins amidships were added to improve
stability, and hydraulically operated valves for free-flooding
the deck areas were eliminated. These changes reduced the
top submerged speed to nineteen knots. Her two diesel
engines produced 2,750 horsepower and sixteen knots on the
surface; the enormous storage batteries produced 5,000 shaft
horsepower for the nineteen-knot submerged speed. Oddly,
the surface and submerged horsepower were almost exact
opposites of the U.S. fleet sub with 5,500 surface and 2,740
submerged. The I-200 class, the first Japanese submarines
with all-welded hulls, had a test depth of 360 feet, deeper
than *Scorpion*, less than *Sterlet* and *Atule*. Its cruising range

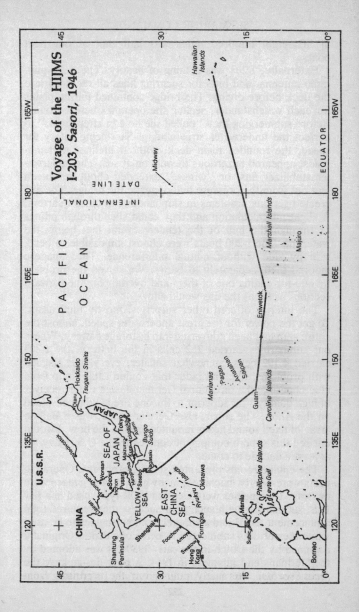

Voyage of the HIJMS
I-203, *Sasori*, 1946

of fifty-eight hundred miles was half that of our fleet boat.

Externally, I-203 was a thing of beauty. The deck gun, radio antenna, and bitts for securing lines all recessed into the deck before diving. The bridge contained fairing plates for each watchstander, sealing the openings before diving. Before submerging they "pulled the hole in after them," to perfect the underwater streamlining. Sacrificing safety for speed, the rounded main deck, without lifelines or handholds, appeared hazardous to walk on at sea. The underwater stabilizer fins, or "wings," extended about seventeen feet out from the pressure hull opposite the bridge. The fins created serious problems in shiphandling in close quarters. A slight miscalculation and they could slice through pilings or through the hull of the tender several feet below the waterline. The I-200 boats were almost impossible to berth side by side without mutual interference. The Japanese moored them separately to buoys. We solved the problem by end-for-ending one of them and overlapping the forward sections as far as the fins would allow.

The interior offered other surprises, mostly unpleasant. To get the power for the great underwater speed, almost the entire ship had been converted into a storage battery. Where our submarines carried 252 cells in the battery, the I-203 carried 4,192 cells, somewhat smaller, every one plagued with problems. She had radar that couldn't tell a blip from blue cheese and a directional German-design radar receiver of high quality—far superior to the one Fred Oyhus designed on the *Atule*. The sonar, also German-made, was a Balkon array of fixed sound heads mounted around the bow. I would not see this superb equipment equaled in the U.S. Navy for at least a decade to come.

The engine rooms presented serious problems. Operating parts were poorly machined; many gaskets and gauges were missing. The engines were German HOR type, used in a few U.S. submarines with such poor success they required total replacement. I-203 had a snorkel to allow engines to be used while the sub was submerged to periscope depth. Originally designed by the Dutch in the early 1930s, it was adopted by the Germans and Japanese in 1944. A poor design gave the Japanese fits, alternately pulling out the eardrums from excessive vacuum or poisoning the inside air with noxious exhaust fumes. The Americans, operating more and more on the surface late in the war, never needed the snorkel, adding it only in postwar construction.

I took special interest in the torpedo-firing system. The Japanese torpedo data computer was far simpler than ours, lacking a position keeper and much of the automation necessary for attacks in a rapidly changing situation, or against multiple targets. I worked with the Japanese TDC until I was able to make a full comparison with ours, meeting a few oddities—ours displayed a "correct solution" light when a torpedo could be fired, theirs the opposite, indicating when one could not be fired.

Throughout the ship, a critical lack of spare parts, blueprints, and machinery histories immediately became obvious. Pieces of equipment were missing. These pre-electronic-era Japanese subs, for example, used voice tubes for communication; several sections were missing. The standard reply was, "Honorable B-29 bomb honorable voice tube factory. So solly."

We had a month to get the ship ready for the midwinter crossing of the Pacific. Commodore Moseley, skeptical from the beginning, didn't believe it could be done. I was inclined to believe him, but I would never let him know. Common sense rarely won over pure guts.

We had one advantage over Speed Currie and the I-201. His boat had been in operation longer, but ours was in better shape, and however good his officers, I thought ours had the edge. They went to work more vigorously and with more imagination. The primary task facing each of us was the engineering plant and, overall, to get spare parts, vital pieces of equipment, and supplies for the long trip. We set about both tasks with enthusiasm. Given the shortages, a lot more than enthusiasm was required.

The date 7 December 1945 in Japan marked itself in our memories for several reasons. First, Commander Submarines ordered the three big plane-carrying subs to Pearl Harbor, escorted by the USS *Greenlet,* the submarine rescue vessel in Sasebo. Departure was scheduled for Tuesday, 11 December, via Guam and Midway. Second, Japanese partisan groups had recently become active, and we learned that an "incident" might occur on the Pearl Harbor anniversary. It actually came a few days later, on a holiday similar to our Independence Day; the target: the occupation forces. As a precaution, we were forbidden to hike on the beaches, ship's boat landing sites were reduced to six, and an armed patrol boat commenced patrolling offshore during darkness. The results of the increased readiness were not unexpected. A *Euryale* patrol opened fire on a darkened small boat that happened to be friendly; and the next night a sailor killed himself trying to load a pistol. Toward dawn an innocent local fishing boat was fired on, wounding two occupants. Somebody decided that unless the Japanese radicals were to become considerably more active, we seemed too trigger-happy to take precautions safely. In a week the routine returned to normal.

Third, I spent the weekend with Phil Berkeley at his quarters. At a big Saturday night party hosted by General Smith, I met several Marine officer friends I hadn't seen in years and enjoyed the evening to the full. Also, General Smith had just received authorization for us to destroy the cargo submarines, some very welcome news the submarine force had not yet heard. The following morning I went to mass at the Cathedral of the Sacred Heart, the only building in the entire business district of Sasebo untouched by the fire bombing. The big thrill was dropping a wad of fifty-sen bills in the collection basket, feeling like a big spender over a net value of about sixteen cents.

Returning from the weekend ashore, I saw a signal from my submarine to the tender, "Please send Fire and Rescue party." I jumped fifty feet in the air, trying to speed up the action. Leaping aboard the *Euryale* launch heading for the scene, I found a potentially serious fire in the battery compartment, not in my boat but in Speed's. It delayed his first trip to sea but the real danger was the effect on the commodore. It wouldn't build confidence about our safety at sea during the voyage ahead.

The first trip to sea for I-203 came on 12 December. Everything except the engines worked far better than we had any right to expect. It felt good to get to sea in a submarine again, and the perfectly streamlined silhouette of the ship looked beautiful. As I passed between the tall bluffs guarding the entrance, feeling the throb of a diesel far below, life really felt good. Having my own command was heady wine.

Success couldn't have been better timed. Orders came from the big boss to take the two boats to Pearl, probably with *Euryale* as escort, tentatively to depart Sasebo for Guam on 10 January 1946. I had just made arrangements to spend a week in Shanghai over Christmas, my first leave period in over two years. Regretfully, I gave it up. To get critical engine spares and vitally necessary battery jar replacements, I immediately sent John Drumm and two petty officers to the town of Maizuru on the Sea of Japan. They will never forget the trip.

Few trains ran, none on schedule. For John we commandeered two flatcars and a passenger coach, all antique, four-wheeled jobs pockmarked with bullet holes. With his land fleet, John flagged down tows on local trains to hitchhike for the fourteen-hundred-mile round trip, carrying C-rations for food and B (beer) rations for survival. The immediate problem was freezing to death. To warm the frosty interior, they built a fire in the aisle, scavenging burnables from seats and fittings. When they struggled back into Sasebo a week later, they were filthy, starved, soot-blackened, frosted, and exhausted. Except for the metal runner down the center of the passenger car, the metal framework, and the four wheels, the car had been totally consumed for fuel. But they were successful; the two flatcars were laden with vitally needed parts and battery jars.

In working with the Japanese crew, Buck Catlin performed magnificently. His duties involved working with the men, and naturally he concentrated on spoken Japanese. I therefore studied the nameplates and meager instruction data to learn how to run the equipment. We took a half-hour course in basic Japanese—how the words are formed, how to break down the symbols and find English core meanings. Buck quickly gained fluency in talking with the Japanese crewmen in the ordinary language of seamen worldwide. After some diligent homework, I gained marginal proficiency in the written word, if only through trying to translate the intricate dating of samurai swords. The Japanese were a major help; virtually all knew some English if they got as far as high school. One small problem was a name for our sleek ship. The Japanese didn't give names to submarines. The men called her the "homesick maru," which the officers thought unfit. I finally suggested "Sasori," *scorpion* in Japanese. My vote was a bit more equal than the rest but it became the popular favorite when Jack Ahearn added, "Perfect—The Sorry *Sasori*."

The next task was fumigation. Rats had become a major nuisance. They had been cultivated as pets by the Japanese crew, but we hoped they would leave now that we were taking the boat over completely. The rats didn't respond to Western-style efforts at elimination. Cheese in a trap wasted time and cheese. With no dairy industry, the taste was unknown. There was no chocolate industry either, but the rats quickly cultivated that taste, and soon located our slim supply of chocolate bars reserved for salvation at sea. For the fumigation, somebody set up a pool, winner take rats and all, on the closest guess to the number of casualties. On the I-400, twelve gunny sacks full of dead rats surrendered unconditionally. Bets ran from 10 to 250, but we caught very few. On the first day at sea part of the answer became clear. As the ship began a heavy roll in a seaway, somebody reported that rats were running from hideouts in the superstructure and diving down the hatch, sliding down the railings just as the Japanese sailors did. Buck remarked, "Well, at least they aren't deserting a sinking ship." I thought the choices of diving over the side or down the hatch were about even-steven, but I made no comment.

Just to let us know it was midwinter, a fierce blizzard suddenly roared out of Mongolia one night. All the submarines were nested at heavy fleet mooring buoys within a mile or so of the tender, but the nests suddenly began breaking up, leaving submarines drifting helplessly at the mercy of the gale. The Japanese skeleton crews aboard were crying for help. The tender could do little. Only the two big launches could survive in those seas; they worked like seagoing tugs until they somehow managed to get everybody safely moored again. One large launch from the tender was lost. We all lost a lot of sleep in one of the wildest, wooliest nights in months.

Christmas 1945 arrived with still no decision on disposal

of the fleet. Phil invited me to a Christmas Eve party with the Marines which turned into a fun-filled evening. The following morning I went to mass at the cathedral. The decorations intrigued me. The creche, surrounded by rubbery magnolia leaves with bright red and white dahlias, looked out of place. Maybe it was because the three wise men came from the *west*. From the center of the nave, a cluster of American flags hung with streamers of other flags to the four corners of the church. There were no Japanese flags, no German, no Russian, but almost all the United Nations, plus Italy, were represented. Returning to the Marine headquarters in time for an eggnog party, I thought the secret formula of rotgut whiskey, storage eggs, and powdered milk produced a fair beverage. Then Christmas dinner at 1400 offered great company and conversation but no vegetables—the Japanese stove had broken down. But I didn't suffer. Getting back to our rice paddy club for several quick volleyball games, I was ready for the submarine Christmas dinner aboard *Euryale* at 1800.

My Christmas gift was a Red Cross box, which I didn't get because there weren't enough to go around, and some enlisted man needed it more than I. The Marines gave me a jug of liquor, which somebody else enjoyed when I unaccountably left it behind in the motor launch, along with a pair of badly needed warm gloves. Lots of the officers talked about having another Christmas party in San Francisco in February or March, complete with tree and all the trimmings, but that was not for me. The holiday would mean nothing without family. My thoughts ran more to spending Valentine's Day on return, to trade hearts and secrets with my lady love.

Christmas Eve on the tender brought an unexpected flurry of excitement. Early in the evening the cooks and bakers, busy preparing for the morrow's feast, noticed a man carrying a case of beer out of the adjacent storeroom. Then another case went by, and a third. Suspicious at last, the cooks quickly guessed that somebody had forgotten to lock the cage. Beer was disappearing at an alarming rate. When the exec got the news, he mobilized the master-at-arms force to find the culprits. By then it was midnight, and as soon as word of the search spread, empty beer cans began sailing out the portholes and bouncing off the hulls of the submarines alongside.

The exec sounded General Quarters, which roused everybody, none very happily. The condition of some of the officers indicated that they too had been doing some illegal toddy-tippling in their cabins. Some certainly weren't in any condition to find or accuse others of violating Navy regulations against consuming alcohol on board. The master-at-arms force had its own difficulties. Occasionally finding a six-pack of "evidence," they set it aside temporarily while completing search of the compartment. Invariably on their return the evidence had disappeared. Finally they found a sailor in the head who had passed out from overindulgence. They threw him in the brig, and as the only real violator in hand, charged him with the crime of misappropriation and use of fourteen cases of beer. When he came up for trial, sanity returned, and he escaped with a warning.

A day or so later, after going alongside a Japanese sub for luboil, *Sasori* went to sea in a snowstorm. It was our first night aboard. In my cabin, the bunk of my predecessor had an ancestral mattress about five feet long and five hundred years old, which we threw over the side. A standard Navy mattress was cut to give me as much length and width as possible.

Most of the wardroom interiors in the Japanese subs were beautifully varnished hardwoods. Of the five *Atule* sailors who had followed me to *Sasori,* one, Gerald Fregoe, had rigged a handsome reading lamp on my newly varnished desk. (The lamp, naturally, had been liberated by the Raiders.) My first letter written at that desk had to go to Henri, and as usual I speculated wildly on how and where to plan our reunion, East or West Coast or at home. Just thinking about possibilities gave me a lift.

For New Year's Eve I again joined the Marines. A large party reached its peak just before midnight with the presentation of awards. Somebody had spent considerable time working up special recognition for deeds of exceptional gallantry during the year. The greatest surprise was my own award. In recognition of the heroic work done by Schratz's Raiders, I was presented with the Japanese "Order of the Sacred Treasure," a beautiful solid silver, eight-pointed star with triangular pendant, suitably inscribed on the reverse side. The citation stated that because the Raiders left so little behind for the Marines to demilitarize, General Smith's task was remarkably easy.

New Year's Day was also a special Japanese holiday. Many of the Japanese submarine officers presented us with small gifts commemorating the occasion. For my part, I sought another kind of gift. For quite some time I had been trying to find a Japanese painter to paint the kamikaze insignia high on the metal fairing around the periscope housing. The Japanese were clearly reluctant. The kamikaze carried a special religious significance. The members, originally limited to aviators, received high honors at special fetes before going on their suicide missions.

When the submarine losses became almost as heavy as those of the suicide squadrons, submariners felt they too should be honored before departure on war patrol. They adopted the same ritual, dressing in white jumper suits with white headbands or *hachimaki,* badges of determination marked with the rising sun emblem. Friends and relatives gathered to honor them with patriotic songs, saki, and special foods before their final departure. The *Sasori*'s insignia had been painted out immediately after the surrender, but the painters finally consented to restore it. Perhaps they thought we, too, would not survive our long voyage.

Meanwhile, work on the engines proceeded day and night with few interruptions. John Drumm and Bob Prine had almost no sleep in the five days before departure; the men had had no liberty since October. And we still couldn't get both engines running at the same time. The big "I" boats had troubles en route to Pearl Harbor but the *Euryale* CO said he planned to leave on time; if we had no engines running, we'd go on a tow line. There was so much power in that huge battery, however, that we could operate for a week without needing the engines to recharge. The daily operations were good fun, too. I let the officers do almost all the shiphandling. Despite the potential hazards from those big protruding stabilizer fins, we had no accidents. My good fortune as a junior officer taught me to let the others have their chance.

On the last day of operations before departure, the

DivCom went to sea with us. He had been out with Speed the day before, and I learned through the grapevine that the battle rations served for lunch, for whatever reason, didn't go over well. Forewarned, we served grilled steaks, and everything ran like clockwork for a change. But both engines still hadn't gone "pickety-pockety" at the same time. That happy moment arrived only minutes before final departure from Sasebo.

Getting under way for the long voyage home was set for 0730 Sunday morning, 13 January 1946. The *Euryale* chaplain knew that on the *Atule* Jason and I had requested services on board before war patrols. I had not requested anything for *Sasori* if only because we had no crew's lounge or other area adequate for more than three people. *Euryale* was also getting under way, and her decks were not available either. The new tender USS *Nereus* had just arrived from the states to relieve *Euryale;* her chaplain volunteered to conduct services on the deck of *Sasori*. We cautioned him that it was not an ordinary submarine deck, but he was sure it would work out fine. It was a bleak, raw, and windy morning with snow flurries swirling around our heads. Even with only a slight roll, the sloping decks, icy in spots, offered perilous footing for a never-to-be-forgotten ceremony.

Backing clear of the *Euryale,* I ran up the Japanese colors, totally improper, and manned the rail with all my men in full dress rendering full honors to the *Nereus* as we passed. Buck literally did the honors, sounding "attention" on an odd-looking Japanese bugle draped with a red sash. It would have made a memorable photograph.

The troubled engines ran like Swiss watches as the secluded harbor entrance and the entire panorama of western Japan slowly disappeared in our wake. An old Navy custom suggests throwing coins over the side upon departure from a foreign port as a good luck offering to bring one back for a future visit. Japan was the first country I ever visited that I never wanted to see again. The Japanese people had been exceptional under circumstances of war, poverty, disease, suffering, and finally surrender and occupation. Westerners may never understand their culture, and my yearning to get back to friends and family again were too much to overcome. I pocketed my coins, turned my back on the scene, and

looked forward to the future. All I wanted at that moment
was for our poor ship, into which so much agony had gone,
to excel over its traveling companion in the fight to get both
across the ocean.

The first round went to the Sorry *Sasori*. About thirty-six
hours out, Speed suffered a steering casualty, suddenly
veering out of formation. Then his engines, which had run
very reliably throughout the training, broke down, one for
an hour then both two hours later. A friendly rivalry had
quickly emerged between the two boats, including the wager
of several dollars on a successful trip back.

Next morning I decided to try the "facilities." My night's
sleep had been a disaster. The bunk was so cramped that I
took the door off the locker forward of the bunk and put my
head inside to gain a bit of length. Very shortly I came alive
in a hurry when a rat tried to nestle in my curls, and almost
broke my nose when I hit the top of the locker. I turned end
for end, putting my feet in the locker, but found it awkward
to sleep uphill. I rose early, and with no shower available,
tried a bath in my cabin from a bucket of water, then a
shave, stooped over a mirror three feet off the deck, with
hot water from the rice steamer in the galley.

The heads were something else. Manufacture of workable
toilets for submarines over the years created more emotional
problems perhaps than any other. In prewar U.S. boats, the
head was located prominently between the engines. When
duty officers brought wives or guests aboard for dinner, they
soon learned to do the necessary before arrival or be prepared to perform with very little privacy. The newer subs
offered a private room, but the number of valves to manipulate before finally blowing the waste to sea often overwhelmed anybody less than a graduate engineer. "Brown-
outs" occurred and ruined more than the evening. The fleet
boat, quite modern by contrast, offered near normal facilities. All waste dropped into sanitary tanks, which were
blown to sea daily.

Japanese practice was primitive. The throne wasn't even
a seat. One carefully positioned himself over a hole in the
deck. The tank below discharged directly to sea, but the sea
valves were so tiny that paper could not be blown through
for fear of clogging. On one side was a wicker basket of slick

papers similar to those used to wrap citrus fruits. After use, the papers were placed in a wicker basket on the opposite side. When a basket was empty, one apparently reversed the procedure and used them again. Whatever risk clogging the sea valves entailed, we decided to follow the Western practice. The *Euryale* fitted an ordinary commode over the hole in the deck, but nothing increased self-inflicted constipation at sea more than this ritual.

While familiarizing myself with the head, I was informed that the refrigeration system had failed. The big ice box was sealed temporarily to preserve the precious store of steaks and other goodies we had gotten from the tender. Other more serious problems claimed my attention. A big typhoon was due to pass through that night. The I-200 class ships, never tested at sea, raised great concern for those stabilizer fins thrashing about in a wild gale. If we were rolling twenty-five degrees and they tore loose or broke the surface on a roll, we had instant tragedy. I didn't want the first dive to be to three thousand fathoms. Early in our sea trials, I asked the Japanese captain for suggestions when heavy seas threatened to tear the stabilizers off. He said, "Oh, you must always dive in heavy storm." My operation order forbade us from diving.

Worries about the stabilizers proved premature. They were far enough under water that they rarely broke surface, and they aided considerably in damping the roll and pitch in favor of a twisting motion. But for each unnecessary worry, a real one soon took its place. The ship "worked" so heavily in the torturing seas that we suddenly discovered that the fresh water was nearly unusable. The lye compound used by the tender to flush out the tanks had accumulated in the tank tops, and the storm shook it loose, making the water so brackish it was unfit for drinking. Only in strong coffee was it even manageable. The big coffee pot thus became the only source of hot water. We bathed or shaved with coffee. A freshly lathered face looked like a coffee parfait.

Meanwhile the refrigeration plant proved to be beyond the capability of ship's force. *Sasori* became the best feeder in the Navy, with steak three times a day as we ate our way through those carefully hoarded foods. Then came C-rations. The officers' steward took what he could to stock up the tiny wardroom refrigerator, but the next morning on rising, a sharp stench assailed my nostrils. Our refrigerator had failed also, and a stinking ooze seeped through the ersatz Japanese gasket, running down on the deck. Fish! With frozen strawberries and similar treasures to be salvaged, the steward had opted for codfish.

Three days before reaching Guam, Speed Currie suffered another engine casualty that put half his plant out of commission for the rest of the voyage. This slowed us to the breakneck speed of six knots, and delayed our arrival an additional day. The reduced speed aggravated the heavy pitch and roll, making life in the cramped surroundings quite unpleasant. My officers were four or five inches taller and sixty pounds heavier than the previous occupants. There was no room to stretch, up, down, or sideways. A big roll brought cups, china, coffee and cream, with 215-pound Doug Gillam in the middle, cascading into me. I went down flat on the deck. When I could verify that my leg wasn't broken, I hated to get up. For the first time since departure, I could stretch out full length.

The storm caused another serious problem. Those thousands and thousands of battery cells became a real hazard. The jars weren't laminated, as is common practice. Made of a single thickness of hard rubber, they were brittle. The Japanese mounted them by securing the bottom one to the deck, then piling seven more on top and securing the top one to the overhead. When the ship rolled, the stacks began swaying, causing the jars to crack and to leak sulfuric acid into the bilges. Neutralizing what we could with soda lime still left a question of the bottom of the ship being eaten through when least expected.

On the evening of 21 January we arrived in Guam to a noisy welcome. The information sent ahead by the tender created an exaggerated view of our lifestyle. The men referred to it merely as "our most rugged war patrol." A special reward, proving that the peacetime organization was again in control, also greeted us on arrival. Some clerk decided that since the "I" boats were not in commission as U.S. vessels, and since we were attached to a technically inactive squadron, our appeal to continue submarine pay during the voyage was rejected, effective on the day of departure from Sasebo. This was a great blow to the men, few of whom were able to take the loss of 50 percent hazardous duty pay without some prior notice. No amount of protest could change the decision.

I planned for the men to have a full day off in Guam. They had never worked harder or for less apparent reward. All of us had lost considerable weight. But the squadron commander, anxious to get back to Pearl, decided to push hard on repairs and be on our way. Nobody got time off. Speed and I couldn't move him an inch.

Four days later, 25 January 1946, we were on our way to Eniwetok, 537 miles closer to home. Speed was soon in difficulty. An engine failed on leaving Guam, and he went on a towline to the tug. Pitching into head seas and fighting near gale winds made it tough for both of us. The lousy weather apparently irritated even the rats. Two annoying guerrilla rodents were driven from seclusion. The growing heat in the wardroom, now almost one hundred degrees, bothered them too. Often during meals, I could look up to the air vent over the wardroom table and see a pair of beady eyes peering down. If they didn't like the food, they'd kick dirt down on us. Using every possible ruse to catch them, we finally had to admit they might be smarter than we were. We named them Grover and Edwin, Grover after my good friend Grover "Chet" Heffner, the squadron supply officer on the *Euryale*. Perhaps to break the disheartening routine of continual equipment breakdowns, I began sending a regular evening Grovergram to Chet concerning his namesake. We requested a ration allowance for the food he was consuming and assistance in luring him to his death through his fondness for Hershey bars. Soon the whole squadron was poaching in on our nightly messages, but problems soon recaptured my attention.

Buck and I, thinking seriously about the morale of our wretched and badly overworked men, decided they needed something to take their minds off their troubles. Jack Ahearn, the communications officer, soon came up with several ideas. First he started a ship's newspaper, the *Sasori Sun*. While in Guam he had some letterhead logos mimeographed and soon was producing a highly interesting and amusing paper. He and I, with the necessary collusion of the Chief Radioman, worked out another idea in deepest secrecy. The press back in America not long before had featured a scandalous affair between Charlie Chaplin and a young lady. We cooked up a fictitious story of a lurid affair between Chaplin and Shirley Temple, offering searing details, highly imaginative interviews with the household staff, and other wild dreams.

Immediately we had a tiger by the tail. Shirley Temple was the same age as most of the men and was worshipped by them to a degree I couldn't believe. To associate her with that old roué was too shocking to conceive. Soon we needed extra editions and special news flashes. We three conspirators carefully controlled all copies and got each back before issuing another. Bull sessions produced wild rumors and exaggerations. For the purpose of taking the men's minds off their problems it was wildly successful, too much so. The leg to Eniwetok took only three days. We assumed that the hoax would be exposed when we mingled with the rest of our small flotilla there. Quite the contrary.

The day before the scheduled arrival, we suffered our first major engine casualty, putting one engine out of commission all night and forcing an additional night at sea before entry into Eniwetok. Once again the engine gang would arrive in port exhausted and ready to throw in the sponge. The lost day meant one less day in port, no liberty, and sixteen hours a day preparing for the next leg to Johnston Island. If we hadn't been heading for home it could never have been done. We were traveling on guts alone.

We thought the squadron staff had far too little appreciation of the challenge involved in taking a radically new design submarine across the world's largest ocean on her maiden sea voyage. Nobody knew what fatal shortcuts might have been taken in construction, unknown to us without a painstaking examination in drydock. Nobody was more aware than we were of the catastrophic state of Japanese industry, the shortages of manufacturing skills, and the low priority of submarine building late in the war. If these problems were known to our seniors, their attitude seemed quite casual.

As we arrived in Eniwetok very early in the morning of 29

January, the commodore was the first to greet us, genuinely pleased at our performance and more friendly than ever before. He obviously was stewing to get to Hawaii as soon as possible. First, he decided to skip the stop at Johnston Island and head straight for Pearl. Since the direct route was beyond our cruising range because of the gross fuel waste through leaky gaskets and plant inefficiencies, he decided that both boats would go on the towline from Eniwetok, me behind the tender, Speed behind the tug. We would keep one engine on the line to ease the strain on the tow and increase speed somewhat. I was twice as anxious to get back and I agreed with his solution. We had already made our brownie points in the good-natured rivalry with the I-201. The strain on all of us would be eased in many ways.

The life of my crew of giants in their Lilliputian home is impossible to convey fully. The Japanese *never* stressed creature comfort in their ships, and we were living at a subhuman level even by their standards. In scores of ways—the constant peril from the huge storage batteries below the living compartments, never free of shorts and grounds, of explosive hydrogen mixtures, of acid eating its way into the keel, of "pearl diving" the engine room bilges each watch to clean out suction valves lacking strainers, of the penetrating stench from decomposing soybean fuel waste, of bathing in a cup of turpentine with an astringent water washdown, of sleepless nights and primitive heads, wretched food preparation and laundry facilities—the strain worked on us all. Without question a high speed target submarine would be invaluable for training antisubmarine forces. The real issue, yet to be faced, was whether the Japanese models, brought up to minimum American standards, would be more costly than a new model built from the keel up. Our experiences at sea under considerable stress went a long way to furnish the answers.

No sooner were the lines secured in Eniwetok than the men swarmed aboard the tender for baths, laundry, food, drink, or merely a good stretch. And everywhere they spread the heartbreaking details of the Shirley Temple scandal. Far from killing our myth, the men on the tender gobbled it up, the gossipers adding details even we couldn't invent. Back at sea the following morning the tales were more lurid than ever, the hatred for the innocent Charlie Chaplin more vitriolic—and the problem of the conspirators more and more impossible to solve.

Under way at 0700, 1 February, we cleared the channel and began maneuvering in a heavy seaway to transfer the towing cable. An hour later *Euryale* took a good strain on the line and headed east toward Pearl Harbor. Before another hour had passed, a sharp crack split the air and the anchor chain thundered out of the hawse into the sea. A vision of my predecessor came immediately to mind: "So solly, Captain. Hon'able B-29 bomb hon'able chain factory. Anchor chain no good. So solly."

To run a new rig, the tender prepared to transfer heavy lines and equipment by motor launch. To speed things up, I offered to put my bow under the stern of the tender for direct transfer of cable and chain. It was necessary to keep my bow within ten to forty *feet* of the *Euryale,* both ships yawing, rolling, and pitching in the seaway. I kept the conn for a half hour, then an hour, and finally decided to let Buck and the watch officers have a try. It took intensive concentration over four long hours to complete the rig and every minute held the possibility of a wrong guess, a wrong bell to the engine room. Anything out of the ordinary could have badly damaged both ships. I felt very proud of our seamanship. Handling heavy equipment on the smooth, slippery deck while rolling and pitching in the seaway was hairy. Huge sharks cruised about us. Some we drove off with gunfire, a half dozen we caught on baited hooks, wondering if they would tow us to sea. No other caution was necessary; everybody did his job without fuss or furor.

When we were finally on our way again, the towline, now foreshortened, began snapping clear of the water, seriously risking a new break. I also needed to use my only engine in commission for a battery charge. The tender agreed reluctantly to slow down. The charge took most of the night. Then early next morning we discovered that the cable was about to tear loose from the hull. I slowed to lengthen the span of cable and had just resumed speed when the I-201 reported that his anchor chain had parted. The new delay took several more hours.

The evening edition of the *Sasori Sun* had a comment about "speeding home."

The Ancient Mariner

Once lived an ancient submariner
  Old and hoary was he
And his face was grim and bearded
  With the salt of many a sea.
"How grew you thus?"
  Fair maiden asked.
" 'Tis short to tell," said he.
  "I was only a lad
When I set out to cross
  The Pacific on the 203."

Jack's daily poems were broadcast each night on his "evening news program" for the rest of the squadron. Then Mother Nature gave us a break. The weather turned gloriously smooth and sunny, a thoroughly enjoyable change. We found time in the wardroom for an Acey-Deucey tournament, the favorite of all Navy games. The CO won, naturally, with a bit of sorcery hinted at by the *Sun* editorial over a few extremely lucky rolls of the dice, each called in advance.

Smooth sailing on a course for home brightened the spirits back aft. But I had one awkward task to complete before arriving in Pearl. The Shirley Temple story had to be killed. It had been a marvelous device to take our minds off our acute problems. Jack sought me out to ask plaintively how we could ever get out of the mess. One of the men told him he wrote his mother asking her not to let his younger sister go to the movies anymore.

On the last day before arrival in Pearl, I thought the time had come. The final issue of the *Sasori Sun* carried the following statement: "Men, I have a confession to make. You've been had. The Shirley Temple story is a hoax. For what I thought were very good reasons, we dreamed up the story, every bit of it, and it just isn't true. It's total bull. And now I've got to ask you to cover for me. You may want to kill me later, but put yourself in my shoes. Something had to be done to get your minds off our serious day-to-day problems. I had no idea she was so much the goddess of your generation. But think. Now she's just as pure as you always believed.'' The reaction was mostly splendid. A few didn't forgive me but most had a good laugh over it—later.

Meanwhile, plans for Pearl Harbor favored first renting a Turkish bath and soaking for a day; second, throwing a big party; and third, getting home on leave or discharge from the service as soon as possible. My own thoughts were anticipation, wonder, and overpowering love. I had no firm plans, no special wishes, just the desire to drop anchor on the front doorstep as soon as possible and turn off the war forever.

The long, slow voyage to Pearl gave lots of time to think. Suddenly I felt tired and homesick. My war had started almost five years before in the North Atlantic, with a high percentage of that time in the combat zone, resulting in thirteen ships sunk and three damaged totaling sixty-three thousand tons. Despite unreliable torpedoes plaguing the submarines, I had never seen an abnormal run and had racked up 48 percent hits, a third higher than the force average. We made a successful mineplant deep in enemy waters, served in dozens of lifeguarding exercises in which seven American aviators were rescued, conducted numerous special missions, and did more than our share in the demilitarization of Japan. All that remained was to reach Pearl Harbor without adding a Japanese submarine to my score—*Sasori*.

The best information on the future of the *Sasori* came from the big I-boats that preceded us to Pearl. They were in caretaker status with skeleton crews, still waiting for a decision by the Allied commission. If Congress funded an overhaul, which I could not see as worthwhile, it would be done in Pearl. The I-200 boats would follow the same policy, also a gross waste in my view. *Euryale* would continue to San Francisco to be mothballed as soon as possible. After a short two years since departure, I felt like the returning ancient mariner. But my immediate goal was far more modest. I wanted to get to Pearl in time to make a Valentine's Day call to Henri.

I almost made it. On 14 February, *Sasori* eased alongside her berth at the submarine base, Pearl Harbor. Bob Prine made the landing, his first ever, and it was a thing of beauty. Buck stood atop the bridge, the small bugle to his lips, red streamers blowing slightly in the wind as we came alongside, all orders given in Japanese. The line handlers had been coached in the few necessary Japanese words, and signals were given by bugle or word of mouth from the bridge. Scores and scores of guests waved from the head of the pier; everything went off like a movie script. Only one flaw marred a perfect performance. The landing was so smooth that few even realized it was in Japanese.

I walked off the ship to a very noisy welcome and soon turned my back on *Sasori* for the last time. I looked only toward home. Orders were waiting to put the subs in caretaker status and for me to return to the West Coast with the *Euryale,* to be met on arrival with orders to shore duty. In minimum time I was luxuriating serenely in my commodore's cabin for the last leg of the crossing, making maximum speed toward San Francisco. I chatted with several other returning warriors about how one meets his family after a long absence when we have been fathers but not parents. The children have looked to the mother, not the father, for guidance as head of the household. One submariner confessed to the mistake of punishing a young daughter the day after he returned, and she didn't forgive him for months. We knew very little about how our wives ran the family as both mother and father, making all the decisions, bearing up under long periods with no mail, appearing serene when icy fingers of fear strangled hopes that they would ever hear from us again. A few of the men found that their wife had left to feather another man's nest. On arriving home, would we hear a little voice cry, "Mother, what's that man doing here?"

I was soon to learn about the wonderful job Henri had done in making our daughters' father into much more than a photo on a mantel. Yet for all the letters, I knew little about the children's speech and mannerisms, the personalities behind the photographs, the many things about children so heartwarming to parents. Many times I regretted the little I had been able to contribute to their development and what a great obligation I owed to the grandparents, not only in offering their home but as stand-in parents when things got too tough for Henri to bear alone. These things I wouldn't fully understand for years. They were part of a vast unknown in long separations whose effects emerged sometimes joyfully and sometimes with pain. I hoped and prayed for guidance.

A small but enthusiastic crowd of spectators was on hand as we moored at the Mare Island shipyard in San Francisco Bay. The wild greetings for the returning heroes immediately after the surrender were long forgotten. From a few I sometimes sensed an unasked question, "Excuse me, sir, what war was that again?"

Whatever the reception lacked in enthusiasm, one spectator in particular caught my eye. A very attractive young lady smartly attired in a Wave's uniform seemed to be calling and waving to me in particular. It took several minutes to realize it was my sister Marian, whom I hadn't seen in years, suddenly grown into a beautiful woman. My promised orders weren't waiting, but Marian was. We spent several riotous days with a crowd of submariners. She was about to be married to a scion of the Old South, a decadent young man of whom I soon learned the family didn't approve. He was due in San Francisco the day after my departure. After trying to keep up with some parched submariners partying day and night, Marian was exhausted. When he arrived, his eager first suggestion to go out for a night on the town met a very cold response. Before the weekend was over, so was the romance. Quite by accident I had done my duty to the family. Marian soon met the real man in her life, married, and lived happily ever after.

Orders arrived for duty in Washington, D.C., in the Bureau of Naval Personnel, with a few weeks leave before reporting. Catching the first plane east, I arrived in Pittsburgh to the welcoming arms of a loving wife and family. In the rush of enthusiastic hugs and kisses, I first saw little Henrie, a year and a half old, and mistook her for Gina, now almost three. Both were absolutely precious dolls. Tears of joy flowed everywhere, my mother in the lead, but we all did our share. I was deliriously happy to be home at long last. At Henri's parents' home, I walked across the threshold and, grasping her in my arms, said quietly, "Honey, the war is finally over."

8

The USS *Burrfish*

Fast and Loose

Shore duty is often a period of rejuvenation from the rigors of sea duty. In our case it gave us much needed time to live together as a family. I welcomed the home life equally with the challenge of Washington duty. I felt stimulated by the opportunity to contribute to the making of policy in the power center of much of the universe. Temporarily, I had laid down the sword; time would tell whether the pen was mightier.

I had three weeks' leave before reporting. After two deliriously happy weeks with the family and the tender moments in first meeting the children—during which I fell asleep every time I sat down—the thought of joining the hordes looking for housing in the Washington area soon urged us to be on the move. The Bureau of Naval Personnel, better known as BuPers, overlooked the Pentagon from a small hill adjacent to the Arlington National Cemetery. We naturally opted for housing in the Arlington area and lucked into a nice house in a new subdivision called Dominion Hills. The house sold for $8,500 new; we stole it for a bit less than $13,000 four months later. (Today it can be had for $130,000. The buyer can be had, too, at that price.)

Henri did a marvelous job in setting up a very warm and comfortable home for the family. We had largely ''period'' furniture—orange crates and the junk used during the children's toddling stages, to be thrown in the trash for some decent stuff about the time when tuition costs prevent buying some decent stuff. Our contemporaries did the same thing, the wives making draperies, the men finishing off rumpus rooms in the basement. This latter activity, a mildly addictive disease, Captain Hyman Rickover scornfully called "pump room fever"—submariners wasting time on trivia that rightfully belonged to professional study.

My new job started off as a near insurmountable challenge. I was allegedly the legal expert for BuPers on officer retirements. On-the-job training consisted of slashing through an incomprehensible thicket of ancient laws and modern court interpretations. I thought the Navy judge advocate general (JAG) did those things, but BuPers needed to know how to ask him the right questions, then apply the answers so that the comptroller general would not object to spending public funds in support of those decisions.

When I arrived in the office, the desk sagged under the weight of a backlog of a thousand wartime cases of officers in hospitals or at home, pending a decision on physical disability retirement and drawing full pay and allowances while waiting for the bureau to act. For that "act" I had a tough time learning my lines. One case went home with me each night to study and try to make some sense about what to recommend. Decisions on each case, after cursory review in the Navy Department, went to the president for final action. After his approval, letters of notification had to be prepared for signature by the secretary of the navy. Any error, even if made in good faith, literally required a special act of Congress to correct. It took weeks before I could complete one case a night, and several hundred new ones arrived each month. In about six weeks, however, I was able to review a case, decide the disposition, and attach a tiny memo at the top, itemizing certain carefully prepared paragraphs to use in putting the letter together. I developed with great care about fifty standard paragraphs requiring only filling in a few blanks for appropriate dates and laws. Using my memorized paragraphs, I could soon outline about a hundred letters a day. A battery of typists then ground out the letters to go to the secretary.

The laws were Civil War relics designed wholly for the long-service career regular. Disability retirement pay was 75 percent of active duty base pay for life, regardless of the degree of disability or length of service, and was not subject to reevaluation. The law was an open invitation to abuse, and several Washington attorneys specialized in appeals, generally setting fees at half the pay of their clients for the time they were able to keep them on active duty, plus a percentage of any retirement pay thereafter. The officers were predominantly reserves who had come on active duty for the emergency. They had little service, and their disabilities, often temporary or situational, frequently were not incurred in line of duty. Administration with justice and fairness became a tightrope act.

The short-service junior officers didn't cause all the problems. Some senior regular and reserve officers created others, first in using pressure from influential friends in government to push a retirement through, second for special treatment to stretch the law to cover. Unfortunately, the JAG made several questionable decisions pyramiding benefits of both temporary wartime and permanent peacetime legislation, which were impossible for the bureau to administer servicewide.

We also wanted to do something special for certain war heroes who asked nothing and deserved far more. The retirement letters had to be suitable for framing. Those retiring after "long and faithful service" got a special paragraph with a few laudatory adjectives. I stretched the dividing line on "long and faithful service" to include my own classmates disabled in the war. A still more special set of adjectives went to heroes like Fleet Admiral Halsey. He couldn't be "specially commended for heroism in combat" and advanced another rank as provided by law; he had already attained the highest rank possible. For fleet admirals, therefore, I added some special flagwavers about the nation's gratitude for service to their country. Then I added one additional bonus. Throughout my career it was always an annoyance to be required repeatedly to "furnish your paymaster two certified copies of these orders." Without adequate typing and duplication facilities it was a perennial pain to get additional copies. In an earthshaking change first used in the Halsey letter, the appropriate paragraph stated, "By separate action your paymaster has been furnished with certified copies of this letter."

After forty years, I still wonder why it wasn't always done that way for everybody. When the Halsey letter went up the line for signature, other senior officers phoned to request similar pretty words when their time came. It soon became necessary to set up a private pecking order among superlatives corresponding to varying degrees of rank, heroism, and national stature.

The task of applying questionable policy decisions in one case to all similar cases became intricate. The bureau sought absolute equity and justice and couldn't run the Navy on any other basis. With competing pressures on all sides, I relied on two strong and wholly congenial sources of counsel and inspiration. My immediate boss, Captain Charles W. Moses, was a jewel. Modest and self-effacing, Charlie was brilliant and highly personable, deeply respected by juniors and seniors alike, and he backed me to the hilt. Second was a fearsome woman, Ruth W. Wickware, serving as liaison between BuPers and the Bureau of Supplies and Accounts and thus holding access to the public purse. She had served in Washington in World War I as a "yeomanette" and continued as a civilian. A dominating, foul-mouthed, and often rude person, she had a love-hate relationship with peers that made strong men tremble. Fortunately, Charlie and I earned her esteem, and she often pulled our chestnuts out of the fire before harm was done.

The first time she entered the office, she sat down at my desk, exposing a considerable area of lumpy thigh road-mapped with varicose veins. Noting my abashed glance, she boomed in a gravelly contralto, "I always give the boys a lot of leg. They love it." The three of us formed a powerful bond in keeping the Navy Department out of too much trouble. If a JAG opinion brought administrative woe, I carefully searched for a test case where public funds might be involved and wrote it up for submission to the comptroller general, asking if he would approve payment. These pivotal cases set limits on questionable policies and avoided potentially serious future problems: we equalized combat advancements between regulars and reserves; we obtained approval of Naval Academy service—not countable for retirement—for certain former enlisted men; we set up a special pension program using money from the Secretary of the Navy Prize Fund, accumulated from sale of merchant ships taken as prize on the high seas since the Revolutionary War. This fund, dormant for a century, became a last resort for disabled veterans not otherwise covered by law. And finally, when nothing else worked, we submitted cases to the secretary's Board for the Correction of Naval Records as a court of last resort.

The not insignificant achievements of the office soon earned considerable recognition throughout the Navy Department. It also brought new demands on our services. Charlie and I spent time briefing the chief of naval personnel for testimony before Congress on retirement legislation. Charlie wrote a layman's guide to the military retirement system. We spent much time trying to cover the subject in the simplest possible language. His pamphlet quickly earned wide distribution throughout all the services.

I came in for a share of speech-writing chores and soon learned that the speech-writer lives in a world of his own. It isn't enough that he be an expert. He must also inject himself into the skin of another person, whose expression and rhetorical style differed from his own. The new defense secretary, James Forrestal, asked for a speech draft for the opening session of a congressional investigation of military retirements.

In my draft I pointed out the Civil War origins of our system; without a retirement system, old Mexican War heroes were kept on active duty long after they had outlived their effectiveness. With a new war brewing, the senior naval officer was a captain who had been on active duty for sixty-three years; the average Navy captain had forty-eight years of service. In the Army, superannuated officers commanded vital forts along the North-South fracture line. To improve the national readiness, President Abraham Lincoln signed the act of 3 March 1861 to retire officers who had grown "incapacitated through long and faithful service," specifically aiming to relieve twelve officers then holding critical commands.

The 1861 law to take care of those twelve was still on the

books to handle three million officers of World War II, predominantly short-service officers. The only amendment came in 1938, to give reserve officers the same retirement pay as regulars. In the speech draft I put together a historically oriented presentation, in what I thought was the defense secretary's finest literary style. To spice up the presentation I used the example of General Winfield Scott, hero of the Mexican War, in command of Fort Sumter, relieved and retired just before the opening salvo at Sumter on 12 April 1861. Secretary Forrestal's presentation was warmly received by the committee. On adjournment I made my way back to the office on a cloud.

Reaching my cluttered desk, I pushed aside a pile of papers to handle a bit of urgent business. The notes I had used for the speech caught my eye. To my horror I discovered that Winfield Scott was nowhere near Sumter in April 1861. He was the commanding general of the army in Washington, seventy-five years old, overweight, too big to get on a horse and too young to retire. With nobody around to call for help, I finally went home and tried a delayed dry martini. Then I relaxed. The Army's turn came the following day. Surely they would recognize the mistake and correct the record.

Next day the Army chief not only mentioned Scott at Sumter but enlarged on Secretary Forrestal's statement. I succumbed to acute terror. The Army had perpetuated my error of fact. That night I tried two martinis, one for each goof. Then I relaxed. Next day the chief of naval personnel would testify. If he repeated the error, the truth no longer mattered. Three times in the *Congressional Record* establishes its own truth.

My error never came to light. As somebody once claimed, reading makes the full man, conference the ready man, and writing the exact man. I made sure I was far better read and conferred before I next put in writing words for another's mouth. That lesson the sooner learned, the better appreciated.

By the time I had a year's experience on the job, I felt confident I could manipulate the hopelessly muddled statutes to serve justice almost regardless of the circumstances. I had developed a profound interest in law as a career.

Charlie, Ruth, and others strongly urged me to request the postgraduate law course then available to regular officers. Ruth, a strong friend of a new JAG coming into office, assured him that in a decade I would succeed to the chair as judge advocate.

My submarine cohorts saw it differently. To ask for shore duty on completion of a tour ashore would foul up my career rotation and would hazard bright prospects in the submarine force. The two officers controlling submarine assignments in BuPers at that time were Johnny Davidson, my skipper on the *Mackerel,* and C. Edwin "Ebbie" Bell, a classmate and close friend. After much mental anguish, I decided to stick with my submarine brethren and turn my back on a law career. But I realized I needed more education to fulfill whatever ambition I had for the future and began to shape my career toward that end, initially by enrolling in master of arts courses at local universities wherever duty took me.

Washington duty also gave me an opportunity to get back in shape with my fiddle, which I hadn't touched since departure from the Naval Academy seven years before. I dug out my Sevcik and Kreutzer studies for some work in the woodshed and soon passed an audition for the Arlington Symphony, the best semiprofessional group in the metropolitan area. I also joined the Washington Civic Opera orchestra, and thanks to regular rehearsals with both groups, I soon regained whatever skills I had. About half the members of the two groups were professional, and many people suggested I join the union and get paid for my play. Not long after, I became president of the Arlington Symphony Association and thought it a propitious time to raise the issue with the union headquarters in Washington. The Navy JAG had no objection as long as it did not interfere with my military duties, but the union found all sorts of difficulties. As a military officer I was a transient, and therefore I would "displace some loyal member from his rightful place in the orchestra." I accepted the principle fully, promising I would not compete if a qualified resident contested my seat. It was no big thing on my part; a worldwide shortage of string instrument players created gaps in every symphony. This is what kept me alive. But the Union said no deal. It not only refused my application to play as a professional but refused, in vulgar, earthy language, to give permission for me to play even as a nonprofessional. I ignored the advice and continued with both groups as an amateur. During this period the Arlington Symphony gained wide recognition as the first symphony orchestra to telecast a concert nationally, via the Dumont network, then the nation's largest.

Washington also offered unusual opportunities in the social whirl. Young military officers were frequently included on guest lists as White House aides for protocol affairs. One evening I was invited to a formal reception at Blair House—President Harry Truman's residence while the White House underwent major repairs—and to another at the Philippine Embassy immediately following. One was stag, the other not. Somehow I managed to confuse the two. I arrived at Blair House with Henri on my arm and we were graciously introduced to the assemblage. Did I detect a slight emphasis on the "and *Mrs.*" as we were announced? Accepting a glass of refreshment, my favorite companion shortly asked, "Did you notice that I'm the only wife here?"

"No, I didn't, dear. I guess you'll have a fine time." She snarled, "I felt sure this was stag. I'll see you in Lafayette Park after your courtesy two drinks—if I ever see you again." It was too late to undo the harm. I added, cheerily, "Just think. You crashed a White House party. An awful lot of folks never get here at all."

After two years in the job, sea duty was again calling. Every morning I joined Johnny Davidson and Ebbie in the detail office for a cup of coffee. Seeing and hearing the pressure everybody put on them for preferred assignments, or to get certain hotshots assigned to their ships, I decided never to bring up the subject of my next duty. They knew me and my record. If they had questions, I was close at hand. By no means did this mean I wasn't on tenterhooks of anticipation. On the verge of a casual comment many times, I managed to hold my tongue.

Then one day Johnny asked if I wanted to talk about what he had in mind. I could scarcely find the breath to reply. They had me slated for new construction again, this time for command of the USS *Pickerel*, a new high-speed "guppy" type incorporating the best of wartime experience and, above all, slated for duty in Hawaii. This was absolutely the finest command available, and I was in seventh heaven. To ice the cake, we would go to Portsmouth again for fitting out. For my exec, they suggested Lt. Cmdr. William E. "Pappy" Sims, a fine officer and a great athlete at the Naval Academy. I didn't know Pappy, but he seemed an ideal choice. Among his many qualifications, he had done postgraduate work, earning a professional degree in aeronautical engineering.

The news of the new command assignment spread rapidly. I was soon besieged with requests from old shipmates trying to get aboard—"We did a great job last time; let's do it again." As much as I wanted to see these fine people again, I didn't favor the idea. The presence of shipmates from previous commands breeds cliques in the wardroom. Even if they don't presume on old acquaintance with the CO, the other officers may sense a difference and feel left out. More important, having worked together in the past, each knows the other's style and neither is likely to learn. For good reason, therefore, I suggested to Johnny and Ebbie that much as I admired these officers, I wanted to start with the slate they proposed for me. I added, "It's the detailer's job to place the officers. If you send me your poorest and I have anything on the ball, I can make an average crew out of them. If you send me any better, I will build a superior command around them."

Thinking it over later, I realized that probably sounded pompous. But I recognized it as good psychology. Giving the detail office full responsibility stimulated them to do their best. In the *Pickerel* officers I made out like a bandit.

We were still a long way from leaving Washington. Zest for my present duty got me deeply involved as usual in everything going on. My last case for adjudication soon became one of the most interesting. Bob Brown, who had gone down with *Scorpion*, was the only son of a congressman. When we arrived in Washington, out of respect for the senior Brown, I offered my assistance to him as a point of contact in the Navy Department to bird-dog cases in which he had an interest. One such case came within the jurisdiction of my own office.

A naval officer, retired as an enlisted man, had been recalled to active duty during the war and earned a promotion to lieutenant. When demobilized, he was at the point of death. The medical officer in command of the hospital assumed, erroneously, that because he was already retired, it didn't matter whether he died active or inactive. The error was soon aggravated by several veterans' organizations in Georgia, and nobody seemed to know the facts or what to do about the case. When it reached my desk it defied solution.

The secretary of the navy had just set up a Board for the Correction of Naval Records, empowered to change a record "to remove an error or correct an injustice." This seemed ideal for my case, and I prepared it for submission to the board. In the officer's record there was no indication that he had ever acknowledged receipt of orders releasing him to inactive duty. Because of the delicate state of his health, this hardly seemed unusual. Acting on this presumption, I built a case for a finding that in the absence of evidence to the contrary, he must be presumed to have died on active duty.

Congressman Brown then asked if I would represent the widow at the hearing. Having prepared the government's case, I thought this seemed like a clear conflict of interest, but nobody seemed to object. On the day of the hearing I drew the officer's record for one last look before testifying. On the very top page was a statement, "I, Cosby Homer Dawson, hereby acknowledge receipt of orders releasing me from all active duty in the Navy."

I couldn't believe my eyes. Even today, so many years later, I have a clear mental image of that letter. After a few moments in deep thought, I made my decision. Tearing the damning evidence from the file, I ate it on the spot. It was an onionskin copy but definitely didn't taste like a hamburger. I then went to the hearing and committed a slight perjury in a case for which I was the legal counsel for both sides. To complicate matters further, the widow turned out to be a gorgeous Georgia peach, much younger than her husband, and so grateful for her windfall that she wanted me to join her in Washington and start enjoying it that night. Controlling my enthusiasm with great difficulty, I managed to beg off.

I hadn't mentioned that our family was increasing. The baby boom was on in Washington; we helped create it.

Margie arrived on a ghastly winter night in February 1947. A light snow began falling in the early evening and became quite a storm by midnight. At almost two—my head had just touched the pillow—Henri roused me to announce that her time had come. We had made a deal earlier that all births would occur in the middle of the night so as not to interfere with major sporting events on TV. I leaped into my clothes and helped her into the car. The snow was now eight to ten inches deep, and the Naval Hospital at Bethesda was sixteen miles away. As we backed out of the driveway, the car immediately slid off the crown of the road into a ditch. I didn't think we'd ever get it out, but somehow we were on our way. We fell in behind a snowplow, followed it for several miles, and arrived without a major crisis. Since Margie was the first for whom I was around for the whole process, it did occur to me that, despite the mental stress, things were a lot simpler for father when he was off at sea.

Margie, a very cute and happy child, earned a warm welcome into the family. The children were all such fun that, as often happens, Henri was due again just as we were scheduled to move from Washington. Nancy did her part by arriving a few weeks early, in late July 1948, to help ease the move to New England. We still hadn't sold the house so I went alone to New London. This was one of those difficult times in the Navy when the wife with four children under the age of six, one a tiny infant, had to cope with getting the house ready for the movers. Dad, meanwhile, drove off in the only car, suggesting as he pulled out the driveway, "And by the way, dear, don't forget to sell the house."

Checking in to the submarine base, I was assigned to the PCO course, the same course of instruction in which I had a special interest at the bottom of the totem pole while on *Mackerel* six years earlier and which I had attended en route *Sterlet* four years before. In the pile of mail awaiting my arrival was a notice of a shipment to be claimed at the local railroad station. It was a bushel of beautiful Georgia peaches, the gift of my last client. Having sat on the dock in the sun for several weeks, every one was rotten and smelled to high heaven. I muttered to myself, "It serves you right, you conniving, perjuring rascal. You don't deserve any better."

A word is appropriate here about our four daughters. While we were in Pittsburgh on leave, I met my high school orchestra conductor. When I mentioned our growing family, his reply was, "Of course they're all girls; you're a musician and musicians have only daughters."

For years it had been noticed that submarine officers rarely had sons—something about the battery acid, snorkeling, or even worse fantasies. Then I learned that my star was doubly crossed for being a musician. A third possibility suggested the Shakespearean implication that seniors who sleep soused sire no sons, but that couldn't apply in our case. I suggested a fourth possibility. Since much of my life was spent in close contact with men, the Lord blessed us with soft, cuddly, and charming girls to fill the void.

The PCO course, with that zealous team of Hensel and Patterson now only a memory, nowhere near met the intensity of the war years. The peacetime submarine force, I soon sensed, felt complacent about a job well done during the war. The underseas force had been a vital if not *the* vital element in the defeat of Japan. It was only natural that the rigor of wartime training would relax. Some senior officers feared that the submarine force, and the Navy as a whole, had done its job too well. With no enemy left on the high seas, the Navy was expected to go into decline. The sea was no longer the first line of defense; to young America airpower was the wave of the future. The defense of the realm shifted from the deep blue sea to the wild blue yonder. Nuclear power for ship propulsion was on the drawing board, but new roles for the submarine lagged far behind their potential.

In Washington, virtually all senior submariners participated in the Submarine Conference, a monthly forum to discuss weapons, technologies, and policies for the future. I had participated in at least one historic meeting on the decision to go ahead with nuclear power. The technological genius of the group could not be questioned. We as a group, however, had less to suggest on the role of nuclear power on national policy in the submarine of the future. Part of the reason was the unnatural domination by Captain Rickover, a pure technician, uninterested in the strategic or political role of the new weapon, and not at all reluctant to discourage contrary thoughts by others.

In a vague way I gradually came to sense these attitudes. I knew I couldn't accept them. I determined that my command would accept no relaxation of standards of performance and would strive in every way to push the frontier of future development toward far higher levels.

After our little family finally cleared Washington, we drove through the familiar haunts of New England and up the scenic coastal road to Portsmouth. Good friends from earlier tours found us a beautiful estate in Kittery Point, Maine, just across the Piscataqua River from Portsmouth. Grayhaven had been built as a retirement home by Andrew D. White, former U.S. ambassador to the Hague Peace Conference at the turn of the century. White founded Cornell University and the Cornell plan followed by other universities; his wife founded Swarthmore. Their magnificent ten-bedroom home was leased to us completely furnished, including a superb library and a set of heirloom Canton china. Acres and acres of grounds offered a breathtaking view of the lower harbor and the seacoast to the south.

White's youngest daughter, Karen, a charming spinster of about sixty-five, lived in a cottage on the grounds and managed the estate in the time she could make available from her consuming interest as an observer and critic of the political scene. We rented this idyllic castle on a year's lease for $85 a month. Karen said the rent was low because nobody had lived there through the winter and she thought we'd freeze. I had checked the house thoroughly. It was soundly built, but when a new furnace had been installed, ten feet of the basement wall had been knocked out and not replaced. I rebuilt the wall, sealed other major leaks, and for the winter closed off the four-bedroom summer wing. Storm windows and plenty of firewood made the winter as snug as could be. With the family comfortably settled in the new home, I was raring to go on the new command.

The early weeks in Portsmouth seemed just too good to last. And they were. The glories of fall color were tingeing the leaftips when I was ordered to Key West to attend the sonar school course for commanding officers. Air travel serving both ends of my trip was largely nonexistent so I went by train and decided to travel in uniform. By coincidence, the American Legion was holding its annual convention in Miami at that time, and the train was filled with an enthusiastic group of partying veterans warming up for the convention. My several rows of very impressive ribbons earned during my many months in combat quickly attracted an audience. The trip became very wet and woolly. Somewhat the worse for wear, I left my new friends in Miami, wondering what the survival rate would be for Legionnaires after four more days of celebration.

The sonar school course was a disappointment, offering too much trivia by an unmotivated staff, a week of material which they managed to condense into two weeks of school. The new equipment on display was valuable, but the administration was juvenile. An interesting phase of the instruction tested recognition of the Doppler effect on sound signals—the increase in tone when the source is approaching and decrease when going away. To a musically trained ear such tests were rudimentary. I couldn't believe that I missed one (out of fifty), and on a recheck they found the school was wrong.

My disappointment by day was made up at night. Enrolled in the course was an old friend and classmate, James H. Elsom, a newly selected destroyer skipper. Jim invited me to go into town with him the first evening for a couple of beers and the floor show at a local nightclub. He had a secret. He had discovered that when one of the slot machines paid off, it could be played again without inserting another coin. Several times we had repeated hits on a single coin, and there was no way we could lose if we continued to play. Jim claimed to be an honest man and wouldn't take advantage of his discovery, playing only enough to cover the bar bill and floor show each night. Thus the money remained in the club. After several evenings we decided to broaden our adventures with a shopping tour to Havana, but fate suddenly intervened.

On the first of November 1948 I received orders to leave immediately for New London to take command of the USS *Burrfish*. The chief of naval operations decided to test the condition of the "mothball" fleet and the state of Atlantic

Fleet readiness as well. Simulating a war emergency, the Submarine Force Atlantic was ordered to carry out the emergency war plan for reactivating the mothball fleet and to place in commission one submarine and a rescue vessel. The order originated in Washington at the stroke of midnight on 1 November; officers and men were ordered from wherever they could be found. A major fleet exercise was then in progress, and the men "found" were mostly in the brig or hospital, plus a few recalled from leave. By plan, the ships were to be fully operational within thirty days.

I left Key West immediately, commandeering military flights via Norfolk, and arrived in New London on 2 November. I went straight to Rear Admiral James Fife's headquarters on the submarine base. Fife lived and breathed Navy. His wife had divorced him many years before; rumor had it that she blamed the U.S. Navy for alienation of affections. I had not served with him previously but knew him well by reputation. The duty with *Burrfish,* he explained, was only temporary; she was due for conversion to a radar picket at the Portsmouth yard in a few months. I would operate her until that time and then resume my duties with *Pickerel.* Fife's chief of staff was none other than Captain Karl Hensel. I looked forward to working with him again. Both Hensel and the admiral welcomed me warmly and offered every assistance, pointing out the significance of the reactivation to war planners and many other people both inside and outside the submarine force.

Hensel asked how soon I would be ready to place *Burrfish* in commission, suggesting 20 November. I replied, "Captain, we're taking these men from operating submarines and they lose submarine pay until the date of commissioning. I hate to penalize the wives and children when it isn't necessary for our great experiment. I suggest a much earlier date."

"What about next week?"

"What about tomorrow?"

We compromised on "next week." I am sure he realized that I was not getting submarine pay at all and wouldn't normally until *Pickerel*'s scheduled commissioning in the spring. Anything I got from *Burrfish* was a Christmas bonus.

When I got to the waterfront the ship had already been pulled out of the back channel and shoved alongside a pier. Once the cocoons were removed from topside equipment, virtually everything else became the task of ship's force, with assistance as necessary from the submarine base. We wasted no time in getting to work. In the laying-up process, all operating parts had been coated with a heavy preservative, which had to be removed with special care to prevent it from getting into the machinery and to avoid casualties from noxious fumes. The layup crew had laid on the preservative with abandon, to our sorrow. Even the wardroom silver and the coffee urn had a heavy coat. In our efforts to make the ship presentable for the commissioning ceremony so soon upon us, the ship soon reeked of solvent, which the best of air circulation could hardly cut through.

My exec, Lt. Cmdr. William C. "Bill" Walsh, previously the squadron engineer in New London, knew every rathole on the base to tap for spares, special tools, and equipment. The next two officers, Lts. Robert Krombar and Robert H. Armour, were Mustangs—former enlisted—with long experience in submarines, very capable, both with a touch of larceny in their hearts—ideally chosen for the present duty. Bob Krombar covered everything but engineering and electronics; Bob Armour handled engineering; and Lt. Walter S. Rose, a Naval Academy graduate, quickly made himself indispensable as the electronics officer.

The commissioning ceremony was one to remember. There hadn't been a commissioning at the sub base since the war, and, with or without invitations, the multitudes descended on us. Every command in the Atlantic seemed to be represented. Celebrities lined the pier, and families, spectators, several brass bands, and miscellaneous guests crowded each other off the dock. But *Burrfish* had only four officers and four enlisted men. The admiral and Captain Hensel came aboard with appropriate honors; following a stirring march by the band, and the chaplain's blessing, the time came for the main address. Hensel gave a stirring talk, a challenging, stimulating oration deserving a far wider audience. It was Thaddeus Thomson's special *Wichita* firebreather updated. Since the date had been chosen to benefit the men, it was unfortunate so few were on hand. Hensel noted this also. As he left the ship, he muttered to me, "All this for *four* enlisted men, huh?"

Within a very few days *Burrfish* was ready for her first tests under way. As we proceeded down the Thames River toward the submarine operating area in Long Island Sound, the throb of the diesels under me gave the old familiar feeling. But it was unfamiliar in one respect. She was my ship, even if only for a few months, and she would soon reflect the reputation, the personality we stamped on her, for good or ill. The first time under way was primarily to shake the men down and get them in the routine of working together.

Getting the ship fully ready for independent operations within a month would require heavy reliance on officers and men who had never worked together before. My high standards of performance applied for a temporary or a permanent command. I would make all necessary demands on the men and I had to know they would deliver.

The operating boats from which they were drawn did not always send me their best. Some on board were serving out brig sentences. We made clear to the weak links that their past was behind them; they were starting anew. But they needed special inspiration to rise above themselves. Bill Walsh and I had to be more than father figures to pull it off. Bill, a highly qualified exec, had laid out a meticulous schedule for testing every piece of equipment on the ship, including firing all torpedo tubes and guns, full-power runs surfaced and submerged, and every operation to be expected of a veteran ship and crew. But the first day at sea forced a major modification.

We had hardly entered the Sound before Bill complained of severe stomach cramps. The seas were rough and, thinking it a bit of seasickness after his long tour at a desk, he minimized the pain. Very shortly it became clear that something far more serious was wrong. I cut the operations short and headed for the barn at high speed, asking for medical assistance on arrival. Bill, as befits a good exec, was the first man ashore, but this time on a stretcher. His appendix had ruptured, and he was rushed to the hospital for surgery.

After a long convalescence, he made a complete recovery, but he never again went to sea on the *Burrfish;* his services as executive officer were terminated, and I received no replacement.

I still had full responsibility for getting *Pickerel* to sea on schedule. I relied heavily on Pappy Sims. I tried to get to Portsmouth on weekends for a look at the ship and to visit the family. We reviewed progress and planned accordingly. I had no cause for concern. Rear Admiral John H. "Babe" Brown, the shipyard commander, had been an All-American in football at the academy and greatly admired Pap for his gridiron skills and for other reasons. A great bond of friendship rose between the admiral and our ship. On the waterfront, the senior man was Cmdr. Ralph Kissinger, a brilliant officer whom I had known and admired from academy days. We built the strongest rapport between ship and yard.

Nevertheless, my responsibilities in New London with no exec created a new challenge. After a long bull session with the officers, we mapped out a revised program to get *Burrfish* ready for sea on time. Bob Krombar, next senior, inherited the exec's job in addition to his previous duties; the other officers took up the slack where they could. Through luck or extra diligence, we had no serious problems. On 19 November, less than three weeks after the reactivation started, I reported to Admiral Fife that *Burrfish* was fully ready for unlimited operations, nine days ahead of the war plan. Delighted, he promised to inspect the boat on 21 November.

We took two days for a final spit-and-polish cleanup and, following an inspection by the admiral and his staff, I reported to the Atlantic Fleet commander for duty. I thought we had earned a nine-day pre-Christmas shakedown cruise. My choice was St. Thomas in the Virgin Islands. To add a little extra incentive toward a quick approval, we offered to detour via Puerto Rico and do a photo reconnaissance of San Juan harbor en route.

The request was quickly approved; Admiral Fife sent for me for a briefing on official and unofficial calls in St. Thomas. Following my mandatory call on Governor William H. Hastie—a recent Truman appointee and the first black to hold the office—Fife wanted me to convey his regards to Vice Admiral Robert C. Giffen, who lived there, and several other officials. Fife clearly wanted to chat that morning, offering suggestions on where we could find items like fine kid gloves, perfume, and sharkskin material for suits at very low prices. Then he added, "And liquor is very cheap, too."

Walking back to the ship, I tried to figure out the significance of the comment concerning liquor. An aggressive teetotaler, Fife had shortened several careers over incidents involving alcohol. I couldn't believe he was seriously suggesting that I bring Christmas spirits back with us in bottles. My DivCom, Cmdr. George H. Laird, was a good enough friend to advise me. He too was surprised, adding only that if I decided to bring back a supply, to add a case for him. This was all I needed. Spread the responsibility, and *always* include somebody senior.

With great enthusiasm we were off on our adventure on 3 December. After the first three days of very rough seas, the weather suddenly turned mild and warm, with a flat, calm sea under a clear blue sky. After several hours of drills, I decided it was time to play. Stopping for swimming call over the side, we lolled away an hour, then enjoyed a double feature movie and a superfine steak dinner. After dinner we tried a bit of fishing for a favorite delicacy, flying fish. A lantern placed on deck for the fish to fly into soon attracted scores of the finny specimens. Cleaned and popped into a pan, they made a delicious but somewhat bony snack.

The fine weather stayed with us to San Juan, too much of it, almost, for the photo recon. We were required to remain undetected throughout, get the job done, and not get rammed into the mud by some old freighter trying to use the channel at the same time. The exercise demanded far more than merely snapping pictures. The submarine must steer a precise course parallel to the desired objective on shore, in close and at a steady speed so as to get the proper 150 percent overlap on the photography. All photography was shot through the periscope, using a special adapter for the standard Graflex camera. The pictures were developed on board immediately, then made into a moulage, which, under a stereo viewer, gave a clear, three-dimensional panorama of the objective area. Aided by Bob Krombar's precise navigation, photo expert Walt Rose did a thoroughly professional job.

St. Thomas is a charming spot and a favorite liberty port for the Navy. Our men deserved some relaxation as a reward for the hard work in getting *Burrfish* into shape so quickly. Following my call on the governor, we were all set to enjoy the area thoroughly. He returned my call on board that afternoon and graciously offered every assistance, including his limousine and driver for a special sightseeing tour of the beautiful island. He had done the same for President Harry Truman a few weeks earlier.

I was particularly anxious to meet Vice Admiral Ike Giffen again. He had been Commander Cruiser Division 7, flying his flag on the *Wichita* in Iceland at the time of my departure on 8 December 1941. I knew his son, Robert C. "Skip" Giffen, Jr., in submarines. The senior Giffens lived in a very attractive home on a small island in Charlotte Amalie, the harbor of St. Thomas. They were conveniently located and knocked themselves out with several cocktail parties, receptions, and shopping tours. The admiral was also helpful in the matter of liquid spirits.

Over the years, when opportunities arose for purchase of inexpensive or tax-free alcoholic beverages, I followed several inflexible policies. First, the rules applied to everybody, officer and enlisted. Second, all sales were cash on the barrelhead. The ship would negotiate the purchases, arrange delivery, and provide secure stowage aboard. Third, prudence suggested including orders from seniors in the chain of command. I stressed to the men the vital importance of exemplary conduct ashore. Despite chain lightning rum at a nickel or a dime a shot, I wanted no drunk or disorderly conduct, no breaches of discipline whatever. I gave the men as much free time as possible and relied on their good judgment. They responded superbly, and everybody had a great time. We felt fortunate in how well the crew had come together in so few short weeks. Considering that most were castoffs or problem children, their response was terrific.

On a shopping trip in this tax-free paradise, I found an absolutely breathtaking set of Spode Thistledown china with service for twelve. But the day it was delivered on board, a beautiful young brunette visiting the *Burrfish* kept intruding into my movie record of the voyage, with no views of her departure. I was chided by my officers for months as to what had transpired to make so magnificent a gift necessary as a peace offering for Henri. There was absolutely nothing, of course; such is the stuff of sea stories.

The day before departure the orders of Christmas spirits, delivered on board and sealed in the magazine, left only my neck still out. Admiral Fife's suggestion about alcohol still bothered me. My doubts skyrocketed immediately after the ship got to sea.

An unusually large crowd gathered for our departure as the ship cleared the channel and headed north. I had planned to hold swimming call as soon as the regular sea watch was set. The day was superb, and a nice sea promised an almost perfect "surf" across the deck. I was about to give the order to flood down and create our beach when I was handed a message from George Laird notifying me that Admiral Fife and an inspection party would board us off the sea buoy in New London at 0700 on the announced day of arrival. There could be only one response. I ordered, "All ahead flank."

Putting aside all thoughts of a swim, I mentally computed whether a full-power run all the way could get us to the sub base the evening before to offload the booze, then back out again to meet the admiral and his inspection party at the sea buoy at 0700 the next morning. The "flank" bell brought Bob Armour up from below in a hurry. I showed him the message and mentioned, "We'll have to hold this speed all the way back so we can offload at the base the night before."

"But we can't, captain; we have only enough fuel for a gentleman's trip back."

When I questioned him further, he confessed that since the ship was to go into the yard for conversion to a radar picket shortly after the holidays, there seemed no need to take on a full load of fuel and then pump it all off again. I replied, "Bob, you rascal, your daily fuel reports indicated we had a full load. That 'flank' bell will stay there until we get back to the base or run dry. You figure out how. You wanted to make a four-hour full power run anyhow. Now you've got the chance for four days of it."

It soon became clear that the race would be very close. Bob began to scrounge for everything greasy he could find to run through those beautiful Fairbanks-Morse engines. (A submarine never pumps bilges overboard to prevent leaving an oil slick in its wake. Bilge pumps discharge into a "collecting" tank for salvage and further use by the engines.) I also suggested that he find one of his men somewhat closer to the Lord who could pray for smooth sailing all the way. A winter storm would kill any chance of getting back early. A good storm would also give us an excuse for a delayed arrival and a change in the inspection schedule, I realized, but I didn't mention that to my engineers.

Luck favored us for a while. The dwindling fuel reserve consoled nobody, however. Despite best efforts, it became clear that we would run dry somewhere inside Long Island Sound, just before entering the Thames River. About that time, the first winter's snow started to fall, then suddenly became heavy, just as the engines died, requiring a shift to the battery. Other problems beset us. Since I was coming in unexpectedly, I couldn't request a pier assignment. And the holiday leave period began that morning in New London. All submarines would be alongside for the holiday break. There might be no berth available.

The situation at that time was tense; it was the witching hour of midnight. We were out of fuel, and the battery would last for only a "one bell" landing on arrival, after which the ship would be helpless, unable to move except at the whim of wind and current. No way would there be enough juice left in the battery for any maneuvering to get alongside. A maximum ebb tide was running, and we could hardly see through the blinding snow. Even if we made it alongside, there would be nobody on the dock to assist with mooring lines.

Peering intently through the snow, we couldn't see any piers, open or not. Then somebody on deck forward thought he saw an empty pier. He was right; he had found an upriver berth, which meant that the strong ebb current would help set us alongside the dock. Making the big turn to head in to the pier, I was lucky in putting the rudder over hard at precisely the right moment. The ship could steer directly for the dock. I backed just enough to kill the momentum. *Burrfish* eased alongside and we had our one-bell landing, a rare happening under the best of circumstances. I had never done it before. A few men jumped onto the dock to assist with the lines and in a few minutes we were soon snugly alongside.

The various messengers hurried about their tasks. One roused the duty officer on the boat across the pier to beg enough diesel fuel to get in a battery charge and to get down the river and back. Another tried to find a jeep to get the precious Christmas "presentos" off the ship. A junior officer, Ensign Theodore F. "Ted" Davis, lived in quarters on the base and provided the perfect solution, at least for the moment. We sent a fully loaded jeep of gurgling cartons for storage in his kitchen. But as soon as the warm air of the kitchen made itself felt, Len Davis saw a huge cockroach staring at her from the top of the pile. With a shriek she muscled the whole shipment into the yard and stacked it alongside the dumpster. No problem. In a few minutes it was so covered with snow it couldn't be distinguished from the real dumpster.

Meanwhile, back on the ship, about 0200 the engines were churning again and a charge was flowing into the battery at the maximum rate. We got under way about six and were out at the sea buoy in plenty of time to greet the admiral and party at 0700. My men, dropping from exhaustion, turned in a superb performance. The inspectors didn't concede a thing. If in a month's time a ragtag outfit can do everything required of a regular submarine in a year's training cycle, and do it very well, the whole training period is thrown into question. They gave us the grade we had earned, however, and we were delighted. Some few wondered how we did it. I learned later that Walt Rose put them off with the observation, "Rome wasn't built in a day, but the captain wasn't in charge of that outfit."

I still hadn't learned why the admiral wanted to meet us at the sea buoy. I couldn't wait to ask the division commander. George's disconcerting reply was, "The order for the inspection didn't come from the admiral. I was trying to give you a break, knowing how anxious you were to get back to your family in Portsmouth. I decided to save you the weekend by completing all training exercises on your way in from St. Thomas. Merry Christmas, and I'll see you next year." I thanked him rather weakly for his thoughtfulness.

Back alongside the dock by early afternoon, we found the Christmas gifts were completely undisturbed despite their unusual open storage alongside the dumpster. Bob Krombar in a rare role as Santa Claus made the deliveries, and our people were off for a happy holiday with friends and families.

There was a special reason for all the trouble and personal risk we went to on that occasion. Normally when submariners began holiday leave, each man was given a ham or turkey to help celebrate the Christmas season. That year, the senior sub skipper was Cmdr. Maurice "Duke" Ferrara, commanding the USS *Finback*. Duke was a fine submariner but less skilled as an administrator. His general mess fund was deep in the red and somebody suggested that all the boats forgo the ham or turkey and transfer the money to Duke's commissary to bail him out. When the leave period started the morning of our return, there was some grumbling by many on the boats who had to go home empty handed. But when the *Finback* sailors went ashore, each man left the ship with a ham or turkey slung over his shoulder. It was the only boat on the river able to show a surplus. Our men at least walked ashore with "presentos" to warm the head as well as the heart.

For the new year, *Burrfish* inherited all the special or offbeat operations that came by. We weren't on the regular schedule and were always available for special tasks or as a substitute. I played fast and loose with the schedule and had a good time doing it. We frequently took the enlisted sub school students out and became quite a favorite because we always gave them far more responsibility than the other boats did, allowing them to handle bow and stern planes or the maneuvering room controls and learn by doing rather than watching. If these operations came on a Friday when I was planning to get to Portsmouth, we told the school authorities we'd get under way at 0530, then we zipped through the operations so fast we were on the way back to the sub base at nine, when the others were just going out.

One Friday I was particularly anxious to get away early, but the divcom phoned to report that a special operation might require our services the next day. The chances were about even that it wouldn't develop; the chances were also about even that an expected heavy fog might cancel all operations. I went back to the ship to talk it over. Bob suggested that I head for Portsmouth as planned, then phone the ship from Boston. We would know then about both the weather and the operation. This seemed like a good solution. When I phoned Bob, his remarks were short and to the point: "No problem, Captain. Have a good weekend, and we'll see you Monday morning."

Returning aboard Monday, I said, "Well, I guess we played that one right. Was the weather really bad?"

Bob replied, "Oh, no, captain. It was clear as a bell."

"You mean the operation was cancelled?"

"Oh, no, Captain."

"You mean you went to sea when I was not aboard!!!"

"Ahhh. Yessir, Captain."

"I can't believe this. What did the DivCom say?"

"Oh, I just pulled the curtain to your cabin and told him you had a hard night and were still in the sack."

"That's even worse! You ruined my reputation as well."

And that's how, should anybody ever ask, a submarine went to sea for a normal day's operations with neither the CO nor XO aboard.

The time finally came in early February 1949 to take *Burrfish* to Portsmouth for conversion to a radar picket and for me to get to work on *Pickerel*. The trip was uneventful, and I had my two commands together at long last.

But once again my plans changed. Within two weeks I had orders to fly to the Caribbean to be an observer on a major fleet exercise involving most of the Atlantic Fleet. My temporary home would be the USS *Juneau*, a new light cruiser. Leaving a very raw and frigid New England behind for a Caribbean holiday had its attractions, but I preferred to think about a modest mansion on the seacoast, a roaring fire in the fireplace, a good book at hand, and the family nearby. Much as I enjoyed the interlude, sunning on deck at sea, or enjoying the brilliant white sand beaches in Trinidad, or even sampling a Planter's Punch with old friends at the local club, it couldn't compare.

I spent much of my time conspiring to get home as fast as possible when the exercise was over. Hence I was doubly pleased to run into Lawrence R. "Larry" Geis, my academy roomie, who had just reported for duty as commander of a carrier air group on the *Kearsarge*. Larry offered to fly me to Guantanamo, Cuba, and from the big naval base I could grab a military flight to the naval air station at Quonset Point, Rhode Island, and a staff car home.

But first I wanted to do some sightseeing over the Trinidad-Tobago area. As usual I was standing in the right spot. A visiting Marine general had a similar idea and invited me to accompany him. Using his wheels to get to an Air Force base in the middle of Trinidad, we first enjoyed a fine lunch, then cruised around Tobago, a small neighboring island— where Robinson Crusoe and his girl Friday became Eagle Scouts—then toured Pitch Lake from about a hundred feet above the ground. One of the seven wonders of the modern world, it was spectacular, but I could have enjoyed the same thrill from a few hundred feet more altitude. Then we overflew the islands of Aruba and Curaçao and the coast of Venezuela before heading back. I enjoyed the trip immensely but regretted not having a movie camera along.

Thanks to Larry's influence, I got back to Grayhaven in record time, just in time for the big St. Patrick's Day costume ball at the club. Having been roasted a very dark brown lying on deck of the *Juneau* under tropical skies, I dragged my old ten-dollar Caimanera white linens and Panama straw hat out of storage and went dressed as a bum. I walked in just as the party began, a water-stained cigarette dangling from my lips and the deep tan seeming totally out of place in the snowy New England setting. The costume was an easy prizewinner.

A few days later I was able to turn *Burrfish* over to a skeleton crew under Bob Armour and Walt Rose and transfer my full energies to *Pickerel*.

9   The USS *Pickerel*

Dipsydoodling on Government Time

Pappy Sims and I felt like old friends from the first meeting. Outgoing and always cheerful, he exuded both ability and strength. I quickly learned that behind a Georgia drawl lay the confident presence of a superior athlete and the rare gift to charm seniors and inspire the adulation of subordinates. In both our short- and long-range aspirations we were wholly simpatico. Capable beyond my highest expectations, he offered the combination of daring and caution I not only welcomed but needed. We made a very strong team. Equally important, Henri and Martha soon felt like sisters.

The other officers gave equal promise. Lt. Ralph F. "Snuffy" Jackson displayed special talents as a fine engineer and top-notch diving officer, truly a diamond in the rough. I shared a special interest with his wife, Jodie, a concert pianist. Lt. Michael M. Elliott, a classmate of Snuffy, became an expert navigator and operations officer, his intensity eased somewhat by his charming wife, Carolyn. Lt. (j.g.) William P. Shuman, the first lieutenant, always enthusiastic, added considerable experience to the ship, and his wife, Giovina, to the wives' activities. The other officers were recent sub school graduates. Lt. (j.g.) Charles F. Richelieu, the damage-control officer, and Ensign Grant B. Apthorp, electronics specialist. Chuck proved his French an-

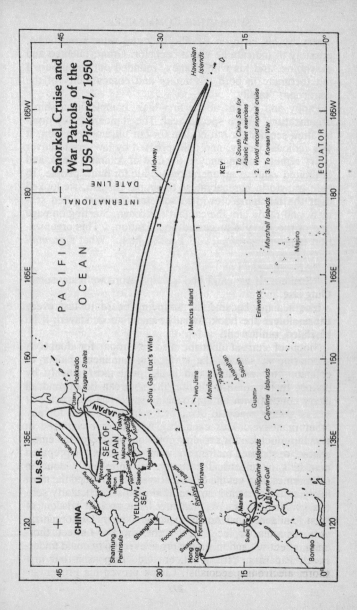

Snorkel Cruise and
War Patrols of the
USS Pickerel, 1950

KEY
1 To South China Sea for
   Asiatic Fleet exercises
2 World record snorkel cruise
3 To Korean War

PACIFIC
OCEAN

INTERNATIONAL DATE LINE

Hawaiian Islands

Midway

Marshall Islands

Majuro

Eniwetok

Marcus Island

Caroline Islands

Guam

Saipan

Anatahan

Pagan

Marianas

Iwo Jima

Sofu Gan (Lot's Wife)

Bonin Islands

Ryukyu Islands

Okinawa

Formosa

Foochow

Amoy

Swatow

Hong Kong

Shanghai

CHINA

Shantung Peninsula

Dairen

YELLOW SEA

Inchon

Seoul

Pusan

Pusan

Wonsan

Otaru

Tsugaru Straits

Hokkaido

Vladivostok

U.S.S.R.

SEA OF JAPAN

JAPAN

Tokyo

Yokosuka

Atami

Nagoya

Kure

Maizuru

Hiroshima

Sasebo

Nagasaki

Philippine Islands

Manila

Subic

Leyte Gulf

Borneo

EQUATOR

cestry by his birth on Bastille Day and wore a mustache, possibly to indicate he was a bachelor. Grant, talented and easygoing, and his wife, Nancy, rounded out the group. I felt fortunate in both the ability and compatibility of the wardroom "family."

Pappy and I went at the first task, completing a ship's organization, with a special zeal. The standard Navy organization seemed far out of date for our ultramodern ship. It was tedious, wordy, and dull, proofed by lawyers to cover every remote contingency at the cost of common sense, and of limited value as an operational guide for living people. To help transform bureaucratese to simple English, we looked over the incoming crewmen, selected the least gifted seaman, and made him the captain's yeoman. Starting on page one of the Navy's suggested organization, "This organization is promulgated . . . ," I asked him, "What's *promulgated* mean?"

"Ah—ah—sir, I ah . . ."

"Strike it. If we can't find a simple word we'll say something else."

The seaman became the sounding board to test every expression in the book. What he understood, stayed; if he hesitated, out it went.

Much of current doctrine also left room for doubt. A submarine at sea on the surface in imminent danger of collision, for example, can avoid peril most quickly by diving. In less than a minute, the ship can be beyond all likely contact with an approaching ship. The submarine at sea is always ready to dive, better prepared than for any other maneuver. This capability was never recognized in standard doctrine for avoiding collision. Whatever the emergency, we stressed realism and common sense. We prepared new bills on electrical casualty, not previously done in submarines, and yet the electrical systems provided the most likely cause or contributor to all mishaps, particularly serious in submarines. We challenged the ancient wisdom of John Paul Jones and Admiral George Dewey. Our organization was a masterpiece, we thought, short and sweet, thorough, effective, and in simple prose everybody could understand. Pap said, "It's great, but God help us in our first administrative inspection."

The work on the organization had been completed largely while I was involved with *Burrfish*. Pap and the other officers and chiefs had done a sterling job in my absence. Thanks to Admiral Brown and Ralph Kissinger, I enjoyed more whole-hearted support from the shipyard than ever before. The Yankee shipbuilder, unsurpassed in his craft, could also be as stubborn as a mule and just as contrary. We offered praise unstintingly and they slaved to justify it; criticism we left to others. Without the distraction of a lurid case of adultery this time, I tried to motivate the officers to stay completely on top of their jobs and to use my authority to do so. Not every detail needed to be brought to my attention. To establish priorities of effort, I suggested somewhat facetiously that I wanted to know immediately about a problem that would amount to something a decade into the future. If it would be important after five years, they were to notify the exec; three years, the engineer. If it would blow away in a year, I expected the younger officers and the chiefs to swarm all over it and reach a solution on their own. The yard quickly learned about my priorities and used the idea to great effect to smooth over problems that could have become annoying if bucked to higher levels.

By late March, *Pickerel* was ready for sea trials. We were entranced with the ship. The submerged power available in the "Guppy"—derived from *G*reater *U*nderwater *P*ropulsive *P*ower—gave us eighteen knots easily. The I-203 made nineteen knots but was no comparison with *Pickerel*, far and away the finest submarine in the world. We itched to get her to sea and open the throttle wide. But many weeks of intensive preparation lay ahead to gain the knowledge to handle her and keep the enormous power in our hands under firm control. Ned Beach, my esteemed classmate, had command of the new *Amberjack* and had done pioneering work with high speeds and steep angles as effective tactics for quick attack and escape. Pap and I saw great value in Ned's ideas and hoped to develop and expand on them. "Dipsy-doodling" at high speeds and steep angles required unprecedented skill in diving officers, planesmen, and others. A small mistake could lose the ship. Every man and the ship's cook had important roles in tying down loose gear and equipment under unique conditions. Emergency procedures for casualties such as loss of power, steering, and depth control had to be worked out to a degree never before approached in a submarine. Of primary importance, I felt that all the officers had to be expert shiphandlers. How to gain that skill in operations in the Portsmouth area presented problems.

The shipyard lies on the Piscataqua River, which made up for its short length by its extremely strong and unpredictable currents. At maximum strength the current ran seven to eight knots on the flood, ten to twelve on the ebb. Channel buoys disappeared from sight at strength of current, leaving only a swirl on the surface. River pilots at the yard never moved ships up or down river except at slack water. Therefore, ships had to get under way at odd hours of day and night, and, when yard workmen were involved, two shifts had to be taken to sea, one idle and one working, because tides rarely coincided with shifts. I decided to find a better way. Ideally for the yard work cycle, we should have gotten under way every morning at 0700 and moored every afternoon at 1400. This seven-hour period also roughly equaled the time span between slack water and maximum current, either ebb or flood, and therefore the maximum and minimum currents in the river.

What would happen when the slack didn't occur at 0700 and 1400? In the worst case, if we got under way when the current was rushing downstream at ten knots and the ship docked heading upstream, it would be impossible to twist her around in midstream against the current before being carried down the river sideways or backwards. And even if we cleared the dock and headed downstream, the ten- to fifteen-knot speed required for normal steerageway, added to the current, would mean a risky twenty- to twenty-five-knot speed over the ground. Shortly below our moorings the river made a sharp turn around the old naval prison. The channel was narrow and very rocky and our 310-foot ship wouldn't bend in the middle. The turn would become extremely ticklish to navigate at such speeds. Nevertheless, I thought I could handle it.

The other half of the problem was just as tough. If we got out safely, what about the return trip upriver? The worst case now was trying to come alongside the dock with the current at maximum flood, hence pushing us rapidly upstream. If we tried to dock with the bow heading upstream, the current might catch the stern and force the ship upstream sideways, toward a low drawbridge just beyond the shipyard. But if a big turn were made so that we could moor heading downstream, the strength of the current would help push the ship alongside the dock.

This gave me the clue. By anticipating the state of the current for the next time under way, we could always moor to head either upstream or downstream to minimize the worst case on leaving or returning. They couldn't both be bad. The interval between slack and maximum current was always seven hours, hence it wasn't possible to get the most unfavorable conditions both going and coming. A maximum current undocking meant a minimum current on return, and vice versa. We could go alongside heading either up- or downstream to avoid the most adverse current. I notified the yard that we would leave at 0700 and return at 1400 each day. The yard officials were delighted; the pilots said we were mad and very quickly would come to grief.

Perhaps I had another reason behind the decision. Either the Boston Red Sox or the Braves—there were two baseball teams in Beantown then—were on TV every afternoon. I could get home in time to enjoy the game every day.

Despite the dire warnings of the river pilots, our system worked fine. I took the conn for all mooring and unmooring until I felt completely confident, then let Pappy try until he had the touch. Then we turned the conn over to the duty officer. This was a major achievement. No submarine had ever allowed junior officers to learn shiphandling under such severe conditions.

Then one day the odds caught up. Backing away from the pier, Bill Shuman allowed the stern to get too far out into the current. In a wink we were heading downstream at about ten knots, sideways. I took the conn, ordered an emergency twist—backing emergency on one screw, ahead flank on the other—meanwhile trying to estimate how soon we would reach the dead man's curve at prison point and how we could possibly go around that point sideways. Easing the backing bell as soon as the wind took effect, we were just beginning to gather steerageway when we reached the eddies around the rocks on the far side of the channel. I turned the conn back to Bill, adding a few suggestions, freely translated as, "Bill, try to be just a teensy bit more careful next time."

The commissioning ceremony was set for 4 April 1949. I had given it a lot of thought. A submarine CO is unique in many ways. I suggested earlier his important role in setting the style, the character of a ship. I believed that I had exerted a significant influence on each of my submarines, even as a tyro in *Mackerel*. But full responsibility falls on only one man's shoulders. The fundamentals of command were old when the triremes of Themistocles put to sea, and one can never measure himself against the challenge of command until he faces it. I lacked no confidence that I would measure up, certainly after the *Sterlet* experience. But since my earliest years I was, through no conscious choice, a nonconformist. It was not enough that I would measure up as a CO; it was necessary that *Pickerel* stand out even among the best of contemporaries. I sought a special character, a panache, an elegance, in everything we did. Such an aura turns on the young officers and petty officers who carry the load on the reputation of a ship. The key to success in setting the style of operations lay largely in the executive officer. Here I thought Pappy became my best disciple. Better, perhaps, each of us was the other's.

The senior guest and speaker at the commissioning was the Honorable Sherman Adams, Governor of New Hampshire, soon to become President Dwight D. Eisenhower's senior adviser. Adams was brilliant, witty, extremely personable, and a fine conversationalist. He and his wife were most gracious guests and contributed to a memorable occasion, especially for the CO and his own charming wife.

There is no question that in our first operations with *Pickerel* we were like teenagers with a hotrod. She handled so beautifully, so differently from any other submarine within our experience, that we soared through liquid space probing her innermost secrets. Submarines during the war dived and surfaced with three- to five-degree angles; we began experimenting with fifteen, twenty, and soon thirty and thirty-five. Slowly, very slowly, we gained confidence to handle her under any conditions—and under casualties both imagined and real. We delighted in taking out veteran submariners, heeling into sharp turns and spirals wholly unlike other ships, which roll outward on high speed turns. Admiral Brown and his aide, Edwin T. Osler, shared our delight during a special cruise, and they became still stronger supporters. The admiral wrote Admiral Fife about *Pickerel*. Pap and I were formally commended by Fife for the outstanding conduct of the ship during the fitting-out period.

Just before completion of the underway tests our parents visited us in Kittery. Dad Schratz was suffering a terminal illness at the time and made the trip only with considerable distress. With great difficulty he made his way through the submarine, but we were not able to take him to sea. Sadly, it was his last trip away from home—just as *Pickerel* was about to make her first. Dad Frank went to sea with us and enjoyed the thrill of a lifetime.

I had hardly arrived in Portsmouth before it was time to leave again. Anxious as we were to be on our own, I was equally reluctant to leave our beautiful Kittery Point home. Dad's worsening condition soon became a major concern. Shortly before departure we made a nonstop drive to Pittsburgh with our four little girls buckled into their car seats. It was clear that Dad had only a few days left.

The *Pickerel*, one recalls, was slated for Honolulu duty. Getting the families out to the islands created many more difficulties than usual, if only because most of the burden fell on the wives. Because the government didn't pay for transportation of dependents who left before the home port was changed, *Pickerel* left before most of the wives. As we headed down the familiar channel for the last time, Ralph Kissinger stood alongside Henri on the dock, summarizing aptly the experiences of the year: "There goes the best ship the yard ever built, and the best crew."

Newport offered no thrills during the torpedo trials, and at New London I was interested mainly in getting home to Pittsburgh for a final visit with Dad. During the few days in New London, we had temporary quarters on the base, left the two youngest girls with Nancy Apthorp, and repeated the overnight rush home with the children. Dad died two days later, just as the ship left for Norfolk. Henri couldn't attend the funeral; I hoped to get there from Norfolk.

With the four children age six and under, Henri began the

long trek to Hawaii, using a combination of rail and air to the coast and a Navy transport from San Francisco to Honolulu. Neither railroads nor airlines had experience with four little travelers so young, nor did Henri. It was a great adventure, however, with only minor mishaps until the last leg. On the transport, Margie developed bronchial pneumonia and upon arrival in Hawaii was taken by ambulance from the ship to the hospital.

Pickerel, meanwhile, rushed to Norfolk, the first port on our shakedown cruise. Here the Navy gave me a two-seater airplane with driver to get me home, but on arrival in Anacostia (Washington, D.C.), he couldn't get clearance for the flight over the mountains. I grabbed a commercial flight; my "private" plane followed the next day. The only memory of the commercial flight was of an attractive young lady sitting next to me, bubbling over with anticipation of a hunting trip with her father, with whom she obviously enjoyed a fond relationship. Finally, she asked why I was bound for Pittsburgh. I could barely blurt out, "I'm going home to bury my father."

I couldn't send word of my arrival until about ten minutes before I flew in. Suddenly showing up in uniform at the funeral home, after scores of people had expressed their sympathy to Mother that I couldn't be there, seemed almost supernatural. Mother had a hard time of it for a few moments, but, a real trooper, she bore up well through the evening and the funeral on Saturday, the day following. Sunday I spent with the family but felt morose, probably because I would be so far away during the difficult days to follow. When the time came for me to leave, Mother planned to accompany me to the airport but changed her mind to spend the time alone.

My Navy plane had arrived the afternoon before but then couldn't get clearance for the return. (The pilot must have been cleared to fly only on bright, clear days.) Just then a Navy VIP plane came in from the West Coast, and I bumped one of the passengers, offering him my plane for his return the following day. I got back to Norfolk just in time for *Pickerel* to get under way for Jacksonville, Florida.

The weather became exceedingly rough as we approached Cape Hatteras. Many preferred to "sack out" rather than eat, but the Hatteras ritual soon changed all that. Traditionally, when a Navy ship rounds the stormy Cape southbound, the word is passed, "Cape Hatteras is abeam; all men are now bachelors."

It is well known throughout the Navy that nothing better calms the seas and raises the spirit of adventure in a young man's heart. Sure enough, the seas calmed, the skies cleared, and everything seemed right with the sailor's world.

Jacksonville offered quite a welcome, with brass bands, gals, and gold braid. But strangely, as we eased in toward the pier, the ship slowly came to a complete stop a hundred yards short of the pier. I still had five knots speed rung up, and Mike Elliott, the navigator, said, "Captain, I think we're aground. I don't think we can get alongside."

The chart indicated adequate depth of water, but a strong wind whistling downstream had apparently blown the water out of the channel. I said to Mike, "When the band is playing and pretty ladies are lining the pier, you never disappoint them. If five knots won't do it, try ten."

Ten knots didn't do it either, but about twelve did, and we churned our way alongside through the mud. When the senior visitors departed, I hosted a lunch for a wardroom full of broadcasters and feature writers. They were interested in the Navy's newest sub and also in her famous exec, who had starred at a nearby university before entering the Naval Academy. One of the press stories in the local paper told of me running the ship from my bunk in a "dank, dark stateroom that looks like a gear locker." We suspected Pap was the source; he took quite a razzing about it and promised to correct the misunderstanding at the next stop.

The next day I made my formal calls on the local dignitaries, pushing off a series of radio interviews on Pap. We then joined to share the publicity at several banquets and receptions. The following morning *Pickerel* was scheduled to take the local reserves out for a cruise. Breaking free of the mud was the first task. We ran the low pressure blowers to the ballast tanks for fifteen minutes; the air, bubbling out the flood holes at the bottom of the tanks, carried the mud away and dug us a channel. To give the reserves a thrill, we worked out a special treat. After each man had a chance to operate the various ship control stations during diving and emergency drills, our experts took over and showed them the dipsydoodles, up, down, and across, with everything but an inside loop, finally surfacing with a huge up angle. Most were exhilarated; a few were scared green. We figured the latter weren't material for submarine duty anyway. Just before sunset we anchored half a mile off the boardwalk at Daytona Beach and sounded swimming call or provided fishing gear for those who preferred. For liberty, both periscopes were available for girl watching.

New Orleans came next, the city of intrigue, the city of sin, the fun city of the deep South. Passing by Key West, I stopped for the daily swim. The water was blue and sparkling, and two "clubs" seemed to be forming among the swimmers, those able to dive off the top of the periscope shears—about thirty-five feet above the water—and those who could swim under the keel—about twenty feet deep.

Steaming up the Mississippi River, we raced a major hurricane streaking across Florida and heading for New Orleans. Despite threatening weather, again a large welcoming committee was on hand. Here we learned the sad news of tragedy from the far north. The newest guppy conversion from the Electric Boat Company, the USS *Cochino*, had gone down north of Norway following a serious electrical fire and battery explosion. Her CO, Rafael C. "Ralph" Benitez, was a longtime friend from academy days. Loss of the ship, including loss of a civilian technician and six men from USS *Tusk* during rescue operations, brought our immediate sympathy. Ralph was a fine submarine officer, and these things never help a career, no matter how accidental.

Because of the weather in New Orleans, rumors floated around about canceling the scheduled reserve cruise so I announced to the press and radio that *Pickerel* would go to sea regardless of weather conditions. When it was suggested that the combination of weather and the loss of *Cochino* might scare off some volunteers, Mike Elliott added that if they knew the thrills we had in store for them, nobody might show up.

The weather abated and nobody missed the cruise. For the long run downriver to deep water, we laid on four-engine speed and averaged twenty-two knots for the 120-mile jaunt. After a busy day with sixteen dives, one for each visitor on all stations plus the dipsydoodle, we then headed for Grand Isle, a fisherman's paradise about fifty miles farther along the coast. After anchoring, a Coast Guard launch, prearranged by a wise exec, met us and ran liberty trips to town throughout the night. Next morning early, a shrimp fisherman came alongside, and when the deck watch offered him a trip through the boat, he gave us an enormous bucket of fresh-caught shrimp. It was Sunday morning, dead calm and sunny. Going back up the giant river, Pap and I spent most of the day on the bridge enjoying a shrimp cocktail every hour, with a simply delicious sauce prepared by a leading machinist's mate. The shrimp were huge, three to four inches long, and succulent.

While lazing away the day, we noted several church services along the shore, including some baptisms in the river. A place on earth more blissfully peaceful at that time was hard to imagine. But our peace was suddenly disturbed. The Mississippi is one of the few waterways in the world on which taking a pilot is virtually mandatory. We thought we'd save the taxpayers some money and do without. But Ole Miss had special rules of navigation of which we knew nothing. Ships don't always drive on the right. They steer the shortest distance from point to point down the tortuous channel, sometimes passing to port, sometimes to starboard. A big freighter heading for a starboard-to-starboard passing almost drove us up on the shore trying to get around us as we tried to pass port-to-port. The tops of tall trees gave us a leafy overhead before he eased off. It gave us a scare, but by the time another came by we had more or less figured out the local passing rules.

After my protocol requirements on official calls were filled, I joined Pap, Snuffy, and Mike for an evening tour of the Bourbon Street nightspots. Pap soon found an intriguing new challenge. Several showgirls did a tassel dance with much swinging of breasts, which Pap thought he could emulate. When he learned the routine, we bought him a pair of paste-ons. His act, with the addition of a grass skirt, wowed 'em in Honolulu.

Houston, Texas, was the next haven. Heading first to Galveston, we enjoyed a movie on deck in the half-light of the moon, took a swim off Galveston, and spent a busy day steaming up the Houston ship channel toward the big metropolis. Here, Pap promised us the greatest hospitality the country had to offer. He had been given such prominence in the press at our other stops, we didn't know what to expect. Surprise of surprises, he got very little publicity; I got loads. The officers knew that I had spent some time in Texas many years ago—I hesitated to say how many, but it was as an infant—and Chuck Richelieu decided to play a joke on Pap. In New Orleans he had informed the press that I was a Texan, and the "local boy" in command of the Navy's newest submarine made every Houston headline and news broadcast. We had a huge laugh over it; the families back in Pittsburgh were astonished.

Pap's friends were unbelievable. The Shamrock Hotel, one of the best known in the region, became our headquarters, with a Cadillac or two always available for transportation. We showed off in the big pool by diving together from the high ten-meter board. By then we were both deeply tanned and in splendid shape, but four hundred pounds is a lot of beef flying through the air, even in Texas. The splash made the local papers.

When we returned to the ship late that night, Mike met us with a long face and some disquieting news. "I just had a phone conversation with a friend in Washington. He claims that *Pickerel* will be sidetracked, kept in the Atlantic Fleet to replace *Cochino,* and not go to Pearl. With half the wives already en route, the men are quite upset."

So was I. Peacetime duty in Honolulu merits a fight well beyond the acute financial sacrifice of sending families out and back without reimbursement. I made a few discreet phone calls trying mainly to avoid putting the idea up to somebody who had not yet thought of it and definitely trying to cool it.

The continuous round of hospitality was hard on the constitution. Pap was a nondrinker, and I thought I might be leading him astray. We almost always went ashore together, and finally agreed on a compromise that he'd train up to two drinks a night and I would train down to two. We tried to follow this practice throughout our tour together. A few times I weakened and had to borrow on a dry day at sea to augment my shore ration, but it worked well. The strain was never greater than in Houston.

The reserve cruise for the Houston area surpassed all the others. On our patented final act, I surfaced at eighteen knots from about five hundred feet, shooting out of the water like a giant fish at an angle of about forty degrees. On board were an Associated Press photographer and some AP and NBC reporters. The latter taped a half-hour recording of a dive which went on the air the following week; the AP photographer pleaded with us for a picture of the steep angle, promising to make us both famous. After the show, I anchored off the big Seaside Pier and beach at Galveston and sounded swimming call. Pap, Snuffy, and I offered to dive off the top of the periscope shears for the benefit of the photographer. It was a great picture except that Snuff turned chicken and jumped. Literally hundreds of visitors asked about it later when they came out to go through the ship.

With no new liberty port scheduled until Panama, we decided to add Freeport, Texas, on the first night out of Houston. The Coast Guard again arranged a berth for us, but as we steamed up the narrow Brazos River, we ran aground quite a distance from the dock. It had only ten feet of water and was less than a hundred feet long. Backing clear, I decided to go up to the head of the river at Brazosville, Texas, turn around in the turning basin, and catch a new berth on the way downstream. The second surprise was that there was no turning basin. I had a 310-foot ship to turn around in a 300-foot channel. The alternative of backing clear out to sea again didn't make sense; the only choice short of hiring a tug was to build up speed, throw the rudder over hard and drive the bow up on the bank, then put a strong twist on the screws to drive the stern upriver until we could back clear and head out. Hotrodders of the highways call this a J-turn, I believe. Our charts, incidentally, showed nothing at all of the river, merely a void with a note that pilots are necessary after dusk. We, as usual, had no pilot.

The turn worked out fine, with one exception. The heavy twist on the screws threw up mud and water and disturbed zillions of ravenous mosquitoes slumbering on the still surface. The men on deck were in danger of being carried off. We got clear, however, found the new dock chosen for us, and again grounded about forty feet off the creaky pier. Passing the lines to the pier, we heaved around on the capstan and pulled the ship halfway in, the dock halfway out. The dock was in the middle of a weed field, abandoned except for the rattlesnakes. But with the town council waiting for us, what else could we do? One of the commissioners and his wife welcomed us to Freeport, then drove me, Pappy, and Snuffy back to Brazosville for a huge steak dinner. The mayor and his wife joined the party, and after dinner we adjourned to his home for some lively conversation. At 0130 we returned for a tour of the ship with our hosts. All hands had a great time ashore, thanks to the royal treatment by the town. The reserves in particular enjoyed the break. As one commented, it was the only liberty they got in two whole days at sea.

Early the next morning we returned to Galveston, disembarked the reserves, and turned south for Panama. Smooth seas and hot sunny days again made ideal cruising. Using two engines at full speed every night, we picked up enough distance to conduct training and kill one hour with a daily swim. For the swim, one change was added to the routine. We were now in tropical waters, shark country, and a duty officer with a Browning automatic rifle took station atop the bridge as a safety precaution while men swam over the side. The danger of shark attack was minimal. We enjoyed "surfing" mainly, diving into the waves rolling across the deck and allowing them to lift us back aboard. By flooding down until the main deck was almost awash, a fine surf could be created as the heavy seas broke across the deck. Nobody swam very far from the ship. There was more danger of injury from the shark watch than from a shark.

Just before our arrival in Coco Solo, the schedule called for running target services for naval aviators trying to track a snorkeling or deep, high-speed submarine target by hemming us in with sonobuoy patterns. I thought these weapons were marginal against a fleet submarine and useless against a guppy, but we all got some good training out of it. Again we tried to cut down the cost to the taxpayers by retrieving the sonobuoys after each exercise. Several officers swam through so much dye marker tracking them down that they carried a greenish tinge for a week.

Ashore that night the aviators reciprocated with first-class hospitality. Here their weapons were far more effective, and we had a rousing good time. Liberty for all hands in the Canal Zone is a thrill for the first or the fortieth time. The men had come to love the routine of swimming or fishing every day at sea and lots of free time in great liberty ports every time the mooring lines went over.

Celebrating the transit of the canal, we formally reported for duty with the Pacific Fleet—with sighs of relief. Nothing beyond the rumor had developed to keep us in the Atlantic to replace *Cochino,* but it set the stage for a great liberty in Balboa before setting course for Pearl Harbor. We set several courses, in fact. *Pickerel* clearly had a fast set of heels. Already we had reason to believe we might be the fastest submarine in the fleet. Or maybe we just put heavier loads on the engines. Only through superior speed were we able to make the unscheduled stops at Daytona Beach, Freeport, Galveston, and Brazosville on the way south, aided by on-the-spot arrangements through the Coast Guard. For the long leg from Panama to Pearl, I hoped to pick up many hours of extra steaming time. First choice of a place to visit was the Galapagos Islands, near the equator off the coast of Ecuador. Second was the island of Villa Gigeda off the southern coast of Mexico, uninhabited and apparently unvisited. Not as far off the normal route, this became our choice.

Navy ships aren't free to gad about the oceans at will. We sent daily position reports to the Navy Movement Control Center, which maintained a plot of all vessels at sea, to Commander Submarines, and, with coded weather information, to the Fleet Weather Center for use in forecasting. The ship's positions for all these reports should coincide. In *Pickerel* they rarely did. And differing from all of the above was a fourth position report the navigator made to me every day at noon, telling where Mike thought we *really* were. By running a few knots faster than the assigned speed of advance, we gained time for the reason we joined the Navy—to see the world.

Easing into the natural harbor of Villa Gigeda, only slightly sheltered from the open sea by a partial ring of green, treeless hills, we picked our way carefully through largely uncharted waters. I dropped the anchor as close in as seemed safe, and the fishermen went to work. Rigs of all sorts appeared topside, using anything and everything for bait. Every line had a bite almost as soon as it hit the water—little fish, big fish, strange ones and common ones. The three ship's cooks set up shop topside to clean and fillet, offering the rest for bait. The chief quartermaster used the head of one for bait, caught a larger one, used its head for bait, and soon was heaving a grapnel over the side with the head of a sea monster for bait. Concerned that if he caught his dream fish, he might end up as bait for the last one, I suggested that he secure the grapnel chain to a deck stanchion so as not to lose the grapnel as well.

In a matter of only an hour or two we had all the fish we could use for the rest of the trip. It was hardly sport fishing unless one gets his thrills just from seeing what strange monsters of the deep he pulls in. Nobody could remember anything like it.

As we entered the Hawaiian Island chain, all sorts of emotions emerged—concern for wives and children, memories of the war, romantic dreams of duty in paradise. After having sailed into Pearl under so many different circumstances, nothing could be more dramatic for me than returning as commander of a beautiful and powerful warship. Life never looked better. Adding to our good fortune, Admiral Babe Brown from the Portsmouth shipyard had just arrived to be the new Commander Submarines and was the first to extend his very special welcome. Kenny Nauman, my DivCom, made us feel at home. It was the first time I had seen him since the *Salmon* episode when *Sterlet* assisted her into Saipan in 1944.

Everybody was curious, naturally, about our new Jules Verne submarine. That had to wait until we greeted families on the dock, each with tales of adventure in the long trek from New England to Hawaii. The band played good old Hawaiian music; hula dancers greeted the crew and convinced them they never wanted to leave. I saw Henri immediately, but only the two older girls. Margie was still in the hospital. So that I would not be concerned upon arrival, Henri decided to leave baby Nancy behind also.

Life in the islands grew on us in a hurry. Splendid beaches and picnic areas surrounded us on all sides. Trips took us to the magic of the other islands, each more beautiful than the previous. The only limitation in our idyllic existence was housing. We were assigned quarters in Navy housing, cheap wartime construction for civilian workers, held together by termites. Because it was substandard, the rent was very low, even below our rental allowance. Henri worked her usual genius in making it comfortable, however, and we were very happy.

Pickerel quickly fell into the training cycle. The intensive workup just completed en route put us well ahead of the pack. I still couldn't accept the peacetime routines noted here and in New London. We executed diving and surfacing exactly as in wartime, a forty-five-second operation; others, I noticed, did a step-by-step procedure taking several minutes. The difference was not of greater safety but of greater caution.

Coming from the Atlantic, we also noted a great difference in the use of the snorkel. Although it was accepted in the Pacific as a useful piece of gear under certain wartime operating conditions, only two other subs in Pearl were snorkel-equipped and it played almost no role in the training. For those less than expert, snorkeling meant inconvenience, discomfort, and slower travel. But it was available for use when necessary, and that need seldom came. It was accepted as a fully tested and reliable piece of equipment when in fact it had never been realistically evaluated by the Navy. Additionally, a serious flaw in the engines caused by snorkeling had not been solved. This was a major concern.

Always anxious to show off our beautiful new ship, we made *Pickerel* available for reserve cruises, visitors, newsmen, and anybody else, especially beautiful ladies. Local broadcasters taped shows on board, always guaranteed an enthusiastic group of crewmen and a smart ship.

As soon as we were settled in our new life, I auditioned for the Honolulu Symphony and the summer "Pops" orchestra and, luckily, made the first violin section in both. Through the symphony we met many of the fine people of Honolulu, expanding our social life considerably. Several were kind enough to offer their beach homes on the other islands. One in particular, on a secluded cove on the coast of southern Kauai, was heavenly. In this idyllic life, the months sped by. Christmas came, and the children welcomed Santa ashore from his outrigger canoe. We celebrated Mele Kalikimaka and a Hauoli Makahiki Hao, hoping for the 1950 new year that things would never change.

Two new officers reported aboard, Lt. David "Ski" Wessinger and Lt. (j.g.) Edward M. Cummings, and a number of men. Ski's skill as a photographer soon made him indispensable; Ed took over the TDC and made an excellent fourth for our daily tennis games. Ginny Wessinger and Mimi Cummings, beautiful and talented, became immediate favorites. The new men had heard so much about fun cruising they wanted their share. They convinced me that the routine of training was boring. Perhaps we were all getting a bit footloose. Proving we were on the right side of the Lord, relief came unexpectedly.

Before leaving Washington, my orders to a Pearl Harbor command gave me the idea for a shakedown cruise to Pearl via the Mediterranean, the Indian Ocean, Singapore, and Hong Kong. I visited the British Joint Services Mission in Washington and painted a rosy picture of fleet exercises out of Malta, Singapore, and Hong Kong with the most modern submarine in the world as the prey. The Brits were enthusiastic; we both went to work laying a proper groundwork.

But Pap Sims had also worked on ideas for the shakedown cruise. Before reporting aboard he put his irons into the fire to visit every whistle stop down the Atlantic coast and through the Gulf for a pilgrimage with old friends and admirers. When my Dad's health became critical, Pap's plan, which would keep me in range of Pittsburgh for a few extra weeks, swayed me and I requested the traditional route. The wheels of the bureaucracy had already begun to grind, however, and my politicking for exercises with the Royal Navy paid off—backward. Early in 1950, three Pearl Harbor submarines, including a high speed guppy, were requested for a combined U.S.-U.K. fleet problem to be conducted between Singapore and Manila. *Pickerel* and *Queenfish* were chosen from Pearl; *Sea Dog,* a San Diego boat, was already in the Far East. Kenny Nauman decided to ride *Queenfish* out and return on *Pickerel.*

I tore myself away from daughter Margie's third birthday celebration on 8 February and headed west, exhilarated by the great feeling of being once more on our own. We played hare and tortoise with *Queenfish* on the way out, alternating as target for radar tracking, surface and submerged attacks, and casualty drills; *Pickerel* added a daily swim call. The *Queenfish* CO, Thomas C. "Thump" Williamson, a classmate both at the academy and at sub school, had a slow-footed boat and soon began to cramp our style of operating on the wide, wide sea. We were due for a twenty-four-hour engineering run and used it as an excuse to draw well ahead and proceed into Manila independently.

I immediately changed course for the Mariana Islands. When the engineering test was completed, we made a sightseeing trip around Pagan Island, then dropped anchor a short distance offshore in Apaan Bay. My official report claimed that we were collecting data for the Hydrographic Office. Perhaps. This was the island from which the Japanese had launched the fighter raids on Saipan while I enjoyed the spectacle as AA fire control officer on *Fulton*. I wanted a closer look. Pap favored landing on adjacent Anatahan Island. That might have been far more exciting. We didn't know it, but about two dozen Japanese survivors of the war were living on Anatahan, under the rule of one Keiko Kusakabe, an Okinawan-Japanese queen bee of Amazonic proportions. She chose one of the Japanese as her consort, which generally marked him for a mysterious disappearance so that somebody else could take his place in the service of the queen. In the years since the war ended, the surviving male stock had been reduced to about fourteen. How a boatload of Yankee submariners would have fared was an intriguing question. Pap would have made a great king, but Martha and I both needed him.

Pagan Island, as far as we could tell through the periscope, was uninhabited. With my trusty exec and a landing party, we paddled the rubber boat ashore for an inspection tour. The day was brilliantly clear, and the bright blue water, black sand beach, and stately mountain peaks towering in the distance made a beautiful setting. We found all sorts of war relics, pillboxes, AA batteries, and slit trenches. We returned to the ship laden with strange flowers, delicious giant oranges, bananas, coconuts, and other tropical fruits, and two five-pound fish, shot with a carbine in the lagoon.

We left the rats, lizards, flies, and crabs in control of the island. The airfield had already been reclaimed by the jungle. A destroyed hangar offered a few souvenirs from plane relics and abandoned landing boats.

While we adventured on the beach, Snuffy, left behind in temporary command of *Pickerel,* had his own problems. He soon found that the anchor was dragging. He got the ship under way under emergency conditions and dropped the hook in a new spot just before we decided to return.

Some of the fresh fruit was disappointing. Two large stocks of bananas were small and green. To allow them to ripen, we secured them to the lookout platforms on the bridge for exposure to the hot sun, taking them below every time we dived. We didn't know that they were cooking bananas and already edible. By the time we found out, nobody thought the effort was worth the reward. But the Hydrographic Office probably appreciated the information that the anchorage offered an unsafe holding ground. We also ran a photo reconnaissance of Pagan, largely to give Chuck Richelieu some experience toward qualification. Four days later, after entering San Bernardino Strait, we rejoined *Queenfish* and did a special photographic operation off Tagiran Point on Luzon.

Since the time the AP photographer in Houston had pleaded to get a shot of the steep angle on surfacing, I had been trying to contrive an opportunity. More than camera equipment was required. We needed an observing ship with sonar gear to track us accurately and coordinate the action of both ships. Things happened so quickly in those wild surfacings that rapid and efficient two-way communications were vital. Off Manila, sonar conditions were excellent, and *Queenfish* thought she had an adequate camera aboard. Ned Beach in *Amberjack* off Key West had surfaced at forty-five-degree angles with no difficulty. We had done thirty-five to fifty degrees many times. I thought we could do considerably better. Obviously it required tremendous concentration, intensive training, and careful preparation of the ship. I had nightmares of a torpedo sliding from the racks and bouncing around the room, the three-thousand-pound air pressure in the flask almost as dangerous as the warhead. They were cinched down with double and triple straps, and every piece of gear in the ship was just as tightly secured.

The ship's test depth was four hundred feet, but we had operated as deep as six hundred feet on several occasions. For the big angle, I decided to start at five hundred feet. The first sharp up angle would throw the stern deep, and I didn't want the aft compartments, the weakest on the ship, to go below six hundred feet. We were making eighteen knots. The diving officer commenced blowing all the forward tanks until he could no longer hold the ship on an even keel, then threw the bow and stern planes on full rise and hung on. It took only microseconds to break the surface; we came out at seventy-two degrees. A tool in the overhead dropped through two compartments before hitting the deck. The only unanticipated casualty involved the gyroscope. Steep angles sometimes spilled mercury from the gyro; this happened so fast there was no time for a spill, but the sudden change in the axis of rotation confused the gyro enough that it almost tumbled. The compass card jumped about forty-five degrees, and the helmsman, trying to regain his course, almost put us on a collision course with *Queenfish*.

As we emerged, two-thirds of the ship—two hundred feet of its length—came clear of the water, then the ship fell back to about periscope depth, coming up the second time on an even keel. I was standing at the forward periscope and suddenly found myself lying on the after one. Most of the men were standing in their bunks. Things were a bit sticky for a few moments. The only "official" photography was from a 16-mm movie camera. The sight bordered on the unbelievable, but because it had no telephoto lens, the largest still print Kodak Hawaii could make was little over postcard size. Only in recent years could laser techniques finally produce a suitable enlargement.

Thump said the view from the *Queenfish* was indescribable. Most of his crew watched on deck as twenty-four hundred tons of ship as long as a football field hurtled into the air at twenty miles an hour. After much animated discussion, the crew went below quietly. Thump claimed he never again had a problem with discipline. All he had to say was, "Shape up or we'll ship you to the *Pickerel*."

On Friday, 24 February, we moored alongside *Queenfish*

at the naval base, Subic Bay, Philippine Islands, having enjoyed sixteen days of perfect weather for the trip out. The incoming mail brought a surprising letter from Admiral Brown to all his guppy submarine COs. He expressed serious concern at the "trend toward excessive angles by his submariners" and wished to avoid by all means the task of writing ninety letters to bereaved widows and parents. He thought ten degrees would serve legitimate tactical needs, and anything over that was unjustified.

Clearly it was hardly the time to call in the press for some sensational photography. We confiscated all the photo evidence from our sister submarine and locked it away. The admiral's aide, Ed Osler, and Pappy Sims were classmates. We had been very friendly since Shipyard days. There was no way to keep the news of the big angle from spreading; Ed promised to let us know when the mood in the headquarters was right to release the pictures.

Subic Bay was a lousy liberty port. Nobody met us on arrival; the tennis courts were hazardous and the swimming pool a disgrace. Every facility seemed to be in the middle of a turf battle between half a dozen senior commanders. Officers seemed to be sent there for duty either because of a very ugly wife or for punching an admiral, or both. The first evening was so hot and dreary at the club that Ed and I decided to walk into Olongapo, the worst, most depraved village in the world. Most of it was out of bounds for the military; all of it should have been. We finally found a stinking, cruddy bowling alley with broken balls, crooked and split pins, and a beat-up alley. We bowled a ninety in one game, very good under the circumstances, and called it a night. It was a pleasure to get back to the ship. Back into town Sunday, after mass we walked up into the hills to see a cockfight. The village, a one-lane open sewer, offered a dilapidated, thatched-roof arena for the matches. The place was overrun with dirty, naked children, mongrels, chickens, pigs, and greasy-haired punks with their prize birds. Fifty seconds of fighting after an hour of haggling to arrange matches made it tiresome. A little went a long way. Never did I think I would spend a sunny Sunday morning sitting in a filthy chicken coop.

On 27 February we left Subic for the first phase of the

exercises with the combined fleets. *Queenfish* and *Sea Dog* were ordered to attack the main body, a carrier striking force, and *Pickerel* the Logistics Group. Ken Nauman was now flying his flag in *Pickerel*. Heavy seas were building, and soon we were heading into the teeth of a full gale. I ordered the bridge watch below, leaving only the OOD, protected by a plexiglass bubble canopy. Though thankful for the bubble, he was still very wet. Engine air suction was shifted to the snorkel intake high above the surface and shielded from the sea. Cascades of saltwater still tumbled down the hatch from the bridge. Then about 1000, a giant sea engulfed the bridge and activated the closure of the snorkel head valve even at forty feet above the waterline. On the bridge, Ed Cummings, the OOD, fought for his life. Tons of saltwater flooded out all radars and the master gyro, leaving a foot of water in the conning tower and several inches in the control room. From the control room I tried for agonizing seconds to reestablish communication with the bridge, fighting the awful fear that Ed might have just terminated a very promising career in submarines. Not till the water had finally drained from the bridge enclosure could we hear a very faint, garbled, and thoroughly shaken voice indicate that the OOD was waterborne but still aboard. A very capable crew of electricians and electron pushers had all the gear back in operation by 1900, just as we arrived at the rendezvous point and began a search for the main body.

At 0428 the following morning we made radar contact with the main body to the northwest at seventeen miles, the enemy heading south at sixteen knots. Our contact report was the first received by the Seventh Fleet commander, who was running the defensive forces. The news was fortuitous. His carriers were just then facing the necessity to launch a search in very poor flying conditions. Our report made it unnecessary. *Pickerel* continued sending amplifying information, avoiding detection by moving eastward around the main body before resuming the search for our primary target, the support force, somewhere within twenty to fifty miles of the main body. The attack phase lasted only from 0700 to 1200, but not until 0900 did we finally make contact on the Logistics Group. We were almost dead astern and twenty-one miles away. Against an air-escorted convoy, the chance of getting into attack position within three hours seemed hopeless. The enemy consisted of two large merchantmen with escorts on each beam and one patrolling ahead. The only hope for an attack was a high speed surface approach on the quarter of the port escort, then going deep and fast into position on the heavy ships after the escort had passed by.

Surfacing, we commenced pursuit at flank speed directly into mountainous seas, the bridge very, very wet. At 1030 we were still eight miles astern. Our small end-on silhouette and the cocoon of seawater and spray as we drove in to attack made the ship almost invisible. The near escort, HMS *Black Swan,* looked prominent six miles away. A British Sunderland flying boat was detected closing; we dived at four miles and continued to close submerged at sixteen knots, twice the enemy speed. On the basis of the air contact, *Black Swan* came back to investigate but, grossly underestimating our speed, rushed by to examine a spot we had left some time ago.

Pulling all those amps out of the battery created another problem. The battery electrolyte temperature had not fallen below 110 degrees since arriving in the tropics. It was then 130 degrees, the safe upper limit, and rising a degree a minute. At 1130, with only a half hour to go to the end of this part of the exercise, we were three thousand yards from the enemy when he made a turn to starboard, again putting us almost astern. We continued in at the half-hour battery rate, but when the electrolyte reached 150 degrees, we took what the gods offered and fired three simulated torpedoes at the SS *Green Ranger* at twenty-one hundred yards range, and three at the SS *Port Charlotte* at three thousand yards range, firing flares from the signal gun to denote an attack. None of the escorts could find us, even with the flares to assist.

By then the maneuvering room was so hot the controllermen claimed they had to pour coffee on the contactors to cool them off. Surfacing a few minutes early to give the battery a break, we offered our sleek ship to the British for services. The escort commander requested that we take station on his beam "to get his hydrophone operators reorganized." To say we were thrilled with the remarkable performance of a guppy submarine on this, her first real test against a fleet, is an understatement. No other sub in the world then could have equaled it.

In the later antisubmarine exercises with U.S. destroyers, limitations on evasive tactics were gradually removed until we were giving them almost everything in the book. The calm sea and superb sound conditions with no thermal layer conceded big advantages to the surface enemy, but we never lost the offensive. Using high speeds, rapid changes of depth, and hairtrigger diving control, we frequently shot to periscope depth for a cold setup and attack on one or both targets, then immediately went deep to evade. I could only marvel at the minor miracles our superb ship could accomplish against first-class opposition. At the end of the exercise it was almost with regret that we headed for Sangley Point for a few days ashore in Manila.

On arrival, Pap and I were invited to the British carrier *Triumph* for lunch. The Royal Navy rice and curry, a specialty in Asia, was judged "just hot enough" when beads of perspiration rose on the forehead but didn't run down the face. The standard dessert was a Malacca pudding, with a Vaseline base, I thought, to assuage the flames. Cocky about the exercises, we challenged the *Boxer,* outmanning us about five hundred to one, to a softball game, and thrashed them, then challenged *Triumph* to a soccer match and beat them too. The British were extremely hospitable and very good sports.

The final phase of the exercises began on 10 March, a sortie of the combined fleets from Manila, opposed by the three submarines. This, our first crack at the carriers, I hoped would be our cup of tea. On station early, we made almost immediate contact at fifteen miles. The carriers *Boxer* and *Triumph* were protected by one American and two British cruisers, with six American destroyers and two British frigates in the screen. We penetrated the screen at periscope depth undetected, then saw two destroyers pull out to counterattack *Queenfish* to the southeast. We were inside the screen but, alerted by the *Queenfish* contact, the formation reoriented, leaving us out in the cold. I worked our way back in at 160 feet, this time making fourteen knots under a sharp thermal layer. Just as we reached a new attack position on the *Triumph*, the entire formation changed course and increased speed to twenty-five knots to recover planes. For the second time we were left in the cold.

An hour later, *Boxer* slowed and returned to base course, leaving us between the two carriers. At 1102 we fired six tubes forward at *Boxer* and the four aft at *Triumph* from a near perfect position. When they saw our flares in the air, the first knowledge they had of a submarine in the middle of the formation, the screen began charging around in all directions. I cleared the area deep and fast, took a few shots on a cold setup on two U.S. destroyers, then headed for Hong Kong and new adventures. The *Pickerel* luck was with us, and we made many believers on the capability of the guppy.

The first visit to Hong Kong is unforgettable. The city is beautifully located in a large bay dotted by small islands and surrounded on three sides by steep mountain ridges. The clean white stone and marble buildings of Hong Kong and Kowloon were shrouded in mist; to the north lay the mysterious Inner Kingdom, the sleeping giant rising once more under the leadership of Mao Tse-tung.

A British boarding officer met us on arrival and made arrangements for my official calls on the governor, commodore Hong Kong, and others. The American boarding officer followed with arrangements for boats, cars, and my call on the U.S. consul. By this time the ship was surrounded by an unbelievable profusion of junks hawking wares of every description. Women nursing children, other children pulling at mama's skirts, everybody toted huge bundles of merchandise to unload on my poor crewmen. Silk with 40 percent rayon, teak carved from packing crates, onyx made from deodorant jars—custom requires one of everything free for the captain for the privilege of allowing hawkers on board. I gave it all to the crew. We finally had to turn the extinguishers and fire hoses on them to keep the deck clear. The only exception was to allow Mary Soo her usual contract on U.S. Navy ships to scrape and paint the hull in exchange for our garbage.

Vice Admiral Russell S. Berkey, Commander Seventh Fleet and a big *Pickerel* fan, arrived a few hours behind us. When he visited *Pickerel* in Manila to return my call, we served him not wardroom coffee but his favorite beverage, a fresh daiquiri. To allay his curiosity about my serving alcohol on board, I confided to his aide that the drinks were a special concoction of fresh limes and rum extract, a tasty nonalcoholic drink. Berkey was concerned with security for a guppy submarine in Hong Kong. We had received final clearance only hours before arrival.

My first act was to detach my favorite Filipino steward, Federico Bugarin, for four days, either to get a job or offer to work in the kitchen at the Parisian Grill in Hong Kong, just for the experience. His real task was to find the secret of its world-famous baked onion soup. I planned to have it on the menu every evening on the trip home until we were sure he had perfected it, then twice a day.

No visitors were allowed on board except to return official calls. The limitation made exchanges of hospitality with the British a bit difficult. After completing some of my calls, I took a long walk through the teeming "old" city with its indescribable aroma of too many people and too little space. After lunch, several of us took a long drive in the country, enjoying the beautiful scenery and a bit of shopping. Cocktails at the American Club put us in the mood for dinner at the Parisian Grill and a superb steak, delicious black rye bread, and a baked Alaska. The cost with tip came to $1.50 each.

Just as the rickshaws got us back to the ship, the British fleet arrived, leaving a stack of invitations for parties, dinners, sports, and other entertainment. *Pickerel* was very popular. Everybody showed a strong interest, even though I could do little to reciprocate. The performance of the guppy sub in the fleet exercise led all the bull sessions; what we couldn't discuss factually we covered in sea stories.

One day ashore I devoted to shopping. For this ritual one best goes unshaven and very casual. I had a wonderful time haggling with the merchants, a chore I relish. After being fitted for two suits and a sports jacket, I asked for the customary presento for mama-san. I couldn't tog myself out without something nice for Henri and suggested a slinky nightgown. He dragged out a gorgeous creation with a long train flowing in its wake. When I suggested maybe a shorty nightie, he said quickly, "Oh, you like quick easy get-at-it? OK, I feex."

Picking up his huge shears, he made as if to lop off the bottom. All the nighties, surprisingly, were the same length. Chinese ladies don't wear them, and explanation of their bedroom habits took an hour of intimate discussion. Since we knew little of the other's language, it took quite a performance to find a normal length gown.

Then I decided to dress Henri from the skin out. The only panties were finely knit but had very large holes all through the weave, looking like the bags for shipping citrus fruit. For a bra, he offered a stack of foam rubber cups to fondle to make sure the fit was right. (The Chinese think of everything.) Then for the home I bought nested rosewood tables and a lot of rattan, after much haggling in two currencies and several dialects. When the agreement was finally struck, the salesman asked, "You're from the merchant ship in the harbor, yes?"

"No, from the American submarine."

"You work in the engine room?"

"No, just tell the deck watch it's for the captain."

He was shocked that he had given me far too good a bargain.

For the return trip, plans were now firm for us to try snorkeling nonstop the whole way to Pearl Harbor. Some of my seniors thought we needed an escort, which didn't make much sense. Everybody's concern was engine failure. Both the Fairbanks-Morse and General Motors diesels had been designed years before a snorkel was dreamed of. They were magnificent engines, but on submerged operations, the air intake pipe wasn't large enough to get all the air needed without pulling a high vacuum; the engine exhaust discharged against considerably higher back pressure than normal. When the seas broke over the head valve, it slammed shut, and until the engines could be pulled clear our ears and noses quickly reminded us we weren't getting air from the outside. Neither were the engines. The unusual stresses on the engines inevitably caused the large aluminum blower lobes to wipe against the housing. No American submarine had snorkeled for a hundred hours before ruining blower lobes in this manner; an engine on a test stand at the Engineering Experimental Station in Annapolis also had wiped. Before leaving Hong Kong, we were near the hundred-hour critical period when we could expect trouble from the blowers. Just before leaving Pearl, however, we had almost wiped one; Snuffy and his experts thought the near casualty might have suggested several answers.

First, inadequate instrumentation prevented observation of critical temperatures and pressures, especially while snorkeling. This discovery hardly seemed important enough so that we could snorkel five thousand miles where others couldn't do five hundred. Second, battery charging while snorkeling created special hazards, especially when the head valve closed. The sudden vacuum in the sub before the engines could be shut down sucked air from inside the submarine, risked damage to the engines, and also developed potentially explosive concentrations of hydrogen in the ship—our private form of hydrogen bomb.

A similar casualty had caused the loss of *Cochino* in the North Atlantic a few months previous. The Bureau of Ships ordered new and restrictive battery-charging procedures to minimize buildup of hydrogen bubbles on the battery by closing the head valve manually at least hourly while snorkeling to shut off the outside air supply. The artificial vacuum created supposedly would purge the hydrogen bubbles from the battery plates before an explosive mixture could form. The additional discomfort on the crew had to be accepted.

While ashore in Manila, Snuffy found a small wet-cell battery in a transparent jar, which we installed in the wardroom. When we purged the main batteries, the test cell got purged too. We saw immediately that the new procedures wouldn't work. The hydrogen bubbles reappeared on the plates almost immediately. The new procedures not only didn't solve the problem of preventing explosive concentrations of hydrogen from forming, they actually produced more hydrogen. Again thanks to the practical wisdom of sailors, we soon devised a wholly different set of procedures. They solved the problem and were eventually adopted throughout the submarine force.

Third, the snorkel safety circuits were overengineered and probably contributed to engine mishaps. To alert the controllermen to pull clear of the engines when the head valve was ducked, we bypassed the safety circuit and used an ordinary glass milk bottle (typical of that era) with a condom (typical of this era) over the mouth, the head painted bright red. When a high vacuum was pulled in the boat, the condom stood up rigidly and the men responded immediately. Their idling brains were more attuned to that frequency.

Fourth, the Navy had never subjected the snorkel system to a rigorous endurance run. We planned to keep two engines on propulsion continuously at approximately 100 percent load for the entire trip, using a third engine for battery charging as needed. This was a heavy load, limited by the manufacturer to four hours maximum, but we had reason to believe the engines were underrated.

Given the difficulties, we had little reason for optimism that we could cross that huge ocean submerged without ever taking the engines off the line. When we left Pearl Harbor six weeks before, it didn't seem necessary to give Admiral Brown official knowledge of our plans. I went no higher than the assistant operations officer to see if we could take a few extra days on the return trip to allow a slow ten-knot speed of advance, the maximum while snorkeling. The only hint I gave was that we wanted to make a realistic test of the snorkel.

The visit to Hong Kong was memorable for all hands. Our men joined many of their British colleagues in the seductive pleasures of both the day and night games, as they say, and in finding Oriental treasures for the folks back home. The night before departure, the British held a "dining in" ceremony aboard HMS *Kenya* to celebrate our departure, after which we made a final speed run on the town to put a fitting climax to the visit.

The morning of 16 March dawned murky and threatening. At 0800, Ken Nauman transferred his flag to *Queenfish;* he didn't want to take the slow boat from China. We cast off the lines and completed a final tightening, bracing, and securing of the topside. A warm "Good sailing and God bless" message from *Kenya,* or at least from those still alive after the royal sendoff a few hours earlier, marked our social cutoff from the outside world. Just past the entrance buoys, the raucous sound of the diving alarm rang through the ship. *Pickerel* sank into the cold, green waters, leveled off at periscope depth, and commenced snorkeling at 0910 local time. The azure waters and bright skies of Pearl Harbor were a very long way off.

The seas were making, and the weather turned very dirty. Three British destroyers ran training exercises on the snorkel, but they soon lost both radar and visual contact as seas built to state six, wind force six. Depth control was fair with the boat trimmed twenty thousand pounds heavy and down one and a half degrees by the bow. Snorkeling was far more comfortable than surface sailing. Two engines on snorkeling and one on battery charge raised the altimeter—measuring the vacuum in the boat—to about 4,500 feet. When the engine could be taken off charge, the "altitude" dropped to about 2,500 feet, normal cruising. The first meal submerged featured "shipping over chow," typical of departure days from a favored port: thick, juicy steaks to our individual tastes, mushrooms, crisp fries, fresh peas, fresh green salad, ice cream and strawberries, and a cup of good fresh coffee. All was right with the world, and we were heading home. The rollicking retelling of adventures during the cruise can't be described to those who haven't shared the experience. With sea stories vying with each other, the meal ran considerably longer than usual. Sitting at the head of the tiny wardroom table and thoroughly enjoying the camaraderie of an exceptionally happy and congenial group, I looked over the officers and mused on the many things that had happened in the short year we had been together. Alas, it would soon be time for some of us to go to other duty. Pap was ready for command in every respect and Snuffy for an exec's job, the younger officers for greater responsibilities as soon as they qualified. My fondest hope was to delay the inevitable.

I stretched my legs with a routine walk through the boat for a little eye contact and a word here and there with the men. I particularly wanted to look at the aquarium in the after torpedo room. Second Class Torpedoman's Mate Bill Jones and the men in the room had purchased a tropical fish aquarium before leaving Pearl. To avoid spillage or worse during the steep up and down angles, he had rigged a set of torpedo gimbals to keep the tank level, but snorkeling caused more serious problems, especially the "purging" routine. Designed to remove the hydrogen from the battery cells, it also removed the oxygen from the aquarium, and if tropical fish have eardrums, it was probably harder on them than on us. Jones had collected some fine new varieties while in Asia and had installed an elaborate aerator system to put the oxygen back as fast as the ship pulled it out. I was pleased to learn that so far his prized fish seemed to enjoy the cruise.

Completion of services to British Sunderland patrol planes on the morning of the second day ended our antisubmarine services. Late that afternoon the high peaks of Formosa came into view; we passed south of the island just before midnight and set course for a modified great circle route to Pearl Harbor. For dinner that evening I had ordered a special treat. Our wardroom steward was about to unveil the secret baked onion soup delight he had learned at the Parisian Grill in Hong Kong. With proper ceremony we tasted the first spoonful. It was delicious, but not delectable. A vital ingredient was missing. Tomorrow he would try again.

For the trip, Pap, with his usual foresight, had procured four cases of popcorn for movietime. It proved to be priceless. We had been fortunate in getting some top-notch films for the trip, including *The Boy with Green Hair* and *The Voice of the Turtle*. Movies were shown in the wardroom every afternoon and in the crew's lounge twice each evening. As everybody knows, a movie without popcorn is hardly a movie. Only half a can was left on arrival in Pearl. For the westerns and shootouts, Pappy and I kept score on the good guys versus the bad guys: ammo expended, hits, and a Vietnam-style "baddie" count.

On 20 March we completed one hundred hours submerged, making good 1,040 miles; we had already surpassed all other U.S. sub records. The tiny island of Rasa, southeast of Okinawa, dropped astern that day, and three days later the uninhabited Kita Iwo Jima was sighted and soon disappeared astern. A periscope liberty offered to any and all brought a number of sightseers to the conning tower to see Kita Iwo, the last landmark to be seen until entering the Hawaiian Island chain scheduled for two weeks hence. We passed the two-hundred-hour mark on 24 March, and on 28 March, three hundred hours and 3,030 miles lay behind us. The engineering plant, and the ship as a whole, ran smoothly.

If any problem emerged it was navigation. Navigation on

long voyages had been a special interest of mine for years. To indicate how primitive the art was at that time, Vannevar Bush, science adviser to the president during the war, in his book *Modern Arms and Free Men,* concluded that "navigation fully submerged is no small task." This we found to be no understatement. A new edition of Dutton, the navigator's bible, fresh off the press, offered little help. The only reference to long underwater voyages was, "If the predicted long range, high speed, underwater voyages materialize, better methods of navigation will be essential. . . . when submarines capable of such performance are developed, the means of navigation will be available."

This was a little less than we might have expected. The primary system available for submerged navigation was Loran, which was only marginally adequate. Some imaginative thinking about the problem seemed vital for the nuclear submarines just over the horizon. I decided to limit Loran information to the CO and XO alone. To train and encourage other ideas, the younger officers took turns for a few days at a time, navigating by any means they could devise. It made for a good drill in deep sea piloting and stimulated serious thinking on the problem of designing a better system. In midocean, bottom contour charts no longer served; morning and evening sights of low-altitude stars and planets, or of the sun when on the meridian of latitude or longitude, were taken through the periscope with some success. I had high anticipation for the usefulness of the subsolar fix technique I published in the *Proceedings* back in April 1945. The accuracy anticipated at that time for much more distant subsolar points, unfortunately, was not borne out by the results. Whatever the method, the navigator gained one big advantage. We learned that while snorkeling, the ship's dead-reckoning position, through improved steering and steady speed, was extremely accurate.

The first unanticipated problem occurred about a week out. Many of the "genuine" teak and camphorwood chests and tables bought from Hong Kong merchants proved to have been for a presnorkeling era. The unusual undersea dampness in the boat soon caused cracking and warping. C'est la vie.

A very special event occurred for the skipper on 29 March.

Few if any of the officers recognized that it was any different. *Pickerel* that day passed very close to the spot where Reggie Raymond met his untimely end in the *Scorpion* gun battle with the armed patrol vessel exactly five years prior. I had saved one of the beautiful floral leis given us by wives and friends on departure from Pearl Harbor, and I put it, faded but still fragrant, into a torpedo tube and fired it to sea in my private memorial ceremony.

Two days later, 31 March, we crossed the International Date Line, and it occurred to many of us that as the first U.S. guppy snorkel submarine to appear in the Far East, we certainly must have been the first to have snorkeled under the date line. A huge cake from the galley marked the ceremony in the traditional manner. But this was an untraditional cake. Cakes baked while snorkeling have special problems. Depending on the engine load and whether or not the snorkel head valve was ducked under the sea while a cake was rising, it sometimes had huge air holes or came out hard as a brick. If this one didn't reach professional standards because of the variable atmosphere, nobody objected.

The routine for all hands by now was comfortable and relaxed. As was my custom, I rose not later than six, showered, and had a morning cup of coffee before taking a look at the weather through the periscope. After a tour of the ship, I spent much of the morning studying charts and pilot information or doing routine paperwork. An avid reader, I averaged a book a day. A lot of acey-deucey and cribbage went on, with the usual tournaments. Back in the aft torpedo room, interest was rising by the hour as one of Jones' prize red swordtails seemed ready to give birth. There wasn't much we could do to help. When the hour came, the young were so small as to be nearly invisible, but Jones had foresight equal to the occasion. He had a special isolation tank available for the new arrivals.

Saturday, 1 April, marked the completion of four hundred hours and 4,150 miles submerged. The incredible performance by the engineering plant made us optimistic that we could complete the entire passage submerged. It became the chief topic of conversation, except women. The smooth roar of those magnificent diesels found us lacking adequate words of praise. They had been running at continuous full load, essentially the four-hour rate, for the best part of a month without a casualty worthy of the name. Each engine bore a pet name—invariably a girl friend of the leading engineman—and was treated like a member of the family. Rarely was a plant given such continuous tender loving care. The exec personally checked temperatures and pressures at least hourly. With about three hundred snorkeling hours on each engine by then, there was probably reason for concern.

Then to our horror the ship's newspaper that morning ran big headlines datelined Washington, reporting that a snorkel submarine in the Atlantic had just completed a six-hundred-hour, six-thousand-mile nonstop submerged trip from New London to Rio de Janeiro. Crewmen and even some of the officers felt a momentary panic. Then somebody spotted the date and the "April Fool" admission that the story was a hoax. Many were too shaken to feel relieved.

Pickerel was now drawing close to the end of the journey. As the ship entered the Hawaiian Island chain, the strain of the long trip and the anticipation of setting a world record began to show. A potentially serious material casualty soon dimmed our dreams and chilled any premature self-praise. The first problem was the increasing difficulty in keeping the radio antennae watertight. They were grounding out, with water seepage into the hull through the cables. I notified Commander Submarines of our difficulty late on 1 April, adding that "this may be my last transmission." Unfortunately, it was. Admiral Brown came up with the clever idea of using us for practice tracking a snorkeler by antisubmarine aircraft from the Fleet Air Wing in Honolulu. They would locate, track, and report our movement on the last thousand miles of the voyage.

When the exercises started the following morning, all attempts to raise the big boss to transmit arrival plans failed. The loss of antennae cost us the Loran signal as well, the only reliable navigational aid. Attempts to jury rig a coupling to receive Loran through the underwater radio direction finder loop antenna failed; a last resort, an attempt to tie in the sonar head on the main deck with the Loran receiver, produced only frustration. At this most untimely moment, a complete overcast blotted out the sun and reduced navigation to blind groping with the fathometer along a poorly charted ocean bottom. One of the search planes was sighted, but we couldn't raise him on the VHF. Our last transmission was now three days old; I felt increasing concern for the anxiety our continued silence was causing back at the headquarters.

A submarine unreported for two days normally triggered submarine casualty procedures. Admiral Arthur W. Radford, the Pacific Fleet commander, questioned Admiral Brown about our overdue status, asking why we should not be ordered to surface until contact could be made. Admiral Brown replied, "That's my top submarine. I know them personally and have absolute faith in them. I accept full responsibility for their safety."

Tuesday, 4 April 1950, the ship's first birthday opened auspiciously with a message from Commander Submarines received two minutes after midnight: "Patrol planes are searching for you. Run awash or broach at frequent intervals until you are contacted."

Meanwhile, a new problem confronted us, a rapidly deteriorating superstructure. The sheet-metal fairing around the bridge was secured with a new spring-loaded fastener designed to allow easy removal for access to topside equipment. We soon found that the constant sea action caused the fasteners to pop out; the metal plates tore loose with an eerie, grinding sound heard throughout the ship. One clanged down the deck and struck the port propellor, reducing the speed a half knot and causing a pronounced vibration.

During the night, several aircraft were detected by periscope at long range, but we couldn't attract their attention on the VHF or with flares or running lights while broached. Finally, just after sunrise, we detected an airman and were able to make radio contact on the VHF. We were thirty miles west of Kauai, heading for the submarine night operating area southwest of Pearl Harbor. Damage to the screw had dropped us behind schedule but still left several hours to kill in the operating area until we passed the goal of five hundred hours continuously submerged at full load on two engines.

By noon on 4 April "channel fever" ran rampant through the boat. Everybody tried to contribute something for the big birthday dinner that evening. The cake, thanks to some very precise depth control during the critical rising time, had a spongelike consistency unusual on a snorkeler. But the last attempt at onion soup failed. The Chinese had outfoxed Steward Bugarin on a vital ingredient. His best attempt was merely ordinary. Relaxing over the birthday cake and coffee, more than one of us felt that it seemed not a year since commissioning but a year since submerging.

The final day was spent cleaning and polishing the ship for her usual smart appearance on entering port. The big moment finally arrived. At 1530, 5 April 1950, *Pickerel* surfaced off the entrance buoys to Pearl Harbor, completing twenty-one days (505 hours) of continuous snorkeling during a transit of 5,194 miles, a fifth of the way around the world submerged. Throughout the 12,000-mile Asian cruise, the engineering plant performed magnificently. The snorkel cruise from Hong Kong added 1,200 snorkeling hours on the four engines, so superior to any previous record as to be wholly without comparison.

Going to the bridge following the surface alarm, my first sensation was a sour odor of marine vegetation and decay permeating the free-flooding topside areas. Next came a feeling of amazement at what remained of our sleek exterior. The plating around the fairwater was missing entirely except for the leading edge, held in place by sea pressure. The metal framework was missing or dangled free. Despite an intensive reinforcing, strengthening and tightening effort prior to departure from Hong Kong, many riveted sections of deck plating and angle iron stiffeners hung loose or had disappeared. Two of the deck hatches were inoperable, fouled by stray metal. The forward torpedo loading skid was torn loose; both of the messenger buoys—which play a vital role in salvage operations—had torn loose. Lacking the protection of the aluminum fairing, grease lines to topside fittings and equipment had carried away; the radio antennae were torn loose or damaged beyond easy repair. The need for a redesign of the fairwater plating seemed obvious. Rigidity was required while allowing access for repair and maintenance; the problem was hardly new. The specially designed fasteners used for the first time on *Pickerel* went back to the drawing board.

At 1600 the lines went over to Pier One at the submarine base, Pearl Harbor, exactly on the minute of the predicted arrival. (Pap and I never kept the families waiting.) The welcome led to an enthusiastic celebration. My twenty-two-day growth of beard, and those of many emulators on board, was not quite up to the occasion. I had to massage it with a typewriter ribbon that morning just to let people know for sure it was a beard. And as invariably happens, once the family has seen it, rarely would it survive the first day at home. Wonderful as it was to get home again to enjoy a few days' rest and relaxation with the families, this time there was a slight delay. I received an unusual request from the boss.

Because of the initial concern about classifying the operation, there was a complete absence of press coverage and photography on our arrival. When the story was finally released a day or so later, the enthusiasm the voyage stimulated in the media worldwide caught everybody by surprise. The demand for photography and background material left only one alternative—go out and do it again for the movies. The third day after the triumphal return we went back to sea, submerged off the entrance, commenced snorkeling, then headed in and surfaced for a proper welcome.

The reaction of people throughout the country astounded us. I spent several days being interviewed, as did many of the officers and men. The *New York Times* wanted a feature story for the *Sunday Magazine,* but at the Navy's request to deemphasize the publicity, staff writer Richard F. Mac-Millan's name appeared, not mine. He did a good job; we eventually sold the international rights and split the fees. Telegrams of congratulations and commendations rolled in from the chief of naval operations, the secretary of defense, the secretary of the navy, and other government and private officials. An especially warm telegram to "his ship" came from Assistant Secretary of the Navy John Koehler, whom we had taken to sea earlier. Sightseers and guests by the hundreds flocked to Pearl Harbor to share the moment, from Admiral Radford to Shirley Temple. My easygoing exec on that historic moment, looking over the throngs of people, made the comment appropriate to the occasion: "All this and we get paid too?"

The visit of Admiral Radford had a special significance. I mentioned earlier the modification the ship made in replacing the vacuum cutout controls on the snorkel with a red painted condom over the mouth of a bottle at the controllermen's station. In my official report, I stated, "As soon as the vacuum increases, the condom stands up rigid, pointing a lurid finger of caution at the controllermen," adding, "No alteration request will be submitted on this item."

When Admiral Brown's deputy, Captain Elton W. "Joe" Grenfell, read the report, he suggested that it be deleted before it went to Radford. Admiral Brown disagreed; Admiral Radford read it and roared with laughter, deciding to see for himself—the first time since the war years that the Pacific Fleet commander personally welcomed a returning submarine. We didn't know, of course, that his main point of interest was a milk bottle and a contraceptive.

The cocky engineers, meanwhile, were so sure of our superiority they bet $500 that no diesel submarine would ever beat our record. Just in case, I took the minimum precaution of writing to Colonel Morse to report our extravagant faith in his Fairbanks-Morse engines. His only recourse, as I anticipated, was to match our offer and, I am sure we both fully understood, he would pick up the tab for the entire $1,000 if the unexpected challenge ever happened. It never did.

Another interested observer was the Bureau of Ships. We had obviously found both the cause and the cure for the blower failures plaguing snorkelers, but the bureau experts seemed reluctant to give us credit, preferring to discover the secret for themselves. The possibility that Hong Kong fuel made the difference was quickly scotched, and a team from the bureau could discover no better reason. Our men were sworn to secrecy unless the bureau would admit that we were pretty smart too. To my knowledge, the stalemate was never broken.

Immediately after our return, I rejoined the Honolulu Symphony. Conductor George Barati was a disciplinarian and allowed no socializing during rehearsals. We were expected to be in our chairs, tuned and ready to play ten minutes before rehearsal time, allowing only a whispered greeting to one's seatmate. Until the storm of publicity following the snorkel cruise, few in the Symphony knew anything of my profession. From my carriage some guessed I might be with the police or the military, in which few found a deep interest. But on this occasion, concertmaster Conrad Lieberman ran up to congratulate me for "this . . . this . . . this . . . wonderful thing you did." He didn't really know what it was but with all the hullaballoo around town it must have been important to somebody.

We were the fair-haired boys around the base, and *Pickerel* operations now took a different turn. The surge of visitors wanting to go through the ship made it routine for us to be assigned the VIP pier, getting under way last and coming home first. Routine exercises brought radio newsmen to tape shows on board; as on the shakedown cruise, I made the boat available for reserve cruises in addition to regularly scheduled training operations. Even these contributed to the "showboat" image.

One reserve cruise took us to Kauai. The date happened to coincide with the final leg of the annual San Diego–Honolulu–Kauai yacht race, and I facetiously entered *Pickerel* in the race, the only entrant in the 1,850-ton sloop class, then snorkeled over to earn a trophy and a warm welcome in Kauai. The head of the reserve unit embarked was a Naval Academy classmate who decided to accompany us on the trip. I had gone ashore to a special party at the Yacht Club; he went ashore with some of his people and came back aboard shortly after midnight, considerably under the weather. A spare bunk had been set up for him in the wardroom, but he wanted a stateroom and none was available. With considerable gusto, he decided to move into the captain's cabin, emphasizing his choice with 250 pounds, all of it loud and drunk. I was still ashore and the duty chief had never faced such a problem before. He knew the two of us were classmates. He also knew my bunk had better be available when I returned aboard. Retreating into chiefs' quarters, he made his plan. Gathering a number of huge sailors anxious to defend the honor of their captain, they grabbed him bodily, dragged him up the ladder, and threw him over the side. Spluttering dire threats, he struggled back aboard. Lo and behold, not a soul was in sight. With a few desperate oaths, he made his way below, showered, and crawled into his wardroom bunk without a sound.

When I returned aboard, absolute peace reigned. Nary a soul could recall anything unusual happening. The ship received a special commendation from the Naval District commander for an unusually valuable and interesting reserve cruise and hoped to be allowed to repeat it the following year.

Visiting us in Honolulu at the time of our return was an aunt of Henri's who worked with the H. J. Heinz Company in Pittsburgh. Telling sea stories about the cruise one evening, I mentioned my frustration in not being able to get the recipe for baked onion soup from the Parisian Grill in Hong Kong. Aunt Hildegarde exclaimed, "Why, I know that restaurant. They order more Heinz beef stock than anybody else in Asia." So the secret finally emerged. The heart of the world-famous onion soup in far-off Asia came from my own hometown. The next dinner on board *Pickerel* once again included a demitasse of onion soup as the first course—really excellent.

But a far more serious problem of food soon confronted us. The chief cook, W. E. "Tom" Thomas, reported that he was deep in the hole in the quarterly mess statement. Any ship under way almost continuously has all hands on board for meals, and the budget simply doesn't stretch. Nevertheless, a shortage usually produces a nasty letter from the squadron to the CO. To forestall any such letter I asked the commodore to take no action while we fought our way out of the red. Much as I hated to do it, the first act was to shift to tropical working hours, starting the day's work at 0700 and working straight through until liberty started at 1400. Breakfast was served at 0600 before most men returned aboard; we served lunch after liberty started at 1400, hoping that most men in the liberty section would miss both meals. Even this deplorable extreme helped very little. *Pickerel* was off on so many foreign adventures that many of our married men had left. I had a crew of bachelors who lived aboard and had nowhere else to go for their meals.

The next inventory showed that we were still losing money. I sent a still more humble letter to the commodore and appointed Pap the commissary officer; he really cracked the whip. He also uncovered some hanky-panky in the food supply system on the base. A few conspirators were overcharging and shortweighting food orders to the submarines for their own profit. We were the new boy in town and became the major victim. We blew the whistle on the scam but we still had a very long way to go before getting out of the hole. *Pickerel* had always been a "feeder"; we cut down the expensive items so far that our people were begging for handouts from the other subs. A solution was nowhere near, but another problem diverted our attention.

I suggested earlier my insistence on absolute realism and maintenance of wartime standards in all our operations. I subscribed to the views of Field Marshal Erwin Rommel in 1944: "War makes extremely heavy demands on the soldiers' strength and nerves. For this reason, make heavy demands on your men in peacetime exercises. . . . Sweat saves blood."

The *Pickerel* attitude sometimes brought grief to administrative staffs. Our annual operational readiness inspection (ORI) was due. I suggested that it might be wise for the various inspectors to read over our emergency procedures beforehand. This sage advice was neglected, however, causing momentary panic during a collision drill. Nobody else followed our procedure of diving to avoid an imminent collision. When several inspectors assembled on the bridge and told the officer of the deck that he was steaming in a heavy fog, we knew the stage was set for a collision drill. When a mythical ship suddenly emerged from the fog at close range, the OOD immediately ordered, "Dive, dive, dive" and sounded the alarm.

Lookouts and inspectors scrambled for the hatch in a panic to get below in a flurry of clipboards and flailing arms and legs. The watch below had been alerted to delay a bit before opening the vents so nobody would be left on the bridge. The dive was executed smartly with a steep down angle, and we were out of any danger of a collision in less time than it took to relate.

Another test then in vogue, presumably to measure skill in depth control, was hovering—trying to maintain a constant depth with no way on the ship. As a test of readiness for war, I thought this was time wasted. Our planesmen were unquestionably expert, and it stimulated us to lay a plan to screw up the records. When the chief inspector passed the word for everyone to stay in place with no movement forward or aft, it again gave the tipoff. The conning officer ordered "All stop." The controllermen rang up "Stop": on their telegraph but continued at creeping speed on the main motors. As prearranged, a man in the forward room slowly moved the speed indicator to zero by hand. There was no way for the inspectors to realize the ship had not stopped. With timers running, inspectors awaited loss of depth control and waited and waited. The diving officer, the epitome of nonchalance, seemed capable of holding the depth forever, utterly unconcerned about the major test of his skill in progress. Turning away from his station, he relaxed, lit a cigarette, and chatted with the inspectors. When a quarter of an hour slipped by, far longer than any other ship could hover, we gave every indication of being able to continue forever—which we were. The chief inspector finally terminated the exercise, unable to comprehend how we could possibly be so much better than the others.

Several years later, as a submarine division commander, I went to great pains to make the annual readiness tests as realistic as possible. Whatever the war plan envisioned for each of my submarines, they received an operation order to do just that. I filled the exercises with every unpleasant surprise I could think of, including use of live depth charges at minimum range without prior knowledge of the skipper. This action triggered a progressive damage-control problem within the ship. I certainly learned more about the state of mind of the CO in carrying such a mission than routine, isolated emergency drills ever would have done.

It took great efforts to get Commander Submarines to authorize use of live ordnance, especially without the knowledge of the CO on the receiving end. Partly his faith in me made it possible, more, I hoped, his recognition of the need for realism in training. I had no doubt the crew could conduct fire or collision drills efficiently; the internal running of the ship was secondary. The real aim sought to measure the foresight of the CO in *his* preparation for war, mentally as well as physically, and to test the war plans. The exercises became great fun and the battle of wits tested us all, particularly me in finding new ways to outwit my skippers. I received several enthusiastic letters on the exercises, but the true measure of success, emulation by other division commanders, did not occur, and after my detachment the ideas passed into limbo.

Pickerel also added realism in special exercises frequently worked up at the club. The top antisubmarine opponent in Pearl Harbor was a new division of escort destroyers headed by an experienced submariner, Cmdr. James B. "Jim" Grady, skipper of the USS *Carpenter*. An expert in both submarine and destroyer tactics, Jim disputed our claims of the superiority of the sub over the destroyer. I gave him a challenge he couldn't resist. I offered to start with the submarine on the surface at ten thousand yards, and with his whole division searching, I assured him he would never catch us.

Jim drooled at the opportunity. Sound conditions in the islands gave a big edge to the surface attacker, and that day was no exception. The BT showed no temperature gradient beneath which we could hide; sea conditions were all in his favor. Jim assumed correctly that I would go deep and head toward him at maximum speed; he headed toward us at over twenty-five knots to establish a "datum" where we had dived. But he underestimated the speed a guppy can produce in a hurry. Diving deep and steep with all the power we had, I headed directly for the four destroyers at nineteen knots. Since the ships were closing at almost a mile a minute, he thundered over us in less than five minutes. Even if a sonar operator thought he had us, we were gone before he could be sure, and then it was too late. Tracking the four surface ships easily with our sonar, I didn't slow until moments after he did. He had already overrun us and never did make contact. With a four-ship, high-speed search pattern, the wing ships very quickly got spread across the Pacific. Within forty minutes, *Pickerel* was back on the surface with nobody in sight within eight miles. I sounded swimming call, then raised *Carpenter* on the radio suggesting he join the fun. The next lunch at the club was on the surface forces.

Late in the Pearl Harbor training cycle, a new plastic snorkel head was installed for evaluation. Designed to reduce the radar image while snorkeling, it promised only moderate improvement when evaluated in Key West. The manufacturer, on his own initiative, then redesigned it to add a plastic streamlining around the *Pickerel* unit, which looked much like an overturned rowboat. We found it to be a remarkable improvement. When we were snorkeling at slow speed, water flowed entirely around and over the valve; the engine air was drawn through a curtain of water in the wake of the "rowboat" and reduced the radar image to near undetectability. During several hours of tests with Jim Grady's ships augmented by close-in air search, radar made contact only when it could be coached onto the target visually at close range. But my evaluation report found only a pigeonhole in the bureau. Nuclear power, just over the horizon, would make the diesel sub and its ear-popping snorkelers irrelevant.

The weeks sped by, and we still were unable to release the photos of the seventy-two-degree surfacing off the Philippines. Then one evening Henri and I were invited to Admiral Brown's quarters for a small dinner party celebrating the Browns' thirty-fifth wedding anniversary. They were a distinguished-looking couple. The expression of mutual love and respect shared over the years and the admiral's toast to a beautiful woman left an indelible memory. Just before we departed at the end of a delightful evening, he put a big paw on my shoulder and asked me to drop by and see him in the morning. When I arrived at the headquarters, he talked of many things. Clearly something was on his mind which he was reluctant to mention. I was about to take my departure when finally he said, "You know that photograph? Well, Admiral Lockwood is celebrating his sixtieth birthday in Los Gatos next week and I would like to present him an autographed copy."

He gave specific instructions as to how he wanted it autographed and then, after more hemming and hawing, added, "By the way, I'd like a copy for myself, too, and I don't care how you autograph that one." I sent the big-angle pictures to him inscribed as suggested. On his I wrote, "To Admiral Babe Brown, proving that ComSubPac knows all the angles."

This we took as permission for release, and the response was sensational. It wasn't until years later, however, that newly developed laser techniques made possible a decent enlargement, first gracing the cover of *Shipmate* magazine in July-August 1983.

Not all of the *Pickerel*'s rollercoaster operations gained the same enthusiastic reception. One day the commodore asked to go to sea with us to show a friend how a modern submarine operated. We were delighted as always, but Pap and I had a difficult time trying to get the guest interested. Finally, I decided that if persuasion failed, I would try fright. We began dipsydoodling with rolls into sharp turns, steep up and down angles, the whole routine. He was thrilled to pieces. But I made a serious oversight.

I had totally overlooked the commodore. He had gone to the wardroom for a cup of coffee just as the ship headed for the bottom at thirty-six degrees, almost throwing him into the forward torpedo room. He was on hands and knees, clawing his way back to control, when the ship headed up at forty degrees, from 550 feet, and the commodore found himself projected almost into the crew's mess. He was again clawing his way uphill to control when a sharp turn threw him into the gyro table, which he grabbed in a death grip. Within moments the diving officer called me to control for an emergency. I dropped down from the conning tower and found the commodore, ashen white, rigid, and utterly speechless, hanging on to the metal table—which probably still bears a full set of his fingerprints in the aluminum. He could neither speak nor move and appeared to have suffered a stroke. I broke his hands free with difficulty and—lifting his legs over the coaming of the watertight door—half carried, half steered him into the wardroom. An emergency message to the base announced our immediate return and requested medical assistance on arrival. It was a matter of several minutes, each one an eternity, before the commodore was physically capable of anything. He recovered quickly, however, and by the time we entered the channel he was almost back to normal, although a bit shaken and unsteady in gait.

The following morning he sent for me, first to present the most expensive and beautifully wrapped bottle of scotch his guest could find in Honolulu. Then with some embarrassment he tried to explain his actions, carefully outlining that he had been in submarines for almost twenty years, reminding me that doctrine both before and during the war called for a one- or two-degree maximum angle on diving and surfacing, that three was reckless, and that for anything over ten degrees the boat was out of control. Indeed, a submarine skipper had been relieved late in the war because he talked about taking ten-degree angles with a fleet boat. The commodore realized that the high power available in the guppy made a major difference. Still, the intensive training required to gain our present proficiency allowed us to grow into it over many months; he experienced it in a matter of seconds.

The incident had important consequences. The commodore sent for me not long after and announced that the *Pickerel* was almost a unanimous choice as the outstanding submarine in the squadron and fully merited the "E" in the annual competition. He was concerned, however, that we had had so much publicity during the year that it would be better overall to share the honors, and he planned to make the award to another boat.

The decision didn't make sense. Winning the "E" meant commendations in the service records of the officers and men and therefore meant far more than a few fleeting newspaper headlines. The commodore's conservative lifestyle was so different from mine that his real purpose had little to do with sharing the notoriety. I made a strong plea for my men in what we both realized was a losing gesture. And never again did he go to sea in the *Pickerel*.

The idyllic life with the family in Pearl seemed too good to last. Beach picnics, excursions to the other islands mixed with intensive work with the symphony and summer pops orchestra made the weeks fly by. Just ten weeks after completion of the snorkel cruise, *Pickerel* was at sea on a fleet exercise halfway to San Diego when we were ordered to pull out of the exercise and return to Pearl Harbor immediately. It was 25 June 1950; war had broken out in Korea.

At the submarine base, Kenny Nauman had just been relieved by none other than Jason Maurer, my old *Atule* skipper. Jason happened to run into Henri while *Pickerel* was rushing back to Pearl Harbor for the new emergency. He couldn't give her any details but implied that we were being sent to the western Pacific. The tone of his voice conveyed more than he intended, perhaps, and she was prepared for the worst by the time we came charging back into port. None of the wives felt ready for a new war, especially when *Pickerel* was the only boat to get the special invitation to participate. Henri had the empty feeling that there had been no peace since World War II. Suddenly it became one long, drawn-out conflict.

10

War Under the United Nations Command

The first streaks of dawn were tinting the morning sky on the other side of the Pacific on Sunday morning, 25 June 1950. At four in the morning a thousand howitzers split the dawn stillness with a shattering roar; ninety thousand North Korean troops backed by 150 heavily armored Soviet T-34 tanks struck in a surprise assault along the entire thirty-eighth parallel, heading south.

The South Korean (ROK) Army, after months of false alerts, had relaxed for a weekend of vacation. Many of the troops had been given fifteen-day leave periods to go home to work the rice paddies. Heavily outmanned and out-gunned, the defenders fell back at all points. The North Koreans, in a multicolumn attack by tank-supported infantry, headed down the two main highway corridors leading to Seoul, only twenty miles away, aided by amphibious troops landed from junks and sampans behind the ROK lines. Despite many instances of great individual heroism, the South Korean defense task seemed hopeless. The capital fell to the enemy, and the entire peninsula to the south lay open to capture.

The United States interceded through the U.N. Security Council at Lake Success, New York, that same Sunday afternoon, and obtained a resolution declaring North Korea the aggressor and demanding "the immediate cessation of hostilities" and withdrawal of North Korean forces to the thirty-eighth parallel. President Truman, on the recommendation of the joint chiefs of staff (JCS), ordered fleet elements sent to Japan and for the Air Force to commence making plans to wipe out all Soviet air bases in the Far East.

The mission of the naval forces initially was to prevent any Chinese Communist attack on Formosa and to dissuade the Nationalist Chinese on Formosa under Generalissimo Chiang Kai-shek from any moves against Mao Tse-tung on the Chinese mainland. Second, air and naval forces should establish a protective cordon around Seoul, Kimpo airport, and the port of Inchon to ensure safe evacuation of U.S. dependents. To wipe out the Soviet air bases in the Far East, Truman understood that plans called for possible use of A-bombs. He pledged not to use nuclear weapons in Korea, but U.S. planes made simulated A-bomb runs over Pyongyang, the North Korean capital. Several months later, in December 1950, nonassembled bombs were quietly transported to a U.S. aircraft carrier on station off the peninsula.

Implementing the presidential decision, the JCS ordered the USS *Boxer* and screening destroyers to Korea to augment the tactical air forces available to the commander of the Seventh Fleet. Admiral Radford, on his own, decided to include *Pickerel* as well.

Our intensive training and high state of readiness paid big dividends. It took only minimal time to top off on torpedoes, fuel, and stores and be fully ready for war. It probably took more time to write the operation order on how to use our services. What a single submarine could do in our newest Asian adventure to stem the advancing Red tide was not entirely clear.

We were given a whole weekend to spend with our families before shoving off to war, and probably needed it. The ship had been under way almost continuously since commissioning, away from the families, and renewed hostilities in the Far East left great doubts as to when we would return. Most of the officers and their families spent the weekend on the beach at Waianae, our favorite. On the windward side, the heavy combers rolling on the beach made body surfing a thrill. The spotless white sand was ideal for volleyball and games with the children. The tang of charcoaled chicken and hamburgers pushed from our minds the question of when we would be together to enjoy such a day again.

At 1100, 3 July 1950, *Pickerel* cast off the lines and headed out the familiar channel toward an Asian unknown. The departure went largely unnoticed locally. A small item in *Time* magazine that week stated that *Boxer* and *Pickerel* would augment U.S. forces in Asia. Nevertheless, a large crowd of people arrived to see us off. I felt sorry for the wives, especially the young ones. Two-thirds of the officers and men had submarine combat experience in World War II, but few of us expected a major war. I could see fear of the unknown in many eyes. Bill Shuman's wife, Giovina, grabbed my hand firmly and with a warm kiss gave a little speech about us going off to war and how much confidence she had in me. It was very thoughtful of her, but it took me by surprise. In the momentary confusion as I walked aboard I didn't even kiss Henri goodbye. When I turned and noted her amazed look, it was too late. My later thoughts of the kiss I missed lingered more than an ardent and loving one properly given.

The speed of advance was a surprisingly low thirteen knots, which allowed plenty of time for the daily swim and to take the scenic route through the islands. Passing close by French Frigate Shoals, we examined the anchorage where Japanese submarines refueled the big Emily flying boats for attacks on Pearl Harbor. We passed near Leysan Island, home of the gooney bird or Leysan albatross, then Mago Bank and Kure. While exploring a new reef off Kure, we almost went aground on it, which, 150 miles south of our assigned route, might have been a bit awkward to explain.

On Saturday, 8 July, the steward prepared a fine birthday dinner for Pap, using food coloring on mashed potatoes for clever decorative touches around a delicious broiled rabbit. Just before the dessert, a quartet harmonized a special "Happy Birthday" over the general announcing system. We found time to run some special all-night snorkel tests requested by the submarine force engineer. Even with daily swims and the extra cruising, we were still ahead of schedule, so I sent a message to commander naval forces, Far East, the new boss, suggesting we arrive nine hours early.

He did us better, advancing our arrival time by twenty-six hours, requiring almost twenty knots for the rest of the voyage, heading directly into the Japan Stream, which set us back a full knot.

I ordered flank speed, a 150 percent overload on the engines, and with the plant flat out, again put the problem into the hands of Mr. Fairbanks and Mr. Morse. The news from the front in Korea was growing desperate, and we assumed a special operation might be afoot. The next day a follow-up message asked how many hours late we'd be. The seas by now were heavy and met us head-on. Nevertheless, I sent, "With wind and sea in present state/Plunging *Pickerel* will keep her date."

I figured we might as well let 'em know from the start that it wasn't just an ordinary submarine coming out to fight the war. We used rhyming couplets for nearly all messages while in Asia. I soon learned that everybody was reading them whether or not they were addressees.

Those superb engines did better than promised. We arrived an hour and a half early for the rendezvous in Tokyo Bay with the escort, the USS *Greenlet,* a submarine rescue vessel. During forty-four hours at full power, *Pickerel* made good 860 miles over the ground at a speed of nineteen and a half knots, never before equaled by a fleet submarine. But we paid a price this time. I tried to make a trim dive before entering port and found that the main engine exhaust valves would not close properly. After mooring alongside the USS *Catfish* at 1835, 14 July, at the naval base, Yokosuka, we discovered that pieces of piston ring prevented the sea valves from closing. These very special gold seal piston rings had to be replaced on all four engines. It took the entire reserve supply in the western Pacific to get the plant back on the line. In addition, one engine had three burned pistons requiring replacement. The engines had been due for a routine overhaul before we left Pearl Harbor. It could no longer be delayed, but my orders called for departure on a war patrol in four days. Once again I had to ask the hardworking engineers for a little extra.

Catfish, under Lt. Cmdr. Corwin G. "Mendy" Mendenhall, was a San Diego boat caught up by the war while making a routine training cruise to the western Pacific.

Mendy, a classmate and a fine skipper, and the division commander, Cmdr. Cyrus C. "Cy" Cole, Jr., awaited our arrival. The third sub in the area was *Segundo* under Lt. Cmdr. John H. "Jake" Bowell. I could hardly restrain my curiosity on our forthcoming operation. To my question, Cy's reply was startling to say the least. "I think there's a good chance this will be World War II all over again, and I want to get first crack at a good R and R spot before the Army and Air Force beat us to it. There's a big Japanese villa in Atami I want you and Jake to try out this weekend to see if it meets our needs."

I thought to myself that burning out my engineering plant to begin a new war over a rest camp made as good sense as anything else in Asia. Jake and I grabbed the morning train to Atami to open the campaign. Atami was a well-known resort village on the slopes of Mount Fuji, overlooking Sagami Bay. I carried a briefcase with shaving gear, a change of clothing, several select steaks from the *Pickerel* freezer, and a bottle of Canadian Club from Cy's ample stock. Left behind, unfortunately, were my sweating engineers, making a more prosaic sacrifice, also for flag and country.

At the villa, Jake and I were met and quickly put at ease by the serving staff as they escorted us to our rooms. My big corner suite offered a magnificent view of the quaint village and peaceful country scene below. The distant sea framed an active volcano on the island of O Shima, its smoking cone darkening the blue sky by day and illuminating the horizon by night. The villa was built as a retirement home, a fortress really, by a war profiteer who grew rich behind the Japanese army in Manchuria before coming to grief as a war criminal. While he served a sentence in Tokyo's Sagumo Prison, his wife ran the villa.

Jake and I had barely gotten into kimonos and were relaxing in our luxurious living room when two ladies arrived, also planning to spend the weekend there, courtesy of the Japanese government. One was a prominent Japanese, Tell Satoh, the first woman member of the Diet, then serving as an interpreter for the U.S. occupation force. The other, her friend Lu Smith, was a British girl recently arrived from India, a civil employee of the Japanese government. After lazing away the afternoon getting acquainted over snacks and green tea—looking like pond slime—we chopsticked our way through an excellent sukiyaki dinner, complete with a raw egg on top. Shortly after dinner, the maid announced that the baths were ready.

I had showered just before leaving the ship and felt only mildly interested but joined the party for my first "hotsy-botsy" bath in the scalding sulfur spring waters flowing from the innards of Mount Fuji. This centuries-old ritual of the Japanese attracts many followers. After a scrubdown until the blood began to show through my skin, I eased myself into the bath, momentarily wondering why I always dropped live lobsters into the water head first. The baths were on the top floor of the villa, and the maids moved the sliding screens aside to let us enjoy the full panorama of sea and mountains at sunset. The magnificent view and quiet sounds of eventide were seductive. We must have steamed off about fifteen pounds before rising to shift into the cold water to close the pores again. Here we suddenly learned that we were sharing the bath with several large carp, fish with deep historical significance but also useful to keep the water pure.

After a most relaxing weekend, we returned to Yokosuka early Monday morning. Cy was anxious to get our reactions to Atami as a rest home for tired submariners. We made some mild recommendations—nice but hardly large enough for more than about eight officers or one submarine ward-room—and suggested that we not jump too quickly at the first opportunity. My devious plan grew plain over the succeeding weeks: every weekend that *Pickerel* was in Yoko-suka, I and one of the other skippers received invitations to test the facilities at a new site—Miyanoshita, Fujiya, Nikko, Yokohama, Atami again—I just couldn't decide, seemingly. But we surely enjoyed the routine of looking, at Japanese government expense.

Submarine operations were a subject of great curiosity. Security was lax, and the hatred between the South Koreans and the Communist North Koreans was little less than between many South Koreans and the Japanese. Street acquaintances, tradesmen, and minor officials were asking pointed questions about the ship, the name of the skipper, and possible missions. And when an Asian bar girl struggled to get a name like mine from a half-drunk sailor, even he got suspicious. I very quickly learned to take extra precautions on security. Up to four hours before sailing, only Pap and I knew the exact day. Any information on the destination and mission was known to me alone. My official duties, plus socializing with old friends, took much of my time. If I accepted social engagements, I couldn't indicate in any way that circumstances might require me to be absent.

The volatile situation on the fighting front in Korea was complicated by unpredictable threats by Chiang Kai-shek on Formosa. The generalissimo was anxious either to intervene in Korea with sorely needed reinforcements or to take advantage of the situation for a sudden attempt to return to the Chinese mainland. It made for the wildest of rumors. My old friend and look-alike Don O'Meara, whom I had seen only rarely since *Wichita* days, was in Tokyo on the Naval Forces Far East operations staff. Don and I spent as much time as possible together, and I at least had the benefit of his best inside information.

After only five days in Yokosuka, *Pickerel* sailed off to war on 19 July, sharing with *Catfish* the honor of being the first submarines to make war patrols under the United Nations flag. By another remarkable achievement, my engineers had two engines back on the line for departure; the other two joined a few days later. I could find no appropriate words of praise for their achievement; they had gone largely without sleep or proper food during almost the entire time in Yokosuka.

The destination was the Straits of Formosa, between Mao's forces on the China mainland and the generalissimo's on Formosa. Dirty weather and very heavy swells delayed arrival on station by several hours and prevented ship's work or even decent rest. The first of two gales struck immediately on our clearing the coast of Japan, the ship buffeted by unpredictable weather between the two storm tracks. By nightfall the best speed on two engines gave little better than steerageway. Midnight found the ship plowing through mountainous swells; the next three days were a dreary and tiring succession of very rough seas, screaming winds, and torrential downpours of rain with half the ship flooded out by seawater down the inductions and ventilation system. I shifted to the snorkel to ease the pounding and allow some food preparation other than cold meals eaten hanging on. Most of us were bruised and near exhaustion. At one point all the other officers, even the experienced sea dogs, were seasick. I ate lunch alone. This in itself was a change. A case of dysentery had bothered me since our return from Atami, with fever, chills, and a rugged case of the trots. Since I was supposed to have an iron constitution, sixty hours of violent pitching and plunging soon convinced me that my disease was not serious. It was Henri's birthday. I couldn't even hold the paper still to write her, never with more sincerity, how sorry I was not to be at her side, anywhere but where I was.

No seaman fails to enjoy pitting his puny strength against the mighty forces of nature. I always enjoyed relaxing in my chair on the bridge, especially during high winds and stormy seas, driving the bow deep into each sea. But this was ridiculous. The heavy rain clouds scudding by seemed to be breaking up overhead. Then I realized they were emptying on us and rushing back for refills.

On Sunday, 23 July, the typhoon finally blew itself out as the ship entered Formosa Straits. At that time, the Chinese Communists held all of the Chinese mainland and were actively preparing for the invasion of Formosa, using junks and a few thousand tons of steamers and minor war vessels concentrated in the approaches to Shanghai, plus five thousand additional junks off Swatow, Foochow, and Amoy. Opposing them, Chinese Nationalist forces held Formosa, the Pescadores Islands, and a few small islands off the China coast. Chiang was actively insisting that he be allowed to intervene to aid the beleaguered U.N. forces in Korea—if only to obligate the United States in his behalf—and to widen the war by returning in force to the Chinese mainland.

The U.S. Seventh Fleet was carrying out national policy by neutralizing the Formosa Straits. *Pickerel* and *Catfish* were ordered to conduct a reconnaissance of the China coast, keeping commander Seventh Fleet apprised of any immediate threat to the island of Formosa by the Communist forces, of any changes in the pattern and volume of coastal traffic, and of any large movement of seaborne traffic within the area. I was to remain undetected, submerged by day, observing radio silence, and not to close the coast of China inside of twelve miles or the coast of Formosa within six miles.

After careful study Pap and I determined that the most likely objective for a Maoist assault on Formosa was near Kyoko in the northwest, second against Rokuku on the north central coast. If Chinese Communist invaders were expected in these areas, they would have to use the shortest sea route and a massive assault across the beaches to gain a toehold before the overwhelming power of the Seventh Fleet could be brought to bear. A drive inland to the mountains from either objective would sever all communications between Taipei, the capital, and the port of Kirun in the north with the populous areas around Takao and Taiwan in the southwest. Because of the heterogeneity of the Communist forces, fair weather would be very important.

On the other hand, should the generalissimo go on the offensive against Mao on the Chinese mainland, the point of attack would almost certainly be in the Amoy-Foochow areas, where Nationalist forces held out in strength on several of the offshore islands.

I therefore planned to patrol off Amoy and Foochow initially, particularly the latter, then to take advantage of the first period of rough weather to cross the strait and examine the Formosa coastal areas. Immediately prior to arrival in the patrol area, however, we intercepted an English-language news broadcast from somewhere in China that fifteen hundred junks off Swatow had moved northward to Amoy. I therefore headed directly for Amoy. After a day submerged off the big port city, however, we learned from radio Taipei that, contrary to the information in my secret operation order, the Chinese Nationalists still held the islands of Quemoy and Little Quemoy covering the approaches to Amoy and that these islands had been under bombardment by Communist shore batteries throughout the day. Since the defenders on Quemoy obviously had a better look at shipping than mine through a periscope twelve miles at sea, I abandoned Amoy in favor of Foochow, where we might discover something useful. Two days later, the prediction of another gale impelled me to move across the Strait to Formosa, hoping that the twelve-thousand-foot mountain ranges would offer some protection from strong northeast winds.

I took advantage of the opportunity to conduct a routine deep discharge of the battery, requiring eighteen hours submerged. I didn't do these tests off Pearl because it wasted a night at home. The operation is simple but toward the end, hydrogen and carbon dioxide accumulate in the boat and the oxygen disappears. I thought it would be a good experience for the younger men who hadn't lived through the long days submerged in World War II. On this occasion the panting for breath seemed wryly humorous. At dinner Ed Cummings tried to tell a story but, breathing so heavily from the effort, couldn't resume eating for ten minutes. A trip to the conning tower was like running up the Eiffel Tower. Young Grant Apthorp, not nearly tall enough for his weight, tried to crank up the whip antenna by hand and was soon in a near coma even though he rested every few seconds.

Two more days of ghastly weather contributed nothing but storm damage. The beautiful plexiglass bubble over the open bridge carried away; much of the deck plating tore loose, including angle iron supports broken or carried away at the welds. The messenger buoy, so vital to escape or salvage at sea, again became inoperable because the protecting mesh screen and stiffeners caved in over it, wedging it in place. I decided the weather could be no worse on the China side and returned to Foochow, picking our way through the fishermen once more.

That day, 29 July, became memorable for at least one of our officers, Chuck Richelieu. But for the hasty departure from Pearl Harbor, it was to have been his wedding day back in upstate New York. We did our best to help celebrate the nonevent. The chief steward baked him a cake with lots of decorative frosting on it and a colorful inscription, "Happy(?) Wedding Day, Chuck." Then during dinner our inimitable quartet sang a cleverly done variation of "I Wonder Who's Kissing Her Now." In the evening Chuck came into the wardroom attired in a beautiful silk dressing robe, a gift from the bride-to-be. We gave him a hard time about all the college boys driving Shirley around in the big new Buick he had left behind with her. He was due for the midwatch that night, and a full moon broke through the onrushing clouds, giving him at least a romantic night to meditate on what might have been.

The following day, 30 July, we received a surprise set of orders to terminate the patrol—two weeks early—and proceed north to rendezvous with *Catfish*, then return to Yokosuka at best speed. Mendy thought he had the fastest boat in the fleet and we took the challenge. We not only beat him but, to emphasize our superiority, I ran a circle around him. We both thought the recall indicated a higher-priority assignment, a new emergency, and wasted no time getting back. One incident delayed me for a few minutes.

On the last day out, the OOD reported sighting a mine close aboard to starboard. Shades of the *Atule!* The biggest gun the guppies carried was a Browning automatic rifle so I ordered—or, more accurately, wished for—battle stations gun action, bringing two BARs-men to the bridge. A half dozen rounds caused it to sink slowly from view. Rejoining *Catfish*, we rendezvoused with *Greenlet*, our escort, at 2100 2 August and moored at Yokosuka the following morning at 0800.

As expected, Mendy and I were ordered to Tokyo to confer with Admirals Arthur D. Struble, Seventh Fleet commander, C. Turner Joy, Naval Forces Far East commander, and my commodore, Captain Donald F. Weiss. As we headed for Tokyo on a dark night in a driving rain, the Japanese jeep driver turned around to bow his apologies every time he hit a pothole, meanwhile hitting two more when he wasn't looking. Between his head jolting from the road and his bowing, our survival seemed doubtful. When the meeting broke up around midnight, we couldn't find billeting. A set of travel orders was needed; ours were classified. We finally went to Don Weiss's suite at the Imperial Hotel for a scotch before finally finding accommodations at 0300. Mendy and I both needed sleep, having been up all the previous night while feeling our way back to port in lousy weather, but early next morning we were at it again, briefing Don O'Meara's people in the operations section. Returning to Yokosuka just before dinnertime, we cut Cy Cole and the intelligence experts in on our activities, by which time I was ready for adventure.

Fortunately, Tell Satoh, with whom I had enjoyed the earlier visit to Atami, invited Pap and me back for the weekend. We grabbed some clothes, a jug, and a few steaks, raced for the train, and got there just before midnight. Unfortunately, the rain continued through the weekend, but during a lull we decided to see the town after walking Tell back to the station. Egged on by the maid, we wore kimonos, bright obis, and getas with three-inch wooden heels. The townspeople were agog at the two fair-haired giants, accentuated by the housekeeper and a tiny maid walking behind us poohbahs to offer an umbrella lest a drop of rain touch us.

We rose at 0400 Monday morning to get back to Yokosuka and finally enjoyed a few days of pleasant weather. All the *Pickerel* officers attended a swimming and dinner party at the club that evening at which dinner and drinks for the evening cost only $1.50. Later somebody suggested a water polo game, and for an hour we enjoyed ourselves hugely. Pap and I evened the sides by drowning about six of the opposition, most of whom decided to leave the game. It got very rough; we had a great time.

While we awaited patrol orders, a new boat from San Diego joined our force, the troop-carrying submarine USS *Perch*. *Perch* had a huge tank aft of the superstructure for rubber boats and amphibious equipment. Her skipper, Lt. Cdr. Robert D. Quinn, a wild-eyed redhead one year junior to me at Annapolis, was a great man for a party. Bob was itching to join me for a weekend at a spa, and we shortly found ourselves at Fujiya. Bob hadn't yet learned in Japan that booze and a piping hot bath allow nature to sweat out the moisture but seem to leave the alcohol in the system. He disappeared from the bath without taking his clothes, and before I could get back to our suite five floors above, the Shore Patrol was already there. They agreed to leave him in my custody. Totally smashed, he was soon asleep.

It took an earthquake to rouse him at 0400 for the trip back to Yokosuka. He had no recollection of the night before. As atonement he offered to drive the jeep back. Roaring away from the hotel entrance, he missed the curve onto the highway, and almost plunged over a steep cliff. I suggested that maybe I should take the wheel. The jeep had only one dim headlight and almost no brakes. We sped through the valleys in the early dawn, laying a cloud of poisonous fumes behind. I was confident we would meet an oxcart broadside and end our days in a giant honey bucket. We arrived tense and exhausted, just in time for another urgent trip to the big boss in Tokyo about our patrol orders. On return I got a full night's sleep, the first time I got back aboard before 0200 since we arrived in Japan.

The next day marked a year since Dad died. I couldn't believe how much had happened since then and how sorry I was that he missed sharing it with us. I spent much of the morning in my cabin with my own thoughts, feeling very lonesome without Henri and the children. How much of our married life I had missed, and what a wonderful partner she had been despite the long separations! I felt the urge to get home again, but there was still much to be done here. I thought about asking her to fly out to Japan for a while, but it would be impossible either with or without the children. After the meeting in Tokyo I asked Don Weiss if he had any information on our relief in Japan. He said three boats were due out in about two months on the regular rotation, but Admiral Radford had sent us out on his own and we weren't part of the rotation. Bob Quinn added, *"Pickerel* and *Perch* will probably fight the whole war and then be the first to do occupation duty in Korea."

On Saturday, 12 August, Bob and I spent another day in Tokyo planning for the hit-and-run amphibious operation in Korea. We studied aerial photos and other intelligence materials to choose objective areas on the east central coast. *Pickerel* would do the reconnaissance and photography of selected objectives, and *Perch* would land an Army contingent to cut off the North Korean logistic support to its forces in the south around Pusan. Then over the weekend final details on the objective areas, patrol instructions, and a communication plan were worked out with Don Weiss and Cy Cole in Yokosuka.

During a lunch break, Bob and I decided to take a walk outside the base for a breath of fresh air and a brew. When we entered a pub adjacent to a geisha house, an attractive girl in a low cut kimono joined us as we sipped a beer. When neither of us showed any interest, she asked Bob, "Don't you rike Japanese girls?"

"Yes, but most of them have no chi-chi," indicating his chest.

"But I have chi-chi."

"No, yours are PX chi-chi."

"No," baring her breasts, "these not PX chi-chi."

Even serious war planning can bring strange consequences at times. The details of the Korean operation finally worked out, the completed plans were delivered to me. *Pickerel* got under way immediately and headed east to a point thirty miles off the coast of Japan, then turned north. During the layover in Yokosuka, somebody had "liberated" a plastic nose bubble from an Air Force bomber to replace the one lost in the storm off Formosa. I don't know how the bomber flew without it, but we did very well with it. A heavy head sea soon gave it a real test and a chance to shoot some spectacular movies from the top of the periscope shears as the bow plunged into mountainous seas. The following day, as we were still steaming north in company with *Greenlet,* we sighted a mine close aboard to starboard but couldn't relocate it after one pass. Shortly after, just at twilight, another was sighted close aboard to port. After only a few shots in passing, we decided to abandon the gunfire to avoid being identified by nearby fishermen. Shortly after, *Greenlet* suffered a steering casualty and suddenly starboarded across our bow. Less than an hour later it happened again. The OOD, forewarned, backed emergency to clear. By the time I got to the bridge, the red lights in *Greenlet*'s passageways were shining in our eyes. Feeling that our escort had become more of a hazard than a help, I took a discreet station well aft.

We had planned to transit the Tsugaru Straits between Honshu and the northern island of Hokkaido on the surface at night, but delays and detours to avoid detection by fishermen and coastal shipping put us several hours behind schedule. At 0500 16 August, with dawn approaching rapidly, I pulled ahead of the lumbering *Greenlet* at twenty knots to get through the narrowest part of the passage before sunrise and then dive and transit submerged at high speed. Aided by a morning mist, we were able to evade on the surface until boxed in by a tanker, a small tramp, and two Hokkaido ferries. Diving to ninety feet at twelve knots, making half-hourly looks and quick navigational fixes to determine the effect of the four-knot current, we made good progress. The heavy shipping minimized chances of snorkeling undetected. After three tries I slowed to allow *Greenlet* to pass ahead, then commenced snorkeling in her wake. Just before noon a final burst of speed brought us into the bright blue waters of the Sea of Japan, having covered forty-eight miles in five hours submerged. I released *Greenlet* from her escort duty and, in a final effort to deceive her personnel as to our destination, headed south at maximum speed toward Pusan, Korea.

For security reasons I had taken extreme measures to keep our destination unknown to all except Pap and Snuffy Jackson, now filling new duties as operations officer and navigator. The photographic mission required all our skills to remain undetected. The lives of many men on *Perch* and her assault team ashore would be hazarded if the location were suspected. We determined that any breach of security would not come from *Pickerel*. On departure from Yokosuka, no word on our destination was put out to the crew. The ship's position recorder in the control room was offset several hundred miles so that anybody trying to plot the position on a chart would find us off the east coast of Japan rather than Korea. All charts were drawn personally by the operations officer; all other charts of the general area were confiscated. No charts were used outside the wardroom except during the actual photography, and even these were disguised as to area. Navigational fixes were also coded to indicate that the ship was off Honshu rather than Korea. Personnel were briefed individually and collectively that many lives depended on maintaining absolute secrecy on the mission. Officers and men gladly acquiesced, making only such comments as, "Well, I hope we get back to Yokosuka soon so I can read the *Stars and Stripes* and find out where we've been."

After heading south toward Pusan for six hours, we reached the southern edge of the patrol area, then headed first northwest and southwest on ten-hour legs, eventually completing a Z-shaped path across the Sea of Japan. (One of the officers asked if I was trying to fool myself on where we were.)

The situation in Korea at that time was still critical. The North Korean offensive had been stalled by a defensive ring around Pusan, with almost all of South Korea, including Seoul, the capital, in enemy hands. General MacArthur, the supreme commander in Tokyo, was preparing a daring amphibious operation against Inchon on the Korean west coast. If it proved successful, the Inchon landing and the drive on the capital would cut off the enemy completely in the west and break the siege of Pusan. The submarine-launched amphibious strike by *Perch* on the east coast was designed to cut the single rail line and highway running along the seashore, where steep mountains fell to the sea. If *Perch* sappers could dynamite a few tunnels and cut the rail line, the remaining source of war supplies for the North Koreans would be cut at a critical moment. As is well known, the Inchon landing marked one of the most brilliant, daring, and successful operations in U.S. military history. The *Pickerel-Perch* operation on the other coast, although minor, remains unknown.

The preparations for the photographic mission proved to be far more difficult than expected. The best maps obtainable offered a hodgepodge of Russian, Japanese, Korean, U.S. Navy, and Admiralty charts, each with a different set of foreign names, few of which agreed with the pilot data or even with each other. All were to different scales, none usable for our purpose. The amphibious staff in Tokyo prepared 30,000:1 overlays from aerial photos, useful but highly inaccurate on orientation and position. Scales on overlapping charts varied. True north was in error as much as thirty degrees. We therefore had to construct on cross-section paper a completely new and detailed chart of the entire forty-mile coastal area to be photographed. This proved to be a huge and minutely painstaking task requiring virtually the entire time at sea for Snuffy and his team.

When adequate charts suitable for navigation were finally completed, photo-reconnaissance plans were made for the twelve points of primary interest along the coast. For the actual photography of each of the twelve potential landing areas, we planned to commence shooting the northern section, working to the south and east, hoping to complete the entire sequence in one day if possible, to obtain the maximum benefit of backlighting. This plan was carried out essentially as described.

On Thursday, 17 August, radar landfall was made on the Korean coast in the area of Aru Somu, not far south of Wonsan. On diving to avoid shipping, we made an amazing discovery. The BT indicated a thermal gradient far greater than anything ever experienced or recorded in the oceanographic literature. The seawater temperature, eighty-two degrees at the surface, dropped sharply to forty-four degrees at eighty feet, then fell slowly to thirty-eight degrees at four hundred feet. The drop was so extreme that the entire superstructure popped and crackled like a giant ice cube tray suddenly thrust under a faucet. Both the periscope barrels produced a heavy coat of frost, and a raw chill permeated the ship. How could we ever hope to prevent the periscope lens from fogging when raised from forty-five-degree sea water into warm and humid air? How could we hope to do any photography through the periscope under such conditions? And never far from the back of my mind, the entire area was ideal for mining.

The mission required, first, highly precise exposures for preparation of photomosaics for analysis under a stereo viewer; second, photos giving worm's-eye views from the periscope similar to what would be seen from a landing boat at various points in to the beach; and third, photographs of the radarscope from four miles off the beach to give a broad view of each objective area. This required gaining a lot of information in a very short time, and every minute was critical.

Surfacing that afternoon for the final run-in to the coast gave a strange sensation. A chilling breath of frost blew through the superstructure and "up the kilts," while one stood on the bridge bareheaded under the fiery blast of a hot summer sun. I felt like a thermocouple. At 2200, photographing the radarscope began. No special equipment was available through the Navy. We used an ordinary Japanese Mamiya Flex commercial-grade camera with a 75-mm, f3.5 lens and a forty-five-second time exposure, and an Argus 30-mm Type I portrait attachment synchronized with the nine-rpm radar sweep. The entire rig was cannibalized from personal camera equipment aboard. The results, blown up, were excellent. By 0200, the entire job was done and turned over to Snuffy's developing team.

From 0254 to 0302 an unfriendly aircraft forced us down, but we were ready shortly after dawn for the first reconnaissance through the periscope. Both scopes had been carefully cleaned and coated with a "fogpruf" paste carried on board for fire and fume emergencies. It worked fine for the scopes except that, having a glycerin base, it sometimes held drops of moisture which caused a lesser evil of blurred or fuzzed images. Nothing else was known to help; we made do with what we had. Both scopes fogged badly after ten seconds' exposure, particularly in high power. The continuing forty-degree variation in seawater temperature between the surface and periscope depth, we thought, would make depth control difficult. Actually, it was remarkably good. A real problem with no solution was the grease in the periscope bearings. The cold caused it to harden suddenly and made both scopes exceedingly difficult to swing around.

Then a new problem arose. The after compartments at 0939 reported hearing a cable pass down the port side. Were we once again operating in a minefield? I put the rudder hard left to clear the screws, and we were momentarily clear, but the level of tension went up a notch. A month later, when U.S. surface forces tried to enter Wonsan, just south of our position, they were delayed for several weeks while sweeping safe channels through Soviet and North Korean laid fields of three thousand new Soviet mines, including sophisticated magnetic bottom mines. Two of our objective areas were within that field. The usual *Pickerel* luck prevailed. We escaped unharmed, and *Perch* crossed those areas off the list of potential landing sites.

The long and difficult day convinced me the time had come to pull clear of the coast and finish on the morrow. Coverage of all but the last two objective areas was complete. One new spot for a possible landing was discovered and quickly photographed. I decided to try again in the morning after more detailed study of the area. Some of the locations photographed were very close to the beach—I took the ship within a hundred yards at one point, the keel gently furrowing the muddy bottom.

On Saturday 19 August at 0315, the OOD sighted three phosphorescent torpedo wakes on the port side which he paralleled at flank speed. I arrived on the bridge in time to witness the show and quickly determined they were porpoise wakes—not good for the heartbeat but excellent training for the bridge watch.

The time had come to head back in again, and at 0540 we dived near Kotan Tan, took position for the last runs, then moved northeast to redo the new areas located the day before. Two fishermen interrupted us just two exposures short of completion of the entire project; I called it a day and headed out to sea at eighty feet making twelve knots.

That night at 0200, orders came in from the command in Yokosuka to head for home at nineteen knots for the thousand-mile journey. I didn't need to be asked twice and bent on the familiar four. Radar landfall on the three-thousand-foot peaks on Honshu and Hokkaido was made at 130 miles, and we were soon in the Tsugaru Straits. This time the elements were with us. A heavy fog allowed a surface transit, and the current, now in our favor, gave us ground speeds of 25 knots on two occasions. The following day, however, luck ran out. Swells from dead ahead rapidly increased. Slamming into them at high speed made progress very difficult. Down in the wardroom, Snuffy and the photo team, working round-the-clock on the track charts, preparing the photomosaics, and organizing the 546 photos, found himself considerably handicapped by the plunging and rolling of the ship, but the job was completed before arrival.

At 0700, 22 August, we moored on time at the naval base, Yokosuka, arriving once more with an exhausted crew. Pap, Snuffy, and I had had almost no sleep throughout. Snuff, standing continuously over a drawing board with the hot deck plates of the battery underfoot, developed a set of ankles the size of fireplugs. On arrival, he slept round-the-clock, got up for a shower and breakfast, then turned in again. I first had to deliver the goods and brief my superiors in Tokyo. Admirals Struble and James H. Doyle were knee-deep in plans for the Inchon landings on the west coast set for 15 September, for which Doyle in particular was unenthusiastic. They were interested not only in getting the *Perch* strike off on schedule but in learning what we had discovered of the North Korean defenses. Our photography proved invaluable.

This *Pickerel* patrol marked the first venture of an American submarine into the waters of an armed enemy since the conclusion of World War II. All endorsees to the patrol report from Cy Cole through Commander Submarines lauded the successful completion of the mission under severe and unexpected conditions. Admiral Brown awarded the officers and men the Submarine Combat Pin and added a special commendation for me, in which I was able to include Pap and Snuffy. Meanwhile, less than a week after return, we were ready for our next adventure.

The all-day conferences in Tokyo left me neither bright-eyed nor bushy-tailed. That evening I dragged Pap loose for some much needed relaxation with Captain Homer Ambrose at his quarters. Homer and Louise were friends from Portsmouth days, a most devoted and delightful couple. We could always count on a warm welcome. Their quarters on the Yokosuka Naval Base were built atop "Unnecessary Mountain," so called because the Japanese could find no reason to build an "unnecessary road" to the top of a scenic but unused peak. When living quarters were eventually built, the name stuck. The Ambrose quarters had a beautiful terrace overlooking the garden, a Japanese bridge over the fish pond, and a panorama of the sea beyond. After a stifling day in town, we relaxed in comfortable beach chairs and allowed the cool breezes to waft away our cares. With good people and a lively conversation over a glass of fine scotch, we watched the moon rise and chatted about many things. They missed the old submarine crowd, and we were starved for the affection of a loving family. Louise always referred to Homer, about the size of a water buffalo, as "My treasure"; to him she was "Precious."

We invited them aboard for a dinner party the following week; they invited us to drive down the coast on Sunday to a fishing village to buy some lobster. Homer also helped us get a *Pickerel* battle flag manufactured in town and framed in stainless steel for mounting in the wardroom. We had just finished installing it when the dinner guests arrived, the Ambroses, Don Weiss, and Cy Cole. Our two stewards knocked themselves out for a superb feast. The *Pickerel* found reason to celebrate. We had just learned that we would be ordered back to Pearl in mid-October, to arrive in good time for the holidays.

The ship had another reason to celebrate. We were finally out of the red in the general mess account. Since arrival in Japan, we had economized in many ways, shortchanged the supply officer now and then, and cadged everything we could from the system. We thrilled people with a free ride to sea in exchange for favors elsewhere; no ship ever ordered food deliveries to the piers without a chance of losing some to our raiders. We even stole from the Japanese and South Koreans.

With the *Pickerel*'s photography in hand, Bob and his amphibians in *Perch* were hot to trot on the amphibious landing. Unfortunately, every time he had an Army or Marine group trained in the art of launching an attack from a submerged submarine, the crunch for people for the Inchon buildup took them away. The delay in completion of his mission had already lost much of the tactical advantage in Korea. Finally, a group of hard-charging Royal Marines was flown in from Singapore and quickly trained. Bob said they had to go as soon as possible; he couldn't afford to feed them. Bob and I celebrated in advance with a weekend at Atami. Pap and Ed joined us, and we had a thoroughly enjoyable break. The weather was gorgeous. We watched the deepening twilight and moonrise from the open terrace, the lights of fishing boats twinkling in the distance, the cherry red eruption from O Shima lighting the sky and blotting out the southern stars. When the mosquitoes tried to carry us off, it was clearly a signal to try the hot baths again, a splendid way to ease an itch.

The next *Pickerel* mission was delayed and we decided to do some training. Jake Bowell and I laid on a three-day exercise for *Pickerel* and *Segundo,* using the *Greenlet* to run target for torpedo shooting by the junior officers. I chose Atami Bay for the operations. *Greenlet* boats chased down the torpedoes after each shot and towed them back to the submarine. We hoisted them aboard and prepared them for the next shot. The first day we worked hard from dawn until lunchtime, then invited Howard "Hod" Fulton, the *Greenlet* CO, and his relief, Maino DesGranges, who had just reported aboard, over for steaks. After a short swim over the side, we went ashore for some golf, Pap and I filling in the foursome. *Greenlet* used her boats to make liberty runs for the "troops." The village of Atami was rarely visited by Americans, and all hands had a great time ashore.

The golf course was high in the hills, reached by a precipitous climb. Designed by a mountain goat, it required clubs either two or eight feet long. One hole was only 80 yards, another 100, but peril lurked near at hand. On the first round my "girl-san" caddie failed to count some of my wild misses, as she was instructed to do with Americans—one of the smaller benefits of winning the war. I had a horrible time with wood shots. On the second and third rounds I used only the irons and played the best game of my life, thanks to no sleep the night before and a couple of beers between rounds. On one of the short holes I missed a hole in one by inches and eagled a 450-yard hole. On the last round I went around in 36. When the last putt dropped in the cup, I decided I'd hang up the clubs after this cruise. Up to then a duffer, clearly I had mastered the game.

After the match, we relaxed on the terrace of the clubhouse. The pine forest on all sides smelled sweet and fragrant, all the more enjoyable because of the quick transition from the seashore below. We spent the evening around an open fire, chatting with three enlisted men from MacArthur's headquarters who were enjoying a few days off. Their tales of life working for the "blue eyed emperor" were the stuff of history. Pap and the others went back to the ship at midnight; Ed and I decided to stay at the hotel for the night and try the golf again early in the morning. Our thoughts were wholly in tune, both half dreaming of the possibilities of Henri and Mimi joining us in a beautiful spot like this for a few weeks. About 0200 the prospect of a hot bath got the better of us. After getting steamed like lobsters, we headed for the sack. I slept like a log until the 0600 call came for the morning golf.

That morning, *Pickerel* golfed while *Segundo* and *Greenlet* went to sea. It was a gorgeous day, the bright sun filtering through the pine trees, the morning dew sparkling like diamonds on the manicured greens. Far below through the trees we could see *Pickerel*, long and sleek, lying at anchor in the tiny bay as the other ships put to sea. This job of being "commodore" of our small fleet had lots to offer—me on the golf course, my ships going to work below. Finishing our game by 0830, we talked a fisherman into putt-putting us back to the ship. I buttered him up in my best Japanese about our both being ship captains. He showed off his catch but refused any payment for services. I insisted, handing him thirty yen in large bills, about a penny. He made the three ceremonial bows on departure, almost falling over the side in doing so.

Shortly after noon on Sunday, 10 September, Japan was hit by an earthquake. I was driving down the coast to get some lobster, my teeth chattering to the rhythm of rutted roads, when the quake hit. Suddenly the jeep ride smoothed out as the earth trembled almost in synchronization. My experience was mild. Bill Shuman decided to go to mass that day, and the quake happened as he entered the huge church doors. Startled, he looked on high and said soulfully, "Lord, I know I haven't been very faithful lately, but this is overdoing it a little, don't You think?"

For weeks rumors of transfers of some of my officers were the subject of many conversations. The first indication was the arrival of Lt. Daniel P. Brooks, a classmate of Snuff's, who relieved him and in due time fleeted up to be my executive officer. Tell Satoh decided to have a lobster and saki dinner in Hayama to mark the occasion. Bob and Dan were already at her summer place; Pap, Snuff, Ed and I followed Sunday afternoon. Also present were her husband, a distinguished gentleman of about sixty, and one or two others. Dinner was a leisurely affair around the hibachi, with the servants doing the honors with the saki bottle. Everybody was in a party mood, and the conversation never lagged despite the language barrier. I was particularly interested in Mr. Satoh. Theirs was a typical Japanese "arranged" marriage; she was probably twenty years younger, a female activist, interested in the world about her. This was so unusual for a Japanese lady, I suspected that her activism presented serious problems within the family. Because she was not submissive in the usual manner, she was the only Japanese female with whom I could feel any friendship or companionship.

I mentioned earlier the grossly inferior position of Japanese women in their society. From the geisha came the companionship, the entertainment, and the ego massage for the dominant male. She was a professional entertainer and, it should be emphasized, not a prostitute. Both the geisha and the Japanese wife filled servile roles in society. I found both to be unattractive socially and cosmetically. The exceptions like Tell were rare.

One of the most beneficial side effects of the American occupation was the liberation of Japanese women. In 1950 they were female but hardly feminine. Public nursing of babies in the streets was commonplace. To converse with each other, they squatted on their hunkers, knees widespread, showing a yard of muscular thigh and ugly white or black bloomers. Lower class women frequently wore blouses open to the waist, making little attempt to cover sagging breasts. When I left Japan in the *Sasori* four years earlier, I was emphatic that I never wanted to return. Though great progress had already been made at all levels of society, after *Pickerel* I still felt reluctant to return.

Perhaps I had been away from my family too long. Equally likely, it was time for me to get away from the "daily smells of Asia," as General MacArthur described it. Over the subsequent years, I returned to Japan several times, most recently in 1986. The nation and its people have changed so much that few in the new Japan would recognize the old. Only because the country had changed so much could I utter these thoughts today. My nephew, Father Regis B. Ging, has been a Maryknoll missionary in Hokkaido for twenty years. The Japan we met through him, the parishioners whom he deeply loves, were a wholly new experience.

On Monday, 11 September, it was time to go to sea again. The preparatory bombing for the Inchon invasion had already begun. Bob and his delayed amphibians finally got off to Korea a few days later and pulled off a highly skilled and successful operation. The *Perch* saboteurs dynamited tunnels in the precipitous cliffs dropping to the sea north of Wonsan and cut the road and rail supply lines in the path of forces retreating from the south. Partly because of the delay of *Perch*, the surface Navy also began operations on the North Korean east coast. The USS *Toledo* conducted heavy bombardment of rail and highway targets; others were hit by carrier aircraft. Raiders from the USS *Horace A. Bass* carried out three night landings destroying three tunnels and two bridges.

The heavy bombardment of Inchon begun on 6 September largely destroyed the defenses by H-hour. The landings went off on schedule on 15 September. The North Korean resistance broke, and units surrendered or fled north in disorder. A second amphibious landing, planned to break the perimeter in the south around Pusan on 21 September, was called off when the North Koreans suddenly turned and fled. U.S. Army and Marine forces reached Seoul on 25 September, three months to the day from the first North Korean offensive against the South in June. South Korean forces, breaking out from the ring around Pusan, commenced a rapid march up the east coast toward Wonsan.

It was time for us to return to the war. Under way just after lunch on the eleventh, *Pickerel* sailed up the east coast of Honshu and through Tsugaru Straits, picking our way carefully through the fishing fleet to avoid detection. Clearing the coast on the snorkel, I headed northeast to Otaru in northern Hokkaido, where we moored at 0650 on 14 September. *Catfish* arrived from patrol two hours later; we transferred mail and conferred on the details of the patrol area with *Catfish* and U.S. Army representatives from nearby Camp Crawford. The business now accomplished, ample time remained for a brisk sightseeing and shopping tour around Otaru and for a beer party for all hands on the dock.

Catfish left for Yokosuka at 1330 and *Pickerel* for patrol at 1500, following the track of *Catfish* toward Tsugaru until dark so as to throw off coast watchers. I then submerged, reversed course, and snorkeled across the Sea of Japan toward Vladivostok. The patrol area covered most of the Sea of Japan south of the big Soviet naval base at Vladivostok. With the Inchon landings set for dawn on the following morning, it was very important to get information about Soviet ship movements toward North Korea.

The northern limit of the patrol area was latitude 45-45N, running from La Perousse Strait north of Hokkaido to a point on the Soviet coast about 250 miles north of Vladivostok. A Soviet-proclaimed restricted area around Vladivostok prevented any observation of Soviet facilities. I planned to concentrate the entire patrol in the region off the Soviet

Union and North Korea, making only one sweep on the eastern side. Because of temporarily mild weather, we headed immediately for the Sea of Okhotsk. Picking our way carefully through the mined area and avoiding detection by the fishermen became a bit nerve-wracking. The sudden drop in temperature on entering the Sea of Okhotsk added physical discomfort as well. The seawater temperature fell to forty-two degrees and the ship interior, suddenly frigid, stimulated a race for warm clothes and heaters used only once since builder's trials almost two years ago. Our Pearl Harbor blood was far from acclimated to this polar region. I used the legitimate excuse of the swarms of fishermen, abandoned the area, and headed for more lucrative hunting to the west.

Off Vladivostok early next morning, 18 September, we began to detect shipping of all sorts by both sonar and periscope. A great many vessels were detected initially by sonar, some at phenomenal ranges in excess of twenty miles. I arrived at several conclusions. The shipping of primary interest to the mission stayed within the Soviet restricted area beyond my ken of vision. I was faced with the awkward choice of failing to carry out the mission if we remained within the assigned area or of penetrating the Soviet restricted area and succeeding in the mission. My decision hinged on the absolute necessity to remain undetected. If we were identified operating in a forbidden zone at that particularly tense time in Asian events, all hell would break loose. Could we remain undetected? Orders called for remaining submerged during daylight, making all observations by periscope or passively by sonar.

At that time I considered myself the most experienced CO in the submarine force. I had worked zealously on my periscope technique since those early days under Karl Hensel. I took great care that we would not be detected by a careless exposure. Hence the first choice was easy. We would penetrate the area as far as necessary to do the job. The difficult question was what to do about the track chart. Should I expose our violation for all the world to see? This didn't seem so monumental either. In all our independent operations we had rarely been where people expected us to be. Why start now? The very long ranges of sonar contact gave me the clue, particularly since the longest ranges occurred in shallow waters. The mission called for analysis of shipping. We therefore reported the position of the ships accurately. The distance from the submarine seemed to be far less important. It was sometimes nearer, sometimes much farther from shipping than reported. The only rule was not to fix the submarine location within the restricted area.

On the second day in the patrol area, 17 September, we eased carefully over the line into the restricted zone. The next day we went boldly, and thereafter we lived there—and were richly rewarded for bending the rules. I didn't need to face the question of the track chart and convicting myself "out of my own mouth" for several weeks, and many things could happen. Very quickly we detected two ships by sonar at long range, then one by scope, then two more by scope, all at the same time. A mirage effect often prevailed in that region, sometimes distorting heights, sometimes giving a false horizon a few degrees above the actual so that ships in plain sight were actually below the horizon and perhaps a hundred miles away. The challenge to the tracking party had no equal, plotting and analyzing the simultaneous movement of five to eight ships spread across hundreds of square miles of ocean, the nearest fourteen miles away. Three of them were actually below the false horizon and couldn't possibly be "seen." Using the periscope with the TDC, sonar, bearing rate, and navigational plots—but no radar, for security— all contacts were sorted out, identified as accurately as possible, and generally photographed.

On surfacing that night, we had a surprise. Seoul City Sue, the Korean War equivalent of Axis Sally or Tokyo Rose, was talking about the *Pickerel*. The chief radioman had her tuned in as we broke the surface but too late to get her entire message. The news release that the ship had been awarded the Submarine Combat Insignia probably tipped her off on our operations.

We began 26 September much like any other day. It was clear and calm as a brilliant harvest moon sank beneath the western edge of the sea, fading before a blood-red sun rising in the east. No breath of air disturbed the stillness. The patrol routine ran its normal placid pattern with sonar easily tracking the light, fast screws of fishing vessels twelve miles away. During the morning a light breeze arose from the west, gradually increasing in force. Shortly after noon the wind backed clear around to the east, with wind and sea increasing to state three—whitecaps and waves several feet high. Sonar conditions deteriorated from superb to stinking. At 1614, a westbound freighter was detected visually at eight miles. No contact could be made on sound. When the range closed to 4000 yards, the "mushy" sound from the freighter seemed to disguise another sound several degrees astern of the freighter, but nothing could be seen through the scope. The merchantman passed and was duly photographed, and another search was made of the sound beyond the freighter, now forty degrees displaced. A surprising sight came into view.

A Soviet submarine was seen clearly a mile and a half away, then a second, then a third. The cable cutter forward, radio antenna from stem to stern, four-inch deck gun, and 40-mm on the "cigarette" deck aft of the bridge made it indisputably Soviet. Our recognition was aided by the Soviet colors flying from the mast. The subs were quickly identified as Soviet "S" class, or "C" in the Cyrillic alphabet; identification was aided by reading the hull numbers C 50, C 53, and C 56 painted on the sides of the conning towers. We were close enough to identify which unit flew the commodore's flag.

On first sighting I had ordered all torpedo tubes ready for firing "just in case." The firing bearing neared with a perfect setup against a prime and unalerted enemy. My orders were quite specific, to attack only in self-defense. At this particular moment in history, the aircraft carriers *Leyte* and *Philippine Sea* had just entered the Japan Sea for the first time, to begin new air offensives on the retreating Communist forces in Korea. The Soviet subs were heading directly toward the carriers. The same course would also take them to the big Soviet base at Vladivostok. Poised on the edge of immortality, I quickly reviewed the alternatives, then gave the order, firmly and with conviction, to shoot—pictures.

It was urgent to get well clear of the area to get off a contact report on the submarines and any possible interest they might have in the carriers. Making a final periscope sweep before surfacing, however, I noted a new contact to the north which, in the rapidly falling darkness, resembled the outline of still another submarine, zigzagging on a westerly course. The navigational lights were standard for a submarine—or a fishing vessel, but fishing vessels don't zig—and a second blur in his wake, also zigzagging. Sonar reported screw sounds similar to those of the previous contacts. The first, viewed as he passed by at relatively close range, appeared similar to the Soviet B-4, a former British sub. The other, possibly an escort vessel, could not be seen in the scope.

Surfacing at 1850, I cleared the area to the south at high speed for five hours, got off a contact report just before midnight, and headed back where we came from in time for the morning dive. The weather had worsened rapidly with heavy thunderstorms all about us. Believing the weather might keep the fishermen home for a few days, we headed back to the Okhotsk Sea, or Little Siberia as it was known aboard, for a quick sweep. Heavy seas and thirty-seven-degree seawater broke over the bridge constantly. Hailstorms and needle-driven rain dropped the visibility to zero. With a full gale blowing and sea state six, these were the days when submarining wasn't much fun. The interior of the ship became frosty with little relief. We were miserable. I gave in and decided to snorkel back toward Vladivostok.

I was fuming mad. The MacArthur headquarters retransmitted the submarine contacts with the evaluation of "possible," almost the lowest they could assign. Only much later did I learn the reason why. Soviet transfers of ships from the Atlantic to the Pacific fleets were made in the summer via the northern route. We had detected the end of the voyage of the submarines coming from the Baltic. The intelligence services still carried those submarines in the Atlantic, naturally. Since we had identified them by their hull numbers, it couldn't be correct because those particular ships were not even in the same ocean. Ergo, doubtful submarines; we couldn't gainsay the conventional wisdom.

Perhaps the Tokyo headquarters was too preoccupied with the rapidly changing situation in Korea. Advancing north from Inchon, MacArthur's forces had fought their way into Seoul. The general himself had flown to Seoul for a quick visit with South Korean President Syngman Rhee on 28

September. On the east coast, ROK troops had broken loose from the Pusan perimeter, chasing the fleeing North Koreans up the coast in full retreat. Even an important submarine sighting couldn't take the attention of the MacArthur staff away from the volatile front in Korea.

The weather finally cleared on 30 September. A beautiful cap of snow appeared atop Rishiri Shima, the first of the winter season. Once more we returned to tracking and cataloging the scores of ships passing by in all directions. The following day, 1 October, began the last week on station. The day was unusual for two reasons. It was my birthday, and it was time for another of the quarterly eighteen-hour sealed-boat discharges of the battery. The day would also mark the biggest bag of shipping detected, tracked, and photographed, needing far more activity than normal during a battery discharge.

The first ship of unusual significance, the freighter-transport *Mikhail Lomonosov,* was known to operate out of Vladivostok. Shortly before, a medium sized Soviet military transport went by, believed to be the *Pyotr Veliki,* on a westerly heading. Painted warship gray and without stack markings, she had a prominent radar dome and flew a broad commodore's flag. At 0945 two Soviet Yak fighters flew by and at 1425 a third Soviet transport, the eighty-eight-hundred-ton *Sibir,* also passed by, westbound, followed soon after by two more fighter aircraft flying very near the track of the transports.

The two wardroom stewards, Bugarin and Jim Davis, worked most of the day preparing a special dinner of rice and curry, my favorite. Pap had procured a number of special ingredients before leaving Yokosuka and the result was superb. First came a fascinating tray of hors d'oeuvres cleverly decorated with "Happy Birthday, Captain," done with red and green food coloring. The table was decorated with our best linens and fluffy napkins setting off the seven condiments, and the feast was topped off with a baked Alaska.

Dinner came near the end of the eighteen-hour dive. Oxygen was very low, leaving everybody puffing like brewery horses. As the dessert was served, the ship's orchestra, mostly harmonicas, began "Happy Birthday" over the announcing system. Singing without oxygen is tough. After the first line, the inhaling was almost as audible as the singing, and no less harmonious. We had a great laugh over it, one "Haw" at a time, pausing for breath in between. The flaming baked Alaska, fueled by hundred-proof brandy from the narcotics locker, had tested OK an hour previously, but when the time came, not even the sulfur tip on the match would ignite. Perhaps sniffing the brandy from the top of the concoction made an acceptable substitute.

I broke out a box of cigars I had purchased in Yokosuka for the occasion. Pap and some of the officers smoked; I never acquired the habit. Cigars are usually taboo on submarines but no matter that day; they wouldn't light anyway. The birthday, incidentally, was my thirty-fifth, the unofficial upper age limit for submarine COs. After thirty-five, presumably, one no longer had the energy, aggressiveness, resiliency, or endurance to run a submarine. I think the consensus on board was that I still had a few years remaining of my lost youth.

Surfacing shortly before 2000, I cleared the area at high speed, picking the way carefully around several large ships, to get off a report of the unusual transport activity. When we returned to the area for a dawn dive, the seas were flat calm with phenomenal visibility and extraordinary sonar conditions. Shipping activity was heavy, with as many as six being tracked simultaneously. Included were two loaded cargo ships, eastbound, with deck cargo resembling landing craft loaded athwartships and hundreds of uniformed personnel topside.

With the great number of ships detected well inside the restricted area, the time had come to face the question of the track chart. This was my last submarine command and my last war patrol. I was already overdue for relief and couldn't pass up the chance for a farewell message. We had spent most of the patrol in the restricted area but none of this showed on the track chart as submitted. Across the restricted area, however, I carefully lettered "Pickerel" lightly in pencil, then for the last two nights before departure we did some careful sea writing to trace the ship's name on the chart, diving and surfacing to dot the *i*. I thought it showed just the right touch.

The Russians celebrated our departure too. On the last day we located a total of twenty-four ships, all traveling singly, at the end of which the tracking party was bleary-eyed, rubbery legged, and not a little stupid from fatigue. My thigh muscles were killing me from the strain of riding the periscope up and down on thousands of observations. At the height of the day's activities, the ever-faithful TDC failed from combat fatigue after 130 hours of tracking in two weeks. It was quickly restored, however, and with the last wrinkle on the track chart, the time had come to head for home, as usual at maximum speed.

Early on 5 October, we moored in Otaru, Hokkaido, and shortly received *Tilefish* alongside as our relief. Her skipper was Jake Vandergrift, a classmate I had last seen after his release from the Ofuna prison camp in the early days after the surrender. I had visited Ofuna on several occasions. It was the Japanese movie colony, its Hollywood, and was near Tell Satoh's summer place. I knew it as one of the worst of the stockades, used as an interrogation center with many interesting ways of loosening tongues. It was strange that Jake and I should meet again on Japanese soil. Jake had made a fine recovery and it was great to see him. Newly arrived from Pearl, he carried stacks of much appreciated mail and packages from our families. Again, however, business came first, and Pap and I put ours aside until later.

The Army team escorted us to Camp Crawford to talk over the patrol with Brig. Gen. Edwin W. Piburn, the commanding general of the Northern Sector. He had a wealth of information of value to the submariners; I suggested that he might wish to send a liaison officer with the submarines on future patrols. He was not only delighted but had an officer on his way to *Tilefish* before she left the harbor.

Of prime importance, we learned of severe losses the Navy had suffered to mines off Wonsan in the field that *Pickerel* had penetrated during the photo mission. The U.S. fleet was held up for several weeks before a passage could be cleared into Wonsan. Two minesweepers were sunk, the South Korean–manned YMS-509 on 28 September, and the USS *Magpie* on 1 October, with heavy loss of life. Badly damaged were the destroyers *Brush* on 26 September and *Mansfield* on 30 September. We would soon learn that in the week following, the destroyer *Small* was heavily damaged on 7 October, and on 11 October, the minesweepers *Pirate* and *Pledge* were sunk within a ten-minute period, again with heavy loss of life. These weeks were the most costly of the war for the U.N. naval forces. I breathed a silent prayer of thanks for our own close escape.

The general turned over the facilities of the camp to us with an example of Army hospitality the Navy may equal but never surpass. A delicious shrimp and steak lunch preceded a round of golf, Pap and I against our Army hosts. They fitted us out in slacks, sport shirts, clubs, and balls and lost the match to us—perfect hospitality; all we lost were the balls. We then showered and dressed for a cocktail party arranged for us by some Army auditors (female) at their quarters. After a quick round of beverages we rushed to the general's magnificent quarters, the largest home in Otaru, surrounded by a Japanese garden built around an intricate system of fish ponds and canals. A huge thirty-five-pound duck graced the center of the table. About twenty guests were present, and after dinner we sang around the piano or tootled on a half dozen brass instruments lying about.

Pickerel was supposed to have gone to sea at 1600, but we phoned the duty officer to report a delay. Six hours later we were just tearing ourselves loose. The general offered his car and driver, and then everybody wanted to see the submarine. I couldn't refuse but had to limit it to two couples, and we were soon searching out the potholes on the return trip. The men never seemed to object to female visitors wandering through their quarters and, after coffee in the wardroom, it was well past midnight before we backed clear of the wharf, to the carefree sounds of a few prolonged Army-Navy cheers. I still had those letters burning a hole in my pocket. I finished them just in time for a short nap before the World Series began on the Armed Forces radio at 0300; I finally got to sleep at six.

At 0800 Sunday, 8 October, *Pickerel* moored at the naval base, Yokosuka. Waiting on the dock, to my great surprise, was "Happy Jack" Irvin, the dour communications expert at sub school so many years ago, my interrogator over the B-29 incident, and now the submarine force intelligence chief. He had flown from Pearl to talk about our Soviet submarine contacts. He was the one individual before whom I least wanted to display that track chart. I counted on Cy Cole to act as a buffer; Cy was unaccountably delayed. Shifting from one foot to another, I made small talk while waiting for him—with a man who usually hates talk both large and small. Cy finally arrived and the moment of truth was upon us. Unrolling the track chart with its brightly colored ink tracings and *Pickerel* inscribed across the restricted area, Cy laughed until he almost had a stroke. Bill stared in disbelief for a few seconds, then said, "That does it. You just talked yourself into shore duty in public relations."

A PR job at that time had the same effect on one's career as leprosy. I couldn't determine whether he was angry or merely furious. Humor was not his prominent attribute. I broke up the meeting as soon as possible; I had to get to the big staff in Tokyo for a debrief. Also, Cmdr. Walter T. Griffith, a highly successful skipper in the war and soon to be my new DivCom in Pearl, was due to arrive shortly for an inspection tour of Far East facilities.

Admiral Joy enjoyed a reputation as a gruff, hard-nosed individual, undoubtedly one reason he was chosen to head the negotiating team at Panmunjom. I always found him extremely warm and cordial, and this was no exception. He again praised the photography of the previous patrol as the finest he had seen. Major General Charles Willoughby, the intelligence chief on MacArthur's staff, also wanted to talk about the Soviet subs. Even more so did I, but he was unavailable. I assured his staff that the identification was positive and that I wanted him to correct the assessment on the basis of photographic proof. I quickly learned that one who makes no errors has none to correct. Weeks later in Pearl Harbor, Captain Edward T. Layton, the Pacific Fleet intelligence officer, explained the dilemma to me. "In the intelligence business, estimates are made from bits and pieces of information which finally begin to form a pattern. If I accept your assessment, I've got to throw out all those bits and pieces and start over."

I replied, "Then the time has come to start over. There isn't a better trained set of eyes in the Far East to identify a submarine than mine. My exec and I not only checked and rechecked the identifying details separately—and agreed on every one when we later compared notes—but we read the hull numbers off the side of the conning tower and have photographic proof. How could we be wrong?''

Unknown to either of us, the Office of Naval Intelligence in Washington had already confirmed the units as the summer transfer of submarines to the Pacific over the Arctic route. But I wasn't to learn that for many months.

In Yokosuka our return from patrol coincided with a real tempest in a teapot. President Truman had written to a congressman of his low esteem for the Marines. ''The Marine Corps is the Navy's police force and as long as I am President that is what it will remain. They have a propaganda machine that is almost equal to Stalin's.''

The story leaked almost immediately and had some terrible repercussions. Many badly wounded fighting men were recovering in the Yokosuka Hospital, Marines, Army, British, Korean, and others. In the Marine ward, twenty-nine men, almost all amputees or double-wounded transfusion cases, had been presented with Purple Hearts the week before; twenty-three sent them to the president with the statement, ''Here are your police badges. Please pin them on your ass.''

Many sent telegrams. Every jeep in the combat area soon appeared with ''P.D.,'' or ''Calling All Cars,'' or other police logos. Most of us, whatever the service, felt just as angry at the president's inexcusable blunder. He soon recognized his error, though, and we were pleased that he had the courage to make a public apology.

Pickerel was now in the countdown for her return to Hawaii. Rumors that we would be retained still circulated, either because we were not in the rotation or because only a guppy was acceptable as a relief. I crossed my fingers and prayed that the last few days would pass quickly until we could be on our way.

Then on 12 October, Fate took a hand. Working at my desk, I was suddenly thrown from my chair to the deck as heavy shock waves reverberated through the ship. Rushing topside I met a small slice of pandemonium. A frigate maneuvering in the harbor struck *Bugara* amidships and almost sank her at the dock. A fuel tank was ruptured, throwing fuel clear over the periscope housing; the pressure hull was dished in five inches. *Pickerel*, moored inboard of *Bugara*, was tossed around enough to snap six heavy mooring lines and cause leakage in both exterior fuel tanks.

The frigate, U.S.-built and lend-leased to the Russians, was returned after the war to be mothballed in Yokosuka. Reactivated for transfer to the South Koreans, she had a partial U.S. and Korean crew with a former Japanese admiral as a pilot. She suffered only minor damage, but the added problem of our leaking fuel tanks could well speed our departure.

I had one other task to accomplish before returning to Honolulu: I wanted a last look at the Korean coast where *Pickerel* and *Perch* had pulled off the amphibious operation. Don O'Meara arranged a plane for me from his P2V squadron. I rose at 0500 to get to Tachikawa for an 0800 takeoff. On reaching the Korean coast, the plane dropped to three hundred feet altitude and headed up the coast. Airmen from the carriers were putting on a show all around us in low-level attacks on North Korean pockets of resistance. Off Wonsan, minesweepers were still busy in sweeping operations. Further north a B-29 strike was in progress. Bombs dropped from 15,000 feet seemed to be falling through broken cloud cover, us, and the carrier planes. To a casual observer the operations didn't seem too well coordinated.

Then the P2V got its chance at the enemy a few miles south of Vladivostok, just inside the North Korean border. Several ships in a small port began firing at us, and the big P2V swung into action like a fighter plane, attacking with rockets, bombs, and strafing runs, diving at a forty-five-degree angle and pulling out about a hundred feet above the ground. Wedged between the pilot and copilot, I squatted down to shoot some movies through the nose of the plane. When the plane pulled out of the dive, I could hear tendons and muscles cracking in both thighs. After several runs, I was so lame I couldn't walk for days. But it was a great experience.

Returning to my ship late that evening, I learned that Snuffy had received orders to be exec of the *Bugara*. Pap and I took him out for a special dinner, and the crew presented him with a beautiful movie camera. Sorry as we were to see him go, Pap and I would not be far behind.

On 20 October I began making my farewell calls. The date had a special significance. General Willoughby had just annouced that the war was essentially won. His intelligence summary to the Far East command stated that "Organized resistance on any large scale has ceased. . . . The North Korean military headquarters may have fled to Manchuria. . . . The enemy . . . continues to retain the capability of fighting small scale delaying actions."

Little did we know that the Chinese even then were preparing to enter hostilities and that a new war would drag on for another four years of dreary frustration and stalemate. In my final visit with Admiral Joy, he expressed his sincere regret at our departure, assuring us that *Pickerel* would be missed. He promised he would look for me in a year "to do the same thing in Indochina." With a last round of dinner parties hosted by VAdm. Berkey, VAdm. and Mrs. H. H. "Tex" MacLean, and the Homer Ambroses, I finally reached the point where I could leave Asia behind, perhaps for the last time. On 24 October, the ship backed clear of the Yokosuka dock and headed out smartly, the new white silk battle flag and homeward-bound pennant streaming proudly in the breeze.

Not well understood by the American people is the major influence exerted by the Korean War on United States policy. It did for the Cold War what the Japanese bombing of Pearl Harbor did for World War II—globalized it. Before Korea, the only United States political or military commitment outside the Western hemisphere was the NATO treaty. By the end of the war in 1955, the United States had several hundred bases in thirty-six foreign countries. As a result of the Korean War, Americans began to perceive the struggle with the Soviet Union as broad and global rather than European.

I had begun World War II in Iceland six months before hostilities formally began and ended it in Japan six months after hostilities had formally ended. I got into the Korean War with the first wave and ended my role with the first wave of victory. Now I was the senior submarine skipper in the Navy and the longest in command. The time had come to step down. In putting down the sword, for the last time I hoped, I found a new eagerness to shift my energies to the political role of military power. My new assignment seemed ideally suited. I was slated to become the special assistant to the director of politico-military policy on the staff of the chief of naval operations. On relinquishing command of *Pickerel,* I walked through the ranks of proud and capable shipmates for the last time and realized that, no matter the future, a piece of me would never leave. I was desolate that my active submarining had come to an end. Nothing equals the unforgettable romance of independent command.

Index